Marengo

Marengo

Marengo

The victory that placed the crown of France on Napoleon's head

By
T.E. Crowdy

Pen & Sword
MILITARY

First published in Great Britain in 2018 by
Pen & Sword Military
An imprint of
Pen & Sword Books Ltd
47 Church Street
Barnsley
South Yorkshire
S70 2AS

ISBN 978 1 47385 920 3

A CIP catalogue record for this book is
available from the British Library.

Printed and bound in England by
TJ International Ltd, Padstow, Cornwall

Pen & Sword Books Limited incorporates the imprints of Atlas, Archaeology,
Aviation, Discovery, Family History, Fiction, History, Maritime, Military, Military
Classics, Politics, Select, Transport, True Crime, Air World, Frontline Publishing,
Leo Cooper, Remember When, Seaforth Publishing, The Praetorian Press, Wharncliffe
Local History, Wharncliffe Transport, Wharncliffe True Crime and White Owl.

For a complete list of Pen & Sword titles please contact
PEN & SWORD BOOKS LIMITED
47 Church Street, Barnsley, South Yorkshire, S70 2AS, England
E-mail: enquiries@pen-and-sword.co.uk
Website: www.pen-and-sword.co.uk

In memory of my parents-in-law
Dennis and Marion Lear
(1942–2014)
(1944–2016)

and

Romain Baulesch
(1953–2015)

Contents

Maps

Picture credits

Mono Plates

1. Napoleon Bonaparte (1769–1821) in 1800 after Appiani. Appiani, Andrea, 'N. Bonaparte' (1800). (*Anne S.K. Brown Military Collection, Brown Digital Repository, Brown University Library*)

2. Alexandre Berthier (1753–1815), commander-in-chief of the Army of the Reserve. Duplessis-Bertaux, Jean, 'Alexandre Berthier Général de Division: Chef de l'Etat-Major, et depuis Général en Chef de l'armée d'Italie'. (*Anne S.K. Brown Military Collection*)

3. André Masséna (1758–1817), commander-in-chief of the Army of Italy. 'Massena, General der Franz. Armée'. (*Anne S.K. Brown Military Collection*)

4. Jean Moreau (1763–1813), commander-in-chief of the Army of the Rhine. 'Général Moreau'. (*Anne S.K. Brown Military Collection*)

5. Michael Friedrich Benedikt, Baron von Melas (1729–1806), commander of imperial forces in Italy. (*Anne S.K. Brown Military Collection*)

6. Anton von Zach (1747–1826), quartermaster general (chief of staff) of the imperial army in Italy. (*Gian Lorenzo Bernini*)

7. Joseph Graf von Radetzky von Radetz (1766–1858), the general adjutant. Mansfeld, H., 'Joseph Graf von Radetzky: Kais. Ost. General Feldmarschall Lieutenant und Chef des General-Stabs der Haupt Armee' (1815). (*Anne S.K. Brown Military Collection*)

8. General Bonaparte on the morning of the Brumaire coup (10 November 1799). Schopin, Frédéric, 'The Morning of the 18th Brumaire' (1851). (*Anne S.K. Brown Military Collection*)

9. The First Consul reviews his troops at the Palace of the Tuilleries, Paris. Desrais, Claude-Louis, 'View of the grand parade passed by the First Consul in the courtyard of the Tuilleries Palace' (1799). (*Anne S.K. Brown Military Collection*)

10. Bonaparte crossing the Great St Bernard with the monks. 'View of the hospice of the Great St Bernard, taken from the banks of the lake; passage of a French

21. French horse artilleryman. 'France, 1799–1800. Campaign in Italy.' (*General Research Division, The New York Public Library, http://digitalcollections.nypl. org/items/510d47df-b5e0-a3d9-e040-e00a18064a99*)

22. Gunner of the Consular Guard. 'France, 1799–1800. Campaign in Italy.' (*General Research Division, The New York Public Library, http:// digitalcollections.nypl.org/items/510d47df-b5dc-a3d9-e040-e00a18064a99*)

23. Officer of the 12th Horse Chasseurs in walking out dress. 'France, 1800–1802.' (*General Research Division, The New York Public Library, http:// digitalcollections.nypl.org/items/510d47e4-3de0-a3d9-e040-e00a18064a99*)

24. French heavy cavalry. 'France, 1797–99.' (*General Research Division, The New York Public Library, http://digitalcollections.nypl.org/ items/510d47df-b598-a3d9-e040-e00a18064a99*)

25. French dragoon. 'France, 1799–1800. Campaign in Italy.' (*General Research Division, The New York Public Library, http://digitalcollections.nypl.org/ items/510d47df-b5dd-a3d9-e040-e00a18064a99*)

26. French line infantry grenadier, 1800. 'France, 1799–1800. Campaign in Italy.' (*General Research Division, The New York Public Library, http:// digitalcollections.nypl.org/items/510d47df-b5db-a3d9-e040-e00a18064a99*)

27. French infantry captain. 'France, 1803.' (*General Research Division, The New York Public Library, http://digitalcollections.nypl.org/ items/510d47df-b602-a3d9-e040-e00a18064a99*)

28. Flag awarded to the 'Incomparable' 9th Light Infantry in reward for leading Desaix's counter-attack at Marengo. 'France, 1800-1802' (*General Research Division, The New York Public Library, http://digitalcollections.nypl.org/ items/510d47e4-3ddb-a3d9-e040-e00a18064a99*)

29. Hungarian line infantry in 1799. Kininger, Vincenz Georg, 'Gemeine der Hungarischen Linien Infanterie, 1799'. (*Anne S.K. Brown Military Collection*)

30. Austrian jäger light infantrymen. Kininger, Vincenz Georg, ,Gemeine Jäger, 1798. (*Anne S.K. Brown Military Collection*)

31. Austrian and Hungarian grenadiers. Kininger, Vincenz Georg, 'Gemeine Kayserliche Grenadiers'. (*Anne S.K. Brown Military Collection*)

32. Austrian artillerymen. Kininger, Vincenz Georg, and Mansfeld, Johann Georg, 'Gemeine der Artillerie', 1798. (*Anne S.K. Brown Military Collection*)

Author's Preface

The Battle of Marengo was the first Napoleon Bonaparte fought as French head of state. Although comparatively small compared to the apocalyptic encounters marking the end of his military career, Marengo has an almost mythical status because of the nature of the victory. Plucked from the jaws of defeat, the victory confirmed Napoleon's military genius and saw his political power cemented.

This new popular account of Marengo is a retelling of the great battle and the key decisions which led to it being fought. Much of the book is dedicated to the battle itself and the days immediately before and after; but in the first half I have explored some of the lesser-known events and paid particular attention to the principal Austrian protagonists and the full part they played in the drama. I have also dedicated a significant amount of space to the enigmatic 'Marengo spy', an Italian double agent who was responsible for much of the confusion on the day of battle – neither commander was expecting to fight the battle as it happened.

This account draws on two decades of detailed research. It uses primary source evidence from the military archives in Paris and Vienna, a wide range of oral history sources, scholarly studies into the battle conducted to mark its centenary, regimental histories, local tradition and the author's visits to the battlefield and principal landmarks on the preceding campaign. The bibliography is accompanied by a short essay detailing the sources, profiling the authors and unmasking their reliability and prejudices. Readers may wish to study this essay and the accompanying bibliography in advance of reading the central narrative.

Wherever possible, place names are given in their modern, familiar style. Some of the military ranks and terminology have long fallen from use. In the revolution, the French banished infantry regiments, instead labelling them half-brigades; colonels too were retitled 'chiefs of brigade'. At the time of Marengo, and before becoming emperor in 1804, Napoleon was General Bonaparte, or the First Consul. References to the 'emperor' are for Francis II, the Holy Roman Emperor and Habsburg monarch. I have followed the Austrian style of identifying infantry regiments (IR) with their number *and* proprietary name, or *Inhaber*. The Austrians also abbreviate the ranks of their generals; for example *Feldmarschallleutnant* is rendered FML.

T.E. Crowdy
June 2017

On the battlefield of Marengo

'We were all young in those days, soldiers and generals. We had our fortunes to make. We counted the fatigues for nothing, the dangers still less. We were carefree about everything, except for glory, which is obtained only on the battlefield.'[1]

Napoleon Bonaparte

On 5 May 1805, Emperor Napoleon I of France rode onto the fields behind the little Italian village of Marengo. Thirty thousand men, all the French troops then in Piedmont, had been assembled there to mark the passage of the French emperor and his empress on their way to Milan, where Napoleon was to be crowned King of Italy three weeks later. How Napoleon Bonaparte came to wear the French imperial Crown of Charlemagne and the Iron Crown of Lombardy – a golden bejewelled band mounted on an iron bar beaten from a nail of the True Cross – was largely due to the victory won at Marengo five years before. This victory stunned Europe and confirmed the general's pre-eminence as the greatest captain of his age: invincible on the field of battle and watched over by a lucky star. It was also a mighty political victory, one which, in the parlance of the time, 'consolidated the French Revolution' and secured Napoleon's position at the head of the French republic. Within hours of the battle ending, it was remarked Marengo had placed the crown of France on Napoleon's head.

On the fields behind Marengo, on a gentle rise in the ground, a large podium had been erected so Napoleon and Josephine might view the troops on manoeuvre. Two thrones were placed upon the podium, which was surrounded by flags and imperial eagles. On this day, Napoleon dressed in the uniform he had worn at the famous battle five years before. He had brought with him his general's habit – a dark blue tailed-coat rich with gold embroidery and buttons, albeit a little faded and, as Napoleon's secretary, Bourrienne, would have us believe, somewhat moth-eaten. On Napoleon's brow was the very same bicorn hat he had worn that fateful day, weathered by the elements on a campaign that saw him march an army across the snowbound Alps. Wearing the uniform was no act of nostalgia, but a simple message to the troops stood before him. Although now raised by the French people to the imperial dignity, the equal of kings, the French emperor remained above all the first general of France; and the victory at Marengo was the foundation of his legitimacy.

Twenty-two battalions of infantry, four regiments of horsemen, twenty-four field guns and their train were assembled for manoeuvres and inspection.[2] Alongside Napoleon were three of his most important marshals: the eldest was 51-year-old Alexandre Berthier, the titular commander of the famous Army of the Reserve which had fought the battle. Alongside him was Napoleon's brother-in-law, Prince Joachim Murat, a tall and lavish cavalry commander, who was apparently always 'dressed for a carnival'; and the svelte Jean Lannes, a hardened soldier dedicated to Napoleon's meteoric career. Unlike the vast majority of the troops assembled (none of these infantry regiments were present at Marengo), the three stalwarts of Napoleon's rise to glory had been present on that fateful day five years before. They had all shared the dangers and had reaped the rewards since.

Another veteran of the battle present that day was Napoleon's stepson, Prince Eugène de Beauharnais. Still just 23 years old at the time of this commemoration, the prince was the natural son of a noble general sent to the guillotine in 1794, and already a veteran of two campaigns in Italy and a military expedition to Egypt and Syria. Under the emperor's direction, Eugène directed the manoeuvres of the blue-coated troops. Long, smart battalions presented arms in salute, wheeling by company and sections from line to column; marching, halting, redressing their ranks; a formidable sight, somewhat different from the dusty, half-starved soldiers who fought like demons in the long battle. After presiding over the manoeuvres, Napoleon returned to the throne alongside Josephine, and from there distributed the awards of the Legion of Honour to soldiers of long, meritorious service, and those who had been decorated in the previous campaigns. He had done much the same the previous summer at Boulogne, where his Grand Army was camped in preparation for the much-anticipated invasion of England.

One wonders if, amid the pomp and splendour of the day, Napoleon allowed himself a moment of introspection. Did he recall the field before him as it appeared on the evening of the battle, with corpses piled amid trampled crops, horse cadavers, smashed carriages and wagons, with the barns and courtyards of Marengo piled high with hundreds of young wounded soldiers and their pitiful cries for water? In his private thoughts, did Napoleon remember how near defeat had come that day; how much of a surprise the Austrian attack had been; how tenuous his grasp on victory really was? He had not expected the Austrians to attack him the way they did, and he split his modest forces on the eve of battle, thus breaking one of his own tactical golden rules. True, all the signs indicated the Austrians were preparing to take flight. So strong was his belief the Austrians might elude him, bolting off to Genoa or marching northward over the Po, that even after his advanced guard was assailed and driven back, he still did not commit himself to battle until it was more than three hours engaged. If the ill-fated Desaix had not been delayed crossing a raging torrent the night before, if his reserve forces had been two or three hours' march further away, how different would Napoleon's fate have been? Would he have maintained his place as head of state, or would he have been replaced by a more successful general, like Moreau? One wonders if Napoleon truly believed, as the official account of the battle came to record, that the victory had been preordained; that the movement of retreat was nothing but a calculated manoeuvre designed to bring about the ruin of his Austrian foes?

It is impossible for us to truly know another man's mind, but if Napoleon had banished any thoughts of doubt, he did at least pay homage and acknowledge his debt to his fallen braves. In 1805, Napoleon was still prone to moments of idealism and grandiose fancy. He issued a decree after the ceremony to raise a monument to the brave dead on the plain of Marengo. Harking back to his Egyptian campaign, the monument would be a replica of the Great Pyramid at Giza, made from large stones and matching exactly the dimensions of the original. Inside the pyramid would be a chamber inscribed with the names of the fallen. A sum of 300,000 francs was allocated to the pyramid's construction, which Napoleon expected would take about three years. In fact it did not proceed beyond architects' drawings and the laying of a foundation stone some weeks later.

In another act of remembrance connected to the battle, the artist Vivant Denon arranged for the transfer of the remains of General Desaix from Milan to a sepulchre on the Great St Bernard Pass. The death of Desaix at Marengo was one of the most iconic moments of the battle, perhaps even the whole Revolutionary and Napoleonic Wars. Shot down at the moment of victory, Napoleon lost a man who would have been elevated to the front rank in the empire; a general totally dependable with independent command. In the thick of battle, Napoleon had to hold back the tears when told of his demise. The formal burial of Desaix's earthly remains also took inspiration from antiquity. It was to be marked with funereal music and the reading of excerpts from Pericles' eulogies for the warriors killed in the Peloponnesian Wars. After the burial there, feats would be staged recalling the funeral games of Achilles on the death of Patroclus. The victors would be awarded specially created medals. This festival of commemoration was scheduled to occur on 14 June, the fifth anniversary of the battle, nearly a month after Napoleon's coronation on 16 May. Napoleon did not actually ascend the Alps a second time to attend. He sent Berthier to represent him instead and the ceremony took place five days late. By then, Napoleon and Josephine were off on an imperial progress through the cities of northern Italy.

Having paid his dues to the battle and the fallen, Napoleon had more pressing things on his mind. War was brewing. He had his Grand Army assembled on the Channel coast and was waiting for the right moment to strike at England, march his army on London and dictate peace terms at the gates of St James's. In the meantime, he was at pains to reassure his new subjects that the visit to Italy was not a prelude to further conflict. Mindful not to provoke the Austrians at this stage, Napoleon had ordered Marshal Jourdan to send an intelligent officer 'with much ear and little tongue' to reassure the Austrian commander in the country of Venice not to view his presence as a threat.[3] Of course, we know these denials were in fact the lull before ten years of near perpetual war, raging on land and sea from the port of Cadiz to the streets of Moscow, terminating only in 1815 on the muddy and blood-soaked slopes of Mont St Jean at the Battle of Waterloo.

Chapter 1

1799: A Secret History

For the French armies in Italy, 1799 was a calamitous year. With the conqueror of Italy, General Napoleon Bonaparte, marooned somewhere between Egypt and Syria, an alliance known to history as the Second Coalition was formed against France. This coalition included the Habsburg Empire, Russia, Ottoman Turkey and Great Britain. While the Royal Navy swept the seas, a formidable Austro-Russian force under the command of veteran Russian Field Marshal Alexander Suvorov ploughed across northern Italy. Defeat followed defeat for the French; the largest coming at the Trebbia (17-20 June) and Novi (15 August), where the French commander, Barthélemy-Catherine Joubert, was killed in a preliminary skirmish. The republicans were driven back along the River Po and ousted from the great cities of Milan and Turin, so by the end of 1799, with the exception of the narrow Ligurian Riviera and the port of Genoa, the French had lost all the territorial gains made by Bonaparte in his famous campaign of 1796-1797. Suvorov and his Russians then marched over the Alps into Switzerland, leaving the mopping up to the Austrians under their commander-in-chief, General der Kavalerie (GdK) Michael Melas. Everywhere the allied armies went, the republican liberty trees were torn down and the revolutionary *Giacobino* firebrands forced to flee. Desperate for some respite from conflict, and with their art treasures mercilessly plundered by the French, the Italian peoples cheered the allies as liberators for unshackling them from the so-called liberty of the revolution.

On the French side, one of the chief scapegoats of this disastrous year was General François Philippe de Foissac-Latour. In his fiftieth year in 1799, a military engineer and veteran of Rochambeau's expedition to assist the rebels in Britain's American colonies, Foissac-Latour was charged with the defence of the fortress city of Mantua. Sat between two large lakes fed by the Minico River, Mantua was one of the great bastions of north-eastern Italy. Surrounded by swamps, it had held out against Bonaparte's army for eight months in 1796-1797. In strategic terms, it was the key to northern Italy. Yet despite its importance, Foissac-Latour surrendered this fortress to the Austrians on 27 July after a three-month blockade. This was nothing short of a national scandal.

After his return from Egypt, and on becoming head of state in November 1799, First Consul of the French Republic, Napoleon Bonaparte savaged

Foissac-Latour's decision to capitulate. Mantua, Bonaparte believed, should have been provisioned to hold out for a year at least. Mantua could have held out, he argued; it should have held out. It was damned near impregnable under the care of a tenacious defender. Treachery was suspected. In the circumstances, it would have been far kinder to have shot Foissac-Latour; but Bonaparte did worse. When Foissac-Latour was eventually released by the Austrians in 1800, Bonaparte cancelled the general's court martial and by an executive consular decree cashiered and humiliated him, stating he was unfit to wear a French uniform. The poor man was never rehabilitated and was dead within four years. Even Napoleon would later concede his treatment of the general was tyrannical and completely illegal; although by the end of this account, we may suspect Napoleon had an ulterior motive in not wanting a formal investigation into the circumstances of Mantua's fall.

But the disgraced general did have a case to answer. Firstly, there were acts of apparent incompetence. Like a good republican, Foissac-Latour had marked the national celebration of 14 July – Bastille Day. He even took the trouble to write to his opponents forewarning them the garrison was marking the fete day and there would be a great deal of firing on the French part. The Austrians were not to be concerned, Foissac-Latour assured them, because the guns would not be loaded with ball: powder and wadding only – a *feu de joie*. The commander of the besieging forces, Hungarian Feldzeugmeister Paul von Kray,[1] acknowledged this advanced warning and quickly rounded up thousands of peasants and soldiers to spend the night working on the siege trenches, safe in the knowledge the French were distracted with political sermons and ceremony. When the garrison awoke on 15 July, the first parallel of the siege lines was more or less complete. After the garrison surrendered, Kray lavished praise upon Foissac-Latour, and even awarded him the right to keep a flag of his choice. Why were the Austrians being so good to him? This favour smacked of treachery; but the thing that really did for Foissac-Latour, the hammer blow against him, was a letter he sent to General Jacques MacDonald, commander of the French Army of Naples. MacDonald recalled the note in his memoirs:

'While at Lucca I received a note from the commandant of the fortress of Mantua informing me that he was blockaded, but not attacked; that he had a good and well-disposed garrison and that the place was sufficiently well provisioned to stand a long siege.'[2]

Receiving this note, MacDonald communicated the message to the other French commanders in Italy and rather than rushing to Mantua's relief, instead went to Genoa, where the armies of Naples and Italy could combine to meet the

Austro-Russian threat. MacDonald was somewhat dumbfounded when he subsequently learnt 'by private means' the cataclysmic news Mantua had fallen. Having been earlier instructed the fortress was in such good shape, MacDonald's fellow generals Moreau and Joubert, and his chief of staff, Suchet, said the news was false and had been spread by the Austrians as a ruse. MacDonald was adamant the news was true:

> 'The details of this event were so precise, the means through which I had received the information so trustworthy, that doubt was to my mind impossible ... Of course, I wished to believe them [Moreau, etc]; but on the other hand, I could not doubt the honesty of my informant.'[3]

MacDonald did not reveal the identity of his source, but in the parlance of the day, an 'informant' or a 'trusted source' generally meant a spy. Indeed, MacDonald had a very good Piedmontese spy; very convincing, as this account will reveal, but also capable of great duplicity, to say the least.

Shortly before MacDonald received the fateful note from Foissac-Latour, a chance encounter had occurred outside the walls of Mantua. It was the evening of 16 June 1799. Making a reconnaissance of the marshes was the recently promoted Oberstleutnant (Lieutenant Colonel) Josef Radetzky. Then in his thirty-fourth year, Radetzky was riding with an old Walloon trooper from the de Bussy Jäger Regiment zu Pferde (Light Horse). This regiment enjoyed a certain notoriety as it contained a number of French *émigrés*, outcasts from the revolution who would only return to their *pays natal* under pain of death. Scouring the marshes, Radetzky's keen eye spotted the figure of a man scurrying through the darkness. The Austrian officer went off in pursuit. Just as he caught up with his quarry, the unidentified figure spun round to face Radetzky, holding a brace of cocked pistols pointed squarely at the Austrian.

Speaking French, the man introduced himself: 'As you want, your friend or your enemy. Before you arrest me, I'll kill you.'

As the man motioned threateningly to Radetzky, the Austrian saw the uniform of a French officer beneath his overcoat and the epaulettes of a captain. At such close range, Radetzky could neither fight nor take flight without the risk of being shot from his saddle, so he dismounted and engaged the stranger in conversation ... and what a conversation it turned out to be.[4]

The man was an Italian claiming to be MacDonald's chief of secret correspondence. He claimed to have given up on the French, whom he professed to hate, and wished nothing more than to serve the imperial cause. Hidden in a hollow compartment in the heel of his boot, he claimed, was a message to Foissac-Latour from MacDonald. The Italian now offered to work for the Austrians and to ensure that not a single message in and out of Mantua would pass without the Austrians having knowledge of it.

The Italian agreed to follow Radetzky back to his headquarters at Roverbella, approximately 10km north of Mantua. The commander of the siege force was the Hungarian Feldzeugmeister Paul von Kray. Matters relating to intelligence were the preserve of the chief of staff, so Radetzky handed the Italian over to Generalmajor (GM) Anton Zach. Along with Radetzky, one of the principal characters of the Marengo story, Zach's background and character will be explored more fully later in this account; but for now it is enough to know Zach was something of an intellectual, in truth more suited to academic pursuits than life in the field; and he loved a good piece of intrigue, the more complex the better.

With the Italian safely delivered to Zach, something of an interrogation followed. In this case the spy's name was later recorded as 'Karl Giovelli', from Alba in Piedmont, the son of a doctor still living there. Karl was the Austrian rendition of Carlo, and although Giovelli was how the name of the spy was written by the Austrians, elsewhere the name is given as Giojelli, or more properly, Gioelli.[5]

Dealing with spies in a military context went back to the days of biblical history, and was a dangerous business on all parts. There were many types of spy. At the most basic level were spies bribed or coerced (preferably a combination of both) into passing through hostile territory and reporting back on enemy troop movements. There were then professional spies; people who made a vocation from the obtaining and selling of information either through some notion of patriotism, or more likely for the thrill and financial reward. Some were even double spies, agents who served both parties and who acted, in modern intelligence parlance, as something of a backchannel between rival commanders. Such complex individuals required careful handling. One of Zach's staff officers in 1800, the Marquis de Faverges, described the chief of staff as a 'crafty old man', and declared, 'I knew no one more skilful at handling traitors and spies.' We may come to reappraise this assertion.

Gioelli unscrewed the heel of his boot and passed Zach the secret message. It was dated Reggio, 14 June 1799, from Léopold Berthier, chief of staff to MacDonald. It described how the Army of Naples was approaching Parma, having taken Modena by storm. Meanwhile, General Moreau's Army of Italy had received considerable reinforcements and was marching on Alessandria with the intention of joining MacDonald. Once the junction of the two armies was complete, the French would 'have all eyes fixed on Mantua'. This was interesting and concerning news, but Zach did not act immediately; he decided to hang on to the spy for a little longer as he digested the facts. This pause was most opportune, because on the very day Gioelli arrived in the Austrian camp, MacDonald's army encountered coalition forces near the city of Piacenza. Over the next four days, a series of engagements took place between Suvorov and MacDonald known as the Battle of the Trebbia. In this bruising encounter, the junction between MacDonald and Moreau failed to occur, and MacDonald was forced to retreat. When Zach learned of the defeat, and knew MacDonald was unable to come to Mantua's relief, the wily chief of staff decided to allow Gioelli to fulfil his mission.

The arrival of the spy was recorded by Foissac-Latour in a work published in 1800 setting out a defence of his handling of the siege. The meeting apparently took place on 24 June. First, Gioelli was interrogated by acting General of Brigade Louis Claude Monnet, then by Foissac-Latour himself. The letter was read and Gioelli verbally gave a very optimistic appraisal of the French army's condition and prospects. By the time of 14 July, the garrison of Mantua should, according to Gioelli, be in a state of preparedness to mount operations in support of MacDonald's advance. He offered to deliver Foissac-Latour's news back to MacDonald and said that he would be returning in the near future with further instructions. The spy made no mention of the Battle of the Trebbia and the fact MacDonald had already been defeated and pushed back in the direction of Tuscany (it is almost inconceivable Gioelli had not heard about the battle while residing in the Austrian camp).

To lend credence to his account, Gioelli volunteered he had met with Austrian officers outside Mantua and, in 'confidential conversations', had learned there was a traitor in Mantua named Carlo Speranza who was corresponding with a former servant outside the city. Employed in the postal service, this Speranza was, according to Gioelli, the Austrians' principal source of intelligence during the siege.[6] The betrayal of Speranza was an interesting move on the part of the spy. On the one hand it demonstrated his trustworthiness and continued loyalty to the French, but it also eliminated a rival source of intelligence to his new Austrian paymasters. Knowing there was a strong likelihood of Speranza being shot, it also demonstrates a cold ruthlessness in Gioelli. As it turned out, Foissac-Latour was not prepared to have Speranza executed on hearsay alone, but as a precaution had him arrested and secretly locked up in the dungeons of the castle of San Giorgio until the end of the siege.

Foissac-Latour took stock of Gioelli and the news he brought. The Frenchman was immediately suspicious of MacDonald's emissary, writing in his account: 'What a spy adds in such a case is always ambiguous, because honour and truth are rarely the virtues of those who get themselves hanged for money.'[7] Why had it taken the spy ten days to cover a distance of about 60km between Reggio and Mantua?[8] How had Gioelli made it through Austrian lines at all, and why did he seem so sure he would be able to leave and return in the future? How did the Italian have such detailed knowledge about MacDonald's strength and intentions? Why would this level of detail be entrusted to a Piedmontese spy? Did MacDonald really trust him, or was the matter dealt with only by Léopold Berthier? There were so many doubts Foissac-Latour entertained on the matter that one wonders why he did not simply lock the spy up or have him shot? The truth is, Gioelli was very convincing and Foissac-Latour was probably not the first, and certainly not the last, to be taken in by him. He states as much in his letter of response to MacDonald dated Mantua, 26 June: 'The letter of your chief of staff, my dear general, very fortunately reached me by your emissary, a very skilful and very intelligent man.'[9]

Believing he was about to be rescued by MacDonald in a matter of weeks, Foissac-Latour's reply was extremely optimistic. It was perhaps over-optimistic, as Foissac-Latour suspected the letter might fall into enemy hands one way or the other and he wanted to play up his strengths. There were hardships of course; they had been on awful biscuits for a month and meat rations were limited to twice every ten days. There had been desertions – about sixty Italians – but the Polish and Swiss troops were doing well, albeit pay had been cut by a third. There was also sickness, with around 500 men in hospital, and this had been made much worse by the heavy rains and the putrid emanations from the surrounding swamps. However, he and his commanders and staff were going to drink a toast to the junction of the Armies of Naples and Italy and their arrival at Mantua. If MacDonald could get word to him of his approach, Foissac-Latour offered to march out with five to six thousand men and a large artillery park. However, he would need certain reassurances if he were not to walk into a trap. 'If your spy was double,' Foissac-Latour cautioned, 'he could bring me down.'

Gioelli used hollow compartments in his heels to hide this message. He exited the city and headed straight for Roverbella, where he handed the message to Zach. The Austrian chief of staff was extremely pleased the spy had come back, and was equally pleased with sight of the hidden message. He awarded Gioelli 50 Ducats from his secret expenditure fund and promised the delivery of further intelligence would be similarly rewarded. Gioelli was sent back to MacDonald with the letter and 'with false intelligence'.[10] This misinformation probably underplayed the Austrians' strength and determination to escalate the blockade into a full-blown siege. In any case, a combination of the letter and the falsehoods Gioelli delivered caused MacDonald to renounce for the foreseeable future his attempts to relieve Mantua, and instead to march off towards Genoa to join with Moreau. This delay proved fatal for the defenders.

Would Foissac-Latour have ever written that letter with full knowledge of events? No. If Gioelli had not been so convincing and upbeat about MacDonald's chances, if Foissac-Latour had known about the Battle of the Trebbia, he would have likely given a more cautious appraisal and a sense of urgency. Instead, his message gave MacDonald a false sense of security. Foissac-Latour's attempt at a ruse backfired. After Marengo, it became common knowledge that Zach had indeed read Foissac-Latour's letter to MacDonald, and this confirmed Gioelli's treachery. However, without a court martial, Foissac-Latour could never hope to clear his name, and he went to an early grave cursing the day he met the Piedmontese spy.

And of course it did not end there. Gioelli became a frequent visitor to Zach, who after Mantua became chief of staff to the Austrian army in Italy. It is almost certain Gioelli was the trustworthy 'private means' by which MacDonald learned of Mantua's fall. When MacDonald and Moreau prepared to leave Italy for Paris, they handed over their commands to Generals Joubert and Championnet respectively. It appears MacDonald handed over Gioelli to Championnet, and so the Italian was therefore free and well-placed to continue his treacherous trade. And so he did. Every time the French attempted a new initiative, the Austrians somehow had the upper hand. Their final attempt to push back the Austrians and retain a foothold in Piedmont came at the Battle of Genola on 4 November. Here again General Championnet was bested by Melas. Of course, he had no idea Gioelli had delivered his battle plan to Zach.

After the victory at Genola, the Austrians pushed on and laid siege to the fortress of Cuneo, an important stronghold in south-west Piedmont on the confluence of the Stura and Gesso rivers. This was the last French foothold in Piedmont, and although late in the season for launching military operations, Zach was convinced its capture would crown an already successful year. The loss of Cuneo would consign the French to the Ligurian Riviera and deny them control of the main road from Turin to Nice over the Col di Tenda. The siege commenced on 7 November.

Behind the scenes, Championnet had fallen ill and would die in a matter of weeks. Command of the French Army of Italy passed to 29-year-old Louis-Gabriel Suchet, previously Joubert's chief of staff. With the command of the new army came the services of the agent Gioelli. Suchet despatched the Italian to Cuneo with an urgent message for the besieged commander, General Claude Clement. As he left Suchet's headquarters at Finale, Gioelli started to suspect his luck was running out and his duplicity was about to be exposed. The spy was somewhat jittery, therefore, when he arrived in the Austrian headquarters at Borgo San Dalmazzo at noon on 2 December. Cunningly disguised as a lemon seller, Gioelli was carrying several documents, including a large, folded Army of Italy proclamation to be read to the besieged troops and a small format, eight-page Order of the Day dated 29/30 *Brumaire* (20/21 November), which included the announcement of a new government under Bonaparte, recently returned from Egypt. Gioelli was given a verbal instruction from Suchet to Clement that a relief force would arrive on 5 December and he was to hold out determinedly until relieved. Having delivered this information, the spy produced a small message hidden in the hollow heel of his boot. It was just 6cm square and sealed with red wax to make it waterproof. Suchet's message was dated Pietra, 5 *Frimaire*, Year 8 (26 November 1799) and read:

'Listen to the man who hands you this note; welcome him; however watch him. Give us your news and reckon that you will soon hear news of us.'[11]

Suchet's warning to watch Gioelli confirmed the French were suspicious of him, but this did not prevent him from carrying out one last service for Zach. In return for the sum of 1,000 Ducats, an enhanced pension and the right to refuse future missions, Gioelli theatrically made his play.[12] He said:

'I leave myself in your hands. Dispose of my life, either take it from me or allow me to pull off a major service. Here is what I propose to you: I will enter this place; I am, as you know, known to the commanders.'

The spy pulled out another small piece of paper, which was blank, except for Suchet's signature. It was in effect a blank cheque. He continued:

'The signature that I am showing you will make the order, which I am going to fill in before your very eyes, seem completely genuine. This order will instruct the commander of the place to yield it to you on the most advantageous conditions he can obtain. I will justify this order and the impossibility of raising the siege, due to the blockages caused by the heavy snow and the wretched state of the army.'

Knowing Suchet was only a few days away from marching to the relief of Cuneo, and with the siege still in its early days, Zach eagerly agreed to the spy's proposal. However, instead of having Gioelli write the order, Zach called for Captain Englebert, an expert in handwriting who could write in a style indistinguishable from Suchet's own hand. The new message read:

'Listen to the man who brings you this note and Order of the Day. If he can, he will tell you of the situation of the republic and of ourselves; receive it and give us your news; the weather is against us.'

Gioelli agreed that, as he handed over the note, he would tell Clement the army was in no condition to come to his relief. He was also to describe the chaos into which the republican army had fallen, with desertions, revolts in Genoa and, finally, that a recent coup d'état in Paris had disrupted everything, leaving the capital in chaos. In short, Gioelli was to paint an utterly bleak picture to the commander of the French garrison.

The spy quit headquarters just after dark and was escorted through the trenches before Cuneo as far as the third siege parallel. From there, Gioelli ran out into the open ground, heading straight at the French outposts. To make the scene more believable, several Austrian soldiers were ordered to fire at Gioelli with blank cartridges. As the musketry crackled into life, the French troops hastily opened the barricades to allow Gioelli through. Establishing his identify with the outpost commander, the spy was immediately escorted to Clement at his headquarters, where the next stage of the deception began.[13]

Until now Zach had retained a healthy scepticism about Gioelli. The spy had proven useful, and his information had prevented the Austrians from making some imprudent moves in the latter half of the year. With the Italian safely delivered to Cuneo, there was nothing for it but to wait and see what, if anything, the outcome of the mission would be. They did not have to wait very long. At seven o'clock that same evening, word arrived that General Clement wished a meeting place for a parley. A rendezvous was arranged at a place named St Angeli at one o'clock in the morning. Sure enough, a French messenger arrived out of the darkness and announced that Clement would send a fully empowered emissary at 8.00 am to negotiate surrender terms. By noon the following day, the capitulation of Cuneo was agreed. Twenty-four hours after his arrival carrying Suchet's message, Gioelli returned to Zach and announced he had delivered the surrender of Cuneo as promised.

By now, Zach was working directly for the Austrian commander-in-chief, General der Kavalerie (GdK) Michael Melas. When he learned of Gioelli's claim to have delivered the surrender of Cuneo, Melas was stupefied at the news. In all his seventy years, Melas had not seen the like. He'd fought the armies of Frederick the Great and Napoleon Bonaparte in his time, but never had he seen an unarmed man walk into a city – a well-provisioned and strongly garrisoned city – and make them lay down their arms as Gioelli claimed to have done. There must have been some other factor, as yet unknown, which had caused Clement to seek the surrender terms. Melas wanted to get to the bottom of the business and instructed Zach to send for Clement's adjutant, Captain Carlo Falletti. Zach sent staff officer Major Daniel Mecséry to find Falletti and establish the events leading up to the surrender.

Falletti was reportedly something of a chatterbox. He almost bragged to Mecséry that the surrender was nothing to do with cowardice. Despite the Austrian blockade, a *confidant* had arrived in the city with news of the events in Paris and a verbal order to surrender. Falletti then pulled out the very same Order of the Day Gioelli had carried into the city, citing this as proof of the story. Following the arrival of the *confidant*, Clement had called a council of war. With the city now under Austrian bombardment and the hopelessness of them being relieved, Clement recommended they seek terms. So it was all true - everything. Gioelli had indeed pulled off an astonishing coup.

Those in the Austrian command who knew the true story of Gioelli's intervention (the group appears limited to Melas, Zach, Radetzky and several of the staff officers) actually felt sorry for Clement when they heard some of the junior French officers calling him a coward as they filed out of the city. The better-informed blamed the arrival of one of General Championnet's spies for the disaster. As the troops piled their arms and marched off, a rumble of guns could be heard in the distance. It was the relief column battling its way to save them, alas too late.

Finally satisfied with the loyalty of the spy, Melas wrote to Graf Tige, president of the Hofkriegsrat (high military council), the body which set military policy on behalf of Emperor Francis II. Melas' long letter detailed Gioelli's colourful exploits since arriving in Roverbella in June. In reward for his services, Melas recommended Gioelli be paid an annual pension of 200 Florins in addition to the 1,000 Ducats already advanced. Concluding his letter, he added, 'Gioelli must be thanked, amongst other important services, for the fall of Cuneo, together with the favourable outcome of the battle of the 4th.'[14]

As the army went into winter quarters, Zach also considered what he ought to do with Gioelli. Although he had promised him the right to refuse future missions, the quartermaster general was reluctant to dispense with the spy's services completely. Gioelli could not be sent back to Suchet's army without risking him being unmasked as a double spy and a traitor, but missions elsewhere in Italy might require his special talents. In the interim, Zach persuaded Gioelli to remain with him in the capacity of a spy-master, responsible for the recruitment and training of new scouts. He appears to have become something of a minor celebrity in closed circles. Radetzky claims Zach took him to Vienna. Elsewhere, it is claimed Gioelli even became known to the King of Sardinia after the Cuneo episode. He also became something of a marked man among the pro-French partisans of Piedmont.[15]

There is a fairly detailed description of Gioelli in the memoirs of Jean-Baptiste Louis Crossard, a French émigré in Austrian service, assigned to the staff of the army in Italy. Crossard identifies Gioelli as a young advocate (lawyer) from Turin excited by the philosophical debates provoked by a new interpretation of Plutarch's work, *Greek Lives*. He was inflamed by republican ideals exported by the French Revolution and quickly became a leading exponent of the cause. On 12 December 1798, the French seized Turin and forced King Charles Emmanuel IV to take refuge in Sardinia. Enthusiasm for the new republican regime quickly waned on the approach of the Austro-Russian army under Suvorov. On 26 May 1799, coalition troops entered Turin and Gioelli found himself at odds with the majority of his compatriots. Narrowly evading the scaffold, Gioelli said he sought salvation in the French army, where he was employed in the offices of the French staff in the section responsible for intelligence. There, Crossard wrote, Gioelli's 'skill, the language which he was natural with, the relations that he had struck up with the different Italian parties, made him precious, and brought him to the attention of headquarters'. However, when the war in Italy went badly for France in 1799, Gioelli began to realize he faced the prospect of exile. If the Austro-Russians could not be defeated, he would never be able to return home. This 'heartbreaking' prospect compelled Gioelli to commit 'a new treason', hoping to redeem the crime of having betrayed his king. Likening Gioelli to Sinon, the Greek who convinced the Trojans to accept the gift of a wooden horse, Crossard described how Gioelli masterfully convinced the members of the council of war in Cuneo that the signed order he bore was genuine and there was no hope of them being saved.

We should urge caution from reading Crossard's account. It is too neat. Spies are by their very nature duplicitous, and as we have already seen, Gioelli was a master of his craft, employing disguises, secret compartments in his heels and so on. He could also be ruthless, as we have seen with his denouncement of the French informant, Carlo Speranza, in Mantua. We must therefore take the tale given to Crossard with a pinch of salt. The secret of imparting a lie or deception is to shroud it in sufficient truth for it to appear plausible. Equally, the falsehood ought to be tailored to the recipient's character, so it reinforces a belief they already held firmly or at least entertained. Crossard was drawn to Gioelli and compelled to record his story because the Italian portrayed himself as an exile, desperate to do anything that might allow him to return home. Although repelled by Gioelli's dishonourable profession, Crossard saw something of himself in the spy, a fellow exile who yearned to return to his native lands. Gioelli therefore played up these similarities. Under scrutiny, there are subtle differences in the tale told to Zach, such as the home of Turin, rather than Alba; Gioelli would also have been hard-pressed to have fled Turin and arrived at Mantua as MacDonald's chief of secret correspondence as recounted by Radetzky. Clearly Gioelli was holding back the full story.

In his memoirs, Radetzky was far less charitable about the Piedmontese agent. Having first brought Gioelli into Austrian headquarters six months earlier, he clearly distrusted him. In later years, Radetzky would write that Gioelli 'was a professional gambler, debauched and set little value on money and sacrificed everything to fulfilling his desires'.[16] Radetzky considered the pension of 200 Florins (then about £45) to be a paltry amount, concluding that spies should either be paid a fortune or hung before they turned upon their masters. Although Radetzky wrote this many years after the event, and with the benefit of hindsight, we detect a certain meanness of spirit against a man who had delivered to the Austrians a string of spectacular successes, and also against Zach, the spy's principal controller. In fact, if it did not exist before, after the fall of Cuneo we detect at this time a distinct hostility towards Zach on the part of Radetzky. This clash of personalities is recorded in many of the Austrian accounts, and one might even suggest this growing conflict would become the undoing of Melas' army in the months ahead.

Chapter 2

Brumaire

It was the seventeenth of *Vendémiaire* in the eighth year of the French Republic. This was the *septidi*, or seventh day of the second decade of the month named after vine harvests; the first month in the year of the French republican calendar, and the name day of the *citrouille* – the pumpkin. The inhabitants of the small Provençal fishing village of Saint-Raphael stood on the pebbly beach and watched with some sense of excitement as General André Thomas Perreimond was rowed out to one of the four ships in the harbour. The French soldiers on board these ships had announced to the gunners manning the coastal artillery that General Bonaparte was with them and wanted to come ashore. The arrival of such an illustrious visitor was perhaps the greatest thing to have ever occurred to Saint-Raphael, before or since, and such was the sense of excitement that Perreimond waived the usual quarantine restrictions; after all, no one on board appeared to be dying of bubonic plague, despite having just arrived from Egypt. In an eerie dress rehearsal of his return from exile in Elba fifteen-and-a-half years later, Napoleon Bonaparte was literally carried ashore and mobbed by well-wishers. It was not every day the conqueror of Italy and Egypt landed on one's doorstep. For his part, Bonaparte was impatient and full of questions. He had heard things were bad in Italy. How bad? What about Paris? He thirsted for news, having been away from France for more than a year and a half. Impatient to get going, to whatever end, at 6.00 pm he set out in a coach in the direction of Lyons, and from there to Paris, where his destiny awaited him. As the coach trundled off, the inhabitants walked alongside it, burning torches held aloft to light the returning conqueror's way.

Before we uncover the events following this momentous 9 October 1799, let us first refresh our memories as to what had gone before. Fully ten years had passed since the powder keg of revolution had detonated in France. A decade before, France had been a feudal society, where the people were divided into three classes or estates. The First Estate was the Catholic clergy; the nobility formed the Second Estate. These two classes owned most of the land, enjoyed fantastic privileges and, crucially, were exempt from taxes. Everyone else, around 25 million people, formed the Third Estate. From the most successful merchant to the scrawniest hawker, these were the people who toiled and were taxed heavily for the privilege. Unlike in England, where the monarch ruled through the shackles (or wise council) of a parliament, the French monarch believed his power on earth was absolute and derived directly from God. An 'Estates General' (a gathering of all three social orders) had not occurred since 1614. However, in 1789, after successive poor harvests and rocketing bread prices, such was the perilous financial position of France that all three estates were summoned to Versailles. The king wanted more money. In a response reminiscent of the American cry 'no taxation without representation', the Third Estate wanted real and meaningful political representation in return for said money. When the latter did not appear to budge, the representatives of the Third Estate formed a National Assembly on 20 June 1789 and made the *Serment du Jeu de Paume* – the Tennis Court Oath – a pledge not to separate until France had a written constitution. This was the great principled act giving birth, for better or worse, to a new European age.

So what about the storming of the Bastille, *Quatorze Julliet* and all that? Well, while the representatives debated, the people became impatient. Many believed King Louis XVI had summoned foreign mercenaries to butcher the good people of Paris and put an end to this unwanted political debate. Being largely recruited from Parisians, the Regiment of French Guards mutinied and sided with the protestors. With Paris awash with rumour and counter-rumour, and the bloodthirsty mercenaries expected at any minute, some of the guardsmen and a mob of their fellow Parisians marched off towards the Bastille fortress looking for gunpowder. It was the afternoon of 14 July. When this mob of 1,000 or so people arrived at the Bastille, the governor of the fortress, the Marquis de Launay, refused to open the gates and hand over the gunpowder. One can understand why. A negotiation ensued, in which the people of Paris exhibited their famous propensity for violent impatience. The drawbridge was cut down, a shot was fired and all hell broke loose. By the end of the day, de Launay's head was skewered on a pike and paraded up and down the streets. For all the fine and enlightened words spoken in the tennis courts of Versailles, the French Revolution ultimately proved to be a succession of bloody, violent acts.

The history of the revolution and the detail of what happened next are a complex subject fit for a lifetime of study, mercifully outside the scope of this account. However, there are a few key events we should remember. One should know the first experiment with constitutional monarchy did not work out quite as planned. Feudalism was abolished; a constitution was written, and rewritten; and there was even a Declaration of the Rights of Man. However, there was a suspicion that the king was not quite as enthusiastic about his changed circumstances as the people had hoped. With their feudal privileges curtailed and the political atmosphere decidedly ugly, the French nobility voted with their feet. They boarded up their chateau and emigrated. In June 1791, the king decided to join these *émigrés*, but was caught in the act and unceremoniously escorted back to Paris. Although Louis

XVI signed the declaration of war against Austria on 20 April 1792, the suspicion was that he did so hoping the Austrians would win and restore his authority.

Then came the *real* revolution. On 10 August 1792, a group of hard-line revolutionaries stormed the Tuileries Palace and massacred the king's Swiss Guard. The monarchy was suspended and the remaining members of the royal family imprisoned. Louis XVI lost all his titles and was given the surname 'Capet' – the family name of the first king of the Franks. On 22 September 1792, France became a republic. On 21 January 1793, at 10.22 in the morning, Citizen Louis Capet went to the guillotine. France was now, for want of a better word, *governed* by the real firebrands of the revolution – the Jacobins. Employing state control over almost every facet of human existence, they sought to eradicate all vestiges of feudal life, replacing Christianity with a cult of the Supreme Being based on the virtues of 'reason' and even introducing a new calendar, an attempt to erase from history the era before the declaration of the republic. Where they encountered resistance (real or imagined) to their radical dogma, they terrorized the population into acquiescence, slaughtering anyone and everyone who offered the least token of resistance. With the country now seemingly at war with everyone (including itself), the French state became something of an armed camp. The churches became stables and foundries. Everything was geared towards supporting the war machine, and with the largest, youngest population in Western Europe at the time, it was not long before columns of blue-clad soldiers were marching on the frontiers with their martial hymns, ready to export the revolution abroad.

The Jacobin 'Terror' effectively ended with the execution of its leader, Maximilien Robespierre, on 28 July 1794. The Terror had turned in on itself and devoured its chiefs. The National Convention went on to approve a new constitution on 22 August 1795, the so-called Constitution of Year III. This created a new form of government, a five-man ruling executive called 'The Directory', with a parliament composed of two houses: a council of 500 representatives (*Conseil des Cinq-Cents*) and a council of 250 senators or 'elders' (*Conseil des Anciens*). The executives were appointed by the senators from a list put forward by the representatives. History has not been kind to the memory of this executive, which is roundly portrayed as only borderline-democratic, stinkingly corrupt and if not incompetent, then at best ineffective.

At this stage, we need to know about one key event in the history of this government: 13 *Vendémiaire*. Not everyone had been happy to see Louis XVI led to the guillotine. Nor were they enamoured by the subsequent death of Queen Marie Antoinette by the same method on 16 October 1793. Hotbeds of royalist support remained, particularly in the west and south of France, and these were stoked up by British agents and *émigrés* in equal measure. Since the death from sickness in June 1795 of the incarcerated 10-year-old Dauphin (crown prince),

Louis-Charles, the legitimate line of succession passed to the brother of the executed king, the Count of Provence and self-styled Louis XVIII. There was therefore a legitimate successor to Louis XVI, and there were many Frenchmen sympathetic to the restoration of the royal line. With the west of France in open civil war, the pretender's brother, the Count of Artois, landed in the Vendée with several thousand British troops: a counter-revolution seemed all too possible. Buoyed by news of this landing, an insurrection in Paris began to bubble over, with several parts of the city openly declaring support for the royalists. On 5 October, one of the Directors, Paul Barras, turned to a young brigadier general residing in the capital named Napoleon Bonaparte and charged him with protecting the government. In turn, Bonaparte instructed a cavalry officer, Joachim Murat of the 12th Chasseurs, with collecting forty cannon from a nearby park and positioning them around the convention building. At 3.00 pm, a crowd of 25,000 royalists surrounded the building. Barras gave the authorization, and Bonaparte commanded the guns to fire. For three-quarters of an hour, they fired canister shot, pummelling the protestors and leaving 300 of them dead on the cobblestones. The government was saved and 'General Vendémiaire' became hero of the hour. In reward for saving the government, Bonaparte was made a full general of division and given command of the Army of the Interior, then the Army of Italy. Barras even introduced him to one of his mistresses, a general's widow named Rose de Beauharnais. Bonaparte married 'Josephine', as he preferred to call her, and thus began one of the great historical love affairs.

At the end of his Italian campaign in 1797, Bonaparte had become something of a double-edged sword for the Directory. There was no denying his talent, or his success. Had anyone really expected the relatively inexperienced general in his mid-twenties to conqueror Italy and dictate peace terms in the heart of Austria? No, and that was the problem. Bonaparte was too successful, too independent, and impatient to boot. This was a very dangerous mix from the point of view of the politicians. Ever since France went to war in 1792, various governments had been alive to the threat of *caesarism*; that a popular and successful general would turn his army on Paris and seize control, as Julius Caesar had done in ancient Rome. There were already signs that Bonaparte might become this very man: so what to do with Bonaparte now there was peace?

At first there was the possibility of an invasion of Great Britain. An Army of England was planned, but then the Directory started to think about Egypt. What if they put together a mighty Mediterranean fleet and sent off Bonaparte and his army with suitably nebulous instructions to form a French colony, create new markets for French goods and perhaps even threaten the British domination of India? Egypt was a land almost no one knew anything about, but to Bonaparte it was an exciting opportunity to emulate the heroes of antiquity, to follow in the footsteps of Alexander and Caesar, and above all, to exercise total power. Far from Paris, he would have free rein to engage in conquest and scientific inquiry. For not only would he take his soldiers, but he would have an army of *savants* – engineers, artists and scientists - and would record the marvels of antiquity for all mankind. The government encouraged Bonaparte to think big with this expedition, and probably breathed a hearty sigh of relief when the fleet cast anchor and set sail from Toulon on 19 May 1798.

With the benefit of hindsight, the adventure was a costly mistake. Things started well, with the capture of Malta en-route. However, once landed in Egypt, the British sank the French fleet in Aboukir Bay on 1 August 1798. This effectively cut off Bonaparte and his army from any chance of reinforcement or return. He defeated the Ottoman Empire's Mamelukes outside Cairo too, but his attempts to appear as a liberator to the Egyptians hit a cultural barrier. Bonaparte considered converting the army to Islam, but admitted he could never ask a French army to make a pledge never again to drink wine. Before long, Bonaparte and his army became viewed as a force of occupation. On 22 October 1798, there was a bloody revolt in Cairo and a brutal response. In the following year, Bonaparte learned the Ottomans were preparing an offensive against the French, so he took pre-emptive action, marching his army into Syria. By mid-March, Bonaparte was encamped outside the city of Acre and became bogged down by a combination of bubonic plague and the Governor of Acre, Achmet Pasha, better known as 'Djezzar' (the Butcher), a man perhaps even more ruthless than the French commander. Supported by a handful of Britons, the garrison held out against the French army, and on 20 May 1799, Bonaparte retired on Cairo, claiming the campaign had achieved its objectives.

Although he portrayed his Syrian adventure as a great triumph (Bonaparte was an absolute genius at self-promotion), the reality began to sink in that he was cut off from France, from the centre of the action, with very few options. He had also learned that Josephine had been unfaithful and was seeing a certain Monsieur Charles. He in turn reacted with a spell of infidelity of his own, having an affair with Pauline Fourès, the wife of an officer on the expedition. While Lieutenant Fourès was sent on an urgent and perilous mission back to France, Bonaparte kept Pauline with him. This was all very much common knowledge, so much so the soldiers nicknamed her 'Cleopatra'. Thoughts kept returning to home.

After defeating an Ottoman army at Aboukir on 25 July 1799, Bonaparte decided to quit his army and return to France. He set sail on 23 August with a detachment of soldiers and some of his closest generals, including Berthier, Murat and Lannes. He left in secret, leaving command of the army to General Jean-Baptiste Kléber, who reacted to the news of Bonaparte absconding with the thunderous remark: 'He's left us with his breeches full of shit.' With outstanding luck (or a secret deal), Bonaparte's two frigates stole past a British blockade and made their way across the Mediterranean unmolested, arriving in Ajaccio Bay in Corsica on 1 October.[1] There was a five-night delay to the journey here, which proved extremely fortuitous because news of the victory at Aboukir reached France just two days before Bonaparte's own arrival.

For the best part of 1799, the Directory had been in a state of turmoil. In Germany, its forces had been beaten at Stockach on 25 March 1799. Switzerland had come under attack and Zurich was taken by the Austrians in June. Italy was becoming a graveyard of its forces and Holland was invaded by an Anglo-Russian force. In the west of France, the royalists had raised the flag of rebellion and a British invasion force was expected to land in support at any minute; while in the south of France, banditry had broken out. New military conscription laws had failed to bring forward the number of recruits needed, while those conscripts arriving in the depots found them empty of stores. The supply services feeding and re-equipping the soldiers already in the field, had failed badly. In places, especially in Italy, men dressed in rags were forced to pillage their rations from the local population. Yet despite this, by the autumn, somehow the country had not collapsed. In Switzerland, the very able General André Massena recaptured Zurich. The Austrians did not press their advantage in southern Germany after Stockach, and General Guillaume Brune was successful in Holland against the Anglo-Russians. It was almost as if the allied coalition just could not land that last, knockout blow. Therefore, by the end of September and early October, there was a period of relative calm. Had Bonaparte arrived sooner in the year, he might have found himself more enthusiastically received by the government, but as it happened, his arrival in Paris on 16 October met with a muted response. His first visit was not to his wife or brothers, but to the president of the Directory, Gohier. Standing before him, Bonaparte said: 'The news that reached us in Egypt was so alarming that I didn't hesitate to leave my army, but set out at once to come and share your perils.'

'General, they were indeed great, but now we have gloriously overcome them,' Gohier replied. 'You have arrived in good time to help us celebrate the numerous triumphs of your comrades-in-arms.'

At this short meeting, a time was arranged for Bonaparte to meet the full Directory the following day. Gohier's recollection of this meeting depicted Bonaparte as attributing all the troubles France had faced to his absence. Then in a vain attempt to assure the Directors his intentions were honourable, Bonaparte placed his hand on the pommel of his sword and promised it would never be raised except in defence of the republic. Was it a threat? Gohier gave a very measured response that played down any notion of crisis. The Executive Directory, Gohier claimed, viewed Bonaparte's 'unexpected return with the same pleasure mixed with surprise that is spoken of all over France'. Gohier went on to assure Bonaparte that only the general's enemies (who were naturally the government's enemies too) could put an unfavourable interpretation on the way Bonaparte had temporarily abandoned the colours for patriotic motives.[2]

The general must have left this meeting somewhat thwarted. The public acclamations which greeted his return must have given him a false impression. In truth, not everyone was pleased to see him. For example, General Bernadotte (future marshal of France and progenitor of the modern Swedish royal line, but at that time a committed Jacobin) apparently suggested Bonaparte should face a court martial for deserting his army in the field and ignoring the strict quarantine laws for those arriving in Europe from plague-stricken countries. There was also a great deal of luck for Bonaparte that his arrival in France had been preceded by news of his victory of the Battle of Aboukir, and not a stinging letter which Kléber wrote to the Directory, condemning the secrecy with which Bonaparte left Egypt, and the deplorable state of the army, its finances and the prospect of fighting the Ottoman army. If this had arrived before his meeting with the Directory, Bonaparte may well have found himself locked in chains.

Temporarily checked, Bonaparte withdrew from public view and began a reconciliation with his wife, if only not to become bogged down in the scandal of a divorce at such a politically sensitive time (Lannes was less fortunate – he found his wife pregnant on his return and a divorce was required). Fortunately for Bonaparte, political change was in the air. Before his arrival in Paris, the Director Emmanuel Joseph Sieyès had been looking to reform the Directory, seeking to reduce it to a three-man body, at the head of which would be a popular general – 'a sword'. The man of choice was General Joubert, but he was killed in action at Novi. Bernadotte was too much a Jacobin for Sieyès to work with, which left Moreau, who turned Sieyès down immediately. Bonaparte's arrival from Egypt was therefore quite opportune, although the two men formed an immediate enmity to one another, with the Director one of those who believed Bonaparte should be shot. Still, political expediency makes strange bedfellows – a plot was hatched.

The coup was planned in two stages for 9–10 November (18–19 *Brumaire* in the revolutionary calendar). Bonaparte's part in the coup was to ensure the loyalty of the Paris garrison. Sieyès, with the help of his fellow Director and ally, Roger-Ducos, would bring over the support of the Council of Elders. Bonaparte's younger brother, Lucien, was conveniently placed as President of the Council of 500. Lucien's role would be to defuse the Jacobins in the assembly long enough for the coup to occur. On the first day, Sieyès declared the government was in immediate danger from anarchists in the capital and both Houses should relocate to St Cloud for their own protection. He motioned for all the troops in Paris to come under the authority of General Bonaparte, who would supervise the councillors' protection.

This move was constitutional, although it was clear what it foretold. Sieyès and Roger-Ducos turned on the other three Directors: Bonaparte's old mentor, Barras, conveniently resigned, while Moulin and Gohier found themselves escorted to the Luxembourg Palace and were held for their 'own safety'. Bonaparte held reviews of the troops, ensured he could count on their loyalty and detached a large body of men under General Murat, to march on St Cloud to assure a satisfactory outcome of phase two of the coup the following day.

The Jacobins now realized a full-blown coup d'état was underway. They had the night to decide what to do. In the morning, as the Council of Five Hundred reconvened at St Cloud, each member swore an oath to support the constitution. A motion was presented that President Lucien Bonaparte should outlaw his brother Napoleon. When Bonaparte heard of this, he rushed into the chamber, which promptly exploded with rage and cries of 'death to the tyrant!'. Bonaparte hadn't expected this, and the red-cloaked councillors were clearly in no mood to be bullied. They surged at Bonaparte, who was spared the fate of Caesar by two grenadiers of the 96th Half-Brigade, who managed to bundle him out of the chamber. One of the grenadiers (Thomas Thomé) had his uniform torn, and claimed he was stabbed in the arm while shielding Bonaparte.[3] The coup was teetering on the brink, but at this critical moment, a quick-thinking Lucien Bonaparte dramatically threw down his robe of office, walked out the chamber and harangued the soldiers outside. He told them fanatics had attacked him and solicited them to enter the chamber and clear out the assassins. The dependable Murat led the troops into the chamber and ejected the councillors out of the ground-floor windows at bayonet point. They were later rounded up and encouraged to vote themselves out of existence. That evening, Sieyès and Bonaparte established themselves in power with Roger-Ducos. The three conspirators titled themselves as Provisional Consuls and began the draft of the Constitution of Year VIII. The first step of Bonaparte's rise to power was complete: now he would have to consolidate it.

While the political processes were ironed out (the constitution would be tested by a national plebiscite in February 1800), uppermost in Bonaparte's priorities were to review the state of the army and the military situation France found itself in. Bonaparte's trusted chief of staff, Alexandre Berthier, was made Minister of War the day after the coup. At the time of *Brumaire*, the military situation had stabilized somewhat. To the north, the Battle of Castricum (6 October 1799) had defeated the Anglo-Russian army, which beat a retreat from Holland the following month. There was then the formidable barrier of the Rhine, with no sign of this being breached. Massena had been victorious against the Russians in Switzerland, and French troops guarded the Valais, which allowed them access to a number of Alpine passes. In Italy, at the time of the coup, Cuneo still gave the French a foothold in the Po valley, albeit the city was under siege. In the west of France, there had been another flaring among royalist rebels, but for now it was contained in the western departments. Ignoring the troops marooned in Egypt, on 22 November the First Consul had some 285,000 men in five armies:

Army of Batavia (Brune)	23,589
Army of the Rhine (Lecourbe)	62,299
Army of the Danube (Massena)	83,590
Army of Italy (Championnet)	56,253
Army of England (Hédouville)	57,505

There were, in addition, another 100,000 men dispersed around the interior of France on various garrison and 'police' duties.[4]

The first priority was Italy. If Cuneo could be held over the winter, then the French would have a solid, exploitable route back into northern Italy the following spring. If Cuneo fell, then the French would have to begin their operations from the reverse side of the Apennines or Alps. Alas, the column sent to relieve Cuneo was preceded by the double spy Carlo Gioelli, who betrayed the French garrison and brought about the surrender of the place. After this reverse, the plight of the Army of Italy was such that no further actions could be considered. Thwarted in Italy, Bonaparte charged Moreau and Clarke with developing a new plan of operations for the French Army of the Rhine. Bonaparte was particularly anxious to drive at the most direct route to the Austrian 'Hereditary Lands' via Bavaria. He therefore instructed these generals to launch operations in that theatre by the end of December. This directive proved somewhat optimistic and nothing came of it.

Before we develop any further discussions on military strategy, there was also the question of peace. First were the entreaties to King George III of Great Britain and Ireland, and to the Habsburg emperor, Francis II. His letter to the British was something of a break in protocol; a direct appeal from Bonaparte to George III, bypassing the normal Foreign Office routes. Dated 25 December 1799, the letter spoke of the need to bring eight years of European war to an end for the sake of commerce and 'internal prosperity'. The British reply came from Foreign Minister Grenville on 4 January 1800. They were not prepared to negotiate with Bonaparte's new government, as it did not appear 'assured'. Further, French aggression over the past decade had been so rampant that the British simply did not believe Bonaparte would deliver real peace, only an interval in which the French could re-equip their forces before launching new aggressions. The reply concluded that Bonaparte should restore the Bourbons to the French throne if he genuinely wanted peace. The tone of the letter was such it was effectively a re-declaration of war on the new French government. The reply from the Austrians was similarly hostile. The Austrians were offered peace on the terms of the 1797 Treaty of Campo Formio. This would have seen the Austrians give up their recent Italian conquests. As one can imagine, they had no intention of accepting these terms while being in a position of apparent strength.

Bonaparte was more successful with Tsar Paul of Russia. On entering the coalition, the Tsar's objective was to restore something of the status quo in Europe. In Italy, this meant the re-establishment of the House of Savoy in Turin. The Austrians had other ideas on the subject and appeared extremely reluctant to see the restoration of Charles Emanuel IV, instead preferring to keep the territories for itself. This irked the Russians, and it is fair to say there was a strong element of rivalry between the Russian and Austrian commanders in the field. The Tsar was also suspicious of the political machinations of the British. Bonaparte sensed, or was informed, about these tensions in the coalition and so made a gesture of reconciliation with Russia. The French had captured around 6,000 Russian troops in Switzerland and Holland, so Bonaparte repatriated them after providing new uniforms and equipment for the prisoners first. Touched by this gesture, the Tsar declared Bonaparte was a man he could do business with, and having been left with a sour taste for coalition politics, ordered his forces home. Russia had therefore been knocked out of the coming campaigns without a shot being fired. It was a massive advantage gained, particularly as neutral Prussia gave assurances it had no intention of joining the conflict on either side. With the British Army ejected from Holland by mid-November, this meant Bonaparte could concentrate entirely on defeating the Austrians alone.

Another success came in the pacification of France's western departments. On 28 December 1799, Bonaparte guaranteed the rebels freedom of worship under the new constitution, and also granted a general amnesty. At the same time, he instructed General Brune to march westwards and back up these concessions with a show of force. If Brune encountered any die-hard rebel leaders, he was to have them shot and, if things still did not calm down, he sent instructions to General Hédouville to burn 'two or three communes' as an example. This carrot and stick approach appears to have worked, and interestingly there was somewhat of a belief among the Chouans that Bonaparte, himself a former noble, might pave the way for the return of the Bourbons. The idea appears to have gained sufficient credence for the exiled Louis XVIII to write to the First Consul directly and broach the subject of his return. Bonaparte replied politely but firmly to this proposal. At this time, he wrote, the return of the Bourbons would lead only to further bloodshed.

Many commentators take a sceptical view about Bonaparte's sincerity in wanting a lasting peace at the turn of the nineteenth century. Although the majority of Frenchmen were sick of war, political infighting, and the economic hardships which follow as the natural result of strife and conflict, did Bonaparte really share this view? Where was the glory in watching hundreds of thousands of young men – many of whom knew nothing but soldiering – return from the frontline without jobs and to an economy which had been teetering on the brink of collapse even before those bourgeois gentlemen in the tennis courts at Versailles demanded a written constitution? How long would Bonaparte have survived politically without new military glories? Regardless of the motivation, having offered peace and been rejected, Bonaparte skilfully used this rejection as a rallying cry to his people. If Frenchmen wanted peace, he said, they would have to fight for it. This became an important motivational factor in the forthcoming campaign.

Returning to the central thread of this narrative, if a continuation of the war was inevitable then a strategy was required. The obvious threat was from the Austrian armies in Germany and Italy. Bonaparte enjoyed a key strategic advantage over these two threats. The further the two Austrian armies advanced westward, the more they were separated from one another by Switzerland. With this alpine country in French hands, the Austrians could not easily support one another. In military parlance, they lacked 'interior lines'. The only way they could combine their strengths was to retreat in the direction of Austria. While holding one enemy army in position with a defensive covering force, Bonaparte could attack and defeat the other army with a local superiority, force it to retreat and then move his forces onto the flank of the other enemy army.

To exploit this geographical advantage, Bonaparte needed a new army independent of those already engaged; one with which he could deliver the knockout blow. The nucleus of this new force would be the half-brigades stationed in the interior, most of which had missed the fighting of 1799 and were still fresh. This army would be raised in secret and centred on Dijon, a central position from where it could fall on whichever front most needed it. The order to form this new Army of the Reserve was issued to Minister of War Berthier on 25 January 1800. Here is the instruction in full:

'My intention, Citizen Minister, is to organize an Army of the Reserve, whose command will be reserved for the First Consul. It will be divided into a right, centre and left. Each one of these three grand corps will be commanded by a lieutenant of the general-in-chief. There will be, moreover, a division of cavalry, also commanded by a lieutenant of the general-in-chief.

'Each one of these grand corps will be divided into two divisions, each commanded by a major general and by two brigadier generals, and each of these grand corps will have, moreover, a senior artillery officer.

'Each lieutenant will have a brigadier general as his chief of staff; each general of division, an adjutant general.

'Each one of these corps will consist of 18-20,000 men, including two regiments of hussars or chasseurs, and 16 artillery pieces, including 12 served by the foot companies and 4 by the horse companies.

'The 14 battalions which form the depots of the Army of the Orient; the 14th, 30th, 43rd, 96th Half-Brigades, which are in the 17th Division [author's note: the military administrative district of Paris]; the 9th and the 24th Light, which are with the Army of the West; the 22nd, 40th, 58th and 52nd, which are also with this army; the 11th Light and the 66th, which are in the new reunited departments, shall be part of the Army of the Reserve.

'The 15th, 19th, 21st, 24th Chasseurs; the 5th, 8th, 9th and 19th Dragoons; the 11th, 12th and 2nd Hussars; the 1st, 2nd, 3rd, 5th and 18th Cavalry; the 7 depot squadrons of the cavalry corps of the Army of the Orient, will be the core of the Army of the Reserve.

'The right will be united at Lyon, the centre at Dijon and the left at Châlons-sur-Marne.

'General of Division Saint-Remy will perform the duty of commander of artillery for the army. Chief of Brigade Gassendi will be director general of the park. First Inspector of Engineers Marescot will command this arm. There will be a disbursing officer [ordonnateur] and four commissaries attached to each of the three grand corps, and a chief orderer attached with the army and residing near the Minister for War, who will perform the duty of chief of staff.

'It is necessary to call to Paris a member of the council of administration of each corps composing the army, bringing the states of the armament, equipment and clothing. They will be assembled in Paris on 15 February.

'You will give orders to complete each battalion as promptly as possible to 1,000 men.

'You will propose to me the officers who will form the staff of this army.

'You will keep the formation of the aforesaid army extremely secret, even in your offices, from which you will ask only for absolutely necessary information.'

Several points should be emphasized about this instruction. Firstly there is the secrecy surrounding the army. Berthier was being asked to form this army without the Ministry of War knowing about it – no mean feat considering the number of units, senior officers, generals, suppliers, etc. who would have to be consulted. Another point is that the army was being formed expressly for Bonaparte's personal use, which runs contrary to the comments of Bourrienne, who stated that the First Consult was prevented by the constitution from commanding an army outside the territory of France (there is nothing implicit in the constitution of Year VIII which backs this claim). A final point of interest to students of Napoleonic warfare is the reference to formations given the name 'grand corps'. Under the First Empire, Napoleon perfected an army corps system. Each *corps d'armée* was an all-arms force under the command of a marshal or senior general capable of independent missions, and was largely self-sufficient. In 1800, Bonaparte was experimenting with this concept, but on a smaller scale to what would become norm in the empire. At this time there was no intermediate rank between a general of division and an army commander. What Bonaparte proposed here was some of the more senior generals being nominated as lieutenant generals (a modern four-star general), with two divisions of infantry under their command, and a central cavalry reserve. By building up the independence of these grand corps, Bonaparte hoped to make his army more flexible, with each corps capable of a degree of operational independence.

By placing the centre of this new army at Dijon, it could theoretically fight in Germany or Italy. However, from the outset Bonaparte looked at a descent on Italy through the Swiss Alps. Italy was the theatre of his first major success, and the loss of northern Italy in 1799 was a dent in French prestige. For his plan to be successful, Bonaparte was heavily reliant on the Army of the Rhine and the Army of Italy coordinating their operations in order to support his dramatic march through the Alps. The largest army was that of the Rhine, commanded by General Jean Victor Marie Moreau, and this was a problem. Although Moreau had supported the *Brumaire* coup, he remained a potential political rival to Bonaparte. The fact Moreau was mortally wounded at the 1813 Battle of Dresden by a French cannonball while talking to the Russian Tsar indicates the type of relationship the two men had. However, the First Consul could not easily dismiss Moreau, because that risked opening a conflict. Instead, it would take careful and patient work to get Moreau to do his bidding.

The critical command was that of Italy. Here Bonaparte sent General André Massena to take charge of a perilous situation. Having beaten the Russians at Zurich, Massena could have hoped for a prestigious appointment, but Bonaparte needed him to stabilize what was left of the Army of Italy and, most importantly, keep Melas occupied long enough for the Army of the Reserve to cross the Alps. Of all the generals then available, Massena was the best man for the job. A native of Nice and a veteran of the earlier Italian campaigns, Massena was perfectly acquainted with the region which would form the theatre of operations in the spring. The celebrated memoirist Marcellin de Marbot called him 'the wiliest of Italians'. He knew the people, the mountains, the passes and tracks (he had turned his hand to smuggling before the war); and he had a passionate, winning mentality, one perhaps second only to Napoleon Bonaparte himself. After his prominent role in the first Italian campaign, Bonaparte called him 'dear child of victory'. His victories in Switzerland in 1799 preserved this strategically important country for the French, and became the bedrock of the First Consul's strategy in 1800. The Austrians were certainly very wary of his capabilities.

Having been appointed army commander on 14 November, Massena only arrived in Genoa on 10 February. His journey to the port took him through Provence, his native Nice and into Liguria. The state of the army was even worse than anyone in Paris could have imagined. Massena's predecessor, Championnet, had died at Antibes on 9 January after falling ill from typhus. Marbot claimed Championnet had really died of grief at seeing his troops reduced to such a pitiful state. Without provisions, order had broken down and the men were left to scavenge as best they could. Bands of soldiers headed for the bridge over the Var and sought a better fate in Provence, claiming they would return to duty when the state could feed them. The officers and generals were little better inclined to serve in such miserable conditions. They requested leave, new postings or simply resigned. The hospitals were bursting with the sick and starving on bare floors next to unburied corpses. In short, the army was disintegrating rapidly. Massena wrote to the First Consul on 5 February with his early impressions, announcing that his army was 'absolutely naked and barefoot' and had been without pay for six to seven months. There was no forage for the horses and a total lack of transportation. On 23 February, he concluded that the country of Liguria was exhausted and he was forced to put all soldiers on half-rations, leading by example. He also reduced the daily ration for civilians to 3oz of bread per day – in modern parlance, the equivalent of three slices of wholemeal bread for a day – around 230 calories. The situation there was critical, and it would take time to turn things around. Discipline would have to be restored. Provisions would have to be found. The men would need to return to their colours. Massena's only hope was that the Austrian army was in a similarly poor condition and would give him the time he needed to perform a miracle.

Chapter 3

The Savona plot

'Go scout out the land leading up to the Great St Bernard Pass,' he'd been told – the pass at the top of the Aosta Valley. 'Check the Great St Bernard. Take your uncle Costa's notes and have a good look round.' That was his mission, his contribution to the imperial war effort during the winter lull.[1] Henri Milliet de Faverges et de Challes, Marquis de Faverges (1775-1839) was a native of Chambéry, the historic capital of the Duchy of Savoy, an alpine region now forming part of France, Italy and Switzerland. Although Faverges was born on the French side of the Alps, at the time of the storming of the Bastille in 1789, Savoy found itself part of the Kingdom of Sardinia, under the reign of Victor Amadeus III (1726-1796), whose capital was in Turin, on the Italian side of the mountains. This kingdom included Savoy, Aosta, the County of Nice, Piedmont and of course the island of Sardinia itself. It is worth remembering that at this time, pre-*Risorgimento* (unification), Italy, like Germany, was a geographical expression only; a collection of independent states of one description or another, not by any means a united political entity.

Controlling many of the alpine passes into the rich plains and cities of northern Italy, Savoy was a key strategic possession. When the wars of the French Revolution broke out in 1792, France quickly moved to annex Savoy. This act of hostility caused Victor Amadeus to join the First Coalition against France, allying himself with the Habsburg Empire, Prussia, Great Britain, Spain and Holland. In his seventeenth year, Faverges upheld his family's long tradition of military service and joined the corps of Royal Grenadiers. For three years, the soldiers of Victor Amadeus waged war in the mountains and alpine passes, preventing the French from descending into Italy; all until a newly wed, 26-year-old Corsican general named Napoleon Bonaparte took control of the French Army of Italy in March 1796. Within a matter of weeks, General Bonaparte and his bedraggled soldiers were victorious everywhere. Victor Amadeus was obliged to sign an armistice and formally quit the coalition, ceding Savoy and Nice to France and permitting the passage of French troops through Piedmont.

Gaining passage through Piedmont allowed the French to sweep along the River Po, through Piacenza, into Lombardy, entering Milan on 15 May 1796, and then Verona on 3 June. The relentless pace of Bonaparte's advance was slowed by the great fortress city of Mantua and successive Austrian attempts to relieve the place;

but by February 1797, Mantua had fallen. By April, the French were marching on Vienna itself and the Habsburgs were forced to seek an armistice with Bonaparte at Leoben on 18 April. This in turn led to general peace negotiations, ratified in the Treaty of Campo Formio which was signed on 18 October 1797, formerly bringing the war, and the military coalition against France, to a close.

There was something of a lull for half a year, and then the irrepressible Bonaparte took much of his Army of Italy off on their oriental interlude. While Bonaparte entertained lofty ambitions of emulating Alexander the Great, Faverges found himself in somewhat of a quandary. Bonaparte had spared Victor Amadeus' throne (somewhat to the surprise of the Italian revolutionaries who had aided the French), but the king lived just a few months more, dying on 16 October 1796. His successor, Charles Emmanuel IV, maintained his independence only a little over a year, until in December 1798, the French occupied Turin and forced him to abdicate to the island of Sardinia. A pro-French provisional government was formed and the Piedmontese Republic was declared. With the abdication of the king, Faverges had a decision to make. No longer bound by his oath of loyalty to the monarch, he chose to serve in the army of another nation. Of noble birth and carrying the scars of several French musket balls in his body, there was little chance of him throwing in his lot with the godless republicans. Instead, he chose Austria and joined the imperial army of the Habsburg Empire.

For most of Faverges' new brothers-in-arms, the lull after the fall of Cuneo was a time to make good and recuperate, to prepare themselves for a new campaign. At this time, Faverges was serving as a staff officer under the imperial army's quartermaster general, or chief of staff, Anton Zach. As an officer on the staff, the winter break was a busy time of planning and preparation. Somewhere over the looming Alps, the French were also preparing. In 1799, Bonaparte had returned from Egypt, then seized power in France in the *Brumaire* coup. The spy reports and open sources indicated the new French First Consul was planning to build a new army in France to reverse the misfortunes of 1799. Thus in the early months of 1800, Faverges set off for the Aosta valley on his mission to put his local knowledge to the test and scout up to the Great St Bernard Pass. He took with him a set of notes written by his uncle, Joseph Henri Costa de Beauregard (1752-1824), a topographical engineer in the Piedmontese Army. He was accompanied on this mission by his 'domestic', an orderly by the name of Jusping – an indiscreet 'comedian' all too quick to dent his master's ego. Faverges forgave him this because the man was a genius at making omelettes and risotto.

Having escaped an encounter with bandits (after eight years of conflict, the mountains were home to all sorts of itinerant desperados) and an angry husband whose wife made keen eyes at the officer (or so Faverges flattered himself), Faverges reported to the local commander at Aosta, General Major (GM) August de Briey, who commanded a body of troops including the Franz-Kinsky Infantry Regiment and some Croatian grenzers – light troops drawn from the empire's borders with the Ottoman Empire. GM de Briey was in his early fifties, a native of the Austrian Netherlands, and with very little military experience – in Faverges' opinion. He appeared to be living reasonably comfortably in a country house, which he shared with a pockmarked ADC and four other 'scatterbrains'.

No doubt irritated by the energetic Savoyard, GM de Briey allowed Faverges to get on with his mission without too much interference. A local guide was arranged: a hunter who specialized in stalking alpine chamois. The two men explored the Aosta valley. This was a region of steep mountains, lakes and glaciers, cut by the Dora Baltea River which flows down from the slopes of Mont Blanc, eastwards to Aosta, before turning sharply south on its journey to the great River Po. For a traveller on the Italian side, the entrance to the valley was protected by the imposing fort of Bard. Only after passing this stronghold could an army venture out of the alpine pass and reach Ivrea, from where one might join the roads to Turin or Milan. After years of warfare, the mountainous valleys were desolate, with agriculture neglected and many houses burned. At the heads of the valley were two road passes, the Little St Bernard (2,188m) and the Great St Bernard (2,469 m), which connected Aosta to Martigny in the Valais canton of Switzerland. At the top of the Great St Bernard Pass was a hospice for travellers, looked after by monks and their giant dogs. Although difficult, this alpine pass was a long-established route for travellers. It had a Roman road and formed the medieval *Via Francigena*, one of the main routes of pilgrimage through Western Europe leading from Canterbury in England to Rome. As was the case with most of the Alpine passes in the winter of 1799–1800, when the French had retreated across the mountains they left detachments of soldiers at the heads of the valleys. Although these detachments were not full garrisons in their own right, they were certainly enough to scout the passes and give warning of hostile moves against them. Possession of them would give the French a strategic advantage in the coming campaign season.

In his memoirs, Faverges states that the Austrians considered the snow-bound Alps an impenetrable barrier in winter. Indeed, some of the mountain passes his guide led him to explore were, in his words, 'neck breaking'. However, as he became used to the conditions up in the mountains, the young staff officer began to show a greater interest in the French position at the top of the Great St Bernard Pass. The huntsman revealed there were paths up over the mountains which would allow them to capture the pass from the French. One was a route up to the 'chalet of Faggian' which led down to Orsières on the French side of the pass. It was then a case of marching up the road to St Pierre and taking the French troops by surprise from the rear of their position. There was another route too; one only practicable in the depths of winter when the snow was frozen solid. It led towards an adjacent valley to the west of the Great St Bernard, where the village of Ferret was located. From there, a precipitous path led almost directly down on top of the hospice. It would have seemed as if the Austrians had fallen from the sky. Faverges began to formulate ideas about seizing the pass from the French.

Returning to de Briey's comfortable headquarters, Faverges outlined the possibility of capturing the pass. Faverges explained the two potential routes and offered the general the choice of which to attack, declaring he would personally lead the venture. De Briey listened to the proposal thoughtfully before giving his reply:

'Madness! Utter Madness!'

Why, de Briey wanted to know, should he risk the lives of his troops on such an ill-conceived adventure on top of an ice-bound mountain? What possible gain could outweigh the inevitable loss of life such an escapade would entail? Somewhat crestfallen, Faverges accepted the general's decision. The two men supped together, then went to a social engagement at the home of Madam Bard. Writing his memoirs years after the event, the Savoyard admitted he then had no idea what part the Great St Bernard Pass would play in the great drama of 1800, but his instinct to deprive the French of the pass was the correct one. De Briey is said to have admitted his mistake too, and apparently later blew his brains out in remorse for not having acted with more audacity. We do not know if this is true or not, but this story is the first of several missed opportunities on the part of the Austrians that year. Much worse is to come.

Faverges remained some time at Aosta until he was recalled to Turin. Arriving in the Piedmontese capital, he went to make his report to his chief, a little before 25 February. The chief of staff was suffering from an eye infection, so Faverges found Zach in his quarters, in a state of undress, sitting in his bed, the blankets covered with maps and various documents. Somewhat affronted by his commander's *toilette*, Faverges compared Zach to a hoopoe bird, a creature known for emitting ill odours and wallowing in its own filth. Nevertheless, he gave an account of his time in the mountains, and may even have outlined his scheme for capturing the Great St Bernard, but he was interrupted.

A second staff officer arrived in the room, Lieutenant Colonel Anton von Biking (sometimes written as 'Piking'). The appearance of this officer was evidently unexpected, and had the effect of an electric shock on Zach.

'What! What!' Zach exclaimed, throwing his bed covers into the air. 'What are you doing here?'

Biking stood in the middle of the room and rolled his eyes. Clearly, he had not expected his appearance to elicit such a response.

'I was recalled,' Biking said at last.

'What! By whom? How?'

'But, by order of the commander-in-chief!'

'By order of the commander-in-chief!' Zach exclaimed. 'Oh my God, the madmen! That imbecile Melas! That blasted Radetzky! Everything has gone to the devil!'

Zach jumped out of bed and hurriedly began to dress. Slightly bemused by the exchange, Faverges thought it would be helpful to tell Zach his cravat was not straight and his shirt was hanging out of the back of his breeches, but the chief of staff was already running up the staircase 'with gouty legs', heading in the direction of Melas, the commander-in-chief. So what had these 'madmen' done to enrage Zach so? This takes some explaining, but it is crucial for our account, because at this moment, rarely discussed in other accounts of 1800, the Austrians may perhaps have just lost the war.

We remember the final act of the 1799 campaign. The spy Gioelli had just brought about the surrender of the city of Cuneo. This effectively cleared the republican forces out of northern Italy. On 5 December 1799, Zach presented the Austrian commander, Melas, a strategic review of the Austrian situation. An excerpt reads:

> 'The fall of Cuneo has made all the enemy's hopes of being able to hold out across this winter evaporate. Their next operation can only be aimed at defeating our army in order to lay siege to a fortress, which would form a secure foothold in Piedmont for them. These fortresses can only be Cuneo or Alessandria. How little capability the enemy now has for such an offensive is only too obvious; we can consequently safely assume that the enemy will abandon all long-distance operations into Piedmont, merely limiting themselves to the defensive, occupying the mountain passes into the Riviera and thus deployed this way, await the spring. They would be acting more intelligently if they went into winter quarters to allow the wreckage of their troops, who have been ruined by their misfortunes, to recover and create a new army for themselves with which to recover Piedmont. For this reason, we can also go into winter quarters like them and promise ourselves some rest.'[2]

Zach added something of a caveat to this assessment. With the fall of Cuneo, clearly the Austrians had the superior morale and physical superiority. Should they not press on into the Riviera and drive the French out before they had time to recover? If they waited until the spring, the enemy would recover. Should they strike now? There was certainly a case to be made for this course of action. However, on balance, Zach concluded the army needed rest and had earned a break to increase its strength, put everything into good order and reorganize.

This assertion is reflected in the account by staff officer Joseph Stutterheim. He recorded the army was 'exhausted', with some regiments reduced by sickness and combat casualties to an effective strength of just 300 men. If Zach had recommended a continuation of the campaign, it would likely have required laying siege to several major cities in the Ligurian Riviera, including Genoa and Savona. This would have sapped the army's strength further and rendered it less able to withstand the inevitable French response in the new campaign season. So the Austrian army went into winter quarters. Having witnessed near continual strife and conflict for four years, the countryside was wasted, so Zach spread the army's cantonments far and wide along the River Po.

For Zach, there was no real let-up in planning for the spring. Early in the New Year, he began to receive reports, some through secret means and others from the newspapers in Turin, that the French were planning to assemble a new army in the Dijon area. It stood to reason this army would march on Italy, perhaps through Switzerland and the St Gotthard once the alpine passes were clear in April. This would leave the Austrians in a difficult situation, caught between the French in the Rivera and those arriving from the north.

In Stutterheim's account, we read that the Austrians knew the snow in the mountain passes over the Apennines generally cleared six weeks before those of the Alps. The imperial army therefore had this small window of opportunity to clear the French out of Liguria and form a defensive line against France along the River Var, before turning round to meet anything coming from the direction of Switzerland. This was the strategy Zach would recommend, and in addition to his spies (Gioelli was not the only one), the Austrian chief of staff ordered officers like Faverges up into the mountains to reconnoitre and report back to him on what they observed there.

At the same time, very much behind the scenes, Zach was working on yet another audacious scheme. Around the turn of the year, two officers in French service appeared in Turin and presented themselves to Melas. The Austrian commander turned them over to Zach for interrogation. They were Brigadier General Giulio Domenico Assereto and his adjutant, Chief of Battalion the Marquis de Sainte Croix. Assereto was a native of Genoa and commanded the town of Savona, the French army's main store. In return for safe conduct for their families, Assereto claimed he could deliver Savona to the Austrians and issue a proclamation to the local population to rise up against the French. It all sounded too good to be true, but with Gioelli's exploits in Cuneo still fresh in the mind, Zach did not discount the idea altogether. In fact he began to explore the opportunity in some detail. The Austrian chief of staff opened a secret correspondence with the pair and invited them to Turin, all the while suspecting them to be royalist agents posing as republicans.

Savona was a tantalizing prize. Unlike the difficult route through the Bochetta Pass to the fortified port of Genoa, the mountains at Savona were somewhat lower. Savona was on the coast, 40km west of Genoa. If Savona could be captured, the French in Genoa would be cut off from France. Working in tandem with the British Royal Navy, Zach saw Genoa could be blockaded by sea and land, with little hope of relief. Meanwhile, the Austrian army would be able to push westwards toward Nice and the River Var, clearing the Riviera of French troops entirely. The cooperation of the British was key, as the narrowness of the Riviera placed French troop formations in the range of naval artillery. Fortunately for the Austrians, the British proved amenable to the idea, with the deepwater port of Genoa a strategic prize for them.

Through the course of January, the secret correspondence continued. Saint Croix travelled into Turin in disguise and announced a third French officer had joined the plot. The newcomer was Chief of Brigade Charles Sans Mascaril, whose principal motivation appears to have been to reignite a love affair with a lady in Piacenza, a city now in Austrian hands. A secret meeting with Sans Mascaril was hurriedly arranged, in which the Frenchman stated that the commandants of Savona and Vado, both Genoese, were prepared to join the plot. Sensing the time might be right to call the army out of winter quarters, Zach began to involve the Austrian commander at Alessandria, Feldmarschalleutnant (FML) Friedrich Franz Xaver Count Hohenzollern, in the planning. Using neutral passports purchased from the Danish Consulate in Genoa, a communication line was set up through Novi allowing these 'men of the night', as Hohenzollern described them, to come and go. Meanwhile, Zach drew up an operational plan and issued it to Melas, who referred the matter to Vienna and received an enthusiastic approval from their political masters.

It was a fantastic plan; a masterful combination of *ruse de guerre* and *coup de main*. Assereto would inform the Savona garrison a reinforcement of troops was arriving by sea. A small flotilla of Genoese *feluccas* was assembled at Livorno (Leghorn), the home base of the British Mediterranean fleet. Sailing under the flag of the neutral Ligurian Republic, these transports would arrive in the port of Savona. On board would be 350 imperial infantry and artillerymen. Two hundred of the infantrymen would be fluent French-speaking Walloons, disguised in captured French uniforms. To lend credence to their arrival, the British would arrange to chase and fire at the transports. Once the disguised troops had run the boats up onto the beach, Sainte Croix would ignite signal fires. Meanwhile, inside Savona, Assereto would arrange for the senior French officers to be invited to dinner out in the countryside that evening. En route to dinner, they would be abducted. If there were any problems inside the fortress, Assereto would be assisted by a small team of seven Austrian soldiers infiltrated into Savona, dressed in civilian clothing and armed with pistols. Led by staff officer Oberleutenant Rumerskirchen, if necessary these handpicked men would overpower the French guards and throw open the gates. At daybreak, two columns of Austrian troops would descend from the mountains, led by local guides and an advanced guard of 200 men under Major Biking (the same whose appearance would cause Zach to explode in a rage). Savona would belong to the Austrians, and the French army would be cut in half long before any assistance could come over the Alps. When he later heard of the plot from Zach, Faverges described it thus: 'What a lightning strike, indeed, one that would have brought us down from the sky like meteorites in the middle of the French army.'

The date of the attack was set for the night of 24/25 February. Ten days were required to bring the troops out of winter quarters and concentrate them, so the necessary orders went out on 14 February. However, in all the elaborate planning one thing had escaped Zach's notice. A small thing no doubt, almost trivial in fact, but one which would arguably not just jeopardize the mission, but ultimately perhaps cost Austria the war.

Melas had set up his headquarters in Turin, and there, with his wife and a certain degree of comfort, he rested from the rigours of a long campaign; a campaign he had not expected to serve in at all, let alone command. Michael Friedrich Benedikt von Melas had been born on 12 May 1729 in the German, or 'Saxon', colony of Siebenbürgen, better known to us today as Transylvania, in Romania. He was descended from evangelical Lutheran priests, but enrolled in the infantry as an officer cadet at the age of 17 and then steadily progressed his career, fighting in the Seven Years' War (1756–1763) and finishing the conflict as a captain of grenadiers. Opportunities then came in the heavy cavalry, the karabiniers and kurrassiers. A war with Turkey in 1788 paved the way for Melas' promotion to general major in June 1789, a month before the storming of the Bastille. Now in his sixties, Melas saw Europe plunged into the bloodiest of wars. He initially served on the German front in the conflict against France, rising to the rank of Feldmarschalleutenant in 1794. Melas was then transferred to Italy, where he experienced Citizen Bonaparte's lightning warfare for the first time. Melas had spells of independent command, but found himself deputy to FML Wurmser. When the Treaty of Campo Formio was signed in 1797, Melas sensed it was time to hang up his spurs, retire to his home in Graz and enjoy the company of his wife ... or so he thought. In 1799, Melas was called out of retirement and asked to command the army in Italy. Melas' first response was fairly emphatic: 'I am in no condition to lead that.'[3] The trouble was that the best generals were already assigned to commands, including Baron Kray, Count

Heinrich Bellegarde, the Prince Johann Liechtenstein and the counts Klenau and Sommariva, the first four to Germany, and the latter for the Government of Tuscany. Command was offered instead to the Prince of Orange. Alas, soon after arriving in the theatre, the prince died in Padua. The glare of the Hofkriegsrat (the Habsburg war council) returned to Melas, who begrudgingly accepted the appointment. Arriving at the court, he told the Archduke Charles' chief of staff he was 'simply going to His Majesty to thank him for his gracious punishment, as he viewed it'. The Archduke was apparently not impressed with the appointment, declaring: 'As army commander in Italy, we now have Melas - alas!'

When the unhappy Melas finally set out for Italy from his home in Graz, he did so with a substantial baggage train and wife in tow, and made slow progress into the theatre. Stutterheim gave a very frank assessment of Melas at this time.[4] He described him as 'a brave old man of more than 70 years, a good soldier, for his part brave'. He was, Stutterheim conceded, 'considered in earlier times a good cavalry officer who understood how to fiddle around with his regiment'; but as commander of the army in Italy, Stutterheim felt Melas was completely out of his depth. More importantly, crucially in fact, Melas' health was visibly in decline. In the winter of 1799/1800, Stutterheim remembered how the old man tended increasingly towards 'leisureliness' and welcomed peace and quiet. Melas was 'workshy', Stutterheim claimed, and would welcome anyone who took the burden of work upon themselves, hardly appearing interested in the content of the orders he signed 'with a trembling hand'. His only relief appeared to be visiting the spa baths at Acqui. This was the man who would have to confront the French First Consul, forty years his junior and one of the greatest military leaders history had known.

While Melas rested in Turin, the younger officers were intent on enjoying themselves. Turin was the perfect place to hold parties and balls. Some even came out from Vienna to take advantage of these brilliant winter quarters, among them a bevy of the most glittering young ladies, including the 19-year-old Francisca, the Countess Radetzky, wife of Melas' right-hand man, the general adjutant, Colonel Count Josef Radetzky. Faverges described the countess as 'young, lively, infinitely pleasant and witty', saying she was in the front rank of society. In turn, her husband, Radetzky, was 'no less brilliant' and 'liked enjoying himself as much as her'. Radetzky is now considered a national hero in Austria and was immortalized by Johann Strauss' march of the same name. Born in his family castle at Trebnitz in southern Bohemia on 2 November 1766, Johann Josef Wenzel Anton Franz Karl, Graf Radetzky von Radetz was descended from a noble old Bohemian military family. Stutterheim describes Colonel Radetzky as the perfect officer, bold and fearless on the battlefield, but with a captivating nature and witty. If anything, Stutterheim believed Radetzky was only at fault because he was 'too much everybody's friend'. He was loved by the soldiers. In terms of his role, as the general adjutant he was Melas' right-hand man and the Austrian commander-in-chief rarely did anything without consulting him first. At the age of 33, Radetzky was perhaps the life and soul of the army. We should state at this point that in Stutterheim's first draft of his Marengo account, he said Radetzky and Zach hated each other.

To understand this conflict of personalities, we must understand Zach's background and personality in more detail. The chief of staff was not, Crossard remarked, 'a man who could be lost in a crowd'.[5] One can take that statement several ways. The chief of staff was not of the old nobility, but from a very intelligent, scientific family. His father was the medical superintendent for the city of Pest in Hungary. Caring for the military hospital in the city and the wider German-speaking community, his father gained the patronage of influential nobles, and was himself ennobled in 1765 by Empress Marie Theresa. Zach was the eldest of three brothers and had for a godfather one of the richest landowners of the country, Duke Anton Grassalkovich. While Zach and his youngest brother became soldiers (Karl was killed in action in 1792), the middle brother, Franz Xaver, became an astronomer of note (the Zach crater on the moon is named after him). Zach apparently shared this interest in astronomy, and also cartography, and maintained an active, intellectual correspondence with his brother, who travelled across Europe and appears to have been somewhat sympathetic to the French Revolution. In the 1780s, Zach was a mathematics professor at the Theresan Military Academy at Wiener Neustadt. His knowledge of mathematics, and his reading and knowledge of military texts, were acknowledged as second-to-none; but where others had received from nature 'the genius of war', Crossard believed Zach 'had received only the faculty to give lessons in it'. Stutterheim described Zach as having the air of an '*arch rector magnificus*' – a university chancellor.

Zach played up this supposed intellectual superiority by exhibiting a haughty tone, and the result was he had few allies among the operational commanders. His propensity for upsetting his colleagues is clearly illustrated in a long, stinging memorandum written in 1798. In this, Zach analyzed the performance of the Austrian Army in the conflicts against Turkey (1788-790) and France (1792-1797).[6] Having failed to produce 'a single great man', the Austrian Army, in Zach's opinion, was hindered by a combination of poor and indifferent leadership, stifling regulations and a great divide between officers and common soldiers. Although probably not widely read at the time, producing such works was hardly a route to gain popularity. As Crossard points out, Zach was not without his faults either. Crossard pointed out Zach's two 'great defects' as a chief of staff – 'he was forgetful and was untidy'. Furthermore, Crossard believed Zach relied too much on theoretical knowledge and lacked the activity to see the ground in person, and to observe and appreciate the advantages and defects it offered. Crossard also reports that Melas once described Zach to Bellegarde in very unflattering terms: 'You see that little fellow, he has a soul blacker than his face.'[7] Given Faverges' comparison of Zach to a hoopoe bird, perhaps there was something in Zach's *toilette* which affronted his colleagues? We do know from Stutterheim that Zach's pedantic manner caused him to become the butt of the junior staff officers' jokes. Zach could not even get on with his deputy, Colonel de Best, the pair being 'sworn enemies'. De Best was generally considered very eloquent and helpful, but he was a friend of Radetzky and apparently did everything he could to thwart his superior's plans.

As chief of staff to the army in Italy, there appear to be three specific events which led to the breakdown in the relationship between Zach and the army's senior commanders. In a letter to Alvinczy dated 5 August 1799, Zach explained the opposition he faced after recommending lifting the siege of Serravalle to free up some extra troops: 'I believed I had already made strides to win the confidence of the field marshals when everything was spoiled by my opposition to the siege of Serravalle. Now I am a pendant, scribbler, diplomatist [author's note: a studier of documents] and a speaker of uncertainties.'[8]

The next incident came after the Russians quit Italy and marched up to Switzerland. Melas saw that his troops were beginning to tire and wished to issue a suitably rousing order to his army, calling for one last effort to drive the French beyond the mountains, promising them winter quarters in Lombardy in return. Probably correctly, Zach changed the order because he felt it revealed too much about Austrian foreign policy; but he does not appear to have explained these changes to Melas in advance. After this, Melas began to increasingly distrust Zach, who was found to be in frequent contact with the Austrian diplomat responsible for foreign affairs, Baron Thugut.

The final blow to their relationship came after Cuneo. We have already seen Zach's recommendation to move into winter quarters after the fall of Cuneo. Radetzky's memoirs tell a different version of events. Apparently, Melas announced his intention to go into winter quarters as he had earlier promised his troops. Zach wanted to continue the campaign through the winter and press their advantage. Melas called a council of his most senior commanders to debate the issue. At this meeting, Radetzky set out the reasons why operations in the mountains could not be continued. There had been heavy losses over the nine-month campaign and the troops were exhausted; food was lacking, as was money; the country was exhausted and offered no means of preserving the army; and there was a lack of clothing and also a lack of animals. The senior generals nodded their heads in agreement with Radetzky's suggestion to leave a covering force of 25,000 men south of Turin at Carmagnola while the rest of the army rested in winter quarters. Having heard

Radetzky's advice, Zach haughtily produced a letter from Baron Thugut which expressly ordered the continuation of the winter campaign and appeared to make Zach responsible for this order. Melas was understandably angry: 'I believe that I, and not Zach, as commanding officer, have the responsibility, and declare that I accept orders not from the minister, but from my lord and emperor, and in his name from the war president.'

This episode is crucially important. The impact of this relationship between Thugut and Zach cannot be overstated. A civilian politician had in effect attempted to overrule the military commander in the field, circumventing the official channels of command by cultivating a relationship with the army's chief of staff.

We have mentioned Austrian military policy was steered by the Hofkriegsrat, the high military council in Vienna. The president of this body (i.e. the war president) was Count Ferdinand Tige (1719-1811), a long-serving cavalry officer, then general. However, the real power behind the throne in 1800 was the diplomat Johann Amadeus, Baron Thugut (1736-1818). A complex character, Thugut appears to have upset as many people in court as Zach did in the army. A commoner by birth, Thugut rose to become one of Francis II's most important advisers. Unmarried, Thugut spurned society. He rarely consulted with anyone, instead taking important papers directly to the emperor. His secretive nature and willingness to highlight the incompetence of others caused great anger among the nobility, who thought Thugut had been promoted far above his natural station. Known as the 'war baron', Thugut was determined to continue the war against revolutionary France. Others, like the Archduke Charles, were much more persuaded by the idea of rapprochement after a long and fruitless war, but Thugut overruled them. Without wishing to become bogged down in the complexities of Habsburg foreign affairs, Thugut saw Prussia as Austria's natural enemy (he was ultimately proven right in this) and, somewhat paradoxically, saw France as Austria's natural ally in opposing Prussian domination over the German States. The French Revolution had destabilized the natural order of things – Austria and France, two Catholic countries, with thrones united by marriage (Queen Marie-Antoinette was an Austrian princess by birth). All this had been destroyed by the creation of the French republic. There is also the small matter of Thugut's many and substantial financial investments in France before the revolution, and the inference that he stood to lose personally from the current state of affairs. Added to this, Thugut was strongly supported by Austria's coalition partner, Great Britain, and he was crucial for gaining British financial subsidies.

In the eyes of a noble like Radetzky, the interference in military matters by two men – born as commoners – must have been an affront. The fact that Zach was awarded the Maria Theresa medal in 1799 ahead of Radetzky must also have rankled, although the latter did not admit as much. What is clear is that from this episode onwards, the relationship between Radetzky and Zach was poisonous.

The above passages have been somewhat of a detour from our central account, but as if from the pages of Tolstoy, we must understand something of the men behind the uniforms and titles in 1800. These were all of flesh and blood, and as culpable to petty jealousies, aspiration and folly as the rest of us. Understanding their foibles helps us to understand the decision-making and actions in the field. A strong leader might have got the best out of the polar opposites of Zach and Radetzky, but Melas was too old, too tired and increasingly too ill to make this work.

Returning to the narrative, while Zach was busy concentrating on the Savona operation, Radetzky and his clique were planning a great ball. This would be the highlight of the winter season, and would be attended by visitors from Austria and Turin's most eligible ladies. What could be more important to a young Napoleonic officer than some society, glamour, perhaps even the chance of marriage? A venue was selected by Captain Albeck of the staff, but unfortunately this house was the very same which Zach used as a headquarters for his planning. When Zach found out Albeck was about to open to Turin society the doors of the building containing the Austrian Army's most sensitive plans and documents, he exploded with rage and had Albeck arrested. The chief of staff then returned to his documents and thought no more about the matter. Meanwhile, another venue was sourced and a date set for the night of 24 February. Of course the night set for the party was the same as the start of the Savona operation.

In winter quarters, no one had consulted with Zach about the timing of the party. They probably had no intention of inviting him after Albeck's detention. Conversely, none of the dancers knew anything about Assereto and the secret Savona plot. Radetzky's inside man on the staff, Albert de Best, had been sent away to Livorno to act as a liaison with the British on the expedition, so he was not in a position to tip off the general adjutant about the clash of dates. The first they knew anything about Savona was on 14 February, when Zach unexpectedly ordered his staff officers out of Turin to join the army columns. There was uproar at the news. This drastically reduced the number of dancers available for the ball, and many saw this as the pedantic Zach deliberately spoiling everyone's fun.

Fortunately for the dancers, the complex operation quickly began to unravel. Zach developed an eye infection, probably conjunctivitis, which effectively incapacitated him for the rest of the month. While recuperating, a supply contractor named von Bienenfeld informed the chief of staff the army's magazines at Ceva, Mondovi and Acqui were severely depleted. To keep the army supplied in the field would take an extra six weeks of planning.[9] While Zach raged about the contractor's incompetence, the weather suddenly turned for the worse. On the night of 13/14 February, there was heavy snowfall on the main Apennine routes, making them impassable even for spies. Even though it was likely this snow would clear after a few days of fine weather, Radetzky took this opportunity to administer the coup de grace to Zach's plan.

While the chief of staff was wallowing in his bed, surrounded by his maps and charts, Radetzky went to see Melas' wife, Josepha. It appears Radetzky was something of a favourite of Josepha's, and perhaps more importantly, the two were both from the old Bohemian nobility. Radetzky explained the difficult conditions in the mountains; conditions her poorly husband would have to endure if the expedition went ahead. Radetzky asked Josepha to have a word with her husband, and get him to see the sense in cancelling the operation until the better weather came. Despite having signed an order to commence the operation a few days previously, when Melas heard about poor weather in the passes, potential supply problems and of course Zach's poor health, he did not hesitate to sign the counter-order Radetzky placed before him.

The first Zach knew about the counter-order was when Biking interrupted his meeting with Faverges. When the half-dressed, enraged Zach finally encountered Radetzky, he was told the attack had been cancelled for three reasons: the bad weather, Melas' ill-health and the chief of staff's eye infection. Despite the willingness to proceed with the operation by a number of the column commanders, some of whom were marching in perfect sunshine, the counter-order had done its work and caused considerable confusion. Everyone returned to their winter quarters.

The opportunity to seize Savona by surprise was lost. The attack on Liguria was delayed, bringing the opening of the alpine passes ever closer. In fact the operation to take Liguria did not begin until 6 April and this delay was to have fatal consequences, as it afforded Massena a little time to restore the Army of Italy to something resembling a fighting force. We know how Zach felt about this turn of events, as he confided in Faverges years after the event (Faverges' brother had by then married Zach's daughter). Faverges remembered how the 'dignified general still pulled his hair out about the missed opportunity'.

Before closing this chapter, we should conclude with a postscript on the adventures of Faverges, as he does not follow us all the way to Marengo. Through the course of March, Zach received reports of French movements on Mont Cenis, the principal alpine route from Turin to France. The Austrian chief of staff sent Faverges to investigate, this time allocating him a small squad of soldiers, which included a Hungarian corporal, a drummer and eight 'crafty' Croats, strapping fellows who could have 'drunk the cellars of Heidelberg dry'. Leaving imperial headquarters,

Faverges headed for the town of Susa at the foot of the road leading up to the pass. He stopped off there to meet another uncle, Télémaque Costa, who had been fighting in the mountains since 1793 and was an expert in ambush warfare. Uncle Télémaque was evidently something of a character: 'He was an excellent man, crazily brave, friend of the peasants, heartthrob of their wives, generous with his money, full of spirit, and delighted every time he could play a trick on the French.' In addition to the latest intelligence, Uncle Télémaque furnished Faverges with some practical advice: the address of two ladies who had 'hosted' him for a long time at Oulx, the next major settlement on the road. Arriving at the town, he invited himself to dinner but was crestfallen to find 'the spinsters were on guard'.

A week or so later, Faverges and his men were attacked in a French raid. While his men sheltered behind willow trees and returned fire, Faverges tried to reach a position of cover. Unfortunately he was struck. At first Faverges thought it was just a bruise, but his leg began to stiffen. When the French pressed their attack, Faverges crawled off into a trench, where he was helped to the rear by a soldier wounded in the hand. Reaching safety, he paid two soldiers to carry him back to Susa, where they deposited him on a cart. By midnight he arrived at his mother's house in Turin. A doctor was summoned and at daybreak Dr Rossi arrived at the house. He made Faverges roll on his stomach and told him to bite down on the sheets and not to move, regardless of how much pain he felt. Faverges described the sensation as being cut with a knife made of violin strings. By the time the operation was finished, Faverges had passed out into a long deep sleep. It was the end of that war for him. For six days they feared tetanus would strike. Faverges' family and companions took turns to maintain a bedside vigil throughout.

Then one morning, just as his mother was reapplying the bandage on his foot, Colonel von Fellen of the Furstenberg Infantry Regiment came into the room. Speaking in German he informed Faverges his younger brother, Clément, had just been killed in a skirmish near Novi. Three officers had been killed in succession, and the men had hesitated. Clément took the lead and apparently shouted to the troops, 'I am only a white beak [i.e. too young to shave]; forward you old beards!' They raced off, but Clément was struck by a ball in the head and killed. He was just 17 years old. Faverges' mother listened to the colonel without understanding a word he said, but a mother's intuition could read on the officer's face what had occurred and she asked him nothing. 'Poor mother,' Faverges wrote ruefully. Many more mothers that year were destined to share her pain.

Chapter 4

French Preparations

The history books record precious little about Sub-Lieutenant Pierre Tourné. In 1800, he was about 28 years old and serving as an aide-de-camp (ADC) to General Henri Clarke, the Franco-Irish head of the Ministry of War's Topographical Office. Tourné had joined the colours in 1793, a volunteer in the 11th Battalion of Paris, and risen to the rank of sergeant-major when he was commissioned and selected for staff work. Evidently intelligent, he was instructed to make a reconnaissance of the route leading up to the Simplon and Great St Bernard passes just a few weeks after Faverges had performed a similar duty on the other side of the icy mountain range.

This mission was particularly important because, with the approach of spring, Bonaparte's attention became increasingly fixed on Switzerland and the opportunities it afford him. Since the fall of Cuneo, the easiest route into the great valley of the Po had been closed to him. Although it was not impossible to fight his way over the mountains from Savona and Genoa, the Austrians would likely see him coming and perhaps mount a counter-offensive in Germany. Then he would be too far away to react effectively. Bonaparte's preference was to keep his Army of the Reserve in the central position, opposite Switzerland. This would keep the Austrians guessing over his intentions, he supposed. He would launch an offensive in Germany with Moreau, and at the same time keep the Austrians busy around the Apennines with Massena. When the Austrians were pinned in position, he would pass through Switzerland with the reserve and fall on Milan, cutting Melas' lines of communication. It was a bold plan – perhaps even startling – and it was full of risk.

The first priority was to find a safe route over the mountains practicable for artillery. From the region around Zurich there were two routes which could be used for a descent on Milan, the Splugen or St Gotthard passes. Bonaparte had the former scouted by his ADC Duroc on 31 January. At the beginning of March, Lemarrois was ordered to look at the former. Bonaparte also wished to examine the shortest routes into Italy through the Valais (the upper Rhone valley) via the Simplon and Great St Bernard passes. The information held in the archives of the *dépôt de la guerre* (military records office) was insufficient to gauge the state of the country, so Tourné was sent with three objectives:

1. To reconnoitre the nature of the roads from Lausanne to Sion and to the St Gotthard; to also reconnoitre the passages of the St. Bernard and the Simplon; to learn if artillery and wagons could pass by these positions.
2. To reconnoitre the situation of all the villages, place by place; to note their population, their resources, especially in fodder.
3. To add to this intelligence everything which Tourné believed useful to collect.

The ensuing report, dated 31 March 1800, was extremely thorough and described something of a lost world cut off from neighbouring regions. The Valais, Tourné reported, extended from Saint-Maurice to the St Gotthard and took the form of a valley 40-50 leagues in length, and ½-¾ of a league wide (a league being approximately 4km, or an hour's normal march for infantry). It was bordered on each side by a long chain of mountains and was rendered almost impractical in winter due to snow. In the centre of the valley flowed the Rhone, which came very close to the mountains in many locations and formed deep chasms or marshes. The inhabitants were extremely poor, eking out a living on scraps of ground with landslides and floods to contend with. Many places had been devastated and burned during the war. What little grass did grow nourished the cattle, which were the only remaining resource of the country. Despite this, the strategic value of the Valais was critical. If the enemy were to capture the passes, there were a number of smaller passes which would allow them to advance into Switzerland towards Germany.

Tourné provided a detailed description of the route he took to the Great St Bernard. Exiting Lausanne, he approached the Valais by following the shores of Lake Geneva. The ground was very fertile and rich, and as he entered the Valais, he found the land was initially broad and fairly flat. At Saint-Maurice, Tourné crossed a stone bridge and entered the Valais proper, continuing on to Martigny, where the road to the Great St Bernard Pass was joined. The road was flanked by the River Dranse, which formed a deep gorge. At Orsières was a branch on the track which led to Ferret, a little pass which turned the Great St Bernard Pass and was guarded by a company of men in the summer months when the route was practical. After Orsières, the path became much steeper, beginning to zigzag past some smaller villages. As Tourné approached Bourg-Saint-Pierre, the road became increasingly narrow. At this village of less than 150 inhabitants, Tourné found mules which could be used for carrying loads up to the final ascent to the pass. The track leading up to Proz was no more than 2-3ft wide, littered with stones and bordered by a steep ravine. Reaching this place, the ground opened up a little and he began the steep ascent to the summit. Tourné described the path as zigzagging with five or six turns and becoming increasingly steep for the last hour-and-a-half to the pass. The snow here only melted for one or two months of a year, and if someone strayed from the path, they would remain buried there. At the pass was a monastery about 80ft in length and 20ft wide. The monks lived on the first floor. On the other side of the pass, the road began its descent. Tourné described a dozen soldiers guarding the pass, with twenty more in reserve at the convent. Although the slope was quite steep, the road was good – 3-4ft wide. If an ascent of the Great St Bernard was attempted, there was only enough room for three or four companies of men at the hospice. There was insufficient firewood, and it was too cold to bivouac in the open. The soldiers would have to reach Saint-Rhemy on the enemy side of the pass the same day they quit Bourg-Saint-Pierre. As for the enemy, Tourné learned with some accuracy that the Aosta valley was guarded by a battalion of the Kinsky Regiment and 500 Croatians. The French held the summit, although the entire Valais was protected by only a single half-brigade (the 28th) of just 2,000 men. When the passages cleared after the winter, it was critical to get more men to defend them, lest the Austrians in the valley below become more active.

The report concluded it was possible to use both the Great St Bernard and Simplon passes, and also the St Gotthard. The key advantage of using the Great St Bernard route, Tourné reported, was it only had 2-3 leagues of difficult terrain at the end. The Simplon was a far harder enterprise by comparison, with steeper roads and a longer difficult section. The Great St Bernard was also nearer to Lake Geneva, and supplies could be ferried to the entrance of the Valais from the magazines in Geneva. From there, the stores and equipment could be carried by mules. Where mules could pass, so could cavalry – although only in small detachments at a time. In terms of bringing vehicles up to the Great St Bernard, Tourné believed it was possible to use light wagons as employed by the locals; but after Bourg-Saint-Pierre, he recorded that 'extraordinary means' would be required to move artillery. 'This enterprise is not impossible to carry out,' he wrote. 'It would be necessary to dismount the pieces and place them on strong, narrow sledges.' These sledges could be transported to Bourg-Saint-Pierre on wheels, but then dragged the last leg of the journey. An experiment had been conducted the previous year moving a howitzer across the Simplon. It had been difficult, but it was possible.

While Tourné was scouting the alpine routes, the Army of the Reserve was beginning to take shape. The secret decree of 8 March 1800 confirmed:

Art. 1. There shall be organized a reserve army of 60,000 men.

Art. 2. It shall be directly commanded by the First Consul.

Art. 3. The artillery shall be commanded by General Saint-Rémy; the park by Chief of Brigade Gassendi; the engineers by the First Inspector of Engineers, Marescot.

Art. 4. Disbursing officer [*ordonnateur*] Dubreton shall perform the functions of Chief Disbursing Officer.

Art. 5. The different organizations and the conscripts that are to compose this army shall immediately take up the march for Dijon; they shall be cantoned in the towns within a radius of twenty leagues.

Art. 6. The Minister of War is charged with the execution of the present decree. He shall use every means to have collected at Dijon all the material necessary for the arming, clothing, and equipping of the reserve army.

BONAPARTE.

On 3 March 1800, Bonaparte had already instructed the Minister of War, Berthier, to begin collecting the necessary stores at Dijon, including 100,000 pairs of shoes, 40,000 coats or greatcoats and other articles of clothing. Also that month, Bonaparte made a series of direct appeals to the nation. If Frenchmen wanted peace, he stated, they would have to pay for it in 'money, iron and soldiers'. While Bonaparte had been in Egypt, France had introduced the conscription law of 5 September 1798. This law stipulated all bachelors from the age of 20 to 25 years were eligible for military service. Each year, the government would decide how many soldiers it required, and a ballot would be held to select them. The first draw would be from the 'class' of 20-year-olds, with the other classes balloted in turn as necessary. Some exemptions were made, and the men had to be medically fit for service. On 8 March 1800, Bonaparte passed a law which placed at the government's disposal all Frenchmen whose twentieth year had been completed on 23 September 1799. This law sought to catch those who had slipped through the net of earlier ballots, and to penalize those unable to serve, imposing fines on the family in order to pay for the uniform and equipment of a man who was fit to serve. Those men who were considered better employed elsewhere, or undertaking studies, were required to provide a substitute, in other words privately contract a fellow citizen to undertake military service on their behalf.

Former soldiers and veterans still capable of serving the country were also invited back to the colours. If they could not rejoin their old corps, they were to travel directly to Dijon where they would be armed and equipped, then formed into volunteer battalions. Those with the means to procure horses were invited to form volunteer squadrons, with the promise that the First Consul would name the officers of these formations personally. On 20 March, Bonaparte addressed all young Frenchmen, saying he had received many letters from young citizens who wished to serve their country. Bonaparte invited them to join the new Army of the Reserve and assured them 'glory waits for them in Dijon'. In fact this call for volunteers to flock to Dijon was something of a smokescreen – a military ruse. Bonaparte knew the Austrians would have spies inside the country, so by naming Dijon as the place of assembly, spies would be attracted to it. And what did they find there? A few hundred old men and boys – hardly an army. Meanwhile, the experienced, battle-ready half-brigades were marching from Paris or the western departments, passing through the Dijon region, collecting their new uniforms and stores, before marching off towards Switzerland. The hastily assembled volunteers were formed into something which eventually became a second Army of the Reserve. The deception appears to have worked, with the reserve being considered something of a laughing stock around Europe.

Of the real army, the 1st Division under General Jacques-Antoine de Chambarlhac was one of the first to march. This was composed of three infantry half-brigades – the 24th Light, with the 43rd and 96th Line, in total 8,055 men under arms. These were divided into two brigades, each under the command of a brigadier general. General of Brigade Jean-Baptiste Herbin commanded the 24th Light; General of Brigade Olivier Rivaud the 43rd and 96th Line. There was in truth little difference between light and line infantry at the time. Their structure and organization was the same – each half-brigade comprising three battalions, each with nine companies of men (eight centre companies and an elite company). In the line, the centre companies were called fusiliers and the elite were grenadiers; in the light half-brigades, they were chasseurs (huntsmen) and carabiniers (carbine-men). By 1800, both types of infantry were equally capable of fighting in a loose skirmish formation (*en tirailleur*), or in line or column formations. The light infantry were generally selected from the smaller, hardier recruits; men who could march day and night, and were practised in scouting work. There was no difference in the armament used by either type of infantry – both employed the single-shot, smoothbore, flintlock, muzzle-loading 1777 pattern musket and bayonet. Rifles were rare, the French seeming to prefer weight of fire to slow-firing accuracy; and grenades were only ever used in siege warfare. The only visible difference between the two types of troops was that the light infantry wore a short-tailed coat and had shorter gaiters, both of which were concessions to better agility. Some light infantry had also begun to wear the shako by 1800, whereas line troops (including grenadiers) mostly wore the felt cocked-hat, or *chapeau*. Chambarlhac's division also included an artillery component consisting of eight 8-pdr guns, and four 6in howitzers. When the guns were added to the ammunition wagons and forges, the division's artillery component actually comprised eighty-three vehicles. There were 103 gunners in the division, with another 200 carters on paper. However, at the point the division left Paris, this last component had yet to be formed, so a call went out for volunteers from the infantry to man the wagons until the division reached Dijon.

Chambarlhac's division quit Paris on 17 March, reaching Dijon in fourteen days. When the army marched, it did so in stages (*étapes*). In this case, the division averaged 26.5km per day, with two rest days. In fact, its *étapes* ranged between 18-35km per day, depending on the distance between the villages it was to be quartered in, or where it would bivouac for the night. In 1800, the French Army did not use tents on campaign. They required too much time to erect, were damp and insalubrious, wasting valuable space in wagons or pack animals in transport. Soldiers were either billeted with civilians, or they bivouacked, which is to say they slept in the open, with whatever rudimentary shelter could be improvised. This informal style of camping inevitably lead to a decline in discipline, and although looting was technically a capital offence, French officers turned a blind eye to all but the worst excesses of their men, who swarmed over the countryside looking for firewood and straw to sleep on.

Among the many thousands of young men in Chambarlhac's division making the march to Dijon was a grenadier by the name of Jean-Roche Coignet. Born in 1776, Coignet was conscripted in 1799 and incorporated into the 96th Line over the winter. He describes how his division came to be known as 'Chambarlhac's brigands' as it marched from Paris to Dijon, burning the staves from the vineyards and the poplar trees in the prairies along the route. After its arrival at Dijon, the division was inspected on 26 March. It was found that 298 men had deserted and a further 198 were hospitalized – a six per cent attrition rate for a two-week march through friendly territory.[1] This appears to have been fairly typical.

As the new army began to take shape, so the strategy for the campaign became clearer to Bonaparte. The following story may be apocryphal, but it is as illuminating as it is entertaining. Secretary Bourrienne is the source, and it forms one of the iconic moments of how we think of Napoleon Bonaparte planning his military campaigns. Bourrienne writes:

'On the 17th of March, in a moment of gaiety and good humour, he desired me to unroll Chauchard's great map of Italy. He lay down upon it, and desired me to do likewise. He then stuck into it pins, the heads of which were tipped with wax, some red and some black. I silently observed him; and awaited with no little curiosity the result of this plan of campaign. When he had stationed the enemy's corps, and drawn up the pins with red heads on the points where he hoped to bring his own troops, he said to me, "Where do you think I shall beat Melas?" – "How the devil should

I know?" – "Why, look here, you fool! Melas is at Alessandria with his headquarters. There he will remain until Genoa surrenders. He has in Alessandria his magazines, his hospitals, his artillery, and his reserves. Crossing the Alps here (pointing to the Great St Bernard) I shall fall upon Melas, cut off his communications with Austria, and meet him here in the plains of Scrivia" (placing a red pin at San Giuliano).'[2]

As cautioned above, this story is not entirely accurate. Indeed, the 1800 edition of the map by Captain Jean Baptiste Hippolyte Chauchard does not even show San Giuliano, which is at the centre of the great plain between Alessandria and Tortona. By his own recollection, Bonaparte thought he would meet Melas at Stradella, where the main road from Alessandria to Piacenza passed through a pinch-point between the River Po to the north and the Apennines to the south. Whatever superiority Melas might have in cavalry and guns, this position would reduce the Austrians' ability to manoeuvre. This would suit Bonaparte's infantry – the main component of the army he was raising.

Regardless of the accuracy of Bourrienne's account, it does not take such a great leap of the imagination to picture the first consul crawling over the map, tracing the main roads and rivers, and inserting pins; and whatever faults might be in the above passage, the plan of action it describes is by and large accurate, and by any measure brilliant. It had so much going for it. Rather than a frontal bloody assault against Melas through the traditional invasion route of the Apennines, Bonaparte would fall behind Melas and sit on his lines of communication with Vienna by seizing Milan. Although difficult to bring supplies over the Alps, Bonaparte reckoned on capturing Melas' magazines and living off those. The beauty of the strategy was the way the First Consul planned to use the Alps as a screen, passing eastwards unseen by the Austrians, his march protected by the covering forces positioned along the heads of the valleys. Given the time available to conceive this plan, with a government to form and his other projects, it was a work of extraordinary genius.

Another interesting move came on 2 April, when Bonaparte replaced Berthier as Minister of War with Lazare Carnot, the so-called 'organizer of victory' in the War of the First Coalition. Berthier was in turn appointed commander-in-chief of the new Army of the Reserve. Son of a noted military engineer, and graduate of the Royal School of Engineering at Méziers, Berthier had acted as Bonaparte's chief of staff in the first Italian campaign (1796-1797) and on the subsequent Egyptian campaign. He was a talented organizer and extremely hard working, but he was something of a worrier, with a noticeable stammer, and frequently chewed his fingernails. By appointing Berthier as commander-in-chief of this army, everyone knew Bonaparte intended to direct its operations personally. Why, then, did he not take charge of it by name? Perhaps this was a political move. To have been an army commander would have reduced Bonaparte to the equal of Moreau and Massena. By appointing his trusted lieutenant to the role, Bonaparte visibly remained First Consul, directing all France's military operations.

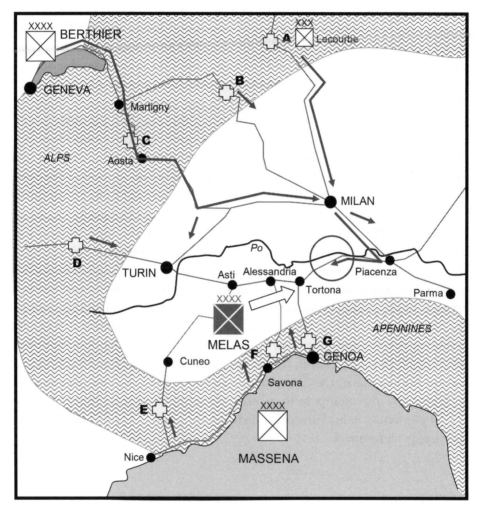

MAP 1: Bonaparte's Strategy – April 1800

While Massena held Genoa and the Ligurian Rivera, Berthier would advance with 40,000 men from Geneva via the Gt St Bernard (C) or Simplon (B) passes. Demonstrations would be made towards Turin, including an attack over the Mont Cenis pass (D), while the main army marched on Milan. The Army of the Rhine would detach 25,000 men under Lecourbe and advance on Milan via the St Gotthard pass (A). The army would then cut the main post road from Turin to Piacenza; and occupy the ground between there and Tortona (area circled). Melas would be forced to evacuate Piedmont and the Rivera, and march on Piacenza to recover his communications with Austria.

As we move into April 1800, the plan of operations crystallized and was brilliantly summarized in a set of secret instructions sent to General Massena by the new Minister of War on 9 April. The Army of the Rhine would commence operations later that month, Carnot wrote. Moreau would command the main body, comprised of 100,000 men, which would cross the Rhine and enter Swabia, advancing towards Bavaria for twelve to fifteen days' march. His mission was to intercept the communications between Germany and Milan, specifically the road from Feldkirch, Coire (Chur) and the 'Italian bailiwicks of Switzerland'. The right wing of the Army of the Rhine, 25,000 strong under the immediate command of General Lecourbe, would first occupy Switzerland, thus protecting Moreau's right flank and defending the route from Rheineck and Feldkirch to the St Gotthard and Simplon passes. Once Moreau had fulfilled his objectives, Lecourbe would come under the orders of General Berthier and march his corps southwards into Italy. At the same time, Berthier would pass through Switzerland, either by the Simplon or St Gotthard passes. The strength of the forces arriving in northern Italy was estimated at 65,000 men, including 6,000 cavalry and 2,000 artillerymen.

When this occurred, Massena was instructed to make diversionary attacks to draw the attention of the Austrians away from Milan. Until this time, Massena was instructed to remain strictly on the defensive, using the mountainous terrain to negate the Austrian superiority in cavalry and artillery. Massena was instructed not to advance into the plains beforehand, as it would be impossible to send him any reserves. In the meantime, he was to conduct a deception operation, exaggerating the strength of his forces, announcing the arrival of fresh troops and generally indicating that the main attack on Italy was going to come from him, not from Switzerland. Of course, the one flaw in this plan was that it supposed the Austrians had not guessed Bonaparte's intentions to use Switzerland, and that Melas would do nothing in the meantime to disturb Massena's diversions. Actually, while Carnot was sitting in his Paris office dictating these secret instructions, Massena was already under attack.

Chapter 5

Melas attacks

Histoy perhaps best remembers Count Adam Adalbert von Neipperg as the man who seduced Napoleon's second wife, the Empress Marie-Louise, and robbed her of any desire to share her husband's exile on Elba in 1814. Neipperg married Marie-Louise (or rather, Maria Ludovica) after Napoleon's death in 1821, and had three children by her (two outside wedlock while the former emperor was incarcerated on St Helena after Waterloo). He cut a fine martial figure, did Neipperg. Bayoneted and left for dead on a battlefield in 1794, he was lucky not to be buried alive in a mass grave, but fortune came in the guise of a charitable Frenchman who noticed he was still breathing and saved him from the burial pit. Having a French mother and been schooled in France before the revolution, Neipperg had an excellent command of his enemy's language, so much so that his saviours suspected he might be an *émigré* or spy. Having been plucked from the jaws of death, he was earmarked to be shot as a traitor once his wounds healed. As it happened, he was swapped in a prisoner exchange instead and returned to his native Vienna wearing a black patch and ribbon over his missing right eye. By the time he joins this account, Neipperg found himself in Italy, the chief staff officer assigned to the column of FML Konrad Valentin von Kaim.

On the eve of his twenty-fifth birthday, that is to say on the night of 7 April 1800, Neipperg took part in a spectacular mission to capture the Mont Cenis Pass at the head of the Susa Valley. Although relatively obscure in the annals of the Napoleonic Wars, the mission must rank among the most daring feats attempted by either side in the 1800 campaign, and we are fortunate to have an account of it written by Neipperg himself for the Austrian Military Journal in 1811.[1] Under the command of Major Joseph Mesko, a Hungarian officer from the 7th Hussar Regiment, Neipperg commanded a portion of the 1,200 men assigned to the mission. All were fit and strong, capable of making an arduous ascent up the mountains to fall on the French position at the head of the pass. With Mesco and Neipperg was Captain Costa of the Piedmontese general staff, and a local hunter. These two locals had an exact knowledge of the area they would be passing through and were critical of the mission's chances of success (Captain Costa was probably Faverges' Uncle Télémaque, the mountain warfare expert and *bon vivant*).

Assembling at Susa, the force drew rations of bread and brandy for three days and then set off under a bright moonlit night. Even with modern roads, from Susa to the pass is 30km, and there is also the matter of a 1,500 metre climb over the same distance. Neipperg and his companions chose a less direct route, climbing first to the Little Mont Cenis pass, which is 2,183 metres above sea level. One should stress they did this at night, without lanterns, in cumbersome woollen uniforms, carrying packs and heavy muskets. It was an astonishing feat. Neipperg remembered 'the cold was very great and paralyzed our limbs and strength.' Despite this, they climbed through deep snow which gave way underfoot, and clambered over the steepest rocks. Everyone had been issued with 'ice spurs' to fit over their shoes, a rudimentary form of crampon; but even then, most of the time they were on all fours, crawling through the snow. Several times they thought avalanches would come down on them. Several men slipped and fell to their deaths in the ravines: Neipperg coldly dismissed these victims as 'clumsy'.

Throughout the ascent, Major Mesko tried to encourage the men, calling out to them, 'Keep it up my children! Keep calm!' in the ten different languages spoken by the troops. The Walloons among the assault team seemed to find Mesko's multilingual exhortations quite funny. 'Laugh as long as you want,' Mesko replied to them. 'Only keep moving forwards! We are on the road to glory, which is just as worthwhile as the one to paradise, and has just as many hardships.'

They eventually reached the summit of the Little Mont Cenis, where they found the remains of fortifications from the fighting in 1795. A two–hour rest was announced and a distribution of brandy made. Some of the soldiers drank the liquor too quickly and fell asleep in the snow. They could not be woken and so froze to death on the spot. The column moved off again in great silence. Everyone was exhausted. Their muskets were soaked and many would have been impossible to fire, but they pressed on to their objective, preferring to face the French rather than have to return back down the mountain. Surprise and speed of movement were their only hopes of success, but if the French saw them coming in the bright moonlight, the mission would be a disaster.

The main French positions on the pass were at a hospice and a post house. In the nearby Saint-Nicolas valley, there were more French at the Inn of the Golden Cross. Mesko's force split into four columns and a reserve. Neipperg was charged with taking the hospice. In the darkness, he saw there was a burning brazier outside the hospice with forty men sat on guard around two cannons. Around half the French soldiers appeared to be asleep. When Neipperg heard the firing commence at the Inn of the Golden Cross, he advanced against the hospice at the assault pace. Arriving within musket range, his men formed up as if making ready to fire. The French outside the hospice were stunned by the sudden appearance of imperial troops. They threw down their weapons and raised their hats in a gesture of surrender. The commander of the position, Chief of Brigade Caffre, was quartered in a nearby house. Neipperg took twenty men and surrounded the building. Sword in hand, Neipperg went into the house and called on Caffre to surrender. The Frenchman was still putting on his boots as Neipperg entered his chamber. Caffre made a move for his pistols, causing Neipperg to retreat. The commotion from the two officers caused some of the imperial troops to run inside the house, and Caffre realized he was out of luck. He handed his sword to Neipperg and surrendered.

By daybreak, the raiding party had captured 1,300 men, mostly soldiers of the 15th Light Infantry, and eighteen gun emplacements. The Austrians did not stop there. They pushed on as far as Lanslebourg, on the French side of the pass, and would have captured Generals Jean Davin and Antoine Valette had a Croatian soldier not accidently discharged his musket on entering the village. Alerted, the two generals fled from their beds and hid in the mountains (Davin left his wife behind, but she was returned to Chambery by the Austrians under a flag of truce). They explored as far as Termignon and Bramans on the French side of the mountains. Neipperg did wonder about sending thirty hussars from Susa to raid Chambéry, but Kaim had cautioned them not to push any further. Their mission had been accomplished. Capturing the Mont Cenis Pass secured the right flank of Melas' army as it finally commenced operations in Liguria.

Following the cancellation of the botched Savona operation, the Austrian army returned to its winter quarters to await the warmer weather expected in the spring. One might imagine this extended break came as a boon to the imperial regiments, many of which had been severely depleted by the campaign of 1799. One might assume an extra six weeks would have seen their strength restored, but it appears this was not the case. Stutterheim's frank account of the campaign in Italy discusses how the Austrians experienced difficulties getting fresh recruits from their regimental depots to the Italian army. The recruits often had only limited training. They were formed into transports of 600–1,000 men and marched off to theatre with very little supervision. The recruits often went without basic necessities. Passing through regions devastated by war, they found little generosity from civilians and were forced to rely on their meagre pay to buy food. Often the recruits would have no means of cooking their food, so they purchased cold meats and bread in the marketplaces instead. At night they were herded into ruined monasteries or churches, where they slept on rotten straw which had already served as bedding for several men before. According to Stutterheim, for every 100 men sent from the Hereditary Lands, barely ten to fifteen actually arrived. He cited the example of the Infantry Regiment (IR) 28 Frölich, where just seventy men arrived in Lucca from a transport of 560 departing Kuttenberg (Kutná Hora) in Bohemia, approximately 1,100km away. Unsurprisingly, these recruits arrived in such a pitiful state that most remained behind when the regiment marched out of winter quarters. In another example, IR 45 Lattermann received just twenty-seven men from 600 sent out of the depot. In Stutterheim's opinion, they would have been much better served if fresh regiments had been sent and rotated with those most affected by the previous year's campaigning. Alas, Austria's resources did not permit this.

With his eye infection gone by the end of February, Zach returned to his maps and planned the strategy for the coming campaign. He had much to consider. Zach knew about the Army of the Reserve collecting at Dijon, and although the formation of this army had been decreed a secret, news of Bonaparte's intentions had reached Zach even before the cancelled Savona operation. Zach had thrown spies far and wide to tell him what was going on behind the Alps. He also knew the enemy was planning to enter Italy by one or more Alpine passes. For example, on 17 February, GM Loudon wrote from Arona on the banks of Lake Maggiore: 'According to the spy reports the enemy with 40,000 men should want to try crossing the Gotthard, Simplon and Saint Bernard at the end of the month.'[2] Even before that, on 28 January, Melas had written to the president of the Hofkriegsrat from Turin explaining that intelligence from spies indicated the French were procuring wagons and equipment in order to the enter the Upper Valais, and that their troops would be concentrated between Martigny and Geneva with this intention.[3] There were numerous local intelligence reports (many of which still survive in the Vienna Kriegsarchiv, but were not published by Hüffer) indicating small but constant troop movements through Switzerland and on the mountain passes. There is evidence some of this intelligence was supplied by Carlo Gioelli. According to Stutterheim:

'General Zach's spy [*Kundschafter*] had secured free access to Massena['s] headquarters. Provided with letters and tokens from this general, he could also go up to the region from Dijon from where he always brought the most certain messages about the strength and movements of the Reserve Army assembling there. Through him we knew that this was unable to undertake a serious operation before the end of April.'[4]

It is debatable if Gioelli dared show his face in Liguria after the Cuneo episode, but Austrian spies were certainly at work. It is more likely that Gioelli was able to operate in Switzerland, and perhaps as far as Dijon. In any case, the weight of evidence suggested something was going to come from Switzerland by one or more routes. According to Radetzky, when this intelligence was reported to the Hofkriegsrat it was largely discounted. Vienna reassured the army it should not be deceived by false news. The Ligurian Riviera was still thought the most likely route for a French invasion. This was the route Bonaparte had taken in 1796. He had magazines at Genoa and Savona, and the southern slopes of the Apennines were warmer for operations than the snow-bound Alps.

Whatever the French intentions, the Austrians fully intended to build on the success of the previous year. There were several options available: for example, they could invade France through the Mont Cenis Pass and advance on the Rhone Valley. Such a move would no doubt cause great consternation in France, but the outcome of it would be questionable. The Austrians would have to leave considerable covering forces around Turin and Alessandria to prevent Massena launching operations from Liguria in the south, and if Bonaparte's new army did debouch from Switzerland, the Austrians' lines of communication would be cut. Zach's preference was to concentrate on the Riviera, on pushing the French westwards, back behind Nice and the River Var. This would give the Austrians a shorter defensive line to prevent incursions into Italy. Knowing there was still a window between operations commencing on the Apennines and those on the Alps, covering forces could be left to watch the Alpine passes, and a strategic reserve maintained in Piedmont to react once the true direction of the French advance was known. By this time Genoa should have fallen, and the Riviera swept clear. Leaving a covering force on the Var, the Austrians would then be able to concentrate their forces in Piedmont and meet the arrival of the French from Switzerland. From an operational point of view too, it was far easier to mount operations over the Apennines than the Alps. Stutterheim indicates there was also political pressure from the British to capture Genoa for the mutual benefit of the coalition partners.

Over the course of March, Zach was left to develop the details of this plan. It was very much a replica of the earlier Savona operation, but without the same level of intrigue and complexity. The imperial army would manoeuvre as if they intended to make Genoa their main target; but they would actually attack at Savona, splitting Massena's line of communication with France. They would then advance westwards along the Riviera, pushing the French back beyond the Var, while a covering force blockaded Genoa. An active correspondence had been maintained with the Genoese General Assereto, and he promised to provoke a peasant uprising to assist with the operation. Assereto also proved an excellent source of intelligence on French movements in Liguria, sending reports to FML Hohenzollern about the poverty of supplies and poor morale among the French.

According to Stutterheim, by the end of March the imperial army in Italy consisted of 86,938 infantry and 14,541 cavalry – a total of 101,479 men. When the various garrisons were detached, around 80,000 men were available for field service. Of these, Zach allocated 30,000 (including most of the cavalry) to stay in Piedmont and remain in observation of the St Gotthard, Simplon, Great St Bernard and Mont Cenis passes. This left 50,000 men for operations against Genoa and the Riviera. The Order of Battle of the Austrian Army on 2 April 1800 shows the principal column commanders and their assembly points:[5]

Operational army on the Riviera

- Ott, with the brigades Eder, Stojanich, Gottesheim and Fenzel, nineteen battalions together, sixteen jäger companies and four squadrons of hussars; assembly point: on the Sturla;
- Hohenzollern, with the brigades of Rousseau and Döller, twelve battalions together, eight companies of jäger and four squadrons of hussars; assembly point: Novi;
- Palffy, with the brigades of Lattermann, Bussy, Sticker and St Julien, thirty-two battalions and four squadrons of hussars together; assembly point: Acqui;
- Elsnitz-Morzin, with the brigades Weidenfeld, Auersperg, Bellegarde, Ulm and Brentano, twenty-eight battalions and four squadrons together; assembly point: Ceva;
- Hadik, with the brigades of Pilatti and Festenberg, thirty squadrons together; assembly point: Acqui.

The remaining troops in Italy were comprised of:

- Vukassovich and Kaim, with the brigades of Nimptsch, Gorup, Knesevich, La Marseille, de Briey, Loudon and Dedovich, thirty-five battalions, twelve jäger companies and thirty-two squadrons together; formed in Piedmont;
- Fröhlich, with the brigades of Riera, Knesevich and Sommariva, eight battalions, two companies and ten squadrons, assembled around Rome and Florence;
- Standing garrisons: two battalions in Istria; two battalions in Terra Firma (i.e. the mainland Veneto region); three battalions in Venice; four battalions in Mantua and Verona; five battalions in Milan, Alessandria and Tortona.

At the outset of the campaign, we should take a moment to reflect on the composition of the Austrian army in Italy. Drawn from every quarter of the Habsburg Empire, it was multi-national, multi-lingual, a mix of Catholic and Orthodox religions and drawn from everywhere from the Low Countries to the Ottoman frontiers. With such a diverse pool of recruits, the imperial army perhaps lacked the same nationalist fervour of the French, but it instead relied on creating a strong regimental esprit de corps.

The flower of the imperial army was its cavalry contingent, although it did not include any heavy cavalry regiments. Instead, the cavalry contingent was composed of light dragoons and hussars. Given the campaign was to be largely fought in the mountainous Apennines, cavalry was of limited use beyond scouting and reconnaissance, so Melas had the bulk of his cavalry acting as a mobile reserve, half watching the Alps and half stationed at Acqui. Although Melas was a cavalry general by designation, the real expert in handling cavalry was FML Karl Hadik. Another gifted cavalry officer, one who would make his name in the forthcoming campaign, was the French-born Colonel Johann Maria Frimont, commander of the Jäger-Regiment zu Pferde, or Bussy Light Horse – a regiment partly populated by French *émigrés*. The imperial army was also strong in artillery, and had well-trained gunners. In addition to the reserve batteries (each of six field guns and two howitzers) and cavalry batteries (four 6-pdrs and two howitzers), each infantry regiment was allocated a pair of 3-pdr guns, which could either be used in the line for local fire support or massed into larger batteries. The imperial army was also strong in technical troops, with specialist pioneer battalions equipped with lightweight, portable bridges called *Laufbrücken*.

The most numerous component of Melas' army was the infantry. The infantry regiments comprised two field battalions each (a Lieb, or life, battalion, and an Oberst, or colonel, battalion), each formed of six companies of soldiers, with a nominal strength of 200 men per company; although, like their French counterparts, these strengths were rarely maintained in the field. Regiments had a smaller third battalion, normally formed of four companies, which usually acted as a depot. The infantry wore a compact, short-tailed white coat, which proved more economic and practical than long-tailed coats of the eighteenth century. The regiments from Western Europe and Poland were classed as 'German'. These wore white breeches. Troops from Hungary, Croatia and the military borders were designed as 'Hungarian' and wore light blue trousers. At this period, the majority of infantrymen wore a crested leather helmet with a brass plaque. The best soldiers from each infantry regiment were the grenadiers. Each regiment provided two companies of grenadiers, selected from their best, strongest and most physically imposing troops. When the army was assembled, the grenadier companies were amalgamated and formed into battalions, six companies strong. These battalions were in turn brigaded. In Melas' army, there were two such brigades of grenadiers, under the command of GM Christoph von Lattermann and GM Karl Philippi von Weidenfeld. These troops were to prove themselves as formidable opponents.

Tactically, we know the Austrians put thought into the forthcoming campaign. On 1 April 1800, Zach issued a tactical instruction on mountain warfare.[6] The key asset was speed. Regiments were instructed not to waste time with musketry. The most effective tactic was believed to be an attack with quick marching, closed-up formations, with military bands playing. Under no circumstances were the columns to disperse. Further, it was only thought necessary to throw a few skirmishers in front of these closed formations. Although the French skirmishers would be able to fire on the Austrian formations as they approached, the losses to skirmishers would be comparatively light if the attack was pushed home rapidly. If a protracted exchange with skirmishers took place, the fighting would likely be 'long and murderous' and, more crucially, would allow the enemy time to gather up his forces and respond to the attack.

It should be recognized that the Austrians did have light infantry specialists, which were necessary for a whole range of *petit guerre* operations, such as acting as an advanced guard, protecting camps and operating in difficult terrain. The army in Italy had numerous companies of jäger (huntsmen) and also several Grenzer (border guards) regiments. The former were drawn from the mountainous Tyrol region and were professional soldiers comprising hunters and backwoodsmen. They typically wore a neutral blue-grey uniform, which afforded a level of camouflage (a concept still fairly alien to European armies). The Grenzers, on the other hand, were men drawn from the military border with the Ottoman Empire, mostly of Croatian or Serbian stock. Although theoretically capable of fighting as line infantry, skirmishing was their preferred style of fighting. In French accounts, they were usually referred to as 'Croats' and had a fierce reputation.

Detailed instructions were issued to the various Austrian corps commanders on 30 March and everything was set. Melas would lead the main column assembled at Acqui. This column comprised the brigades of GMs Lattermann, Bussy, Sticker and St Julien (thirty-two battalions and four squadrons) and would head through Carcare and Altare over the Cadibona Pass for Savona. St Julien (twelve battalions and one squadron) would guard the left flank by marching through Mioglia to take Montenotte mountain. A second column assembled at Ceva under the command of FMLs Elsnitz and Morzin with the brigades of GMs Weidenfeld, Auersperg, Bellegarde, Ulm and Brentano (twenty-eight battalions and four squadrons). These would march through Carcare and turn south to Mallare, leaving GM Ulm around Millesimo to watch the upper Bormida valley and Mount Settepanni, protecting Elsnitz's right flank. The troops earmarked for operations against Genoa were commanded by FMLs Ott and Hohenzollern. When the main column's attack on Montenotte began on 7 April, Ott and Hohenzollern would also commence operations. Assembling in the Sturla valley, Ott's force consisted of the brigades of GMs Eder, Stojanich, Gottesheim and Fenzel (nineteen battalions, sixteen jäger companies and four squadrons). Ott would attack the French position at Torriglia with his infantry and one hussar squadron and secure the Bobbio road. Meanwhile, the brigade of GM Gottesheim (four battalions, all the jägers and

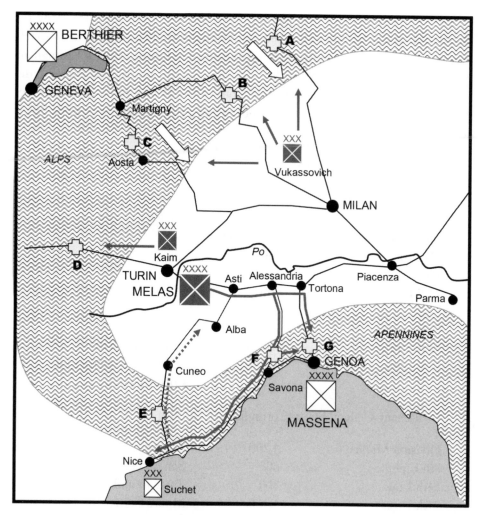

MAP 2: Zach's strategy – 30 March 1800

The army would probe Genoa through the Bochetta Pass (G), while launching the main attack at Savona via the Cadabona pass (F). The army would encircle Genoa and advance to Nice, clearing the French from the Rivera. Kaim would seize the Mont Cenis Pass (D), while Vukassovich monitored the Alpine passes of Gt St Bernard (C), Simplon (B) and St Gotthard (A). When Berthier's 'Dijon' army advanced into Italy, Melas would take the army from the Rivera towards Turin via the Tenda Pass (E), leaving Elsnitz to defend Nice against Suchet.

three squadrons) would attack Recco. A proclamation would be made on 5 April, calling on the Ligurian peasants to rise up against the French. These insurgents would come under the command of General Assereto. They would work with Hohenzollern in demonstrating against Voltaggio and the Bocchetta Pass on the direct route to Genoa.

This was an ambitious plan and exploited Massena's extended line along the length of Liguria. Not knowing where the Austrians would place their main attack, Massena had to string his forces out. He remained in Genoa, while at Cornigliano General Soult took command of the forces in western Liguria, The French order of battle of 5 April 1800 shows the locations of the French forces, and indicates how shockingly low in numbers many of the half-brigades were, with some barely amounting to half a battalion in strength:

Army of Italy, 5 April 1800
Commander-in-Chief: André Massena (Genoa)

Genoa Garrison
Commander: Adjudant-General Degiovanni

41st Line	350 men	
55th Line	250	
73rd Line	500	

Reserve

92nd Line	500	at Sampierdarena
25th Light	1,700	at Vestri di Ponente and Cornigliano

Lieutenant-General Soult (Cornigliano)

Division Miollis:	4,200	Albaro
8th Light	600	San Alberto and Recco
24th Line	800	Tortiglia and Scofera
74th Line	1,100	Monte Cornua
106th Line	1,700	Albaro and Nervi
Division Gazan:	4,920	San Quirico
3rd Line	1,300	Cazella, Buzalla and Savignone
5th Light	500	Voltaggio and Carasso
2nd Line	1,600	Campo Marone, Rivarolo and Ronco
78th Line	1,300	Campo Freddo, Marcarolo and Masone
Piedmontese Grenadiers	90	Teggia
Artillery	40	Bocchetta Pass
Pioneers (three companies)	90	San Quirico

Division Marbot:	4,700	Savona
3rd Light	900	Stella and La Madonna
62th Line	1,500	La Vagnola and Monte-Notte
63th Line	500	St Bernardone and Madonna di Savona
93th Line	500	Savona
97th Line	1,300	Vado and Cadibona
Garrison of Gavi		
45th Line	500	

In addition to the above troops, the Army of Italy also comprised the division of Thurreau (6,400), based at Briançon and guarding the alpine passes as far as Switzerland, including the Mont Cenis Pass.

On 5 April, Melas moved his headquarters to Cairo Montenotte, just 16km from Savona as the crow flies. At dawn the following day, GM Palffy led the attack on the Cadibona Pass on the road to Savona. Zach's detailed planning immediately paid off, as the French around Savona found Austrian columns coming at them from all sides. Given the Austrians' determination to ignore the harrying fire of skirmishers, but to drive forward quickly, the outnumbered Frenchmen had little option but to fall back on Savona or else be cut off in the mountains and surrounded. As the sun set on the first day of the campaign, Melas' troops were fighting on the outskirts of Savona. Realizing his situation was hopeless, General Marbot left a small garrison in the citadel of Savona, and then broke out eastwards through Albissola in the direction of Genoa.

Meanwhile, Massena was given troubles of his own on 6 April. At two in the afternoon, a British frigate began bombarding the port of Genoa. GM Gottesheim began his march through the mountains to get onto the eastern flank of Genoa and reached as far as Bisagno. At the same time, Ott and Hohenzollern probed into the Bochetta Pass. The information reaching Massena that evening could have left him in no doubt that the Austrians had commenced a major operation. His priority was to preserve Genoa, but at the same time he also needed to maintain his communications with the rest of his army. To buy time, Massena launched a fierce counter-attack against Gottesheim in the early hours of 7 April. There was bitter fighting around Monte Fasce in which Gottesheim was pushed back almost to his starting position with significant losses. This was only a minor setback for the Austrians, because they had succeeded in their first major goal – to split the French forces in two.

On 9 April, Melas went aboard the Royal Navy flagship HMS *Audacious* to meet with Lord Keith, the British commander of the Mediterranean Fleet. Melas was aware that Massena's main strength was around Genoa, so he decided to turn the main column eastwards and advance along the coast towards the city, supported by the guns of the British warships. That same day, Hohenzollern began probing southwards towards Genoa. Massena therefore realized the full extent of his problems.

Again, Massena adopted an aggressive stance. On 10 April, he advanced westwards with two columns, attempting to regain contact with Suchet around Montenotte. Leaving 7,000 men to guard Genoa, Massena marched with Gardanne's 4,500-strong division down the coast road, while Soult headed for Sasello with Gazan's 5,000-man division. Suchet had also been ordered to attack from the west, the plan being for all three to unite at Montenotte.

There was desperate fighting at Monte Croce. As the Austrian troops were halfway up the steep slopes, they came under heavy fire from Massena's troops. The French even rolled boulders down the mountain slopes to break up the Austrian columns. The first attack failed; then a second. The third attempt was led by Lattermann's grenadier brigade and the Transylvanians of IR 51 Splényi. This regiment was one of the fiercest Melas possessed, and was apparently known as the *Legion Infernale* by the French. While a brigade was directed to attack the rear of Massena's position, the grenadiers and IR 51 Splényi formed an assault column and made a frontal attack. This time the boulders and musketry failed to prevent Melas' soldiers gaining the heights, and Massena withdrew. The following day, Massena found himself pursued by land and fired on by sea. As his starving soldiers began to break up, the Austrians sent hussars in pursuit. Massena was forced to surround himself with a bodyguard of mounted officers, to draw swords and fight his way out.

The ensuing battles are a tapestry of desperate encounters, where Massena, Soult and Suchet each attempted to unite. The French were able to offer resistance for twelve days, and Soult and Massena were able to link up, but Suchet was driven off towards the Var. On 21 April, Massena toured the forts and walls surrounding Genoa and resigned himself to coming under siege. The French commander instructed the local authorities he was taking command of the city and forming a special commission which would deliberate on rations and public order. Later that day, the imperial army closed in. However, the defences of Genoa were such that an assault on the city from the landward side was all but impossible. The heights around the city were protected by fortresses, and the city had massive walls. The best chance for the Austrians was to starve the city into surrender or provoke its population into insurrection. There were four more weeks before the Army of the Reserve was expected from Switzerland. Would Massena be starved into submission before then?

While the operations on the Riviera continued, a close watch was maintained on the Alpine passes for the 'Dijon' Reserve Army. The hub for processing intelligence from the mountains was FML Vukassovich's headquarters at Arona, on Lake Maggiore. On 8 May, Major Franz Mumb of the general-quartermaster-staff provided a detailed summary of the intelligence thus far available. It left no doubt that the French were preparing to advance through Switzerland:

'Our best spy [Kundschafter] has now provided the news 3,000 enemy troops have arrived in Martigny, which are said to be designated to advance over Mt Bernard. Another 3,000 are supposed to be marching up, which are designated for the upper Valais Canton and are supposed to be advancing over the Simplon.

'Without doubt, on the basis of these movements the St Gotthard will also probably be attacked with the greatest force from Altdorf via the Urserental valley. Therefore the troops positioned here have been deployed in such a way that in the event of an attack everything can be available at the appropriate point with the greatest speed; at the same time, scouts have recently been sent out to obtain more accurate information ...

'I view this as the result of the enemy crossing the Rhine and as protection for the march of the enemy General Berthier, which judging from his actions should be hurrying to General Massena to relieve him.

'If it were now merely this, then certainly their forces facing these positions would not be so worrying, and I therefore hope we are in a position to hinder an advance in this case. At the same time, I confidently hope His Excellency General Baron Kray will defeat the enemy who have advanced to Stockach, therefore if this attack turns out well, then the enemy will certainly be forced to fall back on other plans again.

'Just as I take the view, that the operations in the Riviera at this moment are as important as they are difficult and very extensive, and that the army must keep its forces together, yet I cannot hide my concern that for the division here, a small reserve both of infantry and cavalry is almost indispensible in the event of an enemy attack. I am therefore most fully confident that the army command will give proper consideration to supporting this division all the more, since as a result of their advance, the enemy could immediately spread out in the plains of Lombardy and Piedmont.'[7]

Major Mumb's analysis was sound. He saw how events in Germany were having an impact on Italy, and what might be the outcome of the French breaking through the Alps. As Mumb was writing this letter, Zach was already planning ahead and writing to FML Ott from army headquarters at San Stefano, opening with:

'The definitive report, which I have received that General Berthier will advance into Piedmont, which is however to remain completely secret, makes it necessary for me to consider how I will be able to reinforce General Kaim.'

Zach went on to instruct Ott that reinforcements due to strengthen him must instead be sent elsewhere. That same day, 8 May, Melas wrote to Lord Keith, asking for the British to transport IR43 Thurn from Livorno to Ventimiglia as quickly as possible. The message is interesting because it shows army command then thought the Mont Cenis pass was the most probable route of attack by the French:

'I have very certain notions that General Berthier proposes to debouch into Piedmont by Mont Cenis, with a part of the army which you know, Mylord, they collected at Dijon.'

According to Stutterheim, Melas received on 18 May the first positive report that the 'Dijon' Reserve Army had appeared in the Alpine passes. This report came from the outpost commander, Captain Zivnik, and was dated Aosta, 15 May 1800. It read:

'Zivnik announces the enemy is ready to descend in two columns from the Great St Bernard, and at least 6,000 men from the Little St Bernard. A trusted peasant who reports the latter reports at the same time the enemy has requisitioned 600 mules.'[8]

At this moment, Melas' headquarters were at Nice, approximately 350km from Aosta. On receiving the news, a letter was sent by Melas to the Hofkriegsrat detailing the army's response:

'As it is now confirmed both by reliable spy [Kundschafter] reports as well as by enemy movements, that the enemy general Berthier is advancing in the Valais Canton to enter Piedmont and towards Aosta, and has also pushed back our outposts positioned on the Great St Bernard, so I have ordered FML Baron Kaim to concentrate his troops with the proper caution towards that point, where the enemy's main force is believed to be breaking through, not to allow himself to get involved in any real clashes in the mountain gullies, but to prepare all the more for the main action in the plain.'

Melas would move his headquarters from Nice to Turin to coordinate this, and march troops up from the Var, via Cuneo. In the meantime, FML Elsnitz was instructed to remain around the Var watching Suchet, but was instructed not to get in engaged in any major battles. However, he was to mislead the French into thinking an advance across the Var was being planned. According to Stutterheim, if Elsnitz was seriously attacked, he was instructed to slowly fall back onto the line of the Apennines and entrench himself in the mountains.

On 19 May, Melas sent a second letter to the Hofkriegsrat which clarified his thinking:

'In the last reports made to the Hofkriegsrat, I have not been able to deny myself the request not to be uneasy about the account of an advance by the enemy General Berthier towards Piedmont, as I have already taken serious measures against this operation, about which not the slightest doubt remains in my mind, and also I do not intend to reduce my forces by isolated outpost actions, but to attack the enemy with a concentrated force. In fact with this intention, I have left Nice today and will arrive in Turin in a few days, in order to give the appropriate direction to forces commanded by the two FMLs Kaim and Vukassovich and my already concentrated cavalry … My main intention is at this time wholly directed, for a start, only to gaining time against Berthier, because each day gained is a perceptible loss to Massena and I hope to be able to give Your Excellency good news about Genoa even earlier than I see myself able to make a decisive move against Berthier.'

From reading this letter, it is clear that the Austrians had a coherent strategy. The arrival of Berthier was a cause of unease, but was not a surprise. Whatever Vienna had thought about the 'Dijon' Reserve Army, Melas' command had been under no illusions about the threat from it for months. They had thought about their response in detail. The Austrian reluctance to fight in the mountains might be queried with hindsight. If they had raced reinforcements towards Aosta, they may have bottled the French army in very difficult position. However, there was logic to this decision. Firstly, the Austrians could not be truly sure where the main blow would fall. It appeared to be the Great St Bernard, but the Mont Cenis Pass and the other major Alpine passes had all given indications the French might attack. Perhaps more importantly, the covering forces under Kaim and Vukassovich were strong in cavalry, and so the Austrians supposed they would be at an advantage if they fought the French in the plains of northern Italy, rather than in the mountains, where infantry would have the advantage. The Austrians therefore wanted to deliver the main blow in the plain, with the maximum forces possible. According to the Piedmontese officer, Count Cavour, there was something of a mantra among the Austrians: 'Let them come onto the plain, we shall beat them.' Apparently,

Zach was extremely pleased with the direction of the French advance, and foresaw being able to assemble the army in time to offer battle outside Turin on the left bank of the Po in the area of Volpiano. Zach was so confident of what was about to unfold that he loudly declared: 'I have got them in a bag.'[9]

Melas does not appear to have entirely shared Zach's enthusiasm. The old general had really felt the strain of seven weeks campaigning in the mountains. He had flashes of his younger self, but age and illness increasingly got the better of him. On 22 May, he wrote a letter to Tige, president of the Hofkriegsrat. It was almost pleading in tone. His body was wracked with pain, and although the improving weather was helping him cope, having been so long away from the Teplitz baths in Bohemia, he felt himself succumbing to weakness. If circumstances prevented Melas from using the spa at Acqui, this weakness might gain the upper hand, he cautioned. Although he did not explicitly ask to be relieved, Melas' letter could have left Tige in no doubt that the commander of the army in Italy was struggling to cope with the demands of the campaign.

Chapter 6

Over the Alps

We have seen how Bonaparte developed his strategy for the coming campaign, skilfully positioning the Army of the Reserve so as to be poised to support Italy or Germany, using Switzerland as a great curtain behind which he could hide his manoeuvres. Although his preference was to attack Italy, no final decision had been made until news of Melas' attack on the Riviera was confirmed. On 24 April, the First Consul wrote to his Minister of War, Lazare Carnot, setting out the strategic situation. If Massena was defeated and pushed back to the line of the Maritime Alps, it was critical the Army of the Reserve attacked Piedmont or the Milanese to divert Melas' attention from Massena, and to cause him to return to the defence of Lombardy and his military stores. In equal measure, if Massena was able to defeat Melas, then the Austrian army would be fatally weakened and unable to resist the advance of the Reserve. The letter instructed Carnot to direct Berthier to move the Reserve to Geneva 'with all diligence', and to transport to Villeneuve all the munitions and wine then assembled at Geneva. Bonaparte instructed Berthier to cross the Alps via the Great St Bernard or Simplon passes and to enter Piedmont and Lombardy. At the same time, Bonaparte instructed Carnot to reiterate the order for Moreau to attack the Austrians in Germany. Bonaparte added: 'Let him know his delay essentially compromises the safety of the Republic.'[1]

The First Consul also wrote directly to Berthier with some specific guidance on how to implement the order from Carnot. If he used the St Bernard, Berthier would find himself much nearer to Lake Geneva and would therefore enjoy better lines of supply; however, he asked Berthier to assure himself of the nature of the roads from Aosta to the River Po. Although Bonaparte promised to send more specific instructions once he had heard from Massena, he gave Berthier a very strong and encouraging directive:

> 'Nothing in Italy will be able to resist the 40,000 men you have. Whether the Austrian army is victorious or defeated, it cannot, in any case, sustain the shock of a fresh army.'[2]

Berthier received Carnot's order two days later, on 26 April. Before receiving these instructions, he was still uncertain about using the route over the Great St

Bernard, and appears to have favoured taking the longer route via Lucerne, where he could join forces with General Lecourbe of the Army of the Rhine. Together they could fall on Italy via the St Gotthard Pass, while Watrin's division crossed via the Great St Bernard to act as a link with Massena's army. On receiving the order from Paris, Berthier realized the urgency of the situation and immediately issued instructions to the various corps around Dijon to march towards Lake Geneva. The following day, Berthier wrote to Bonaparte stating he would 'sacrifice everything for Massena'. However, there came a note of caution: he had been expecting a delivery of five million cartridges and lead, but none had materialized. The only ammunition wagons he possessed were those which arrived with Chambarlhac, so even if the cartridges did turn up, he had no means of transporting them. He asked if Moreau's ammunition wagons at Sampigny might be directed to Dijon and Auxonne instead? He concluded on a more upbeat note: 'We will do the impossible.'[3]

As Berthier penned this letter, Bonaparte received a report from Oudinot, chief of staff to the Army of Italy, dated 17 April. It confirmed Melas had attacked Massena on all points, particularly at Savona and Genoa. Uncertain if Massena would be able to make contact with Paris, Oudinot felt obliged to write on his commander-in-chief's behalf. While he painted a picture of extraordinary heroism on the part of Massena and Soult, Oudinot's letter left Bonaparte in no doubt of the army's predicament. It spoke of Melas' 'astonishing superiority' and of columns marching on Genoa, leaving no doubt the Austrians were planning to invest the place. The fort of Savona only had provisions for ten days, and the army was already suffering from hunger. Although Suchet was attempting to re-establish communications with Massena, the British navy prevented any help being sent by sea to Genoa directly. This letter must have reinforced Bonaparte's determination to take rapid action.

While Bonaparte's preference had always been to take Milan, Oudinot's report gave him doubts. The First Consul wrote to Berthier telling him Milan might not be their destination after all, but instead they might have to march on Tortona to disengage Massena at Genoa. If defeated by Melas, Massena would have no choice but to shut himself up in Genoa, where he had an estimated thirty days of provisions. For this reason, Bonaparte instructed Berthier to use the St Bernard. From Aosta they could march on Genoa, or head to Lake Maggiore and Milan if necessary. Furthermore, from Lake Geneva to Aosta was only four days' march, so he would be closest to his lines of supply. The First Consul committed the rest of this day to finding bullets moulds, lead and money for the army as it arrived in Switzerland.

As the army marched on Lake Geneva, an extraordinary effort was made to find the necessary supplies. At one point Berthier complained he was about to attack the Austrians without a single cannon. In the other letters he pleaded for the First Consul to quit Paris and join the army. Bonaparte remained in Paris, firing letters off demanding resources for Berthier. Throughout this period, he remained anxious for signs of movement from the German front. On 5 May, he at last received positive news. Moreau had defeated Kray at the Battle of Stockach on 3 May, and with the Austrians in retreat, the route to the St Gotthard would be clear for a second descent into Italy. This appears to have swung the First Consul's strategy back in favour of an advance to Milan. It certainly gave him the option. Receiving the news by telegraph, Bonaparte congratulated Moreau and told him the Minister of War would soon be joining him. He told Moreau the position of the Army of Italy was critical, and Massena only had provisions to hold Genoa until 25 or 26 May. Bonaparte then sent word to Berthier that he was leaving Paris at midnight, and would stop only a few hours in Dijon before travelling to Geneva to join the army. 'Everything is going perfectly,' he added.[4]

While the army raced towards the Alps, General Armand-Samuel Marescot had conducted a second detailed reconnaissance of the Great St Bernard Pass. He presented his report on 8 May. The road was practical for infantry, cavalry and wagons as far as Martigny, where the ascent began. From there until Bourg-Saint-Pierre, the road was practical for infantry, cavalry, light vehicles and light artillery. From Bourg-Saint-Pierre to the summit, the road was practical for foot soldiers, mules and cavalry, albeit with great difficulty. The only way the army could get its equipment and supplies beyond this point was by hiring peasants and mules. The artillery could be broken up and mounted on litters, and dragged across the pass. To prevent the men from falling sick from drinking melted snow, stores of vinegar and brandy would be necessary for purifying it. The main hazard was posed not by the enemy forces in the Aosta valley (their forward posts were 2km from the summit), but by avalanches, which were capable of engulfing several battalions at a time. The most favourable time for crossing would be at night, under moonlight, or in the morning before noon when the sun started to melt the ice. The peasants had assured Marescot that the slightest movement of men or animals, or even a voice, might be enough to trigger an avalanche. If so, it might prove necessary to fire artillery off in order to initiate the avalanches in advance. There was another hazard to the enterprise. On the Italian side of the mountains, on the main road from Aosta to Ivrea, was Fort Bard. This fortress could hold a garrison of 400 men and was mounted on a tall rock face, making it impossible to assault. The scale of this problem does not appear to have figured highly in the French plans. There was also a significant risk if Moreau did not support the enterprise by detaching sufficient troops through the St Gotthard.

Having departed Paris on 6 May, Bonaparte had arrived at Geneva on 9 May, moving to Lausanne on 12 May. The First Consul conducted a series of reviews of the various divisions of the Army of the Reserve then quartered around the eastern side of Lake Geneva. On 13 May, he inspected the divisions of Chambarlac and Loison on the plain of Saint-Sulpice. He then travelled to Vevey to inspect Boudet's infantry division. He was satisfied with the quality of the uniforms, but was extremely angry to find a great many conscripts had deserted the 30th Line, taking with them their packs and muskets. Instructions were sent to General Mortier in Paris to search for these miscreants. Bonaparte then ordered a live firing exercise to ensure all the men present had tasted gunpowder and felt the kick of a musket before climbing the Alps. He took the soldiers into his confidence, explaining why they were going to fight: 'I offered peace to the Emperor; he did not wish it. We now have to take it by the throat.'[5]

On 14 May, the First Consul was joined by Minister of War Carnot, who had travelled directly to Lausanne from Moreau's headquarters. Carnot had arrived at the Army of the Rhine on the morning of 10 May, the day after the Battle of Biberach, another victorious encounter over the army of Kray. When Carnot presented Moreau with instructions to detach 25,000 men to enter Italy by the St Gotthard, the latter complained he would have to curtail offensive operations and might not be able to hold such an advanced position if such a significant number of troops were taken away from him. When Carnot pressed Moreau on the urgency of following this instruction, Moreau went about selecting troops from all over his theatre of operations, many of which were a significant distance from Switzerland; some as far away as Mainz. He made an excuse for this, saying he did not want the Austrians to realize he was detaching a sizeable part of his force to Italy. These troops would be placed under the command of General Moncey, not Lecourbe as earlier planned. This placed the First Consul's project in dire trouble. Bonaparte could only risk a march on Milan if the approaches to the St Gotthard were secured and he could rely on a strong reinforcement coming down from Germany. The First Consul was forced to write to Moreau on 14 May in strong terms, stressing Massena's perilous situation and pointing out that the Army of the Reserve was also weak. If Moreau did not provide General Moncey with 18,000–20,000 men and have them enter Italy in the last week of May, then Genoa might fall, with the loss of 14,000 soldiers. This eventuality would require Moreau to send a far larger force into Italy. Bonaparte urged him to execute this order promptly so that Genoa might be saved.[6]

At this very moment, Lannes was already on the mountain at Bourg-Saint-Pierre, preparing to lead the army's advanced guard over the pass on the night of 15–16 May. At the age of 31, Lannes was a perfect choice to lead this difficult venture. He was known as the 'Roland of the army', after the heroic paladin of Charlemagne immortalized in the epic poem *Chanson de Roland*, and was considered the bravest man in the army. He was calm under fire and possessed accurate judgement even in the direst emergency. He was of average height, slender and wore his hair in a powdered queue; but swore like a trooper in any company, with his vocabulary described as a 'rolling artillery'. His advanced guard comprised General Mainoni's 'brigade' (in fact just the 28th Line, the half-brigade which had been guarding the Alpine passes in this region over the past year) and Watrin's division, composed of the 6th Light Infantry, 22nd and 40th Line. Brigadier General Rivaud would be attached to the advanced guard with the 12th Regiment of Hussars and the 21st Chasseurs. For artillery, Berthier had reckoned on Lannes having four 4-pdrs, two 8-pdrs, two howitzers, four Genevan 4-pdrs and six 2-pdrs which were already on the St Bernard. The guns at Bourg-Saint-Pierre would need to be dismantled, their carriages, wheels and limbers carried by men and mules, while the heavy barrels were mounted on sledges and dragged by ropes. Lannes complained that the process of preparing the artillery was much harder than expected and he did not have enough ropes. Lannes also issued his troops with strict instructions for the ascent. The path was so narrow that they would form in two ranks only. Mounted officers would have to go on foot, with their horses led. To avoid avalanches, they would make the climb at night, and fifty lanterns would be carried to illuminate the route. Everyone was to remain quiet for fear of avalanches, but at the steepest points, soldiers were authorized to lean on their muskets for support.

From Bourg-Saint-Pierre to the summit of the pass was a climb of 800 metres, over a distance of 13km. Initially it was difficult, but manageable. However, the last 4km were particularly steep, with a little path zigzagging its way up rocky outcrops to the top of the pass. At the summit was a hospice for travellers founded in the eleventh century by Saint Bernard of Menthon. This hospice was managed by a congregation of monks and their enormous dogs, which were famous for rescuing travellers caught in snowdrifts. With the order's headquarters at the foot of the pass in Martigny, the First Consul arranged for all his soldiers to receive a piece of bread, a portion of gruyere cheese and a cup of wine on reaching the summit (the monastery's archives show the first troops received two cups of wine). After such an exhausting climb, this refreshment would prove an invaluable boost to sustenance and morale. As Horse Grenadier Joseph Petit would say of the wine ration: 'No one, not even the most avaricious among us, would have exchanged that single draught for all the gold in Mexico.' Everything was therefore set for the campaign of the Army of the Reserve to commence.

On 15 May, Lannes began the advance to Aosta. The brigade of Malher (22nd and 40th Line) led the way, pausing briefly at the summit, where the monks had placed the food and wine on tables in front of the hospice. The march continued past a large frozen lake behind the summit until the first Austrian forward posts were encountered in front of Saint-Rhemy. These were driven back on Étroubles, where sixty Austrians had set up a post. Again, these were quickly brushed aside by Lannes' troops. The following morning, Lannes reached Aosta at 11.00 am. Here the Austrians made more of a stand with 400 men, but Lannes sent a battalion of the 6th Light to turn their position. The Austrians fell back into the town and made something of a stand on the bridge there. Eager to keep up the momentum of his advance, Lannes ordered a bayonet charge, which quickly finished the matter. From the prisoners and captured post, Lannes was able to glean some intelligence. Nice had fallen to the Austrians, he reported to Berthier, and there were very few Austrian troops in the valley. The nearest large force of Austrians appeared to be six or seven regiments of cavalry at Turin, but almost the whole imperial army was reported to be around Genoa.

Behind Lannes' division, Rivaud's cavalry brigade was next to pass, setting out at two in the morning from St Pierre on 16 May. Two hours behind this brigade was Boudet's infantry division. Berthier sent a progress report to Bonaparte, admitting the sledges constructed for the artillery were useless. The local peasants showed the French troops how to use the hollowed out trunks of pine trees to create a cradle for the heavy gun barrels. It then took sixty men to drag each gun barrel to the summit of the pass. He also asked for more mules to be sent to Saint-Rhemy because a backlog of artillery and stores was building up there for want of transport. The work was back-breaking. Within a few days, the commander of the artillery, General Marmont, wrote to the First Consul complaining the peasants had abandoned the project because the work was so hard. He had been forced to 'lavish' money on them to get them to start work again. Berthier estimated it was costing 500 francs in labour per gun; although he need not have worried too much about the cost - the peasants were never paid.[7] The mules were proving difficult because they were fearful of treading on ice and kept dropping their loads. In any case, there was a shortage of mules, because those sent to the summit were not returned to Marmont, but were kept with the soldiers passing into Italy. The mule drivers were deserting by the dozen through a lack of shoes and coats, and the mules were dying of starvation because no one had thought to feed them. Marmont wrote how he commandeered a battalion of the 59th Line and a detachment of 600 men from Loison's division to support the movement of the artillery, and he claimed it was only thanks to the blows of the officers that anything was achieved at all (corporal punishment had been banned after the revolution). These soldiers were now so 'tired, harassed and discontented' that it was impossible to use them again. Marmont recommended drastic action be taken. Behind Loison's division were the infantry divisions of Chambarlhac and Monnier. In order to get the artillery across, Marmont recommended the whole division take part, with officers at the head of their men, carrying everything up to Saint-Rhemy.[8]

This course of action was adopted. Gunners were assigned to direct the operation, a task they took on with particular zeal. Witness the following episode reported by Grenadier Coignet of the 96th Line:

'Nothing could be more difficult than our journey. Always climbing up horrible slopes and very narrow paths. The stones cut our shoes. From time to time we stopped, then walked again. No one spoke a word. When we reached the ice, it was still worse. Our gunner was no longer master of his piece. At every moment it slipped towards the ravines, and it was necessary to stop, to put it back on the right path. Without the example of our chief, we would have lost courage ... We reached the permanent snows. There it went better; our cannon slid nicely. We were going faster. General Chambarlhac came by and wanted to increase the pace. He approached the gunner and assumed the master's tone. He was badly received. "It is not you who commands here," replied the gunner. "It is I who am responsible for the piece, and who alone directs it. Go on your way." In spite of these words, the general advanced as if to seize the gunner. "General," cried the latter. "If you do not withdraw, I will knock you out with this trail spike or throw you into the precipice!" Chambarlhac thought it prudent to move along.'

Meanwhile, Lannes had pushed on, fighting another action at Châtillon on 18 May. Again the Austrians blocked the road, and again an impatient Lannes drove them out of their position with a bayonet charge. The following day they reached Fort Bard, where the French really faced their first major problem of the campaign. The fortress blocked the passage out of the alpine valleys into the fertile plains of northern Italy. With supplies having to be carried all the way from Lausanne, it was essential the French broke out of the Aosta valley in order to find food, and also to coordinate with General Thurreau, who has been ordered to advance over the Mont Cenis Pass. At first glance there appeared to be little hope of this. The fortress contained two levels of gun batteries, which dominated the road below. This road was bordered by rocks on one side and by the Dora Baltea River on the other. The road itself was cut by three drawbridges, each of which needed to be secured in order to transport the artillery. Berthier rode forward to look at the position for himself, realizing they had underestimated the scale of the obstacle before them. He concluded that they should attempt an assault, but if this did not succeed, it would be necessary to find an alternative route past the fort in order to prevent the army from starving. A goat track had been discovered at Arnad which led over Mount Albard down to Donnas, but this was not practical for the artillery. Unless the fortress surrendered, Berthier would be entering Italy without any artillery.

While Lannes' advanced guard and Boudet's division were sent to Donnas, on the night of 21/22 May an attack was made on Bard. A small force of grenadiers from Loison's division and some engineers climbed down the rocks, following a water pipe, and were able to get inside the village. There they lowered the drawbridges and forced the Austrians there to retreat into the safety of the fort. The guns inside the fortification opened fire, but the French were able to shelter inside the buildings. However, it was impossible to get the artillery past the rain of shells, canister and grenades thrown down by the defenders.

On 22 May, Lannes occupied Ivrea, where he captured several small calibre Austrian guns and their ammunition wagons. He issued strict instructions to his soldiers against pillaging. For two days, Lannes remained at this place supported by Boudet's division waiting for his artillery to arrive from Bard. Berthier was desperate to get the guns through to the advanced guard. Initially they thought it might be possible to dismount the smaller 4-pdrs and carry these over Mount Albard. An artillery officer was instructed to do this, but he refused. The commander of the army's artillery, General Marmont, feared the guns had already been badly treated being dragged over the St Bernard and did not want them broken up again.[9] On 22 May, an attempt was made to pass a gun below the fort under the cover of darkness. It was dragged by men rather than horses because if someone was struck, they could roll away: injured horses had to be removed from their harnesses. The artillery chief of staff, Sénarmont, complained that all thirteen of the men who attempted to do this were wounded by a hail of musketry, grenades, fire pots, etc. On 23 May, Berthier agreed to an experiment using an Austrian 3-pdr gun. This would have its wheels covered in straw to muffle the noise of its passage. Unfortunately, the attempt was thwarted by heavy rain which caused the straw to fall away. A third attempt appears to have been successful, with Berthier writing to Lannes on 25 May confirming he had received two 4-pdrs and an ammunition caisson. This success would be repeated over the coming nights, allowing a trickle of light artillery into Italy. It was extremely hazardous work. On one occasion, an Austrian shell landed directly under an ammunition wagon being escorted through. Disaster was only averted by a soldier who managed to cut the fuse with his sabre and prevent the shell from exploding.[10]

On the morning of 26 May, Lannes instructed Watrin and Boudet to have their men under arms at daybreak. Lannes had been authorized to force a passage over the Chivasso River, convincing the Austrians this new army was destined for Turin, and from there the Ligurian Riviera. Watrin's division led the attack, with Boudet's troops drawn up 800 metres in reserve. The 6th Light Infantry led the attack, opening with a direct assault on the bridge. The Austrian artillery opened fire on the French column, which struggled to gain a foothold on the bridge. The Austrians launched a counter-attack and drove the Frenchmen away. Lannes was told of a nearby ford, and sent the 6th Light to the left of the bridge to find it. At the same time, he sent the 22nd and 40th Half-Brigades to the right of the road to create a diversion. The 28th Line were ordered forwards to threaten the bridge, should the Austrians weaken their centre. The Austrians began to retreat, covering their withdrawal by a cavalry screen. Boudet was called up and told to advance in the direction of Romano. As the French advanced, they were met by a huge force of Austrian cavalry, perhaps as many as 4,000 strong. This cavalry charged the French infantry, passing between the intervals in the French battalions, before peeling away and rejoining the retreating infantry. This was the first significant clash of the campaign, and somewhat ominously for the Austrians, their superiority in artillery and cavarly did nothing to blunt the French bayonets.

Having crossed the Alps and advanced from Ivrea in the direction of Turin, it would have been reasonable to suppose Bonaparte's intention was to do battle with the Austrians and relieve Genoa. Thurreau's attack on the Mont Cenis Pass on 22 May increased the focus on the Piedmontese capital. As we have seen, such a move would have been welcomed by the Austrians, whose strategy had been to avoid fighting in the mountains, instead luring the French out onto the plains in front of Turin. A battle on the plains was their desired intention, but Bonaparte had no intention of obliging them. Although he kept his options open, and did not discount marching on Genoa, the First Consul had always had his eye on Milan, the great capital of Lombardy. Its capture would be partly political – it would read well in the bulletins – and partly practical, as it would no doubt contain provisions for his army. The real prize, however, was strategic. By occupying Milan, Moncey could advance from Switzerland over the St Gotthard Pass, thus substantially reinforcing the Army of the Reserve and opening a new line of communication for it. From Milan, the road network extended out across Italy, affording numerous routes to advance. Most crucially, Bonaparte thought his capture of Milan would act as a lure, tempting the Austrians out of Liguria and the Apennines and onto ground of his choosing. He did not want to fight the Austrians on the plains, but around Stradella between the mountains and the Po. To believe that the First Consul had any intention of marching to Massena's relief is to misinterpret the entire point of the campaign. A direct advance on Genoa would not accomplish any of Bonaparte's high-level strategic aims.

General Lannes had led the advanced-guard over the St Bernard and down the Aosta Valley. His troops now became a covering force, making demonstrations around Chivasso in the direction of Turin, while Thurreau pressed along the Susa valley. At the same time, Murat was given command of a new advanced guard which would spearhead the march on Milan. Murat's command consisted of Monnier's infantry division and the cavalry brigades of Kellermann and Champeaux. They were supported by General Duhesme, in command of the infantry divisions of Loison and Boudet. Although the approach to Milan was only lightly defended by the Austrians, there were two major rivers to cross – the Sesia and Ticino. Both rivers flowed southward from the Alps to the Po, and both were swollen by icy meltwater coming down off the mountains. The Army of the Reserve had no bridging equipment available and few engineers, so the key to Murat's success was a lightning advance, and to hopefully find the bridges over these rivers still intact. Alas, arriving at the Sesia opposite Vercelli, the French discovered the bridge had been burned and the Austrians were in observation on the opposite bank.

On the evening of 28 May, Duhesme reached Vercelli and made a reconnaissance of the river crossing. Duhesme placed two batteries of guns opposite the Austrian position and directed Boudet's infantry to ford the treacherous river above and below these batteries. At 3.00 am on 29 May, the Austrians opened fire on the French works across the river. The French retaliated in kind. General Festenberg, commanding the Austrian forces, was convinced the French were going to force the crossing with boats, so ordered his infantry to fire blindly into the darkness. Meanwhile, Boudet's infantry started to ford the river. The 9th Light Infantry went to the right with Murat. The current was very strong and the infantry was only able to cross after the cavalry formed a supporting chain across the river. Boudet's second brigade, under Brigadier General Guénand, crossed the river on the left. Again the river current was very strong and several men were drowned. However, by seven in the morning, Boudet's force was across the river and converging on Festenberg's position. Faced with the prospect of encirclement, the Austrians withdrew in the direction of Novara, pursued by the 9th Light. With the river crossing secured, a 'flying bridge' was hastily assembled at Sesia in order to allow the bulk of Murat's forces to cross. Not much more than a raft, the flying bridge was a large, flat floating platform, moored to either bank, which used the river current to propel the raft from one side to the other. At Novara, Duhesme requested engineers, pioneer troops, surgeons and basic medical supplies to be forwarded urgently to the advanced-guard. Having prioritized bringing artillery over the Alps, and with Fort Bard still blocking the route for vehicles, specialist equipment was in very short supply.

The next obstacle was the Ticino, a wide river with steep banks, numerous rivulets forming wooded islands. There were two main crossing points over this river; the first at Turbigo and the second further downstream at Boffalora. The Austrians had retreated by the latter route and had burned the bridge there. The Austrians were also able to bring up additional forces to contest the crossing.

After spending 30 May at Novara reorganizing, the French pursuit continued at dawn the following day. Murat took the bulk of his forces towards Turbigo, Duhesme heading to Boffalora with the 9th Light Infantry. Arriving at the river, Murat was able to procure some boats from sympathetic locals. He was able to ferry two companies of grenadiers from the 59th Line over to one of the wooded islands. These troops fired on the Austrian position while additional troops were ferried across. The Austrians quickly withdrew behind the Naviglio Canal, where they received reinforcements from FML Vukassovich. The Austrians mounted a counter-attack and were able to drive the French out of Turbigo. A fierce contest ensued, with neither party gaining an advantage.

Meanwhile, Duhesme reached Boffalora. Although the Austrians had destroyed the bridge, they had moored several boats on the riverbank and these were seen by the French. The 9th Light had organized a company of swimmers, and these were directed into the water to seize the craft. Under enemy fire, the swimmers faltered. One of them was swept away by the strong current and drowned. Witnessing this hesitation, one of the Ninth's surgeons, Charles Vanderbach, threw himself into the water and made for the boats. Eight more Frenchmen jumped in and followed him, their comrades providing covering fire. The boat was secured and taken back to the right bank; it was quickly filled with soldiers and sent across to secure another boat. At this the Austrians withdrew, reporting to Vukassovich that his flank had been turned. Under the cover of night, the Austrian commander withdrew towards Milan, garrisoning the citadel and then withdrawing to Lodi.

On 2 June, Murat entered Milan unopposed at 4.00 pm, riding at the head of six cavalry regiments. Monnier's infantry division was directed to blockade the citadel, while Boudet was sent to secure the Romana Gate on the south-eastern side of the city. Elsewhere, the detachment from the Army of the Rhine was already on its way to the Lombard capital. Much smaller than Bonaparte had anticipated, General Moncey had begun to cross the St Gotthard on 28 May with the divisions of Lapoype and Lorge, with a cavalry reserve, all amounting to around 11,000 men. Bethencourt had also entered Italy, crossing the Simplon Pass on 26 May with another 1,000 men. The capture of Milan was therefore a key strategic objective achieved. They had entirely wrong-footed the Austrians by marching to Milan, and there was more good news to follow. On 2 June, the garrison at Fort Bard surrendered after two weeks' resistance. The remainder of the French artillery was at last able to enter Italy. Earlier that day, after five days' march, Lannes had entered Pavia. He was stunned to discover the contents of one of the main Austrian stores. This included 200 guns of various calibre with their carriages and wagons (all had been spiked), shells and cannonballs, 1,000 barrels of gunpowder, infantry cartridges, muskets, stores of bed sheets and blankets, grain, flour, and 4,000–5,000 quintals (hundredweight) of candles. Lannes had also learned Genoa still held out, but was under heavy bombardment and on the verge of surrender. Lannes wrote to Bonaparte: 'There is not a moment to lose if you want to march on him.'

Zach's master plan had been to park the imperial army outside Turin and await the arrival of Berthier's army. The Austrian quartermaster general had assumed the Army of the Reserve would march to the relief of Genoa and the Riviera. Now the First Consul had turned eastwards, Zach was utterly at a loss to know Bonaparte's intentions. From Milan, would the French strike towards the Hereditary Lands of the Habsburgs directly or march to cut off the Austrian line of retreat? According to Stutterheim, Zach sent a 'very well-tried spy' to find out. Stutterheim also states this spy had been used for deceiving the French army in the previous campaign. His name was Carlo Gioelli.[11]

Before describing the encounter of the spy and the First Consul, we must first retrace Bonaparte's steps. From Lausanne he moved to Martigny on 17 May, and for three days remained with the monks who had their headquarters in the town. It was at Martigny that Bonaparte heard about the difficulties posed by Fort Bard. On 20 May, he set out to rejoin the army, riding a mule conducted by a local guide named Pierre Nicolas Dorsaz. A day later he was at Aosta, where he remained for four days, before reaching Verrès on 25 May. He was at Ivrea on 27 May, Vercelli on 30 May, Novara on 1 June and then entered Milan on the following evening.

On 3 June, the day after the First Consul's arrival in Milan, Gioelli requested an audience with Bonaparte. The details of this meeting are given in Bourrienne's memoir. Although this secret agent is not named in the text, when Stutterheim read Bourrienne's account in 1830 he immediately realized it was Gioelli, writing: 'It is amusing to read in the fourth part of the memoirs of de Bourrienne, what the latter relates about the spy, and gives a benign proof of the slyness of that Italian.' The account reads:[12]

'The First Consul passed six days at Milan. On the second day, a spy, who had served us very well in the first and admirable campaigns in Italy, was announced. The First Consul recollected him, and ordered him to be shown into his cabinet.

"Here you are," he exclaimed. "So, you have not been shot yet?"

"General," replied the spy, "when the war recommenced, I determined to serve the Austrians, because you were far from Europe. I always follow the fortunate; but the truth is, I am tired of the trade. I wish to have done with it, and to get enough to enable me to retire. I have been sent to your lines by General Melas, and I can render you an important service. I will give an exact account of the force and the position of all the enemy's corps, and the names of their commanders. I can tell you the situation in which Alessandria now is. You know me: I will not deceive you; but, I must carry back some report to my general. You are strong enough to give me some true intelligence, which I can communicate to him."

"Oh! as to that," resumed the First Consul, "the enemy is welcome to know my forces, and my positions, provided I know his, and he be ignorant of my plans. You shall be satisfied; but do not deceive me: I will give you a thousand Louis, if you serve me well."

'I then wrote down, from the dictation of the spy, the names of the corps, their amount, their positions, and the names of the generals commanding them. The First Consul stuck pins in the map to mark his plans on places, respecting which he received information from the spy. We also learned that Alessandria was without provisions, that Melas was far from expecting a siege, that many of his troops were sick, and that he lacked medicines. Berthier was ordered to draw up for the spy a nearly accurate statement of our positions.'

To recap, we first met Gioelli at Mantua in 1799 when he was working for MacDonald as his chief of secret correspondence. We then had his involvement in the Battle of Genola and his audacious coup causing the surrender of Cuneo in December 1799. Stutterheim confirms 'Zach's spy' was still active in 1800 and was travelling as far as Dijon to report on the Army of the Reserve. We also have the testimony of Crossard, who remembered Gioelli as a Turin lawyer who had fallen in with the French on the fall of the Piedmontese republic and the capture of Turin by Suvorov's Russians. We also cautioned that the back story given by the spy might very probably be false, albeit, like all good deceptions, hung on some elements of truth. If one closely scrutinises Crossard's description of Gioelli, it never really rang true – Turin fell to the coalition on 26 May 1799. How could Gioelli have reached MacDonald in Tuscany, and then been at Mantua on 16 June where he first met Radetzky? Physically, the journey could have been made; but to suppose MacDonald appointed a recently arrived Piedmontese civilian as his chief of secret correspondence and entrusted him with a captain's epaulettes and a vital message to Foissac-Latour does not seem credible. We must therefore conclude that Gioelli had been working for the French far longer than he admitted to Crossard.

From Bourrienne, we now know Gioelli was previously known to Bonaparte and had clearly worked with him before during the 1796-1797 campaign. Gioelli was from Alba, part of the province of Cuneo, in Piedmont. The people of Alba proclaimed themselves an independent republic on 26 April 1796 after the arrival of Bonaparte's army. Many Italians supported the French Revolution, but the republic was very short-lived. Bonaparte surprised the revolutionaries by signing the armistice of Cherasco on 28 April, restoring all of Piedmont to Victor Amadeus

III. The more ardent revolutionaries scattered, and many joined the French or acted as spies on their behalf. It appears Gioelli was one of these young men who found themselves displaced.

It should be stated at this point that Bonaparte was an avid user of spies, both militarily and politically. His handling of secret intelligence was brilliant and one of the cornerstones of his success (something nineteenth-century writers wrongly downplayed because of the dishonour associated with espionage). In his first campaigns in Italy, Bonaparte employed Jean Landrieux as head of his *bureau secret*, which looked at military and political intelligence.[13] In 1800, Bonaparte was similarly disposed to employing spies. Although the registers of secret expenditure were generally burned at the end of a campaign, plenty of references to the employment of spies exist in de Cugnac's compilation of documents relating to the Marengo campaign. Below is a selection:

26 May: Watrin's spies reported Melas' arrival in Turin the day before, and his being stunned by the movement of the French army. A spy in Vercelli reported the arrival of 20,000 Austrian troops, confirming their quartermasters had arrived to prepare supplies and lodgings.

27 May: Berthier instructed Duhesme to send spies in the direction of Casale, providing 1,000 francs to pay for them.

29 May: Brigadier General Bethencourt wrote to the First Consul asking for money to pay for spies and local guides.

31 May: Kellermann reported a Piedmontese 'patriot' (i.e. pro-revolutionary) had informed them Casale and Valenza were poorly defended. That same day, Citizen Cavalli reported: 'A trusted person, having arrived from Turin, brought the following news: General Melas had departed on the night of the 9th for Alessandria, on the road to Asti; All the guns of the city have been taken away, and they have been carried into the citadel; The Austrian outposts are at Settimo; The government Supreme Council was insulted by the people at the moment when they were about to visit General Melas; The city is in a great fermentation.'

1 June: Lechi informed Murat everyone believed General Moncey had come down from Bellinzona, but his spies had not returned to confirm this.

2 June: General of Brigade Carra-Saint-Cyr at Ivrea reported his spies believed the Austrians were going to move against Ivrea, but he was not persuaded.

One can see there was a web of espionage following the French advance across northern Italy. Most of these spies were local ones, recruited by the various column commanders, or pro-French informants they encountered. It would take a special spy to have dealt directly with the opposing commanders. The Austrian author Hermann Hüffer also recognized the hand of the Cuneo spy in Milan, although not from Bourrienne, but another source entirely. There is a second version of the meeting with the spy written by French author Édouard Gachot in his 1899 work *La deuxième campaign d'Italie (1800)*. Gachot wrote extensively on the Italian campaigns and based much of his richly written accounts on information he said he collected in travels through Italy and Switzerland. These local sources collected within 100 years of Marengo are extremely interesting, but equally difficult to verify today. Gachot claimed to have found a pamphlet (*opuscule*) called *l'art d'espionnage* (the art of spying) while travelling through the Aosta valley. He claims this work was published in Milan in 1807, with a limited print run of twenty copies. The document was, Gachot claimed, the first-hand account of a spy he named as François or Francesco Toli (or Tolli).[14] Although much of the dialogue is different, it substantially follows the same content, with Toli exchanging information on the Austrians in return for the strength and location of Bonaparte's army. It concludes with the two men agreeing to meet on 10 June at the city of Pavia.

Where Gachot's account is wildly different from Bourrienne is its description of an earlier meeting between Bonaparte and the spy, while the First Consul was at Martigny on the Swiss side of the Great St Bernard. The account includes a fantastic description of the spy infiltrating the French army by climbing the Alps. When interviewed after being captured, the spy provided Bonaparte with the following account:

'You know, General, I know my profession. Disguised as a priest, I had presented myself at the Great St Bernard. A sentinel aimed at me, and would have fired, I presume, if I had not executed a prompt retreat. Unable to arrive at Vélan, I ran to Gignod, at the entrance to Valpelline. A guide of my friends accompanied me to the path of Col de la Balme. I spent sixty hours crossing Mont Avril in the snow and on the ice. Exhausted and injured, I descended, clinging to the rocks, towards the Val d'Entremont, and then on the path to Bagnes. Thirty soldiers guarded the bridge at Mauvoisin; I was able to thwart their surveillance by crawling at dawn. I was about to see the village of Orsières when some cavalrymen sent for reconnaissance fell upon me. They would have killed me if I had not asked to be taken to General Bonaparte.'[15]

There is much about this account which rings true, albeit circumstantially. It is entirely plausible for Zach to have used Gioelli in Switzerland and beyond, rather than in the Riviera, where he was known. The route described by the spy is extremely accurate, and is traceable today using modern mapping software and satellite photography. If one couldn't get past French sentries on the Great St Bernard, the next valley to the east does lead to Mont Vélan via Étroubles. Failing that, one has to travel almost all the way back to Aosta before taking the branch to Valpelline. The spy's epic sixty-hour climb over Mont Avril is also a viable track, still in use by mountain walkers today. In Gachot's account, the spy states he was working for Vukassovich, and sure enough, this general was responsible for collating the intelligence on Switzerland. The spy then provides Bonaparte with a description of Vukassovich's strength and position. If this account is true, it perhaps changes our understanding of the First Consul's decision-making after crossing the Alps. If Bonaparte was indeed told of Vukassovich's dispositions and intentions, then perhaps his lightning march on Milan is all the more understandable.

However, this first encounter is not mentioned in Bourrienne. Nor has it been possible to locate the principal sources cited by Gachot. For example, in 1898, Gachot told the editor of *la Revue du Foyer de Lyon* he had seen a note by the *prévot* of the religious order at Martigny stating the spy had visited Martigny on 18 May, and the *prévot* (Louis-Antoine Luder) had stated that the spy Toli had been known to Bonaparte in 1796-1797. This note does not appear to be among the archives today. In fact the accounts written by the monks indicate Bonaparte arrived and locked himself away in silence for three days, and was only seen to leave the room to go to the refectory. He is said to have ordered some movements to confuse enemy spies, but there is no record of him actually meeting a spy.[16] Bourrienne writes how they waited in solitude for three days in the greatest boredom. Surely the arrival of a spy in such sensational circumstances would have merited comment, particularly as Bourrienne later refers to the spy as 'famous'. In the absence of the original documents to corroborate this account, one suspects Gachot used an element of artistic licence, perhaps even amalgamating several stories into one. For the purposes of this account, the most important fact is that we definitely know Zach sent his most trusted spy to investigate Bonaparte's strength and intentions. This spy met Bonaparte in Milan and returned to Austrian headquarters with a somewhat inflated order of battle, also revealing the French were bringing troops down the St Gotthard. However, even with this information, it would have been very difficult at this stage to establish what Bonaparte's intentions were. Was Mantua his real target, or Genoa?

To conclude this section, another contemporary source appears to confirm the presence of the spy in Milan as reported. General Duhesme commanded what had become the French advanced guard, which had pressed on from Milan to Lodi. It comprised the infantry divisions of Loison and Boudet, and was supported by the cavalry reserve under Murat. In his 1814 work on light infantry, *Essai historique sur l'infanterie légère*, Duhesme described the confusion Melas must have experienced trying to understand Bonaparte's objectives, with his fast-moving columns seemingly advancing on all fronts:

> 'This manner of irregularising the march of the divisions had the advantage of speeding their movements and of deceiving the spies of the enemy; for an agent of Melas, who left Milan to make his report, two days after our entry, what would he have seen? What could he have brought back? The French army was almost entirely between Milan and Lodi. The vanguard had already passed the Adda and was heading for Cremona. But in a day the scene had changed. General Murat, from Lodi, where he had marched, had made the head of the column turn right on Piacenza.'[17]

It appears more than coincidence that Duhesme discusses what an 'agent of Melas' might have discovered leaving Milan two days after the French entry into the city. One suspects Gioelli had to pass through Duhesme's troops on his way to cross over to the right bank of the Po using the bridge at Piacenza. To give way to fancy, one can imagine the Italian spy riding up to Duhesme's sentinels and showing the passport issued to him by the First Consul; and then a few hours later, producing a second passport at the Austrian outposts, this time signed by Zach. Such was the life of a Napoleonic double spy.

Chapter 7

The Fall of Genoa

The siege of Genoa proved one of the unhappiest episodes of the Napoleonic Wars. On being blockaded, Massena had declared he would rather die under the rubble of Genoa than surrender it. The city had a population of perhaps 90,000 souls in 1800. Massena's garrison numbered 9,600 men, with a further 18,000 sick and wounded in the city's hospitals. Against him was FML Ott with a covering force of 24,000 men, and of course the ships of the British Royal Navy which blockaded the port from the sea. The city defences were so extensive, Ott was unable to batter a breach and mount an assault, so resorted to war by starvation rather than bullets.

Massena received limited intelligence from the outside world during the siege. He pinned his hopes on the Army of the Reserve arriving by 30 May; which meant holding out for forty days. At the outset of the siege, the city had sufficient grain and pulse for fourteen days. A search of the city recovered enough for an additional fourteen days, and a few local merchant ships were able to break the naval blockade. The French also mounted raids to capture supplies where they could, sometimes followed by civilians who harvested grass outside the city for making soup. On 14 May, Massena made one last effort to counter-attack against the Austrian positions around the city, but it had failed and General Soult was captured on the slopes of Monte Creto. The city was then bombarded by Neapolitan gunboats through the night. Terrorised and angry, people fled the harbour quarter and ran into the city squares. Fearing an uprising, Massena was forced to place artillery in the squares to prevent large assemblies.

By 20 May, supplies were so low that bread was withheld from the civilian population and became the sole preserve of soldiers manning the walls. The only meat came from the horses in the city (even those suffering from disease), including those belonging to the officers. Once the horses were consumed, the city's cats, dogs and eventually the rats fell victim to the knife. As a daily ration, the soldiers received just a quarter of a pound of horseflesh and a similar ration of horrible bread. To ensure the grain lasted longer, this bread was made from a sickening mixture of flour, sawdust, starch, hair powder, oatmeal, linseed, rancid nuts and cocoa. Straw was taken from the floors of the hospitals and added to the mix. The soldiers dragged chairs up onto the city walls as they were too malnourished to stand all day. The only thing which saved them was the continued availability of wine. As for the Genoese, they made do with boiled leaves, grass and nettles, seasoned with salt. Great vats of soup were cooked in the public squares for those too sick to cook for themselves. Once the gardens were stripped of vegetation, they boiled old bones, leather and other skins. Up to 400 people were dying every day from starvation and disease, so a mass grave was opened behind the Carignano Church, and the corpses covered with quicklime to prevent the spread of disease. It was an absolutely desperate situation, and when 30 May came and went with no sign of Bonaparte's army, Massena finally began to contemplate his options. On 1 June, the French commander notified the Austrians he wished to negotiate.

Generals Ott and Schellenberg were with Colonel de Best at Stutterheim's lodgings when this news arrived. The four of them were overcome with joy. The siege had been so long and terrible, they felt it might never end. They had just begun debating the terms on which they would negotiate with the 'stubborn' Massena, when the door to Stutterheim's quarters flew open revealing Major Funk, commander of the artillery in Ott's corps. The major's face was pale and he held some papers in his hand. 'Clear out of Savona; spike the guns; throw the ammunition in the sea,' he stammered.

The papers were snatched out of Funk's hand and passed round the room by the dumbfounded occupants. They were a series of orders from the artillery directorate instructing Funk to evacuate Savona. These orders were followed by a message from Elsnitz to Ott, dated Breglio, 31 May. It indicated he was evacuating the Riviera, heading in the direction of the Col di Braus with less than 9,000 men. As they pondered these messages, orders arrived from imperial headquarters. Two letters from Melas in Turin, dated 31 May, were handed over. The first began:

> 'Now the enemy has also broken out from the St Gotthard and Simplon passes with a significant column, which has come from Germany and has already driven FML Vukassovich back, I am forced to abandon the whole Riviera and lift the blockade of Genoa.'[1]

The order explained Elsnitz had been ordered to retreat via Cuneo to Alessandria, and cavalry patrols were being sent along the coast to inform all Austrian detachments to concentrate. Ott was instructed to send Gottesheim's brigade to Piacenza with all speed via Bobbio, to garrison the citadel and hold the bridgehead over the Po there. In terms of breaking off the siege at Genoa, Melas' instructions were somewhat muddled:

> 'During your retreat, the Bochetta must be garrisoned, the first march will happen at night; the rearguard can only depart at dawn and must halt on the Bochetta, in order to protect the entire retreat. I will still be

able to stay here for a few days; consequently the retreat is not necessary immediately. Consequently, this decision is to be kept most secret in the hope Genoa will still surrender.'[2]

The second letter, dated midday on 31 March, was somewhat contradictory to this:

'From my previous missive, Your Excellency will know the blockade of Genoa must be lifted. From the present letter, Your Excellency is ordered to effect your retreat into the plain of Alessandria immediately.'[3]

Pausing for breath, Stutterheim and de Best took stock of the situation. They now knew the French had descended from Switzerland in force, with confirmation more troops were arriving from Germany. They also knew Elsnitz was withdrawing from the Var and appeared to be under some pressure. However, Elsnitz would not arrive in Alessandria until 10 June, and so, if the objective was to concentrate the army, Ott still had some time to conclude negotiations with Massena before withdrawing. Melas had clearly written these instructions before he knew Massena was about to yield the city. Stutterheim indicates they sat in his room and weighed up the risks before replying at ten in the evening:

'I have just received Your Excellency's two orders of 31st May, which order me to lift the blockade of Genoa. Some hours ago, I sent a courier to Your Excellency with the response of General Massena, who appears to wish to enter into a capitulation.

'I presume that FML Elsnitz has begun his retreat today. If the enemy in that area marches off towards here it is certainly impossible for them to reach this area before the 5th; thus I intend to remain here for tomorrow and the day after, and to start my withdrawal on the night of the 3rd/4th, so I can arrive in [the] area around Alessandria on the 6th.'[4]

Ott turned to his staff officers and warned them to maintain the greatest silence over what had happened in Stutterheim's room; outwardly they would carry on as normal and tell no-one. It was clear, however, that a deal had to be done with Massena by 4 June at the latest.

The Austrians knew the negotiations with Massena would be difficult, and they did not start well. A rendezvous was arranged at Rivarolo. Ott was represented by de Best, the British Admiral Lord Keith by Flag Captain Beaver. Massena sent Adjudant General Andrieux to represent him. The Austrians put on some musical entertainment for the French officers who accompanied Andrieux. At the time, Austrian military bands played a style of music known as 'Turkish'.

This was based on the music of the Ottoman Janissaries and was typically a high-tempo march, with a great deal of percussion, shrill woodwind and horns. As the band struck up, the famished Frenchmen defending nearby Fort Tenaglia assumed the Austrians were advancing to attack the valley below them. The Frenchmen opened fire and the Austrian gunners replied in kind. Down in the valley below, clarinets were thrown asunder and everyone at the rendezvous scattered. Andrieux had his horse shot from under him before anyone could send word to cease firing.

When the conference finally resumed, each of the emissaries stated the opening negotiating position. Massena had told Andrieux he would be willing to evacuate Genoa, but if the word 'capitulation' was mentioned, negotiations were to cease. There would be no surrender on his part. This wasn't necessarily a problem for the Austrians. If they had to take the garrison into captivity, this would require guarding forces, and their key objective was to take possession of the port as swiftly as possible. However, there were still a number of important details which needed to be decided. Negotiations were put off until 7.00 am the following day. This was to provide time for the emissaries to notify their superiors of the various opening positions.

On 3 June, Andrieux offered the first draft of a convention. Reading the detail, Massena wanted all the French shipping in the harbour to go free. The Austrian and British representatives stated that the ships must be taken as prizes. Furthermore, while the allies were content with the garrison returning to France, they wanted Massena to become a prisoner of war. Lord Keith had apparently said the French general was worth 20,000 men. No one would budge on the point, and so the emissaries agreed the only course of action was to arrange a meeting between Massena, Keith and Ott to let them finalize the terms of the evacuation in person. A meeting was set for the following day at the small chapel in the middle of the Cornigliano bridge on the western approaches to the city.

The continued negotiations were a boon to Massena. Every day he could delay the inevitable was a day won for the First Consul. Massena had no real idea what was taking place outside the city walls, but he did know the reserve army was now in Italy and he could still cling to the hope of a relief. At the same time, he knew 4 June would be the final day of resistance. There were no more rations for his soldiers after that. Resistance after this date would condemn his men and the civilians to death by starvation. Meanwhile, Ott wrote to Melas advising him negotiations had begun, but one or two more days were needed to conclude them. Ott asked Melas whether he ought to continue with the talks or evacuate Genoa immediately? He awaited his response.

When Melas received Ott's two letters dated 1 June, he had naturally been ecstatic at the news Genoa might fall. He responded at once:

'Your Excellency's note of the 1st June which has just reached me, gives me the most joyous expectation of being able to gain Genoa by capitulation.

'The order sent by me at the end of the past month was based on raising the blockade. Consequently, I can only nurture the pleasant hope that Your Excellency will have left no opportunity unused in these changed circumstances, which could lead to our capture of Genoa. Therefore, if by now the negotiations are not concluded or broken off, you are to do everything possible and to give whatever conditions, in order just to take us into possession of the city, which in the present moment not only provides us with the desirable advantage in terms of occupying it immediately, but also lets us obtain the great gain, that Massena with so many thousands of men no longer stands in the way of our operations, and consequently your march to the army cannot be hindered.'[5]

Melas then outlined how after the negotiations were concluded, Ott would rejoin the army at Alessandria, before moving against the French who were seemingly advancing against the Hereditary Lands. After writing this letter to Ott, Melas wrote another letter, this time to GM Mosel at Alessandria. This general was to move at once to Piacenza and take control of the city, making every effort to garrison the citadel and, most importantly of all, the bridge over the Po by which Melas' army was going to attack the rear of Bonaparte's army.[6]

On 4 June, the interview with Massena took place. The French commander gave off an air of apparent gaiety at the proceedings. He certainly did not appear as a man whose army was on the brink of starvation and ruin. He attempted to come between the British and Austrian negotiators, taking them to one side in turn and talking secretly with them. He flattered Keith, telling him Britain and France could govern the world if they could only come to an understanding. He mocked the Austrians, telling Keith if he would allow just one boat of grain to enter Genoa, the Austrians would never set foot in the place. Keith, for his part, humoured Massena. He told him on several occasions, 'General, the defence you have made has been so heroic, that it is impossible to refuse you anything you ask.' In fact, despite the praise he lavished on Massena, Keith later concluded the French general was 'the greatest brute in all Christendom'.[7]

By the end of the negotiation, it was agreed Massena's army would march out with its arms and baggage in the direction of Nice. When it rejoined Suchet's troops, it would become active again. Two last points of contention remained. The first was that Massena wanted to send two messengers to Bonaparte informing him Genoa had been evacuated. This would be a crucial piece of intelligence to the First Consul, because it meant up to an additional 25,000 Austrians were now free to commence operations against the Army of the Reserve. Naturally enough, Ott did not want to allow this, but Keith talked him round to it. The second point was the ships in the harbour, particularly those loaded with Massena's private possessions. In the end, the allies conceded these points. Referring to the shipping, Keith told Massena: 'Though law forbids me from allowing any vessels to leave an enemy port, let us speak of them no more, I will make you a present of them on my part.'

One final drama was to arise. At the moment Massena was about to put pen to paper, there was a sound like gunfire rumbling from the direction of the Bochetta Pass. Massena leapt up, declaring: 'Here comes the First Consul with his army!' The French general threw down his pen and returned to the city, leaving Keith and Ott standing dumbstruck. In fact it was only thunder, and Massena eventually returned to sign the treaty.

As Austrian troops took possession of the Lanterne (lighthouse) Gate, a terrible spectacle took place. Several thousand Austrian prisoners had been incarcerated on hulks in the harbour a few weeks before and had suffered the most miserable plight. At the beginning of the siege, when the French had captured Austrian soldiers, they had returned them on parole. While the officers observed this parole, Massena believed the soldiers were simply returned to the ranks and were being sent to fight again, the result being that soldiers were captured and released numerous times. Massena wrote to Ott and complained he felt he had little choice but to place all prisoners on hulks in the harbour, with artillery trained on them in lieu of the guards he could not spare. In addition, he said the prisoners would receive exactly half of the daily ration given to French soldiers, which would amount to an eighth of a pound of poor quality bread (approximately 200 calories) and the same amount of horsemeat (150 calories). Massena invited Ott to send food to supplement these rations, but this was suspected of being a ruse in order to obtain food for the French garrison. The result of this impasse was that the soldiers starved. Marbot stated in his memoirs that the prisoners yelled with rage at their hunger, eating their shoes and knapsacks in desperation – cannibalism was also rumoured.

Stutterheim confirms their unhappy plight, adding that they ate the ropes on the ships, their helmets and equipment straps. They descended into mad laughter and some threw themselves into the sea in attempt to end their suffering, but were plucked out of the water by the French and returned to the hulks. According to Stutterheim, Massena made an example of the prisoners after a prisoner transfer in which the Austrians secured the release of Austrian soldiers, but gave Massena in return non-combatant hospital workers and commissaries. Apparently, Zach was the instigator of this ruse, and as Stutterheim acknowledges, no commander of a besieged place would want 'useless bread-eaters' when there was already a lack of food. When Massena took 3,000 prisoners at the action of Monte Fascio on 11 May, he consigned these men to the hulks. Ott agreed to provide these men with food, Stutterheim contested, but only in a neutral place where they could be sure the food was not being distributed to French soldiers. Stutterheim was aghast when he saw the prisoners released:

'For centuries, among civilized nations, unfortunates were never so much injured as these. The sight of these wretches, when they were brought out of the fortress, was miserable and outrageous. Hardly one man in ten was able to walk alone. Holding on to the walls, these pale corpses crept, death on their lips. Many had lost their speech; others lost their sight or hearing. More than a hundred fell dead on the wayside to Cornegliano. The food they had given them could no longer save them. Only a few, who, with the most strength, were fortunate enough to come to the care of kind hearted and sensible people, who gradually brought the patients round with warming and nourishing food, escaped from the death which struck others more certainly, the hastier they reached out for food. I myself saw several of them give up the ghost with a piece of meat or bread between their teeth, which they were no longer able to chew. As splendid as Massena's defence of Genoa was, this cruelty against those innocents filled the heart of every man with disgust.'[8]

On 5 June, the French garrison marched out. On the same day, Vogelsang's division marched towards Novi; Schellenberg's division departed on 6 June, while Gottesheim's brigade was directed on Piacenza, taking the route through the mountains via Torriglia and Bobbio. Prince Hohenzollern's division remained in Genoa, approximately 7,000-strong. Melas' firm intention was for the main part of the army to unite at Alessandria. The divisions of Kaim and Hadik were already marching there with the cavalry, and Elsnitz was on his way from the Var. All the written orders suggested Ott was to do likewise.

However, at this point, the 'fog of war' descends on our account. With the passage of two centuries, it becomes very difficult to properly understand decisions made by the Austrians. According to Radetzky's memoirs, as the negotiations with Massena continued, Melas became impatient and wanted a decision: either the surrender should take place or the blockade should be lifted. The account adds that Zach was ordered to go to Ott, and to accelerate the outcome one way or the other. Radetzky states Zach arrived in Genoa after the signing of the convention, and also says he had with him the spy 'who had played Cuneo into our hands'. According to Radetzky, on the report of the spy, Zach redirected Ott's troops towards Stradella, where he hoped to catch Bonaparte's troops in the rear if they attempted to march on Alessandria.

Stutterheim does not mention the arrival of Zach. The former had remained behind in Genoa with the émigré Crossard, concluding business while the divisions of Vogelsang and Schellenberg set off. His account states the two divisions heard at Novi the rumour the enemy had crossed the Po in the area around Piacenza. Stutterheim claims the two divisions then took off towards Tortona without orders. The first Ott knew about this was on the evening of 7 June when arriving in Novi himself. As ever, it is difficult to square the conflicting accounts. If Zach had been to Genoa, this would almost certainly have been recorded. The authors of three of the most important Austrian accounts – Geppert, Stutterheim and Crossard – were staff officers in Genoa at this moment: all remain silent on the fact.

It appears certain that Ott's troops left Genoa with every intention of reaching Alessandria. However, when Vogelsang quit Novi, he marched on Tortona. We know this from the memoirs of Crossard, who was detailed to ride ahead of the column and find a crossing point over the Scrivia. This river is a torrent, with a wide stony bed forming something of a shallow scar across the landscape, over 100km long. The river bed is normally quite dry, but is prone to sudden floods of water coming down from the mountains. When Crossard encountered it, there had been a storm so the river was swollen and fast-moving. Crossard was at a complete loss what to do when he saw a long column of country carts pass over the river heading for Alessandria. The four-wheeled carts were quite low and had a long and broad apron, perfect for forming an improvised bridge for infantry. The staff officer stopped the column and had the carts chained together across the river. When Vogelsang's column arrived, Crossard directed the cavalry and artillery to ford the river, while the infantry marched over the cart bridge. Darkness fell around 9.00 pm and the troops were still in the process of crossing. The last battalion to cross met with an accident. The carts formed something of a dyke and the pressure of the river caused the chains to break. With some difficulty, the men thrown into the river were saved, and Crossard did not believe anyone drowned.

By now, General O'Reilly and Gottesheim had made contact with Ott's leading elements. They reported they were being followed by 6,000 enemy troops, which had crossed the Po, but they would attack and repulse the enemy if they were supported. Ott's chief of staff, Colonel de Best, recommended Ott march his troops towards Voghera as quickly as possible. Alas, the rush to go to O'Reilly's assistance and the lack of pre-planning took its toll. On 8 June, Ott's corps awoke at Voghera in a state of utter confusion. The two divisions had become intermingled in the night. Even individual regiments had broken up. Nearly 17,000 men were in disarray. Stutterheim complained this was a recipe for disaster, spending the rest of the day splitting the two divisions and forming a new camp at Broni.

While this reorganization took place, Crossard remarks that Ott was 'without news of Melas' and did not know the location of Bonaparte or his army. A prudent man might have held off and sent for instructions before walking into the unknown. However, just before nightfall, General Vogelsang prepared a small reconnaissance force under the French émigré, Captain de Bellerose, of the de Bussy Light Horse. His instructions were to probe forwards and find the enemy wherever he found them. It was a dark night; there was no way of accurately estimating the location and strength of the French forces. The captain spurred his men forwards and ultimately rode into the French outposts and was killed. His lieutenant returned to headquarters, stating the republican army was approaching.

On the morning of 9 June, Ott received reports that O'Reilly had been involved in a small outpost skirmish, after which the French had fallen back. It did not appear serious and the French retreated from this encounter. However, when the head of Ott's column reached Casteggio at 11.00 am, he ran into the French advanced guard supported by a strong column. This did not appear to be the weak force O'Reilly had described. At this point Zach arrived. It is the first positive confirmation we have of Zach meeting with Ott. Gioelli was probably with him (as Radetzky described), because by now the spy would have returned from his mission to Milan, and was setting off to meet Bonaparte at Pavia as the two had agreed. Gioelli had likely informed Zach the French were in fact moving against the Po and not advancing toward Austria, and Zach would therefore have realized the danger of the imperial army's communications being cut.

Making an assessment of the situation, Zach was nervous about giving battle. When asked what to do, he appeared to dither, taking a cautious approach and avoiding an engagement. According to Stutterheim, a voice rose up from the assembled officers (probably de Best) and said: 'Who is going to run away from these fellows? Come on – we stay!'[9]

Acting more like a hussar than a general, Ott concurred: 'My outposts are attacked; I march to their aid.'

Against all expectations, a serious battle was about to be fought.

Having taken Milan, Bonaparte put in motion the next phase of his strategy. The main post road from Turin to Mantua followed the right bank of the Po, passing through Asti, Alessandria, Tortona, Piacenza and Cremona. To intercept this vital line of communication for Melas's army, the First Consul sought to block the road in three places. Duhesme would take Loison's division from Lodi to Cremona; Murat would take Boudet's division and the cavalry reserve to sieze Piacenza, where the post road was intersected by the main road from Milan to Parma and Bologna. Lannes would force a crossing of the Po at Belgiojoso and occupy

Stradella. Victor would remain in reserve, ready to exploit whichever crossing could first be captured.

In the early hours of 5 June, Boudet's division quit Lodi and marched more than 30km down the Via Emilia until they reached the Po opposite Piacenza. The bridge at Piacenza was guarded by a large earthwork bridgehead fortification mounted with gun platforms and a large *cheval-de-frise* blocking the road. Brushing aside the Austrian forward posts, Boudet attempted to capture the bridgehead by sending the 9th Light Infantry onto the flanks to draw the defenders' fire, while mounting a frontal assault on the main gate with the grenadiers of the 59th Line. The commander of the town was GM Mosel. He had some notice of the French advance and had prepared the defences well. In addition to mounting guns in the bridgehead itself, he placed some on the far bank of the Po, creating an enfilading fire along the flanks of the fortress. Boudet's troops came under heavy artillery fire as they advanced towards the fort for fifteen minutes. The assault on the gate quickly failed; however, the 9th Light took shelter in the ditches surrounding the fort and were able to fire through the embrasures at the crews serving the guns.

At the start of the action Mosel had about 400 fit troops, a mixture of line infantry, Tyrolean Jäger and fifty horsemen from the de Bussy Light Horse. Although he was able to arm some convalescents, the citadel there required a garrison of 600 men, let alone protecting the entire city. Mosel suffered 120 casualties in the first attack on the bridgehead and was naturally concerned the French might sieze the bridge. Piacenza was filled with stores and equipment, including the army's treasury and the Imperial Chancellery containing all of the army's records and correspondance. Mosel had these evacuated to Parma for safekeeping, and while waiting for reinforcements to arrive, decided to evacuate the bridgehead at night and break the boat bridge over the Po. While a covering fire was maintained from the opposite bank, the guns in the bridgehead were evacuated, then a portion of the bridge was removed. Unfortuately for Mosel, his rearguard of eighty men was captured almost single-handedly by Captain Hippolyte Cazeaux of the 9th Light. However, the bridge was cut and Murat was left extremely frustrated.

On 6 June, Lannes began crossing the Po upriver at Belgiojoso. Led by General of Brigade Mainoni, the 28th Line spearheaded the crossing, using several boats which had been gathered. This half-brigade formed a protective cordon behind which some engineers could build a 'flying bridge' – a large raft tethered to the river banks, propelled across the current of the water. At 10.00 am, the Austrians sighted the French and attacked. There was a vigourous contest in which Lannes had to intervene to prevent the Frenchmen being pushed back into the river. The Austrians broke off in the direction of Stradella, and then returned mid-afternoon with some artillery. By then the French had transported five companies of the 40th Line across the Po to reinforce Mainoni. In the coming clash, the French took the initiative and attacked the Austrians, driving them off the field after hand-to-hand fighting. The moment Berthier heard Lannes had troops across the Po, he ordered the army headquarters to Pavia, and directed Victor to march to the newly constructed flying bridge. Berthier also instructed Duhesme to move on Cremona and capture the Austrian magazines in the city, or if this was not possible, to cross the Po elsewhere and march in the direction of Stradella to rejoin the army.

Murat continued to be frustrated at Piacenza. The strong current of the Po made repairing the bridge impossible. No boats could be found in the vicinity of the bridgehead, and the Austrians maintained a hampering artillery fire against the French, who had too little ammunition to reply effectively. Adjutant-General Dalton took a patrol of the 9th Light about 10 miles downstream and gathered various boats. These were collected at Nocetto in preparation for an operation the following day. In the early hours of 7 June, Boudet took the bulk of his forces to Nocetta and began crossing the Po. They took up position on the main road about 2 miles east of Piacenza. Inside the city, General O'Reilly arrived at the head of two squadrons of the Nauendorf Hussars. He had been instructed to take command of the city and had ridden ahead of his main force to do this. In so doing, he lost contact with his infantry, who had run into Lannes opposite Belgiojoso. The only infantry support he received was 600 men from IR 14 Klebeck, who arrived via the Bobbio Road. The Austrian scouts now reported the arrival of Boudet on the right bank opposite Nocetto. To complicate matters, O'Reilly was informed a large artillery convoy of about 1,500 vehicles was about to arrive in the city on its way to Parma. O'Reilly detailed one of his hussar squadrons to protect this convoy and sent an urgent message for it to make all speed on the Parma road to avoid being captured by Boudet's troops. O'Reilly decided to evacuate Piacenza and to save as much of the field artillery as possible.

Things now began to move very swiftly. The French scouts spotted the artillery convoy and also noticed a column of Austrian infantry coming up from the direction of Parma. General of Brigade Musnier took his brigade, composed of the 9th Light Infantry, to sieze Piacenza, sending one battalion of the Ninth to pursue the artillery convoy. Musnier advised Boudet to bring the 59th Line up in support as soon as it was across the Po. As the first two battalions advanced on Piacenza, they were attacked by the remaining squadron of the Nauendorf Hussars. The French infantrymen closed up their columns and advanced towards the approaching hussars. The Ninth had come under heavy artillery fire around the bridgehead and suffered their first significant casualties of the campaign. Boudet's journal says the men called for vengeance when faced with the Austrians horsemen. Musnier ordered the columns to lower bayonets and they charged the hussars, who broke off their attack and fled back to the city.

At the bridgehead, Murat's impatience was at fever pitch. He asked his engineers to re-examine the bridge. Chief of Battalion Pastre of the 59th called for volunteers to swim across to the other side of the bridge. The distance was not so great, but the Po was swollen with mountain water and rainfall. Six of the swimmers drowned and Pastre was plucked out of the water unconscious. Murat need not have been so impatient. Musnier was now inside the city with his light infantrymen and running through the streets. The general took the Ninth's carabinier companies and made for the far gate on the Stradella road. At the same time, IR 14 Klebeck entered the city by that gate. Hemmed in by Piacenza's streets, the two adversaries clashed, with the Ninth quickly gaining the upper hand. O'Reilly's wife was in the city. On balance, the Irishman thought she would be safer remaining than going with him, so the general left his wife behind and made off with a small bodyguard. The remainder of the city garrison locked themselves in the citadel.

With the covering batteries removed, Murat's engineers were at last able to start building a flying bridge. As the French cavalry reserve began to cross, Boudet took the 59th Line and his hussars to meet the Austrian column coming up from Parma. Murat went to watch the action and was overjoyed at how Boudet's soliders fought like 'madmen', launching a bayonet charge against the Austrians despite being under artillery fire. As they were assaulted from the front, Boudet had his howitzers lob shells at the rear of the Austrian column. He then personally led a charge of the 11th hussars to complete the Austrian rout. Murat reflected in a letter to Bonaparte that his troops had taken around 2,000 prisoners, killed fifty and taken thirteen pieces of artillery along with two flags. Considerable stores were taken from the magazines, and thirty large boats filled with provisions of all kinds had been seized. He also had O'Reilly's wife in his custody, and informed Bonaparte she was 'tolerably ugly'. More imporantly, the River Po was now passable because the flying bridges had been established and all the cavalry was across ready to support the next action. They had also captured some despatches carried by a courier, but because none of them could read German he had sent the letters onto headquarters with his report.

Elsewhere that day, Duhesme had fought Vukassovich's rearguard and occupied Cremona. Inside the city, they seized a grain store and a large supply of equipment. Bonaparte had achieved his aim of cutting the Austrian line of retreat to Mantua, and the capture of Piacenza was particularly important because it controlled much of the road network in northern Italy. The army was now in a position to occupy Stradella and wait for Melas to attempt to recover his line of communications. This is exactly as he had foreseen the campaign developing. However, this achievement was to be soured by the contents of the captured letters Murat had sent. Bonaparte had spent the evening of 7 June inspecting some of the troops who had come down from the Army of the Rhine. He went to bed afterwards, but was awoken shortly before dawn by Bourrienne. Bonaparte had a rule that he never wanted to be woken unless it was bad news which required his immediate consideration – good news could wait. This was bad news - the letter revealed Genoa had fallen.

Bonaparte initially disbelieved Bourrienne's translation, but he eventually accepted the news and made his plans accordingly. He sent the following information to Berthier:

'General Murat has forwarded to me at Milan the dispatches captured from the enemy. I am occupied in getting them examined; they contain some very interesting details.

'A letter from Melas to the Aulic council, dated the 5th June, from Turin, informs me Massena capitulated on the 4th. His troops are not prisoners of war; they are on the march to join General Suchet. It appears, however, that Massena has embarked on a frigate so as to arrive more promptly at Nice.

'General Melas also confesses in his letters that Baron Elsnitz has been unable to effect his retreat by the Col di Tenda, because one of his brigadier generals has been overthrown at the Col di Braus, and that line of march has been cut off. He has conducted his retreat to Oneglia. General Melas states he hopes Elsnitz will arrive in Ormea on 7th June.

'Elsnitz has only 6,000 men of his division with him, and 3,400 men of Morzin's division; total 9,400 men; of whom he will have to leave 1,000 men at Cuneo, 1,000 men at Savona and 300 at Ceva.

'General Hohenzollern will remain at Genoa.

'General Ott, with 9,000 men, will return by the Bochetta and Ovada to Alessandria.

'Thus, it appears it will not be before the 12th or 13th of June that the enemy will be able to assemble his forces at Alessandria and then it will have only the following forces:

- Elsnitz's division, 7,000 men
- Ott's division, 9,000 men
- Hadik's division, which is currently on the Orco, 6,000 men
- Total: 22,000 men

'Move forward some parties boldly and crush all the troops you encounter. The advanced-guard can push on to Voghera.

'Cross the cavalry and artillery so all the divisions may be complete, having their cartridges and everything in proper order.

'Even though my carriage is ready and half of my guides have left, I will wait for your return of post.'[10]

There are several interesting parts to this letter. The first is the abandonment of the plan to hold a position at Stradella and to advance to Voghera. The second is that the original of this letter (published by Hüffer) makes no mention of the strengths of the various corps. It is probable the First Consul based these numbers on the information provided by Gioelli. It is also worth stating these numbers underestimated the Austrian strength quite considerably. Having sent this letter to Berthier, Bonaparte then wrote to General Suchet and the Army of Italy. Unaware of Suchet's strength and position, he gave a very simple instruction to him: to hold in check a corps as strong as his own. When he did reach Ceva, he was to discover the location of the Army of the Reserve and manoeuvre to rejoin it. The key issue with acting on this intelligence is that Ott had of course been redirected from Alessandria, also to Voghera. The French were therefore about to advance into a battle they did not expect to fight, against a force considerably larger than they had been informed of. With O'Reilly's troops added to those of Ott, the French would face a force near to 18,000 men strong.

Already that day, Lannes had begun moving on Stradella via Broni. By then O'Reilly had passed this position, having escaped Piacenza the day before, leaving a small rearguard at the latter position. The Chief of Brigade of the 28th Line was Jean-Marie Roger-Valhubert. Rather imprudently, he rode ahead of his half-brigade and entered Broni alone, only to come face-to-face with the Austrian rearguard, about 200 strong. Valhubert found himself separated from the Austrians by a thick hedge. Being mounted, he could see them, but they could not see Valhubert was alone. In a moment of supreme sangfroid, Valhubert menacingly called on the Austrians to surrender. They begrudgingly complied with his wishes and layed down their arms. When no French soldiers materialized, the Austrians realized they had been duped and began to retrieve their weapons. Valhubert bounded the hedge on his horse and fell into the middle of the group, grabbing the commanding officer by the scruff of the neck and placing the point of his sword against his back. He instructed the Austrians to lower their weapons, and they complied. At this point, Valhubert's own troops arrived on the scene and secured the prisoners. They rested at Broni while the remainder of Lannes' troops caught up with them. It was there that Berthier's instructions arrived, directing Lannes on to Voghera the following day, supported by Victor with Chambarlac's division.

On 9 June, the French advanced in the direction of Casteggio. At 6.00 am, Brigadier General Gency led the 6th Light Infantry towards Santa Giulietta, following the main road. On their left was a long line of hills, the beginning of the Appenines; on their right was a largely flat plain, extending 10km to the Po. The terrain was extremely broken, cut with ditches and stone walls, and although largely flat, visibility was greatly reduced by rows of trees, from which vines were hung like garlands. When the French light infantry spied the Austrian forward posts at Santa Giulietta, they at first withdrew, but then returned in strength, pushing them back to Rivetta, 2km east of Casteggio. At this point they encountered more of O'Reilly's force and so they paused again, waiting for the rest of Watrin's division to arrive. At 11.00 am, the French began to probe O'Reilly's defences, so the Irishman decided to fall back on Casteggio, where the buildings would offer a better means of defence. So far these encounters with the Austrians were exactly what Lannes had expected – nothing more than a weak rearguard which should be pursued to Voghera. There was therefore some sense of alarm when Vogelsang's division appeared, with the battalions deploying like clockwork right and left of the main road before scaling the heights above the French position. The French then came under strong artillery fire.

The French responded by deploying two battalions of the 6th Light and had them march obliquely towards the north of Casteggio, drawing the Austrian fire from the main road. Watrin led the other battalion of the 6th Light and the 40th Line to the south, up onto the line of hills. Lannes remained in the centre, on the main road with the 22nd Line, four pieces of artillery and the 12th Hussars. Somewhat impatiently, Lannes ordered a battalion of the 22nd Line to march straight at Vogelsang's position on the hills. They went off at the *pas de charge* through the tall crops, but came under the most severe artillery fire. As they retreated in disorder, Lannes ordered the 12th Hussars to charge the Austrian light infantry in front of Casteggio. This charge scattered the Bach and Am Ende light battalions, and the French hussars penetrated the lower part of the village. They then came under attack themselves by the Bussy Light Horse and Nauendorf Hussars, and were forced to cut their way out from being surrounded.

Lannes sent an urgent request to Victor to come up in support. In the meantime, Mainoni arrived with Valhubert and the 28th Line. Watrin directed them up on the extreme left flank to support Mahler. Initially, the French began to roll up the Austrian battalions on the heights, but Vogelsang had kept four battalions in reserve and these were now committed. In the village below, FML Schellenberg arrived with part of his division and formed a line along the Coppa stream. The remainder of the division (five battalions) were left at the village of Montebello. Lannes was now outnumbered and hard-pressed. The Austrians attempted to get cavalry over the heights and beyond the French line, but they found the 28th Line holding the extreme left of the French line. Valhubert led his grenadiers in a bayonet charge against the Austrian horsemen and saw them off. Ott did not press his advantage as strongly as he might have, perhaps because French prisoners had erroneously told him Bonaparte was present with the French. Neither commander really knew what he was faced with, but both had imprudently attacked.

At 2.00 pm, Olivier Rivaud's infantry brigade arrived. Rivaud directed the 43rd Line onto the left to support Watrin. He deployed one battalion of this half-brigade in a closed column and deployed a battalion either side of this in skirmish formation. These were directed at Vogelsang's battations, supported by Watrin's troops and the 28th Line. Rivaud led the central battalion, which he forebade from firing, instead relying on the masses of skirmishers either side of him for fire support. Victor meanwhile directed the 24th Light Infantry over to the extreme right to support the 6th Light Infantry, which had made some good progress working round the Austrian flank.

In the Austrian centre, Schellenberg could see the French making progress on both wings, so he ordered his reserve battalions up from Montebello, but they ran so quickly they were exhausted by the time they arrived on the battlefield and needed a moment to rest. The French continued to press, so Schellenberg gave the order to retreat to Montebello and hold a new line. O'Reilly's light troops were ordered to protect this retreat by defending the village. When Lannes saw what was happening, he ordered the 96th Line to make a frontal attack and capture Casteggio. The charge was beaten and the 96th stormed over the bridge, chasing off O'Reilly's light troops in the direction of Montebello. Rivaud also pushed his troops on, entering a desperate fight with Austrian infantry in a large farmhouse complex up in the hills. With Casteggio now in French hands, the battle moved to Montebello. It was evening now, and Ott had at last begun to think more prudently. He ordered Schellenberg to form a rearguard at Montebello while the rest of the corps headed to Voghera to regroup. Fighting continued until nightfall, when the last of Schellenberg's troops were at last able to disengage and make good their escape.

For much of the campaign it had been raining. On 7 June, General Duvignau's cavalry brigade quit Milan and stopped outside Pavia, in the rain. Among the officers in the brigade was Galy-Montaglas of the 12th Chasseurs. As memoirs go, his is perhaps unique in having been censored by its publisher for its extremely pornographic descriptions of the Milan brothels which Montaglas and his comrades visited the night before. Montaglas did not like Duvignau at all. The general was in his thirtieth year; he had been greviously wounded at the Battle of Valmy in 1792, where he was ADC to General Rochambeau. Although well versed in war, he caused something of an upset by bringing his wife on campaign with him. While the regiment sat outside Pavia in the pouring rain, Duvignau apparently disappeared for an hour while he 'took his pleasures with *Madame his wife* in the city'.[11] From this place of comfort, Duvignau angered everyone by sending orders for the regiment to continue its march until it reached the village of Belgiojoso. There, Duvignau sent further instructions for the regiment to set up outposts. Montaglas was put in charge of this, and he was infuriated to find the army was already massed in this area. Why didn't Duvignau know the location of the rest of the army, Montaglas asked? He concluded: 'Very often, generals do not know what they are doing and soldiers are always victims of their ineptitude.' They continued on their way, 'wet as ducks', until they reached Piacenza, where the Austrians still held the citadel and would occasionally fire at the French crossing the river. Somewhere in the muddy quagmire which passed for a road, Montaglas lost his pet dog, Countess. He was inconsolable for the moment. On 9 June, on the road to Stradella, they met Bonaparte, who was on his way from Milan to join the army in the field for the first time in the campaign. That night, while Lannes and Victor's troops were firing the final shots of the Battle of Montebello, the regiment's foragers returned with the most wonderful discovery. That night, Montaglas estimated the 340 men of his regiment drank 'at least three thousand bottles of wine'. While they drank, some fattened hens were cooked and bread was distributed. The light cavalry had a certain reputation to uphold.[12]

Bonaparte arrived at Stradella on 9 June and established his headquarters there. The half-brigades which had fought at Montebello needed rest and resupplying, and some time was needed for the divisions of Gardanne, Boudet, Monnier and Lapoype to arrive from Piacenza. Bonaparte therefore decided to concentrate his army between Stradella and Voghera before deciding on the next course of action. It was at Stradella where Bonaparte most likely met with the spy Gioelli. The First Consul posed the spy a series of questions about Melas' intentions and the status of the imperial army's concentration at Alessandria. We will return to these questions in detail in due course.

Bonaparte then went to visit the battlefield at Casteggio. In his bulletin, he admitted 600 casualties, which is higher than the 500 Berthier reported, but still appears light compared to the Austrian admission of 4,275 killed, wounded and taken prisoner.[13] Indeed, Lannes famously said of his troops, the 'bones cracked in my division like glass in a hailstorm'.[14] During the tour of the field, he encountered a surprise visitor, General Louis Charles Antoine Desaix. The last time the two men had seen each other was in Egypt. Desaix had led an expedition up the Nile which discovered the ancient city of Thebes and the temple of Karnak. By the time he returned to Cairo, Bonaparte had already quit the country and returned to France. Desaix was one of the great French generals of the revolutionary era. He was a year older than Bonaparte and had risen to prominence under Moreau on the Army of the Rhine. However, he became captivated by Bonaparte's first Italian campaign, and in 1797 had transferred to serve under him. Of all the men who served him, Desaix had a special place in Bonaparte's estimation. With Desaix, Bonaparte did not have to fear a political rival; in the military sense, they were kindred spirits, obsessed with the pursuit of glory.

The two men went to Bonaparte's quarters at Stradella and spent a great deal of time discussing events since they had last met. The key item for Bonaparte was the Treaty of El Arish which Desaix had put his name to on 24 January 1800. This was an agreement between the local British commander, Sir Sidney Smith, and General Kléber agreeing to the repatriation of the French army from Egypt. This had been an extremely unhappy episode for Desaix. Kléber obliged him to conduct the negotiations, which Sir Sidney Smith had been instructed not to indulge in. Despite repeated warning from Lord Keith, the negotiations had continued and Kléber ordered Desaix to sign the treaty on his behalf. On 3 March, Desaix quit Egypt, eager to return to Bonaparte. Despite having been issued with passports by Sir Sidney Smith and the Ottoman Grand Vizier, Desaix's ship was intercepted within sight of Toulon by a British warship and taken to Livorno. There, Desaix was treated extremely harshly by Lord Keith until the latter was instructed to honour the agreement and let the Frenchman go free. Desaix was still enraged by the whole experience and desperately wanted some form of revenge on the British. When Desaix returned to France, he immediately asked to join Bonaparte. The First Consul advised Desaix to go to Paris and await him there – the campaign was going to plan and it was not essential he take part. However, Desaix could not be held back. With an entourage which included his aides-de-camp Savary and Rapp, and two boy servants he had been presented by the King of Darfur (western Sudan), Desaix crossed the Little St Bernard Pass into Italy.

On Desaix's eventual departure from Bonaparte's quarters, Bonaparte's secretary, Bourrienne, was surprised how long the two had been talking. To this Bonaparte replied: 'Yes, I have been a long time with him, but I had my reasons. As soon as I return to Paris, I will make him minister-at-law. He shall always be my lieutenant: I would make him a prince if I could. I find him quite an antique character.'

Next morning, Bonaparte and his entourage passed by the battlefield of Montebello again on their way to Voghera, which had been captured the night before by the 21st Chasseurs.[15] An interesting event occurred at this town, which is widely reported. One of the Horse Grenadiers of the Consular Guard, Joseph Petit, reports they saw the First Consul on a balcony, standing with Desaix and an 'emigrant officer' who had come to parley with them. Seeing the imperial uniform, Petit says the troops cheered 'vive Bonaparte!' and the bands struck up with military songs. Savary confirms this, writing: 'We met Austrian parliamentarians at Voghera, whose special mission seemed to be to ascertain whether our army was truly marching upon them. The First Consul had them detained long enough for them to be seen. He even attempted to show them General Desaix, who was known to one of them, and dismissed them.'

On 11 June, the French army was reorganized, and Desaix was provided with a corps of his own.

Organization of the army on 11 June 1800

General Lannes:
      28th Line   under the orders of General Mainoni
      6th Light   under the orders of General Watrin
      22nd Line
      40th Line
General Desaix:
      9th Light   commanded by general Boudet
      30th Line
      59th Line
      19th Light   commanded by General Monnier
      70th Line
      72nd Line
General Victor:
      24th Light   division of General Chambarlhac
      43rd de ligne
      96th de ligne
      101st Line   commanded by General Gardanne
      44th Line
General Duhesme:
      1st Light   commanded by General Lapoype
      29th Line
      91st Line
      1st Provisional Half-Brigade
      2nd Provisional Half-Brigade

Finally that which composes Chabran's Division.
Reserve:
      13th Light   division of General Loison
      58th Line
      60th Line
General Moncey:

All the troops coming from the Rhine which are not part of Lapoype's Division.

The staff of General Desaix will be that of Boudet's Division.

The staff of General Victor will be that of Chambarlhac's Division; meanwhile one can draw on the adjudant-generals and their lieutenants.

General Murat commands all the cavalry, including the 12th Hussars and 21st Chasseurs. I have charged this general with attaching a squadron to the corps under the orders of General Lannes, one for the corps of General Desaix, one for the corps of General Victor, a company to the Division Loison, a squadron to the corps of General Duhesme.

The following day, on 12 June, Murat confirmed the organization of the cavalry brigades:

Brigade of General Rivaud.
    The 11th, 12th Hussars, 12th, 21st Chasseurs.
Brigade of General Champeaux.
    2nd Chasseurs, 1st, 8th Dragons.
Brigade of General Duvignau.
    15th Chasseurs, 7th, 9th Dragoons.
Brigade Kellermann.
    The heavy cavalry.

I have attached to the division of General Desaix the squadron of the 1st Regiment of Hussars.

To General Victor, the 3rd Cavalry.

To the Division of General Duhesme, the squadron of the 7th Chasseurs.

To General Lannes, a squadron of the 5th Regiment of Dragoons.

To General Loison, a company of the 5th Regiment of Dragoons.

A company of the 5th Regiment of Dragoons to General Headquarters.

Everything was now set for Bonaparte to advance the army out beyond Voghera towards Alessandria. Victor would assume the role of advanced-guard, with Lannes following in support. Desaix would act as the reserve. However, as the march began, Melas' intentions were still a complete mystery to the First Consul. The questions posed to the spy needed answers as soon as possible.

Chapter 8

The Armies Concentrate

O n the afternoon of 11 June, Hadik and Kaim's troops arrived at Alessandria from Turin. Before departing the Piedmontese capital, these forces had consisted of twenty infantry battalions and thirty-three squadrons of cavalry. En route to Alessandria, they left some forces to strengthen the Turin garrison and placed a rearguard at Asti, which would follow later. They actually arrived with just nine and two-thirds battalions and eleven squadrons. That same afternoon, Elsnitz also arrived in Alessandria: there was widespread shock at the state of this force. Melas had left Elsnitz in Nice with 19,000 excellent soldiers, but fruitless engagements and a difficult retreat through the mountains had reduced his corps considerably. Provisions had run out on the way. Desperate for food, men had been seen gnawing on roots and the bark off the trees; many sat down and simply starved to death on the spot. Some even deserted and fled to the British fleet, either ending up transported to Spain or enrolled as mercenaries in the British Army. There were hardly 4,000 men in a condition to fight – the majority of them being Morzin's grenadier division. Another 3,000 had completed the march, but were barefoot and completely exhausted. Coupled with Ott's heavy losses at Casteggio, the great imperial army was a mere shadow of the one which had commenced operations on 6 April. All Melas had wanted was to concentrate the army as swiftly as possible before delivering battle against the Dijon Reserve Army. Now he was sat at Alessandria, with Frenchmen all round him, encumbered with baggage, sick and wounded soldiers, cut off from his lines of communication and his home. He had never wanted this command, and must have cursed the day he was invited to accept it. Melas wrote a gloomy letter to the Hofkriegsrat outlining his current situation:

'This afternoon the divisions under Kaim and Hadik, together with the remains of FML Elsnitz's force, which now mostly comprises of the eleven Grenadier battalions, have arrived at the camp of Alessandria; only GM Nimbsch still remains with the rearguard at Asti. FML Ott's force is positioned on the left bank of the Scrivia, between Torre Garofoli and San Giuliano and likewise a very weak division under FML O'Reilly comprising mostly of light troops is positioned at Sale.'

At 3.00 pm on 11 June, Melas called a meeting of his senior commanders and staff to debate what to do next. It was a lively session. According to Stutterheim, there initially appeared to be two options open to Melas: either defeat Bonaparte in battle or move the army to Genoa and take a defensive position at the foot of the Apennines at Novi, just as Joubert and Moreau had done against them the previous year. According to Stutterheim, some of the participants in this meeting were 'vehemently shouting' that risking the outcome of the army and the fate of Italy on a battle was irresponsible. Even if Bonaparte was defeated between the Bormida and Scrivia, the Austrians would still find themselves at a disadvantage. This was very true, and Bonaparte knew it. If defeated, he could retreat back towards Stradella, drawing Duhesme's troops towards him. There was a split. Many, Stutterheim added, did not know what to say, and offered no solutions, instead preferring to curse Zach for placing the army in this position. Among those cursing Zach was Melas himself. Stutterheim said the commander-in-chief's hatred of Zach was now at its peak, although Melas still followed his advice, albeit with great indignation.

During the meeting, a third alternative was presented by staff officer Major Anton von Volkmann. He urged avoiding an open battle, but instead advised the army should cross the Po at Casale and then recover its communications by crossing the Ticino. If the army set out for Casale on the night of 13/14 June, the infantry could cross first, leaving a rearguard in the citadel to protect the bridge. From there, the infantry would take the Verceilli road, overpowering the French detachments on the way. Meanwhile, the cavalry would leave a strong presence at Alessandria and make a false attack towards Cascina Grossa before withdrawing and rejoining the army. On 15 June, the army would head for Novara, in effect following the route taken by Murat to Milan. The army would split into two columns, one following the Navliglio canal into Milan, screening the right flank of the main column marching on Nerviano with all the train and artillery. A few days more and the army would be reunited with Vukassovich, the lines of communication with the Hereditary Lands would be re-established and Milan would have fallen back into Austrian hands. Moreover, Bonaparte's communications with Switzerland would be cut. The French would be without provisions, and with all the major fortresses in Piedmont still in Austrian hands, what could they have done? They would have negated Bonaparte's strategic *coup de main* and robbed him of a swift, decisive victory. According to staff officer Adam Neipperg, General Hadik in particular insisted 'with great firmness' that this plan should be adopted.

It appears Zach had considered a similar plan, but he wanted to cross the Po at Valenza and march on Pavia. Neipperg believed this plan was inferior and would have been difficult because there was no bridge at Valenza, and two French divisions were believed to be in this area. It would have been very simple for these troops to lock themselves up in Pavia to defend the Ticino. The terrain in this area was extremely swampy, and the fields cut with ditches. The wagons and artillery would have found movement very difficult, as would the cavalry.

There was an impasse.

Enter once again the Piedmontese spy, Carlo Gioelli, who now comes to play a crucial role in the drama. Since Casteggio, Gioelli had been to see the First Consul. He returned with news on the French positions and intentions (which were probably fabrications on the part of Bonaparte). The intelligence he provided was summarized as follows:

> 'The enemy has crossed over 6,000 men at Bosco under General Gardanne. These have attacked FML Ott on the 9th. The whole enemy army crosses the Po at Piacenza on two rafts. They want to attack us here, but the spy believes a column has been sent across the mountains to Novi, which will continue to turn us across the Bormida. No enemy are in Pavia; in Milan only the blockading corps, in Pizzighettone he believes there is nothing.'

This intelligence appeared to support the proposed crossing of the Po rather than a move on Genoa, via Novi. More importantly, Gioelli revealed to Zach the information Bonaparte had asked him to find. Sometimes, one can gauge an opponent's intentions and fears from the questions they ask their spies to ascertain. Stutterheim writes:

> 'A very well-tried spy, dispatched from Turin to Milan, by whom he had repeatedly tried to deceive the French army command, and had also fortunately deceived them in the previous campaign, arrived at the headquarters at Alessandria, sent by Bonaparte himself. He recorded several points, which the consul demanded to know. The three most important were:

> '- Will the imperial army cross the Po?

> '- Where is Hohenzollern?

> '- Has Elsnitz already arrived at the army?'

Although Zach knew the spy was in contact with Bonaparte, he clearly believed Gioelli's first loyalty was to the Austrians. Based on this premise, Zach hatched a plan so brilliant he believed it would save the army. From Stutterheim's first account, we find more details on Bonaparte's questions. The First Consul wanted to know if the crossing point on the Po would be Valenza or Casale? He also wanted to know Hohenzollern's route itinerary, if the latter was intending to march out of Genoa and rejoin the army. Clearly, Bonaparte had already foreseen Volkmann's plan. He had already guessed the Austrians would consider trying to escape him. This could be the First Consul's undoing.

Zach instructed Gioelli to tell Bonaparte the battle at Casteggio had struck fear and confusion into the Austrians, and they were preparing to cross the Po, before attempting to fight their way westwards over the Ticino, by way of Pavia. To lend credence to the story, Zach told Gioelli to truthfully report the arrival of Elsnitz at Alessandria. The Austrian quartermaster general also provided Gioelli with a bogus document showing Hohenzollern's supposed march up from Genoa, arriving at Novi on 13 June and Alessandria on 14 June. Gioelli was to say the Austrian army was still in camp at Alessandria, and still sorting out its baggage. If the French moved quickly, and marched towards Casale via Sale, they could intercept the Austrians as they were in the act of a major river crossing. The imperial army would be totally destroyed.

If Bonaparte swallowed the bait, Zach would achieve his original goal of drawing the French army out onto the open plain, where the Austrian superiority in cavalry and artillery could be best employed. Zach would pin the French at Sale, and then sweep round behind them with a formidable column of troops. The French would be surrounded and driven into the Po. It was a brilliant plan, one which would prove his own intellectual superiority and put an end to Bonaparte's reputation as a military great.

Yet there was a flaw. Gioelli now had two paymasters, and whatever Zach thought, Gioelli could not afford to openly betray either party. Bonaparte had offered Gioelli a substantial sum of money (far more than Zach was paying him), so Gioelli refused to tell the First Consul an outright lie.[1] Gioelli told Zach he feared being caught out over this fiction of crossing the Po. Annoyed by the spy's reluctance, but utterly convinced by the brilliance of his plan, Zach led the spy into an adjoining room and called for Colonel Pemler and Major Hohensinner of the pontoon corps. He ordered them each to take their bridging equipment to Casale and their train to Valenza, and begin the construction of bridges over the Po. Zach made them responsible for the slightest delay in carrying out this order. When the two officers had left, Zach turned to Gioelli and said: 'If you do not wish to announce our passage over the Po to the French Headquarters, others will now bring this news.' Of course, Gioelli did not want to lose Zach's money either, so on receiving the assurance that the Austrians were committing bridging equipment, Gioelli agreed to complete the mission.

Afterwards, Zach wrote a series of orders confirming the pioneers and pontoon builders needed to begin bridging the Po. He also instructed Major Culoz to take one his battalions of infantry to Casale, leaving that very night. As he wrote these

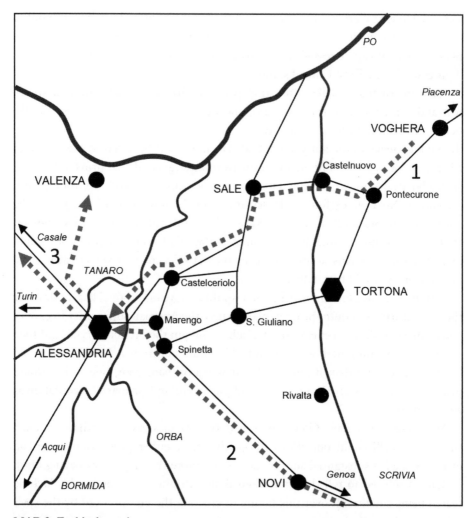

MAP 3: Zach's deception

1 – Ott retreats to Alessandria from Voghera via Sale, acting as a lure to draw Bonaparte onto the plain between the Scrivia and Bormida; 2 – fictitious march of Hohenzollern from Genoa; 3 – Austrian escape routes via Casale and/or Valenza.

orders, one wonders if it crossed Zach's mind that Gioelli might betray him? Would the spy deliver again, as at Cuneo, or would the spy's luck or loyalty finally run out? Stutterheim tells us that in the final days of this campaign, the pressure had started to tell on the Austrian chief of staff. He was at once the leader of every operation, but did not have the authority or power to give weight to the commands he issued in Melas' name. He was, Stutterheim said, well aware that battles could be as easily lost by ill-luck as gained, and that if the coming battle was lost, he alone would be blamed. This agonizing responsibility weakened him. His anxiety could not have been eased by his over-reliance on a spy.

On 12 June, preparations began for the great battle ahead. While Zach penned the battle plan, orders were issued for the army to move into a new camp on the western side of Alessandria. This move would take place on the afternoon of 13 June. In the meantime, engineers began working on the decoy bridge at Casale. Major Culoz arrived with four companies of infantry in support, and sent a report that the French on the left bank were believed to have withdrawn to Vercelli. Work also began on the construction of a pontoon bridge across the Bormida fifty paces below the existing boat bridge. A key part of Zach's plan was to lure Bonaparte onto the plain between the Bormida and the Scrivia. Ott's troops had therefore been withdrawn from Voghera, across the Scrivia to the village of San Giuliano. O'Reilly had withdrawn along a more northerly route, passing through Sale. On the evening of 12 June, Ott was ordered to withdraw from San Giuliano and to cross the Bormida, to unite with the remainder of the army. O'Reilly was also ordered to withdraw, and to take up a position at the hamlet of Marengo.

Before uncovering the plans and movements of the First Consul, now is an opportune moment to explore the ground over which the coming engagement would be fought. Although many of the historic buildings survive in our times, agricultural methods, the construction of the railways and modern roads and large industrial sites have changed the appearance of the countryside considerably. It is therefore necessary to reconstruct this region as it would have appeared that fateful summer. The region between Tortona and Alessandria forms a large lowland plain, bordered to the north by the River Po and to the south by the northernmost slopes of the Ligurian Apennines. The eastern and western extents of the plain are formed by rivers draining down from the mountains into the Po: the Bormida and Tanaro to the west, and the Scrivia torrent on the east. In 1800, the plain was dotted with vineyards, orchards, smallholdings, farm buildings, isolated country houses, hamlets and several churches. The main roads were often lined with mulberry trees and hedges. Many of the roads and tracks were raised on banks to prevent them flooding, and the plain was cut with drainage ditches and brooks. At its widest extent, the plain is approximately 16km wide and measures 25km north to south.

From a strategic point of view, the plain acted as something of a hub for the road network in this part of Italy. The main post road from Turin to Piacenza passed through the centre of the plain, through Alessandria in the west and Tortona in the east. The main road from Genoa came up from the south-east of the plain, branching at Serravalle, from where one could travel northwards to Tortona and join the main road there; or north-west to Novi and Pozzolo Formigaro before joining the main road at Spinetta. The northern routes from the plain in the direction of Pavia converged at the town of Sale. To the north-west of the plain were roads to Valenza and Casale, both of which offered crossing points over the Po. An army in possession of the great plain could theoretically march in whichever direction it chose. Following the main road, the distance from Alessandria to Tortona was approximately 20km in 1800, or five hours' march for infantry, well within what could be accomplished in a single day. A horse might cover the same distance in less than three hours at a walk, or if well-mounted, half that time at a trot.

Terrain often dictates the shape of a battle, so it is worth investing time in studying this plain in some detail. In June 1800, a traveller on foot leaving Alessandria by the Tortona Gate and following the main road would find the road edged by a reasonably flat meadow – a perfect space for assembling large bodies of troops, just as Zach planned to use it on 13 June. Just over a kilometre away, the traveller would encounter the Bormida River. The course of this river has changed significantly in two centuries. Whereas now it flows northwards to the Po in a fairly straight course, the French 1810 *Dépôt de la Guerre* plan drawn by Giraldon shows the Bormida as a substantial, meandering river, with muddy banks, wooded on the left (western) bank.

The main road crossed the Bormida by a bridge formed from a number of anchored riverboats. On 12 June, this boat bridge was supplemented by a second crossing made from sixteen military pontoons about fifty paces above the main bridge.[2] On the east bank, the main road passed through a defensive *tête-du-pont* (bridgehead) fortification - an earthwork guarding the road and protected after Casteggio by fourteen guns. There was just a single exit from this bridgehead, and the ground in front of the works was marshy and cut with ditches, making it very difficult to approach, except by the main road. After exiting the bridgehead, the main road followed for a short time the course of the Bormida until it met the junction of the Pavia road. At this junction, the traveller could turn left and follow the Pavia road approximately 4km through marshy ground to Castelceriolo, a village which controlled access to several good roads to the north and east of the plain. Shortly after this junction there was another road on the right: a track winding its way southwards to the farm of Stortigliona.

Further along the main road one encountered the first of many vineyards, this first one extending either side of the road. Described in the French 1810 map as *vignes à l'Italien*, the traditional method of viticulture was to plant vines amid rows of mulberry trees and then festoon the vines from the trees' branches. This practice kept the vines raised above the humid soil and better exposed them to the sun. (In more arid and mountainous areas, the vines were kept low in order to absorb the heat from the ground.) The leaves of the mulberry trees were in turn harvested for feeding silkworms – Italian silk being particularly prized by the British market at this time. In between the rows of mulberries, the Piedmontese peasants created small parcels of land for growing vegetables, and these would have small irrigation channels cut around them. At the turn of the eighteenth century, the method of growing vines on rows of poles appears to have been increasingly commonplace. In some parts of northern Italy there was a custom to grow vines on tall willow poles as much as 12ft high. These poles resembled a forest of sort. Lejeune's 1801 painting of the Battle of Marengo shows rows of knee-high staves being stamped into the ground by advancing troops. Having been the scene of fighting in 1799, and with the general disruption which comes to agriculture from warfare, some of the vineyards on the battlefield may indeed have been very young in June 1800, planted that spring to repair damage and losses of the previous year. Still, the rows of upright and interconnecting stakes would have formed a hindrance to horses and carriages, and may have broken up infantry formations attempting to move across them. The main road afforded a clear route through these impediments, and was therefore a vital military artery.

A kilometre from the bridgehead, the traveller drew level with the farm of Pederbona to their left (sometimes Pedra Bona in French texts). From this point, looking to the right of the road, the traveller would see the farm of Stortigliona about 900 metres in the distance to the south. These two farms readily lent themselves as strongpoints from which the main road could be dominated. A second field of vines sat behind Pederbona, extending south-west and in front of Stortigliona. Continuing eastwards along the main road for ten more minutes, the traveller would pass through meadows before the village of Marengo came into sight. Maps from the 1770s show a farmhouse complex called Stampina to the left of the road, more or less halfway between Pederbona and Marengo, but no mention of this place is made at the time of the battle, and presumably it had fallen into ruin by then.[3]

About 300 metres from the village of Marengo, the road cut through the Fontanone brook. The Fontanone formed a key part of the landscape and must be described in some detail. North of the main road, the Fontanone headed in a more or less straight line for 2½km towards Castelceriolo. Passing to the west of this town, the brook looped to the right and then joined the Tanaro towards Montecastello. In the other direction, the Fontanone made a sharp turn westwards, for about 400 metres, then turned southwards again before terminating in the fields towards Cascina Bianca. Half a kilometre north of Marengo, the Cavo del Fontanone brook branches from the main Fontanone and runs parallel to it, creating a second ditch.

This brook, often simply described as a ditch, formed a boundary between the Bormida and the plain. The two crossing points over this ditch reinforced the strategic importance of Marengo and Castelceriolo. Without possession of either of these two points, the movement of artillery and baggage to or from Alessandria would be extremely problematic. Relatively inconsequential in modern times, the Fontanone presented more of a hazard in 1800. The Austrian Pioneer regimental history records the Fontanone as being an eight-metre wide, swampy marsh with high and steep banks which could only be walked through with difficulty, with water over chest height.[4] The French 1810 map shows the Fontanone in front of the Barbotta farm as being surrounded by marshy ground and muddy banks. To the west of the main road, the waters appear to have been shallower, but still substantial, and edged with green plants, aquatic rushes and willow trees. After the heavy rains which preceded the battle, one must not underestimate the difficulty of crossing it.

Looking ahead from the Fontanone, one would see the high, red brick walls of the farm at Marengo about 300 metres away, with a brick tower rising up behind it. The road into the hamlet of Marengo was on the other side of the farm, turning left from the main road. In 1800, the hamlet consisted of half a dozen buildings, in the middle of which was a tall brick tower said to have been built by Theodoric, King of the Goths. In 1800, the tower is believed to have housed silk worms. The farm was surrounded by high walls with an internal yard and numerous barns and buildings. It belonged to the hospital of Alessandria and was used to generate revenue for the poor.

At the time of the battle, the hamlet's inn consisted of two floors, each of which had three small rooms. The first accommodated the innkeeper and his family. The ground floor consisted of a kitchen with cooking stoves and spits; this led into a communal dining room, followed by a final room which was reserved for travellers of distinction measuring about 3.5 by 5m. The ground floor windows were protected by rusting iron bars. At the front of the inn was a small garden, in the middle of which was a well. Near to the well was a granite bench. A small branch of the Fontanone brook came into the garden. Adjacent to the inn was a long stable covered with a roof of red tiles. On the northern side, illustrations show there were great open sheds. The hamlet was more or less surrounded with ditches and gullies which emptied into the Fontanone and helped to make the village something of a citadel. The land around the farm was uneven, partly wooded and cut with ditches. These ditches were necessary because the ground around Marengo is the drainage site for all the surrounding fields. The water table is very low, perhaps not much more than a metre below the surface.

The ground between Marengo and the farmhouse of Barbotta a kilometre away appears flat today, with large open fields. Tenement maps from the eighteenth century show the land either side of the road parcelled into small allotments, so the ground would have actually been much more broken up at the time of the battle. There is also a large pond behind Marengo which has long since vanished.

Two kilometres further, the Barbotta road reached Castelceriolo. This was a larger village with the castle of Ghilini on its western side. Dating from the twelfth century, this castle was a brick-built, fortified manorial home of the Ghilinis, a local noble family. Castelceriolo was as much a key possession as Marengo, because from there one could head east towards San Giuliano Nuovo or northwards towards the village of Sale.

Returning to the main road, just beyond Marengo were a series of junctions. The first was on the right, heading southwards towards Frugarolo some 6.5km distant. A few hundred metres more and one came to an important crossroads. The Alessandria-Sale road headed north-eastwards for 3km to Castelceriolo. To the south was the village of Spinetta and its church of the Birth of Holy Mary. This route was known as the 'new road' and passed in a south-easterly direction for 1.8km to the village of Longo Fame. From here, the traveller could turn eastwards and walk all the way to Tortona approximately 15km away. The road heading eastwards from the crossroads was known as the 'old road'. This road by-passed Spinetta and joined the main road after 4km, just to the west of the town of Cascina Grossa. The junction of the old and new roads has now been more or less obliterated by the construction of the railway in the nineteenth century.

The plain also appears reasonably flat today, but there is a noticeable rise and fall towards the centre of the plain. At the western junction of the old and new roads, the ground is approximately 95m above sea level. However, from the junction of the old and new roads it began to rise gently, reaching a high point of 105m above sea level at the Rana farm, 2km behind Marengo. This rise stretched from the old road southwards to the new road, at Pistona. On this westward-facing slope of this small hill was a belt of vineyards starting at the farm of Fournace, extending down past the old road, past Spinetta and over the new road to Lunga Fame. This belt of vineyards was approximately a kilometre wide. Between the vineyards would have been fields of wheat and other agricultural produce. Wheat in those days could be grown to a height of 6ft. Thus, although the terrain east of Marengo might now appear reasonably flat, in 1800 an officer on horseback at Marengo studying the field through a telescope would have been unable to perceive anything beyond 2km ahead of him. This ridge of high ground running northward from the main road towards the Rana and Fournace farms is almost imperceptible today, because a modern main road has been driven through it and an industrial estate placed squarely on the high ground. In 1800, the mulberries, vines and the rise in the ground would have created a defile, or bottleneck, for an army to negotiate.

On the reverse of this slope were a number of farm buildings to the north of the old road, including Li Poggi, Buzana and Guasca. To the south, between the old and new roads, was the farm of Valle, with Pistona below that. Although the French 1810 map does not show the farmhouses at Pistona, Captain Pittaluga's 1896 study does, and in the battle of 1799, there are Austrian references to the small rise at Pistona.[5]

East of this line of farmsteads was an open space approximately 3km long and 2km deep, with a gentle gradient falling eastwards. The old and new roads intersected at a point between the Ventolina farm to the north and Cascina Grossa to the south. The latter was a village clustered around the church of San Rocco. It was connected to the main road by a long, straight, tree-lined road 700m in length. On the east side of this road was a small field about 100m wide, after which came a great belt of vineyards which rose from behind Cascina Grossa, up between the farms of Ventolina and Piccinina, then beyond Villanova.

Continuing eastwards from the tree-lined road at Cascina Grossa one arrived at the village of San Giuliano after 3km. Halfway to San Giuliano there was a clearing in the vines, approximately 1.5km wide and extending 800m north and south of the road. There were more vines beyond San Giuliano, and the road continued for 3.5km to the enormous farm complex of Torre Garofoli. In the same way that Marengo guards the entrance to the western half of the plain, Garofoli dominates the eastern side. The farm is approximately 150m in length and consists of numerous buildings, barns and granaries grouped around two large courtyards, with a large gatehouse at its eastern end. In places it is three stories high, and a tower on the north side of the complex affords excellent views back towards San Giuliano and the plain to the north. Stutterheim says there was a mill stream on the eastern side of Torre Garofoli, and that beyond this point the ground became broken up and was difficult for manoeuvre, much the same as the countryside between the Bormida and the Fontanone.

Three kilometres along the main road from Garofoli, one reaches the eastern extent of the plain. The Scrivia appears as something of a wide scar running north-south through the landscape. Ordinarily the river is quite shallow. At certain times of the year, in some places one might simply walk across it. However, after heavy rain in the mountains beyond Novi and Serravalle, the Scrivia quickly floods and forms a torrent, the waters flowing with unstoppable force. The river then presents somewhat more of an obstacle. The safest crossing points were on the main road, due east of Garofoli and to the north of the road from Sale opposite San Giuliano Vecchio. A kilometre further and one reaches the city of Tortona, dominated by a fortress on the heights overlooking the town.

It was over this plain on 12 June that columns of white-clad soldiers marched steadily westwards, finally fulfilling the order to concentrate the Austrian army at Alessandria. That bloody episode had cost Ott the loss of 4,275 men, including six staff and ninety-eight line officers, killed, wounded and captured. Had Ott left Genoa earlier, perhaps he could have saved Piacenza, or maybe he would have been cut off altogether. It is difficult to guess the outcome of historical 'maybes'.

Elsewhere that day, more problems were arising. The outpost commander at Acqui, Rittmeister Civrani of the 1st Kaiser Dragoons, had become apprehensive of his position. He only had a small force of forty-five troopers and had heard reports that General Suchet would soon be upon him, following up on the retreat of Elsnitz. He sent out some patrols, and when they returned he wrote about his misgivings to the commander of the Alessandria garrison, GM Skal:

'The enemy still has his position at Dego; yesterday evening they sent a patrol to Spigno, where provisions were requisitioned. Yesterday, the enemy also sent a patrol to Squaneto in the valley towards Cartosio; where some head of cattle were taken from a peasant; after that, the patrols returned to their positions again. My bugler came back, together with the corporal and put the enemy strength at 700 men. The local Piedmontese troops have established a picket at my request towards Cartosio, where my left flank can be better guarded, because I cannot occupy all the mountains with my cavalry and could easily be outflanked from that side.'[6]

This letter might not appear alarmist in tone, but Dego was only a day's march from Acqui, itself just a day's march from Alessandria. Did this mean Suchet was only two days away, with nothing but forty-five dragoons and some Piedmontese to protect the route to Alessandria? It was yet another eventuality for Zach to consider – the Army of the Reserve, reinforced by the Army of the Rhine, and the Army of Italy were about to converge on Alessandria any time from 14 June. The moment of decision was near.

Chapter 9

'This time we have this Bonaparte'

On the morning of Friday 13 June, Melas contemplated the events to come. His men had achieved great things under his command, but on the eve of the great decisive battle, he had misgivings. The shock of seeing Elsnitz's command so poorly handled, and the negative effect of the battle at Casteggio, had dented his troops' confidence. Melas also knew he was up against Bonaparte, a young man of considerable talents and energy; a new sort of general – a grand risk-taker. Behind him, advancing swiftly, were the forces under Suchet – the reinvigorated Army of Italy - and no doubt Massena was not far from rejoining them. Caught between two armies, cut off from home, low on supplies: how had this come to be?

Sat in his headquarters, Melas drafted several letters, almost as if he wanted to perform some sort of confessional act. At the very least it was an attempt to limit the damage. The first letter was addressed to Thugut, Zach's cherished sponsor and the key exponent of war against the French. Ultimately, the letter was never posted - it was too pessimistic, even by Melas' standards – but it perhaps serves as a window on the mind of the Austrian commander that day:

> 'Because of the two enemy armies, which are far superior in the number of troops, the army which has landed up here, greatly reduced by the Riviera expedition, finds itself extremely limited.
>
> 'Courage and determination, the former comrades to our successful advance, will now also be companion of our fierce attack, in order at least to reopen the lost communications with the hereditary lands.
>
> 'Should in spite of this, the superiority of the two enemy armies bring it the defeat of an army so reduced only by constant hard-fought battles, then I ask that its worth not then be undervalued, if stripped of any expectation of help and only sure of six days' provisions, this army then will be bound to be rendered the unfortunate victim of the stronger force.'[1]

A second letter was drafted, this time to the president of the Hofkriegsrat, Tige. Melas admitted this message would probably be captured, and therefore gave away very little operational detail. After mentioning a 'decisive action' was about to take place, he wrote:

'Should luck mark this step with success, then I hope to advance along the right bank of the Po and to recover the line of communication to the Hereditary Lands.

'Should however the close proximity of the two enemy armies shatter the persistent courage and steadiness of the troops under my command and thereby tip the scales to an unexpected outcome of the battle, then the complete defeat of the army is all the more certainly the sad fate, when only six days' of supplies secures them from complete destruction.

'I must endeavour to bring this to higher attention most quickly, so that even the defeat of the army can be viewed only as a consequence of the far superior forces of the enemy.'[2]

Zach was apparently in an equally fatalistic mood. He called together the staff officers for their instructions. Stutterheim was present and remembered how Zach spoke to them like 'a priest, who was preparing the convict for his imminent death'. Zach also detached the 2nd Erzherzog Josef Hussar Regiment to Casale, just in case the French attempted to force a crossing there. This just lost the army 1,097 men, along with those already committed to Asti and Acqui.

However, Zach's unhappy spirit began to lift by the early afternoon. Carlo Gioelli returned to Austrian headquarters and confirmed he had delivered the deception to Bonaparte. Gioelli also gave Zach an update on the French movements. The main thrust of their advance appeared to be towards Sale, while only Gardanne had been directed to San Giuliano in the middle of the plain. The key piece of information was that Bonaparte had detached some of his army towards Novi in order to intercept Hohenzollern's fictitious march from Genoa. So that was it; Bonaparte had fallen for Zach's ruse. He had sent away part of his force to Novi on a fool's errand. Zach erupted in joy. He was heard excitedly shouting at the top of his voice: 'This time we have this Bonaparte!'[3]

Digesting Gioelli's intelligence, Zach sat down to write the final battle orders for the following day. Such was Gioelli's importance to Zach, he even referenced the intelligence provided by 'the spy' in this document:

'The main column, where I will position myself, will be assembled in the following way:

'Advanced Guard:

'From the General Staff: Hauptmann Quosdanovich, Oberleutnant Wittgens, Oberleutnant Bechini, Oberleutnant Richard.

'Oberst Frimont of the Bussy-Jäger zu Pferde:

3rd Bach Light Battalion	1 battalion
4th Am Ende Light Battalion	1 battalion
1st Kaiser-Dragoons	2 squadrons
Bussy-Jäger zu Pferde	2 squadrons
Cavalry artillery	1 battery
Pioneers:	1 company

'Main Column:

'From the General Staff: Oberstleutnant Piking, Major Volkmann, Major Neipperg, Major Mecsery, Hauptmann Martini, Hauptmann Fürstenberg, Hauptmann Troyer, Hauptmann Hirsch, Kapitänlieutenant Neugebauer, Oberleutnant Postel, Oberleutnant Meninger.

FML Hadik
GM Pilatti:

1st Kaiser-Dragoons	4 squadrons
4th Karaczay Dragoons	6 squadrons

GM Frederich Bellegarde:

IR 53 Jellacic	2 battalions
IR 52 Erzherzog Anton	2 battalions

GM Saint Julien:

IR 11 Michael Wallis	3 battalions

Brigade GM de Briey:

IR 47 Franz Kinsky	2⅓ battalions

FML Kaim:
GM Knesevich

IR 23 Grossherzog Toscana	3 battalions

GM Lamarseille

IR 63 Erzherzog Joseph	3 battalions

FML Morzin:
GM Lattermann:

Grenadiers	5 battalions

GM Weidenfeld:

Grenadiers	6 battalions

At this point are all the unallocated pioneer companies.

FML Elsnitz:
GM Nobili:

3rd Erzherzog Johann Dragoons	6 squadrons
9th Lichtenstein Dragoons	6 squadrons

GM Nimbsch:

7th Hussars	8 squadrons
9th Erdödy Hussars	6 squadrons

The Artillery Reserve

'The second, or left column: consists of the force under FML Ott and will be assembled in the following way:

'From the General-Staff: Major Stutterheim, Hauptmann Habermann, Hauptmann Reinisch, Hauptmann Babel, Oberleutenant Crossard, Oberleutenant Esbeck, Oberleutenant Nageldinger, Oberleutenant Gatterburg.

'Advanced-Guard:
GM Gottesheim

10th Lobkowitz–Dragoons	2 squadrons
IR 28 Fröhlich	1 battalion
Cavalry artillery	1 battery

'The Column:
FML Schellenberg
GM Retz:

Two twelve pounder cannons together with an ammunition wagon	
Pioneers	1 company
IR 28 Fröhlich	2 battalions
IR 40 Mittrowsky	3 battalions

GM Sticker:

10th Lobkowitz–Dragons	4 Squadrons
IR 51 Splényi	2 Battalions
IR 57 J. Colloredo	3 Battalions

FML Vogelsang
GM Ulm:

IR 18 Stuart	3 Battalions
IR 17 Hohenlohe	2 Battalions

Then the necessary artillery reserve

'This column will pass over the lower, local boat bridge over the Bormida and take their line of march along the shortest road to Sale.

'The third, or right column:
'consists of the following troops:

'From the General-Staff: Major De Brez (Piedmontese), Major Nugent, Hauptmann Odelga, Hauptmann Voith, Hauptmann Bittner, Oberleutnant Häring, Oberleutnant Erben.

FML O'Reilly
GM Rousseau:

8th Nauendorf-Hussars	3½ squadrons
5th Hussars	2 squadrons
Cavalry artillery	1 battery
4th Banater Grenzer	1 battalion
1st Warasdin-Kreuz Grenzer	1 battalion
3rd Ogiliner Grenz Regiment	1 battalion
3rd Ottocac Grenz Regiment	1 battalion
8th Würtemberg Dragoons	1 squadron

'This column will pass over the upper pontoon bridge over the Bormida and take their line of march through Frugarolo and Bosco towards Novi.
    'The attack being undertaken is based on the following reports:

'1) That the enemy main column, between 12 and 15,000 men strong, has moved forward to the Tanaro and is advancing along it;
'2) That the enemy has left no more than 1,000 men under General Gardanne on the main road to San Giuliano, presumably as a decoy, to conceal his movements behind it;
'3) That yesterday (13 June) a column was sent back from Garofoli, in order via Cassano to reach Novi, where in the view of the spy, they could arrive early today.

'Now our manoeuvres are aimed at reaching San Giuliano with the main column, to pursue all the enemy units standing there back towards Garofoli with the advanced-guard and to make him believe, that our attack is directed there, but from San Giuliano, it will turn left, in order to reach the road which runs from Sale to Alessandria; on this we will meet the enemy main force and as our entire force comes onto that road, defeat them.

'An unexpected appearance in the enemy flank must have a huge effect; we can hope to surprise the enemy column, cut it in two or take it completely in the rear, to drive them back to the Tanaro and the Po. Determination and rapidity must secure us a glorious victory.

'The second column under FML Ott is too weak against the enemy, should the overthrow of the enemy main column be expected of them, but he must endeavour to harass them, halt them and if he is himself attacked, to retire slowly, all the more so to decoy the enemy in that event. His line of retreat goes along the Tanaro on to the Bormida bridgehead, which he is then to occupy and so, defend it to the last man together with the left flank of the Bormida.

'The third column is likewise merely designated to advance against the enemy, so far as it is possible, towards Novi, engage them and then to retire as slowly as possible into the Bormida bridgehead, cross the Bormida and cover the left bank of the Bormida upstream of the bridgehead.

'These two flank columns are consequently our decoys, behind which we will execute our main strike with God's help.

'During the march of these two flank columns, I hope to judge from their fire, how far the enemy may have already advanced, which will serve me, located with the main column as a guideline, as to where to fall into the enemy flank; irrespective of that, frequent reports following on one after the other.

'Today the Casale, Asti and Turin (Piedmontese regiments) also march into the Alessandria garrison; GM Skal has to maintain a garrison force in the bridgehead during this attack.

'Hauptmann Sokolovich and Oberleutenant Bellichy will remain with GM Skal.

'The FMLs and generals are to make even today all conceivable efforts, so that their columns can be formed up quickly, so as not to lose any time when marching off.

'The third column already has its infantry across the Bormida; it is only necessary that the cavalry belonging to this column are shifted over when it gets dark, so that it can march itself, two columns are not going over one bridge.

'The troops will march off at midnight; after an hour of unbroken marching, the heads will halt, so that the columns can close up and the troops form up in a column of divisions.[4] When the day just begins to dawn, the columns will continue their marches further to attack.'

In summary, the key parts of the plan were for O'Reilly to watch the Novi road, and guard for the arrival of the French column sent to Novi. Most crucially,

Ott's column was to advance on Sale and pin the main French force, falling back towards the Bormida if necessary. The main weight of attack would come from the central column falling on the left flank of the enemy. Stutterheim's account has Zach saying: 'If luck favours our intentions, so the enemy is thrown in the Po and without retreat.' If nothing else, it would open the road to Piacenza, or so Zach supposed. The main advantage of this plan was the element of surprise. If the spy was to be believed, Bonaparte was fixated on the idea the Austrians were planning to escape him by crossing the Po at Casale. It would be the French who would be strung out on the march, not the Austrians, and this element of surprise was crucial to their success.

With the final commitment to give battle made, Melas' mood also began to lift in the afternoon despite a front of wet weather which moved in. In the time-honoured tradition, he decided to make a tour of his army on the eve of battle. Before this, he had Alessandria's magazines opened and issued the army with rations of rice, meat and wine. They also emptied the last remaining depots, handing out new shoes and replacing or repairing damaged equipment. There was no point holding anything in reserve before this battle.

The tour of the camp went very well. Melas may have had his faults as an army commander, and clearly there were many other places he would have preferred to be that fateful Friday, but once he was in the saddle, before his men, he was energized. The smell of open fires, tobacco smoke and the comradeship of soldiers, this was Melas in his element, not the politicking, strategizing, pen-pushing existence he was so often condemned to endure in his headquarters. As he arrived at each regiment, the men would surround him to hear his words translated into the various languages and dialects by the officers standing alongside his horse. When he reached IR 23 Toscana, Melas was observed by a captain named Wenzel Rauch. This regiment was living under something of a cloud, as it was the subject of an investigation after an action near Novi the previous November. The regiment had been operating in open order and had got into difficulties – regimental honour had been called into question. Standing before the regiment, Melas told the men the investigation would now be dropped, and he would personally vouch for their courage and bravery. Having wiped the slate clean, Melas now told the Toscana Regiment he would place particular trust in their bravery, and expected every man to do his duty in the coming battle. As one can imagine, Melas' words were greeted with wild enthusiasm by the men. Indeed, Melas had boosted the men's morale to fever pitch.[5]

Crossard confirms the high morale of the Austrian troops on 13 June. Of the troops committed to battle, only Ott's corps had suffered serious reverses at the hands of the French, and even these troops had fought with a certain glory:

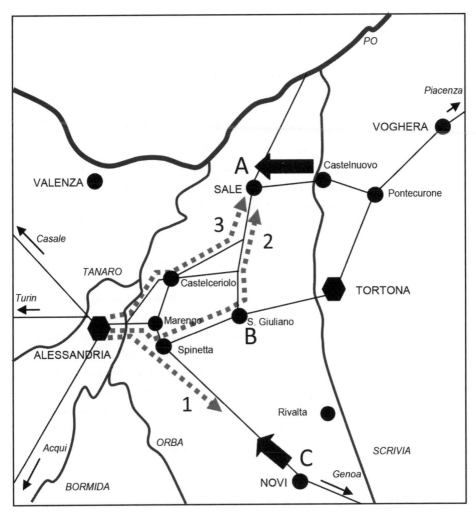

MAP 4: Zach's battle plan – 14 June

A – supposed main line of French advance; B – small French covering force at San Giuliano (Gardanne);
C – French column due to arrive at Novi on morning of 14 June to intercept Hohenzollern.

1 – Austrian right column (O'Reilly); 2 – Austrian main column (Melas); 3 – Austrian left column (Ott).

'The good spirit with which the Austrian troops were animated could only inspire them with audacity, the presage of victory. They had been abundantly supplied; the fatigues had not weighed upon them; their number equalled that which the enemy might have; all probabilities were therefore in favour of Melas. It was also these probabilities that General Vogelsang took for a certainty.'

Radetzky also played a key part in the army's preparation for combat. While Zach had been left to develop the battle plan, Radetzky had written a rousing Armeebefehl (order of the day) in Melas' name to be read to the troops before moving into the new camp. The order read in full:

'As we approach with every hour the decisive moment, in which only courage, bravery and steadiness can underpin the laboriously won glory of such an exceptional army, punish a recklessly advancing enemy and repel the coming danger to the threatened fatherland, then I do not believe it superfluous to repeat several comments which have already been made and to expect with all the more certainty compliance with them, when the army not only has given continued agreeable proof of the confidence placed in me, but has also increased with each day my present trust and regard towards them. I am satisfied beforehand, that the generals will most conscientiously keep the regimental commanders to good order, observance of their sacred duties, bravery and determination, at this time, commend to them the proper following of orders as their honour and duty and at the same time task them with the impressing vigorously on their subordinate staff-rank and line officers, then these on through the lower ranks to the common soldier, who listens so willingly to the speech of his superior, what each man has to do, to work together for the maintenance of the honour of the army and to assure it of victory in advance already, which the enemy has already sought so often in vain to make us doubtful of and has sought to tear from us.

'It will primarily be a matter of moving against the enemy with concentrated forces; consequently the troops are in no way to dissolve into skirmishers, but must remain closed up even in pursuit of the fleeing enemy, who even in flight can rally and renew their attack. I expressly order that under no circumstances are flags to be sent out of the battle line, but the troops must advance with flags flying and bands playing, whatever the weather might be; we have sworn loyalty to the flags, we will defend them to the last man.

'The playing of music invigorates the courage of the advancing force, informs the enemy of a determinedly advancing force; besides which, it is useful for the troops units, especially in restricted ground, as a reliable indicator of their position in the line and even at the moment of breaking up and scattering the unit, as the only means to rally again. It is therefore only too strikingly obvious that the sending back of musicians can bring with it disadvantageous consequences.

'Any kind of stopping short in the face of an advancing enemy or their bold skirmishers grants the enemy a few calm moments to be able all the more certainly to damage us. Only determined advances will disconcert even the boldest enemy.

'I suppress the thought that possibly there could still be those in the army who would forget their duty, who take no interest in the army's honour and who may turn their backs on the enemy; necessity requires however that such is made impossible, which weakness of spirit and heart can effect against better expectations; therefore on the advance it is ordered that proportionately small reserve detachments, who must use their weapons against this kind of forgetfulness of duty without hesitation and to fire into, but on the other hand deal with individual deserters in accordance with martial law on the spot.

'I am convinced, that the honestly wounded soldier will not except in the most extreme circumstances withdraw any of his comrades out of the battle to assist him, but will move back alone as well as possible; should however it be necessary to obtain help, then at most one man will accompany the wounded man, who must pass him on to the rearward reserve detachment and be sent back to his position in the line, so that faintheartedness finds no opportunity to conceal itself under the guise of brotherly love.

'I continue in the pleasant belief, that as its fighting units concentrate, the army will find a new trust in its strength and in our fellow countrymen, who can look forward in all confident expectation to the approaching battle, to provide new proof that nothing can shatter our courage and that nothing can diminish the trust we have in ourselves.

'Only victory can lead us to a restful time, which I will then use with all my ability, to grant to them all those things, which can only ever be permitted to a brave soldier and to the granting of which the Monarch so willingly gives his permission.'[6]

After reading this order, there could be no doubting the seriousness of what lay ahead. Again there was a reminder not to attempt to fight the French in skirmish formation. They were to drive at the French lines in closed formations. The longer they attempted to trade skirmish fire with the French, the heavier the casualties would be. The regimental bands would have to brave the cannonballs along with the soldiers, no matter how much the colonels wanted to preserve their expensive musicians from enemy fire. The wounded would also have to make do, and most grimly of all, there would be squads of soldiers – detachments from the grenadier brigades – instructed to shoot on the spot anyone they suspected of cowardice.

Above all was the caution not to underestimate the French who 'even in flight can rally and renew their attack'.

Radetzky's words filled the men with encouragement and determination. While the men began to prepare to move out to the south of the city, all the army's baggage was directed to a wagon park located north of Alessandria. Everything was ready. However, just as the head of the column began to reach the Bormida camp around 6.00 pm, the unmistakable sound of artillery fire came from the direction of the fortified bridgehead. No one in the column had any idea what the guns were firing at. Something had clearly gone wrong.

On the morning of 13 June, or rather 24 *Prairial*, as the republican French styled it, the French prepared to venture forth onto the plain before them. At five in the morning, Berthier wrote a note to Lannes, who was taking his five half-brigades towards Castelnuovo Scrivia:

> 'We have had no report from you tonight, Citizen General, which makes me think there is no news beyond what you wrote yesterday to the first consul. His intention is that you should attack and overthrow whatever is in front of you. General Victor is moving towards San Giuliano. General Desaix's reserve is in front of Pontecurone.'

Arriving at Castelnuovo-Scrivia, Lannes' troops found 1,500 enemy sick and wounded abandoned there. Victor crossed the Scrivia slightly further upstream, opposite Ova. The bridges over the Scrivia had all been destroyed, but the river was shallow enough to be forded, waist deep, albeit there was quite a strong current.[7] Ahead of the infantry, the cavalry also moved forwards to probe and scout ahead. Brigadier General Champeaux reported:[8]

> 'The reconnaissances of the night have produced nothing new. Those on the side of Castelnuovo Scrivia went without encountering the enemy, and those on the side of the mountain on our left could not be pushed as far as we wanted, the roads approaching the mountain being all cut with ditches. A deserter was found on this side without being able to give us any information. A dragoon of the 9th Regiment has broken his arm while going to Tortona for the distributions that could not take place.'

The 12th Chasseurs had spent an uncomfortable night in the middle of a field next to the Tortona road. The ground there was so hard they had trouble knocking in the pegs for tethering their horses. As well as having to sleep in the rain, they had not received supplies or forage for their horses. About an hour before daybreak,

General of Brigade Duvignau took the usual precaution of mounting his brigade up, ready for the orders of the day or signs of enemy action. Nothing happened. After two hours of bored inactivity, the brigade was ordered to dismount and prepare soup. At 5.30 am, General Berthier appeared and so Duvignau ordered the '*à cheval*' (to horse) to be sounded. Later, an officer from the 1st Hussars attached to Murat's staff arrived and asked for a report on the night's activities. Duvignau provided this. Then a second aide to General Murat arrived with the order to move forward to Castelnuovo Scrivia. The brigade formed a column and marched off up the track to this place, where they found Adjutant-General César Berthier waiting for them. He directed the brigade over the Scrivia to where Murat was waiting for them on the other side. Once they had crossed the river, the brigade formed line and received an impromptu inspection by the commander of the cavalry. Afterwards, Murat told Duvignau to follow the road westwards in the direction of Sale.[9] At the same time that Duvignau's brigade set off, the 11th Hussars were sent off to join General Gardanne, commander of the new advanced-guard, who was heading towards the suspected Austrian position at San Giuliano.

As the army was put in motion, the French chief of staff, General Dupont, penned a brief note to Carnot, the Minister of War. It confirmed the puzzlement the French experienced trying to guess the Austrian intentions:

> 'The enemy is assembled before Alessandria. It is uncertain whether he will give battle; but we will force him to take a stand. The battle of Montebello is more important than it first appeared. It has the happiest consequences for us … p.s. Almost always on horseback, I am compelled sometimes to postpone the account which I owe you of our operations.'[10]

The First Consul was very much ill at ease with the situation. At 8.00 am, Bonaparte learned at Castelnuovo Scrivia that the enemy has assembled all his forces at Alessandria, and there were no posts at San Giuliano or in the plain. This news increased his uncertainty. Had Melas crossed the Po already? Was he heading for Genoa, or Acqui? The apparent refusal to fight in the plain of San Giuliano, where the Austrian superiority in artillery and cavalry would be best served, indicated Melas was intending to escape the First Consul.[11] Bonaparte's state of mind is perhaps best described in Victor's memoirs. The First Consul knew Melas had concentrated his army at Alessandria. He knew Elsnitz had arrived, and the intelligence reports, including captured letters, indicated Melas was planning to give battle; but there was no sign of the Austrian army holding the plain. According to Victor, Bonaparte simply did not believe Melas would be audacious enough to attack. More than anything else, Bonaparte feared Melas would escape. If the Austrians evaded battle, instead of the war being ended in one great stroke, it would drag on and bring about what Victor called 'new military and political chances'. Doubts might arise over the infallibility of the First Consul, and his power base in Paris would be shaken. The whole point of the march over the Alps was to dazzle – to show his superiority in military matters, especially over Moreau; but if the Austrians eluded him, what then of his reputation?

Victor believed Bonaparte doubted Melas would attack him because of 'the word of a spy, to whom he gave too much confidence ... This spy, one day returning from the enemy's headquarters, where he had an access which should have made him suspicious, had assured him that Melas' intention was to pass onto the left bank of the Po.' Victor noted that this reliance on the spy almost proved fatal. The exact timing of Carlo Gioelli's meeting with the First Consul is unknown, but the circumstantial evidence points to mid-morning on 13 June. Gioelli told Bonaparte everything Zach had instructed him to say the day before, and also handed over Hohenzollern's false itinerary for the march from Genoa. The spy was dismissed and his information digested.

Bonaparte did not swallow Gioelli's false intelligence entirely. He was too skilful a user of spies to entrust his entire career to the word of a double agent. Even if he was overly generous with his trust in Gioelli, the First Consul had to consider the possibility the Austrians were feeding the spy false intelligence. This was all part of the game. According to Victor, the key doubt in the spy's intelligence was the lack of corroboration by the reports from General Chabran, who was placed in Chivasso and Crescentino. Zach's ruse at Casale had been noted, but Chabran was seemingly unimpressed by what he saw. On the night of 11 June, Chabran had written to Lieutenant General Moncey saying the strength of the enemy at Casale had increased. He also reported the boats between the Chivasso and Valenza had been collected 'under the cannon' of Casale. Everything indicated the Austrians were threatening to build a bridge there, but Chabran was not sure of it, and said he would inform Moncey if he discovered what the enemy's projects actually were. Even an Austrian cannonade on his troops opposite Casale did not cause Chabran to be overly concerned.[12] As late as 3.00 am on 13 June, Bonaparte was notified by Chabran that the Austrians had not deployed the bridge and had made no dispositions which indicated an imminent crossing. It was all extremely puzzling.

Instead of crossing the Po, perhaps Melas was considering a return to Genoa. From there Melas could strike out towards Piacenza via Bobbio, or perhaps he was intending to turn round and defeat Massena and Suchet? Perhaps the spy's intelligence was a ruse to make him look in the other direction? The only thing for it was to send the light cavalry out to scour the plain and look for the Austrians. If the Austrians resisted and contested possession of the plain, it would indicate Melas was considering a battle. If the Austrians withdrew beyond the Bormida, perhaps the spy was correct after all. As a piece of insurance, Bonaparte despatched

Desaix to Serravalle with Boudet's division and a cavalry detachment. If the spy's information was accurate, then Desaix would meet Hohenzollern that night on the road to Novi. If Hohenzollern was not there, then Desaix could face the other way and block Melas' escape route from Alessandria to Genoa. Meanwhile, Bonaparte began directing all his infantry away from Sale towards the centre of the plain at San Giuliano.

At midday, Bonaparte had reached Sale with the cavalry of his guard. They found nothing there. General Duvignau arrived there soon afterwards with his light cavalry brigade. News then came from San Giuliano, where Gardanne's division had been directed. The Austrians had evacuated the hamlet and were not to be seen on the plain. Bonaparte headed southwards to take a look for himself.

At 1.00 pm, Gardanne was joined by the remainder of the infantry commanded by Victor and Lannes. It was raining, and the men were permitted a short rest while the First Consul, his guard, the general staff and an 'enormous suite' (as Horse Grenadier Petit described it) swarmed around the three farms which comprised San Giuliano. Victor interviewed some peasants still at San Giuliano who, being braver than most of their fellows, had decided to await the approach of the two armies rather than flee. They told him that the Austrians had departed the night before, but were still present with 4,000 men not two leagues away, at the hamlet of Marengo on the western edge of the plain. At 3.00 pm, Bonaparte ordered Victor to take his corps and attack the Austrians. Gardanne would lead, with Chambarlhac's division following behind. Lannes would remain at San Giuliano, while Monnier's division would move forward to Torre Garofoli on the eastern edge of the plain. The division of Lapoype would arrive at Ponte-Curone later on in the day to replace Monnier as a reserve. With Chabran opposite Casale, and Desaix at Novi, Bonaparte had every angle covered, except for an attack against Suchet.

Duvignau had initially remained at Sale, but was subsequently ordered to join the advance on Marengo:

'I was ordered to go to San Giuliano with the cavalry, and to hasten its march. The enemy was at Marengo, he occupied the village, that of Spinetta, the banks of the Bormida, and had his army at Alessandria. I therefore forced the march. General Murat joined me and marched at our head as far as San Giuliano. I had on the right and on the left, scouts of the regiments under my command. Those of the 12th Chasseurs ventured too far and part of them were taken by the enemy.

'At three o'clock in the afternoon we found ourselves in the beautiful plains of San Giuliano, the only plains we have encountered in all Italy, where cavalry may be usefully employed. We saw before us the village of Marengo, and we burned with the desire of soon being there.'[13]

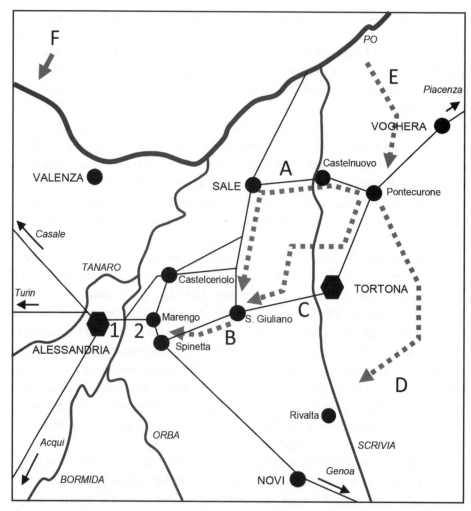

MAP 5: French movements, morning and afternoon, 13 June

A – Route taken by Lannes to San Giuliano; B – Victor's advance on Marengo; C – Monnier directed to Torre Garofoli on eastern edge of plain; D – Desaix's march towards Novi, avoiding Tortona citadel; E – Division of Lapoype arriving at Pontecurone; F – Chabran watching Casale and Valenza.

1 – Location of new Austrian camp; 2 – Austrian rearguard (O'Reilly).

Advancing westwards, Victor's infantry reached the intersection of the old and new Alessandria-Tortona road, level with Cascina Grossa on their left. Chambarlhac's division remained in reserve, taking position on a plateau. Grenadier Coignet remembered the division formed a line and the men piled arms. He could not see the rest of the army, he said, only ADCs flying in all directions in the lower ground around them.

Gardanne's division was directed forward towards Marengo. At this point one should clarify the division was quite small, brigade-sized really, officially mustering 3,691 men according to the French order of battle. It comprised two infantry half-brigades, the 44th and 101st, with a small detachment of fifty-three men from the 102nd. In Gardanne's after-action report, he downplays the size of the division further, stating they were about 2,000 men strong. Gardanne's adjutant general, Achille Dampierre, also emphasizes the weakness of the force, later describing it as '*cette prétendue division*' (this so-called division).[14] Although weak, Gardanne split his force, providing Dampierre with 500 men to follow the new road in the direction of Spinetta (Dampierre complained he actually only had two to three hundred by the time he detached skirmishers and guards for the artillery). Gardanne would advance with the rest of the division, led by the combined grenadiers on the right, following on the new road; behind them, the 24th Light from Chambarlhac's division would follow in support.

General Duvignau's cavalry brigade supported the advance, advancing in an open column of platoons. Having earlier described the plain around San Giuliano as being the best in Italy for cavalry, it is interesting to read the difficulties his brigade had in keeping up with the infantry as it advanced up the old road:

'I kept the head of my column level with that of the infantry as long as the ground permitted me. The infantry and the artillery followed a great track, and my cavalry was obliged to march through broken ground. Several times I marched in line and at the trot, always scouting my left, and searching the houses, the clumps of wood, and somewhat the enemy cavalry which was on my left retreating as I advanced. The ground became more and more cut up with broad, deep ditches, with difficult access, with defiles where two regiments had to pass man by man. Scarcely reformed, which was very lengthy, the vineyards, on which it was necessary to use the sabre because they were entwined, presented new obstacles. All these accidents of terrain delayed the march of the brigade; add to this the fatigue of the horses which had been without oats for many days. It was necessary to take the trot to keep up. I succeeded, however, and I was there when the fire began at Spinetta.'

The Austrian advanced guard at Marengo was commanded by FML O'Reilly. The Irishman clearly had his pickets out beyond Spinetta, but his main position was at Marengo, along the line of the Fontanone brook either side of the hamlet. Knowing the Austrian army planned to advance through Marengo in the early hours of the following morning, one would suppose O'Reilly would have taken greater caution to inform himself of the French advance; but it is unclear if O'Reilly knew what

Zach's great master plan was at this very moment. He may well have believed he was in fact still the army's rearguard and that he would continue to fall back on Alessandria following FML Ott and Vogelsang. The Austrian accounts are split on this. Stutterheim was incredulous that O'Reilly was apparently taken by surprise in broad daylight, while Crossard suggests O'Reilly's orders were to fall back on the bridgehead if attacked. In either case, his key fault was in failing to inform Melas that the French were advancing from San Giuliano in significant numbers and preparing to attack.

French reports are somewhat confusing on what occurred next. Duvignau says there was an obstinate struggle at Spinetta, after which the Austrians fell back on Marengo. No one else appears to talk about an action at Spinetta. Dampierre claims he was first to arrive at Marengo, and with his 'picket' of about 400 men he captured the position, taking two guns and some caissons. It is almost as if Dampierre played no part in the action at Spinetta, or he got Marengo and Spinetta confused. Gardanne elaborates, claiming the Austrians had 4,000 men and seven guns defending Marengo. Victor's ADC, Joachim Jérôme Quiot, put the Austrian numbers more accurately at 3,000 with four guns. The latter claimed the action commenced at approximately 4.00 pm and was over within half an hour. Gardanne suggests the action took nearer an hour. It is difficult to square the accounts with one another, but it appears that at some point O'Reilly's troops opened a fusillade on Gardanne's column. The Austrians perhaps saw the 24th Light manoeuvring menacingly behind Gardanne, and then rapidly withdrew towards the bridgehead when Dampierre appeared on their right flank. An account attributed by de Cugnac to Bonaparte's ADC, Lauriston, summarizes the action thus:

'We marched on the village of Marengo in very good order. The enemy was as strong as us. He had moreover a numerous artillery. He made a very lively fire; but at length he was compelled to yield, and pushed very vigorously up to the Bormida. The general had ordered me to go forward to see what was going on and report to him. I advanced to the right of Victor's division; I entered the village of Marengo with the skirmishers at the moment it was taken.'

One peculiar account of the battle given by Coignet, while perhaps little more than camp-fire gossip, is interesting nonetheless. He claims the 24th were sent forwards and were seriously mauled by the Austrians. Coignet claims the half-brigade had shot some of its officers at Montebello when ordered to advance. In retribution for this, when the 24th came into difficulty during the attack on Marengo and had to form square, the First Consul deliberately left the half-brigade unsupported and exposed. Coignet says his unit, the 96th half-brigade, was sent forward at 5.00 or

6.00 pm to disengage the 24th. When they arrived, the light infantrymen greeted the 96th with insults for not coming to their assistance sooner. They had, Coignet reckoned, lost nearly half their men in the action. Rumour or not, this account is difficult to square with the other versions of the action; however, it perhaps indicates that the action against O'Reilly was not as one-sided as Dampierre portrays.

The First Consul certainly witnessed the taking of Marengo. Duvignau confirms Bonaparte was with the forces which advanced on the place. Horse Grenadier Petit was also there:

'The consul, with his horse guards, and pieces of light artillery, skirted Marengo. We saw him almost the whole time, at a distance from us, traversing the plain, examining the terrain with attention, by turns profoundly meditating, and giving orders. The day began to close in, and we had been on horseback from the moment it broke. We had also been soaked to the skin, for none of us, the consul not excepted, had put on a cloak. We were often obliged to set foot to the ground to stretch and revive our limbs, which had been benumbed by the wet and the uncommon cold. We were joined by several deserters, and some scattered prisoners who had been taken; among others, an officer of Bussy's legion wearing the cross of St Louis. The general questioned them with considerable earnestness. All the prisoners were astonished, when informed that the person they had just been speaking with was Bonaparte.'

Before continuing with the pursuit of O'Reilly's men towards the bridgehead, it is important to consider the impact of the Austrian retreat on the First Consul's thinking. By retreating from Marengo, the Austrians had ceded to the French the entire plain. Since crawling over his maps in Paris, Bonaparte's strategy had been based on avoiding combat with the Austrians on open ground. As we have stated many times, their greater strength in artillery and cavalry meant the plain favoured the imperial army in an open battle. It was now inconceivable that the Austrians were intending to give battle. With the time now approaching 6.00 pm and in heavy rainfall, Bonaparte withdrew from the battlefield, leaving matters to Berthier and Victor to resolve. His 'profound meditation' had led him to believe Melas was intending flight.

As O'Reilly's troops fell back on the bridgehead, the French went in pursuit. Dampierre admitted they advanced with too much ardour right up to the foot of the entrenchments on the Bormida. He described the bridgehead as looking more like a town than a field fortification. The Austrians had mounted fourteen guns in this bridgehead, and these spat a hail of ball and canister at the French. Nonetheless, Dampierre's skirmishers were soon on the banks of the Bormida. General Duvignau was ordered to support the attack, and to advance at the trot. The brigade soon got into trouble from the many ditches which cut up the ground. A staff officer arrived from General Victor, telling Duvignau to hurry up, but the frustrated cavalry officer complained he could not move more than 20m without encountering a large ditch filled with water. Somewhat exasperated, Duvignau finally reached General Victor and Berthier, who were directing the attack.

Across the Bormida, the Austrian commanders at last received a message from O'Reilly that he was unable to hold Marengo. As they rode forward to observe the situation, the Austrian staff saw cannonballs raining down on the infantry arriving at the campsite. No one knew what to do. Should they attempt to camp as instructed or prepare for action? Radetzky had a clear head. He advised Melas to launch a counter-attack with Ott's troops, and offered to lead Schellenberg's division in person. Melas agreed with the plan and gave Radetzky four battalions and the Lobkowitz Dragoons. As they marched off, Zach appeared. When he saw Radetzky marching off to round up the troops, the quartermaster general asked Melas what the general adjutant was doing and had him stopped. He was aghast. Despite the cannonballs flying over from the other side of the Bormida, it was almost as if Zach simply could not believe what was happening. His plan had clearly stated the French were at Sale. The orders had been issued and could not be changed. Zach declared that the French tirailleurs were nothing but a small force, and reiterated: 'The main enemy force is positioned at Sale.'

Fortunately for the Austrians, common sense eventually prevailed. The regiment closest to the bridgehead was IR 51 Splényi, the infamous *légion infernale*. The regiment was now just 700 strong, and had taken many casualties while acting as the rearguard at Casteggio. However, it was still extremely motivated, and fearsomely tough. At the moment the bullets began to fly, the regiment formed itself across the road, facing towards the French. When Zach finally realized the bridgehead was actually in some danger, he consented to Radetzky leading IR 51 Splényi out to launch a counter-attack. The 1st Kaiser Light Dragoons were sent in support and three batteries of guns were moved up to the river bank to fire in support of the artillery inside the bridgehead.[15] The Splényi regimental history describes how the regiment fell upon the French advanced guard:

'With a contempt for death provoked by the courage of despair, the brave sons of Siebenbürgen [Transylvania] pressed forward against the French, and with our brave artillery, the regiment succeeded, even before nightfall, in repelling the attack, and driving Gardanne away from the Bormida.'[16]

The counter-attack succeeded, but at some cost. Radetzky had his horse shot from under him, and staff officer Hauptmann Troyer was wounded too. IR 51 took about fifty casualties, including the commander of the regiment, Oberst Von Eros, who was mortally wounded when a cannonball struck his lower torso. By 10.00 pm, in the darkness, on the broken and unfamiliar ground, the two adversaries stopped fighting. The rain continued to come down, and the Frenchmen sat down on the wet earth and tried to find some means of sleeping.

On the French side, Dampierre described how, 'after we had gone within range of a pistol shot, in the midst of a shower of bullets and grape-shot, we had to retire at nine o'clock in the evening, and go and bivouac within range of the cannon of the entrenchments.' The memoirs of Marmont, commander of the French artillery, claim he tried to support the attack of Gardanne's division, but his artillery was driven off by the Austrian guns on the far bank. Having lost a few men, Marmont went looking for Gardanne to find out what he intended to do: 'I found him in a ditch, having taken no measures either to attack the bridgehead or to prevent the enemy from leaving and debouching. Thereupon I left him, having no orders to give him, and the night being near.'

General Duvignau left the 12th Chasseurs planted in the middle of a vineyard while he went off to find new orders from Victor. After a long search, Duvignau found him at the presbytery of Spinetta, where he had set up his headquarters. When Duvignau arrived, Victor was meditating on his concern that he was in such close proximity to the enemy and yet unaware of their designs. Therefore, Victor ordered Duvignau to scout the Tanaro on the right of the position. He was also to place the 6th Dragoons behind Marengo near to the 43rd Line and to keep the 12th Chasseurs in the plain on the left, with forward posts detached in front. He was then to contribute to a grand-guard on the main road, supporting the grenadiers of the 43rd Line with the 6th Dragoons, in order to guard two pieces of artillery placed in front of Marengo.

Duvignau left Victor and rejoined the 12th Chasseurs at 10.00 pm. After taking a number of them for the Tanaro patrol, he went to set up the guard provided by the 6th Dragoons. Duvignau then had an accident approaching midnight. He had been mounted since 6.00 am, and his horse had not rested or eaten. When attempting to jump a ditch, the horse fell and overturned on the general. Heavily bruised and spitting blood, Duvignau was taken to Marengo. When his condition did not appear to be any better, he went to Spinetta, where Victor authorized him to go to the rear for treatment. In his absence, the men of the 12th Chasseurs suspected Duvignau had in fact deserted them to be with his wife, whom he had left at San Giuliano. The angry troopers stayed in the fields until midnight, when the commander, having had enough of Duvignau's presumed antics, marched them off towards Marengo to bivouac for the night. They were still 'enraged by hunger' and again had nothing to eat, so they spent hours wandering around in search of sustenance. A patrol was sent out under the command of Captain Détré to make a search along the banks of the Bormida; he took fifty troops with him and formed a picket.

Earlier that day, Desaix had been ordered to take Boudet's division south to Serravalle, the point at which the road from Genoa exits the Apennines and enters the great plain. Bonaparte had issued these instructions after meeting with Gioelli and having received the reports of his cavalry patrols. If the spy was correct, then Desaix would meet Hohenzollern's corps marching up from Genoa in the direction of Alessandria. Bonaparte's instructions to Desaix arrived at Pontecurone just after midday on 13 June. Desaix was then found at the home of the Marquess of Durazzo. He had spent a very agreeable evening with the marquess, but appears to have departed in a fateful mood. According to the bulletin of 25 *Prairial* written by the First Consul, several times that day Desaix said to his ADCs: 'I have not been fighting in Europe for a long time. The balls do not know us anymore; something will happen to us.' While these exact words might have been a flight of fancy on the part of Bonaparte, Desaix's sense of foreboding that day was also recorded in the memoirs of the writer and engineer-geographer Victor de Musset, who stayed with the Marquess of Durazzo several days later. As Desaix departed the home of the marquess, the farewells were long. At the moment Desaix went to mount his horse, he bade the marquess goodbye with the words: 'Until we see each other in this world.' After a moment of silence while climbing up onto his horse, he added, 'Or the next.'[17]

Having received the order to march, Boudet's division quickly prepared itself. The division's adjutant-general, Dalton, managed to scribble a hurried note to the army's chief of staff, Dupont, begging for more ammunition:

> 'I inform you, my general, we were unable to obtain at Voghera more than 20,000 cartridges which, joined to the 30,000 we received during the course of yesterday, and to 13,000 that we have in reserve, make 63,000 out of 83,622 which we need to complete the division to 50 shots per man. You see that we lack another 20,000 still, not including that which would be necessary for us to have in reserve. The division leaves at this instant to direct itself on Serravalle. I beg you, my general, to send me as soon as possible, as much as you can.'

Following the Via Emilia into Tortona, the road to Sarezzano is not much more than 30km. However, Boudet's division could not take the main road because the citadel of Tortona was still in Austrian hands. In order to avoid the citadel's guns, it was necessary for the division to take a circuitous route, looping round to the south of Tortona and passing through the village of Sarezzano, before striking westwards to reach the Scrivia opposite Rivalta, there joining the road towards Genoa. This meant the division would have to use smaller roads and tracks, and would have to pass over hilly ground around Sarezzano – this village being more than 200m higher than Pontercurone. It was also extremely wet, and no sooner had the division marched off than the rain began to lash down.

Desaix's force was composed of the brigades of Musnier (9th Light) and Guénand (30th and 59th Line). The 30th Line had only recently caught up with the division, having been left as part of the blockading force at Milan. It was composed only of two battalions, and the majority of the soldiers were conscripts. The other two half-brigades had seen a great deal of action since leaving Milan, notably at Melegnano, Lodi and Piacenza. The brigade had eight guns: a battery of light artillery from the 2nd Horse Artillery under the command of Chief of Battalion Duport comprising two 6in howitzers and four 8-pdrs, and two 12-pdr field guns.[18] The 1st Hussars were attached to the division, as was a detachment of the 3rd Cavalry, both units approximately 120 strong.

The cavalry led the march, followed by the 9th Light. Boudet followed with Guénand's brigade and the artillery. After the passage of the horses and the light infantry, the tracks they followed were churned into mud. By the time Boudet reached the hills around Sarezzano, the guns were only moving with great difficulty. The infantry had to help the mounted gunners push the guns and caissons through the pouring rain. It was to no avail; the guns were stuck fast and Boudet had no option but to call Guénand's exhausted brigade to halt, remaining for the night between the villages of Sarezzano and Carbonara Scrivia.[19] Meanwhile, the head of the division reached the banks of the Scrivia around 5.00 pm. Instead of a ford opposite Rivalta, they found a raging torrent. Rainwater had drained off the rocky hills and quickly turned the Scrivia into a fast-moving and treacherous body of water. A few of the hussars waded across to the left bank, which gave the carabiniers of the 9th Light an idea. The result was recorded by Dalton in his daily report:

'The 9th Light with the 1st Hussars, which marched at the head, arrived on the edges of Scrivia after five o'clock. We attempted the passage of this river which was very swollen at the moment and we were only able to succeed in crossing some infantrymen by making them hold onto the tail of the horses. Twelve men were swept away in an instant; we saved them with difficulty, but they lost their weapons. The general was forced to make camp on the right bank. The 30th and 59th Line had stayed on the mountain of Sarrezano, under the orders of General of Brigade Guénand, to protect the artillery.'

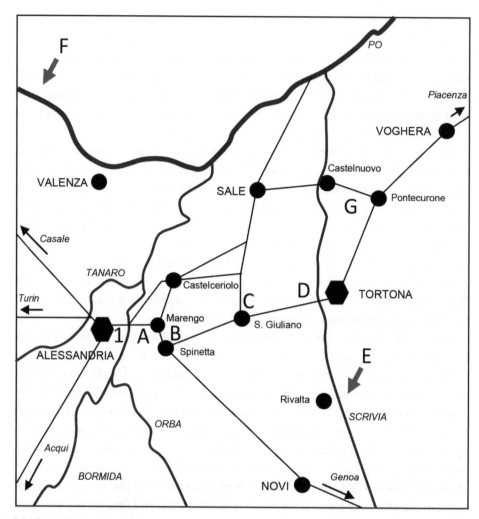

MAP 6: Night of 13/14 June

A - Gardanne; B – Victor; C – Lannes; D – Monnier and the Guard (Torre Garofoli); E – Desaix at Rivalta; F – Chabran; G – Lapopye.

1 – Austrian camp.

Boudet's journal reported only a single company of carabiniers made it across the Scrivia to join Desaix at Rivalta. The remainder of the 9th Light did not spend the night idly, but began looking for boats. In local tradition, a priest came to the aid of the Frenchmen. This was first recorded in 1842 by Pietro Oliva:

'[Desaix] already despaired, when a priest of that country showed up to Desaix, telling him he would call all the villagers, the boatmen to help him. In response to his words rushed farmers, fishermen, boats were sought, and wagons from everywhere, and the French gradually came to the opposite side of the Scrivia.'[20]

The priest has been identified as Don Guasone from nearby Castellar Ponzano - a Francophile who supported the revolution. Many of the peasants who came to Guasone's aid were dependants of the local Castellani-Merlani family, who had lost a son fighting for the French at Novi the year before. The result of this activity was a boat, by which the remainder of the 9th Light were able to cross the river early next morning.

While this work had gone on, Desaix was naturally concerned. If Bonaparte's intelligence was correct, the Austrians might already be at Novi, just 10km away. With the torrential rain, and the roar of the Scrivia, Desaix appears not to have heard the guns open up at Marengo around the same time he arrived at Rivalta. This would only have added to his agitation. Before the fall of night, Desaix sent his ADC, Savary, with a detachment of hussars to explore as far as Novi and report on enemy activity. Savary arrived back in the night, stating there was no sign of Austrian troops in the town. At 2.00 am, Desaix ordered Boudet to make a strong reconnaissance with his infantry in the direction of Serravalle, urging him to take an entire brigade if he felt it necessary. Boudet reported back that he had already sent a staff officer, Captain L'Héritier, with a detachment of thirty men from the 3rd Cavalry to investigate the town.[21] Boudet advised Desaix to await the return of this patrol before committing his infantry. Desaix agreed and changed the order. When L'Hériter returned, he reported imperial troops at Serravalle, but not at Novi – where he had only seen republican troops (Savary's escort?). This information was important. It meant the forces of Melas and Hohenzollern had yet to unite. A message was sent urgently to headquarters, probably arriving before first light.

Chapter 10

That Miserable Ditch

In the early hours of Saturday 14 June, the Austrians counted their losses from the action the evening before. In total they had lost 448 casualties to the fray. Perhaps more importantly, the attack had disrupted the march to the new campsite, and the heavy rain had not helped matters either. Although the situation had been stabilized, and the French skirmishers had been driven away from the bridgehead, with Marengo now in enemy hands, the plan to march off at midnight would be folly. Zach sent a verbal order out to the staff officers with the column to delay the attack until 8.00 am. This would give the imperial troops a few hours of daylight to reorganize themselves and eat breakfast before the battle.[1]

Austrian losses, 13 June:
(officers/men)

	Dead	Wounded	Missing/ PoW	Total
Mariassy Jäger	0/1	1/2	4	8
3rd Bach light. Batt.	0/5	2/12	9	28
4th Am Ende lt. Batt.	0/6	2/30	16	54
IR 57 J. Colloredo	0/4	2/73	0	79
IR 28 Frohlich	0/0	0/0	3	3
4th Banat Grenzer	0/7	1/49	41	98
5th Warasdin-Kreutz	1/4	6/98	11	120
Bussy Jäger zu Pferde	0/0	0/0	0	0
IR 51 Spenyi	0/4	3/48	3	58

Grand total: 448 men

Other than the casualties, the evening battle unsettled some in the imperial camp. A Piedmontese officer, the Franchino di Cavour, witnessed it and was disturbed by the apparently high motivation of the soldiers of the French compared to their Austrian foes:

'One thing truly worthy of remark is, that at the first attack which took place on 13 June, all the French outposts affected to shout, while going forward: "We desire peace or death." Unfortunately few people are able to feel what a fatal effect these magic words ought to have produced on the minds of the Austrian soldiers. Many of their officers were tired of war and convinced the Great Consul sincerely wanted peace. I am certain that the misfortunes experienced under the walls of Alessandria have their source in the propagation of the idea the French want peace.

'At the commencement of the affair of the 13th, I was so affected with the dull and dejected air of the Austrian soldiers, that I ventured to approach a general, to whom I said in a very reserved tone: "Your Excellency, do you hear the cries of the French? They make a terrible fire while crying for peace. Would it not be possible to destroy the bad effect which this may produce upon the soldiers by haranguing them warmly?" The general shrugged his shoulders and laughed. He doubtless did not know the republicans have beaten and plundered Europe only with harangues, tricks, and songs.'[2]

During the night, the Austrian command team debated events. The appearance of the French on the Bormida perhaps indicated Bonaparte was attempting to link with Suchet and the Army of Italy. According to a letter written by Radetzky shortly after the battle, the Austrians had learned Massena had joined with Suchet at Nice and had advanced with 16,000 men. The advanced guard of this force was believed to be operating around Acqui with the intention of cutting off Melas' communications with Genoa. This intelligence must have been deeply unsettling to the Austrians in Alessandria.

Despite Zach's continued insistence that the French were at Sale, Radetzky was concerned at the prospect of a head-on attack to clear the French out of Marengo before the main column could even properly begin its march towards San Giuliano. If the combat the evening before was anything to go by, this frontal attack would require a great deal of sacrifice. He proposed turning the French left by building a pontoon bridge over the Bormida further upstream than the bridgehead. Melas and de Best agreed with him, but Zach had gone to bed exhausted. When they found the quartermaster general and woke him, he also agreed to the change in plan; however, by then it was too late. Radetzky had summoned Captain von Hagen from the Pioneers and discussed the project in detail. At the beginning of June, the bridging train at Alessandria had a total of fifty-one pontoons. Of these, sixteen had been used to create a second bridge over the Bormida, and a further twenty-four had been sent to the Po in order to lend credence to Zach's deception plan. Only eleven pontoons remained – not enough to create another bridge. The only way Captain von Hagen could build Radetzky a new bridge was by dismantling part of the existing pontoon bridge, and dragging it upstream. With dawn beginning to break it was impossible, von Hagen declared, to attempt such an operation without the French noticing what they were doing. Radetzky called off the idea.[3]

Outside, the night gave way to a fine Italian sunrise, one which exuded a warmth thus far lacking on the campaign.[4] The skies were clear and there was a cooling westerly breeze. Summer had arrived at last. As Stutterheim gazed up at the heavens studying the weather, all around him the Austrian soldiers began preparing their breakfasts – mostly chewing on bread rations. With the commotion of the night before, and the impending prospect of a major battle, few would have slept much beyond a few hours; but these were hardy young men, disciplined and inured to hardship. They had marched and fought their way from every corner of the Habsburg Empire; down through Italy, across mountains and rivers, through cities, they had driven the French back before their bayonets. Now called back to their ranks, they prepared to march out again.

Despite Radetzky's protestations, there was no change to the plan. The enemy's main force was at Sale, and the troops in front of them at Marengo were only a weak band of skirmishers. Few would have known it, but 14 June was Zach's birthday. He had come into this world fifty-three years before, and he was determined to end this day with a glorious victory over Bonaparte, or to die in the attempt. The quartermaster general apparently spoke with Hadik and told him as much. According to Cavour:[5]

> 'What is very true is that General Zach said before the battle to General Hadik, whom I got it from, that if the battle was lost he was determined to be killed.'

Such sentiments might appear very noble, but such a fatalistic and blinkered frame of mind indicates Zach was determined to implement his plan, no matter what happened.

Elsewhere, the mood was better. Crossard was watching the troops prepare to cross the Bormida:

> 'The soldiers looked gay, and I never saw better dispositions in troops marching to the enemy. General Vogelsang said to me: "I doubt whether Bonaparte will come out of this fortunately; you see the gaiety of the soldiers; we have forty thousand men, an excellent and numerous cavalry, a formidable artillery."'[6]

Once the first division passed the bridges, Crossard saw Melas arrive with his staff. The Austrian commander-in-chief was once again in his element riding among his men. He approached Crossard and spoke with him for the first time

1. Napoleon Bonaparte (1769–1821) in 1800 after Appiani. (*Anne S.K. Brown Military Collection*)

2. Alexandre Berthier (1753–1815), commander-in-chief of the Army of the Reserve. (*Anne S.K. Brown Military Collection*)

3. André Masséna (1758–1817), commander-in-chief of the Army of Italy. (*Anne S.K. Brown Military Collection*)

4. Jean Moreau (1763–1813), commander-in-chief of the Army of the Rhine. (*Anne S.K. Brown Military Collection*)

5. Michael Friedrich Benedikt, Baron von Melas (1729–1806), commander of imperial forces in Italy. *(Anne S.K. Brown Military Collection)*

6. Anton von Zach (1747–1826), quartermaster general (chief of staff) of the imperial army in Italy. *(Gian Lorenzo Bernini)*

7. Joseph Graf von Radetzky von Radetz (1766–1858), the general adjutant. *(Anne S.K. Brown Military Collection)*

8. General Bonaparte on the morning of the Brumaire coup (10 November 1799). With him are his wife Josephine, brothers Joseph and Lucien, General Berthier, Murat, his son-in-law Eugene and politicians. *(Anne S.K. Brown Military Collection)*

9. The First Consul reviews his troops at the Palace of the Tuilleries, Paris. The core of the Army of the Reserve was composed of fresh troops stationed in Paris and the interior. *(Anne S.K. Brown Military Collection)*

10. Bonaparte crossing the Great St Bernard with the monks. *(Anne S.K. Brown Military Collection)*

11. (*Above*) French army crossing the Alps. Gun barrels are mounted onto hollowed logs and dragged across the ice. *(Anne S.K. Brown Military Collection)*

12. (*Right*) Consular Guard grenadiers and a hussar at the monastery on the Great St Bernard pass. *(New York Public Library)*

13. French artillery convoy snaking its way down from the Alps towards Fort Bard. The Austrian defence of Bard severely hampered the arrival of artillery and ammunition. *(Anne S.K. Brown Military Collection)*

14. The Battle of Casteggio-Montebello, 9 June 1800. This unexpected clash set up the Battle of Marengo, five days later. *(Anne S.K. Brown Military Collection)*

15. Louis Charles Antoine Desaix de Veygoux (1768–1800). *(Anne S.K. Brown Military Collection)*

16. Adam Albert, Count von Neipperg (1775–1829). *(Anne S.K. Brown Military Collection)*

17. The French counter-attack at Marengo, 14 June 1800. *(Anne S.K. Brown Military Collection)*

18. Horse grenadiers of the Consular Guard at Marengo. They delivered the knockout blow to the retreating Austrian army. *(New York Public Library)*

19. Officer of the Consular Guard, by Hoffmann. *(Anne S.K. Brown Military Collection)*

20. Officer of the Horse Chasseurs of the Consular Guard, by Hoffmann. *(Anne S.K. Brown Military Collection)*

21. (*Above left*) French horse artilleryman. (*New York Public Library*)

22. (*Above right*) Gunner of the Consular Guard. (*New York Public Library*)

23. (*Left*) Officer of the 12th Horse Chasseurs in walking out dress. (*New York Public Library*)

24. (*Right*) French heavy
cavalry. Throughout the battle,
Kellermann's heavy cavalry
outfought the numerically
superior Austrian cavalry.
(*New York Public Library*)

25. (*Below*) French dragoon.
(*New York Public Library*)

26. French line infantry grenadier, 1800. *(New York Public Library)*

27. French infantry captain. *(New York Public Library)*

28. Flag awarded to the 'Incomparable' 9th Light Infantry in reward for leading Desaix's counter-attack at Marengo. *(New York Public Library)*

29. Hungarian line infantry in 1799, by Kininger. *(Anne S.K. Brown Military Collection)*

30. Austrian jäger light infantrymen. *(Anne S.K. Brown Military Collection)*

31. Austrian (left) and Hungarian (right) grenadiers. These infantrymen were the most formidable in Melas' army. *(Anne S.K. Brown Military Collection)*

32. Austrian artillerymen. The Austrians' numerical superiority in artillery was a key advantage at the beginning of the battle. *(Anne S.K. Brown Military Collection)*

33. (*Left*) Austrian light dragoon. (*Anne S.K. Brown Military Collection*)

34. (*Below left*) Imperial Austrian hussar trooper. (*Anne S.K. Brown Military Collection*)

35. (*Below right*) The General Adjutant – a position held by Radetzky in 1800. (*Anne S.K. Brown Military Collection*)

36. (*Above*) View of Marengo from the north-east. (*Author's photograph*)

37. (*Right*) The Fontanone in front of Marengo. (*Author's photograph*)

38. (*Below*) The Tower of Theodoric at Marengo. (*Author's photograph*)

39. (*Above*) View towards Castelceriolo, where Ott's forces deployed. (*Author's photograph*)

40. (*Below*) Torre Garofoli – Bonaparte's headquarters during the battle. (*Author's photograph*)

41. Desaix's mausoleum at the monastery on the Great St Bernard (detail). (*Author's photograph*)

since the fall of Cuneo. The émigré had angered Melas by writing to Thugut about various projects, but now Melas let bygones rest – he needed everyone to perform at their best.

Contradicting Crossard's upbeat reflections on Austrian morale, Neipperg thought the soldiers had a look on their faces which 'would have made one believe we were driving our soldiers to slaughter rather than to glory'. Despite Melas' fine words, which he acknowledged, Neipperg blamed this feeling on the distribution of alcohol before the battle: 'As usual, they were given bad wine, which, far from awakening their ardour, often numbed it even more.'[7]

At 8.00 am, the deployment onto the right bank of the Bormida began. A glaring error was immediately realised. While there were two bridges across the river, there was only one exit from the bridgehead. This was all well and good for an army crossing from the right to left banks, but it immediately caused confusion for those marching towards Marengo. A degree of traffic management was required, and this slowed the speed of deployment considerably. Fortunately for the Austrians, Gardanne's troops did very little to dispute their passage. Their line was drawn up away from the artillery in the bridgehead, about a kilometre along the main road. Ahead of the main column was an advanced guard commanded by Oberst Frimont of the de Bussy Light Horse. His troops advanced first and cleared away the French outposts, then he moved to the left to allow space for Hadik's troops to deploy.

The frontal attack on Marengo was led by FML Hadik with Bellegarde's brigade; his troops formed the first line. Infantry extended across the road, and the cavalry formed up on the wings. FML Kaim came behind Hadik, forming a second line, followed by the two grenadier brigades. In Melas' report, he states that the reserve remained in column on the road. There was very good reason for this. Today, the scene of the first clash is formed of large, flat fields. Neipperg describes the appearance of the battlefield in 1800 as being 'scattered with trees and new plantations', and the ground 'resembled a rather thick wood'.[8] Hadik drew up a line of guns in front of his line – mostly battalion guns attached to the infantry, but also Frimont's cavalry battery. These guns opened fire on the French line ahead of them while the Austrian deployment was completed. The battle was now well and truly engaged.

At 9.00 am, the regimental bands in Hadik's infantry regiments struck up with their popular Turkish music. The flags were unfurled and the advance on Marengo began. The senior officers rode conspicuously at the head of their troops, and Hadik placed himself at the head of Bellegarde's brigade, which was composed of four battalions, two each from IR 52 Erzherzog Anton and IR 53 Jellacic. As had been stated in Zach's order, the troops advanced quickly, and did not stop to deploy skirmishers or exchange fire. Ahead of them, Gardanne's line fired a succession of volleys and then began to withdraw in the direction of Marengo, firing as they went.

Everything was going to plan until Gardanne withdrew behind the Fontanone brook. Hadik's troops now came under a crippling fire from the direction of Marengo, but also an enfilading fire against their right flank. They bravely continued forward, taking fearful casualties until they reached the edges of the Fontanone. This obstacle was known by the Austrians, but it had been underestimated. The rainfall the previous day had filled it to bursting point, and the ground around it was extremely swampy and thick with hedges and vegetation. On the extreme right of Hadik's line was the Hungarian regiment, IR 53 Jellacic. Reaching the Fontanone, their regimental history describes them coming under a 'murderous French fusillade':

> 'The Fontanone ditch was reached. Its considerable depth and swampy state did not check our battalion. Fired by the example of their superiors, they respected no danger, and rushed from the high banks into the ditch.'[9]

At this point, the brook was at its shallowest, probably waist-deep in water; but the mud and the intense volume of fire stopped the regiment in its tracks. Trying to urge his men across the ditch, the commander of the Oberst Battalion, Major Lalance, fell seriously wounded from his horse and was taken captive. The next senior officer, Captain Emerich Marx, took command of the battalion and tried to rally his men. Further up the line, IR 47 Franz Kinsky also reached the banks of the Fontanone under heavy fire. Their regimental history records:

> 'At the head of their unit, Colonel Vermatti, and all the officers of the staff, boldly made their way towards the enemy's fire, and they repeatedly attempted to attack: the brave colonel, as well as the Lieutenant-Colonel Kövesdy, were wounded with many officers and a large number of men in the murderous struggle close to the brook.'[10]

In the face of the French musketry, Hadik realized his attack had lost impetus and cohesion. His men were being gunned down relentlessly for no gain. The Austrian accounts use words like 'disastrous hail of bullets', 'terrible fire' and 'violent fire'; Stutterheim described the attack as 'one of the bloodiest ones which one saw in this war'. Hadik felt there was no choice but to order the withdrawal and regroup. No sooner had Hadik given the order to withdraw when he was struck in the ankle by a cannonball. With his leg shattered, he had to be carried from the field. As his line withdrew, FML Kaim advanced his line to provide cover. It was now approximately 10.00 am.

The full importance of O'Reilly giving up Marengo the evening before was now realized. The French were clearly in larger numbers than expected; and the first line of the main column had been shattered by enemy fire before it had even reached the starting point of its advance on San Giuliano. Did it not occur to Zach the French might have moved from their position at Sale? Clearly not. When he later discussed the opening hour of the battle with Faverges, he set out the reasons for failure in that first hour as follows:

> 'Although the enemy, from the first hour, was everywhere driven in, the attack was only weakly pursued … The miserable ditch which separated us, almost dry usually, flowed this day with seven or eight feet of water, thanks to a clumsy bleeder ditch made in the Bormida.'

Nowhere in this account does Zach take any responsibility for ensuring Marengo had been properly defended the day before, nor for the fact he had not scouted out the terrain the day before the battle and had not identified the hazard presented by the Fontanone, should Marengo have fallen into enemy hands. He clearly knew about the ditch, and unless he was completely locked away in his bureau all day, he presumably knew it had been raining very heavily the day before and the waterways were swollen. As Neipperg declares:

> 'It was impossible for our general staff not to know the ground and the ditch which cut it, the plans of the whole country having been drawn, and the army having been manoeuvring there continually for nearly a year.'

Added to the problem of having only a single exit from the bridgehead, the Austrian chief of staff had already made critical errors.

As if this was not enough, at 9.00 am, Rittmeister Civrani arrived from Acqui and told Melas his outpost had been attacked by Suchet that very morning. Although he had in fact only been probed by a small force of French dragoons, Civrani imagined he had come under infantry attack (probably some of the dragoons had dismounted and used their muskets to skirmish with the Austrian outposts). In the face of this perceived onslaught, Civrani had fled to Alessandria convinced that Suchet's main force was about to arrive. When Melas heard this, it played up to his fears of being encircled by the French. The Austrian commander was in no mood to take chances, so he ordered GM Nimbsch to recross the Bormida with his entire cavalry brigade and a battery of artillery, then to take up a new position at Canteloupo and watch developments. Thus, 2,341 hussars were removed from the battlefield, and had to file back through the bridgehead, thus delaying the crossing of Ott's column.

We must now review the first phase of battle from the French perspective. Victor had placed his headquarters at the presbytery of Spinetta the evening before, but he had gone out in the night to attempt to discover what the Austrians were planning to do. The night was clear and peaceful. The slightest noise could be heard, and so, around 1.00 am, Victor heard the unmistakable sound of the enemy army stirring and preparing to give battle. Victor ordered his men to stand to. Back towards Spinetta, Grenadier Coignet was with the 96th Half-Brigade. When Victor's order to stand to arms was received, he remembered the effect it made on him:

> 'One cannot form an idea of the effect which the sound of drums at this early hour produced upon us. It was a thrill like the one the soldier feels at the first cannon shot. Everyone rushed upon the stacks of arms. It seemed as if the enemy was within a stone's throw of us. One did not believe that one was safe except with a musket in his hand, and in the ranks of his companions. The lines were formed throughout the plain; it was a general make ready. In my life I will not forget that moment. I was still a young soldier, and I was only half seasoned. Besides, I do not pretend to maintain that the first moments of a battle have always left me indifferent and calm; I claim, on the contrary, that the bravest soldier feels, on this solemn occasion, an emotion close to fear.'

As twilight gave way to dawn, Victor recalled that 'one of the most radiant Italian suns illuminated the scene'. Looking over towards Alessandria, Victor could see Melas' army before him:

> 'We perceived then all the Austrian army under arms: a third was ranged up between Bormida and Alessandria; two other thirds were held at the back of this place. To the eye it appeared to be 25,000 infantry and from 6 to 7,000 cavalry; its artillery was great.'

Victor fully expected this great host to put itself in motion and attack him, but nearly four hours passed before the advance began. This prolonged inactivity was a cause of surprise to the French soldiers watching. When the attack came, it was Gardanne's advanced guard which bore the brunt of it. This 'division' (really no more than a weak brigade) had formed a line perpendicular to the main road, level with the farmhouse of Pederbona. According to Dupont, Gardanne was called 'Grenadier' by the First Consul, on account of his size and courage.[11] His after-action report has a certain laconic style to it:

'The advanced guard was attacked on the 14th, at nine o'clock in the morning, by the first line of the enemy army, about 15,000 strong, advancing in good order, under the protection of a numerous artillery. I have nothing to add to what General Victor ought to have said about the manner in which the vanguard disputed the ground step-by-step with such a superior enemy.'

Prior to the Austrian attack, Adjutant General Achille Dampierre had placed his small detachment in front of the farmhouse of Stortigliona, 900 metres to the south-west of Gardanne's position at Pederbona. Already weak, this detachment had been further reduced by the 'desertion' of around 100 men from the 101st Half-Brigade, who decided to return to their parent unit. This left Dampierre with less than 300 men from the 44th, one cannon (with no ammunition) and a platoon of light infantry chasseurs. Dampierre watched the Austrian attack begin at 9.00 am and said the firing was along all the line half an hour later. He placed half his men in a sort of entrenchment near the farmhouse, with the other half in a series of gullies on the right. These gullies allowed the men to be hidden up to head height. Dampierre was more conspicuous, sat on his horse between the two groups. It was not long before the Austrian deployment brought imperial troops within musket range of Dampierre's men. They fired into the flank of the Austrians and saw men falling in the ranks after every discharge. Although the Austrians were more preoccupied with attacking Gardanne, Dampierre's detachment did not go unnoticed, and he was about to experience a very long day.[12]

The real mastermind of the defence of Marengo was Victor. Some of the commentators on the Austrian side criticized the French for not attempting to dispute their exit from the bridgehead. However, this would have brought Victor's troops within range of the fourteen guns in the earthwork, and of artillery fire from guns located on the opposite bank of the Bormida, just as had occurred the previous evening. Victor had something far more subtle in mind, and more deadly. He had fought on this ground a year before, and where Zach had neglected to properly inform himself of the ground, Victor was alive to all the possible advantages the terrain provided. In his memoirs, he described the importance of the position, with Marengo and the Fontanone forming a 'very sharp angle in the plain' and affording good communications and outlets onto the plain. If the line of the Fontanone could be held, with the strongpoint of Marengo being the central point of defence, then Victor hoped to hold the Austrian advance long enough for support to arrive from the divisions stacked up on the main road to Tortona behind him. In fact, given the Austrians' superiority in cavalry, keeping the imperial troops bottled up to the west of Marengo was Victor's only hope of salvation. If he had retreated, he would have surrendered the road network and faced the risk of being encircled.

At the moment the Austrians began to advance out of the bridgehead at 8.00 am, Victor sent Captain Deblou to warn the First Consul that 'a decisive battle was to take place'. He sent his artillery in front of Gardanne and instructed Gardanne to take the 'first shock' of the enemy in his current position. At the same time, he placed the 8th Dragoons to the left of Marengo and supported this regiment with Brigadier General Kellermann's brigade of heavy cavalry when it arrived at 9.00 am. Chambarlhac was instructed to line his division in reserve so its right was at Marengo, its centre in front of Spinetta and its left at the Fontanone.

Victor watched as the Austrians advanced without any skirmishers, instead being preceded by artillery, all of which advanced with a firm and rapid step. It was as if the Austrians would simply overwhelm Gardanne with a combination of artillery fire and their huge superiority in numbers. However, Victor was too canny a general to allow this to happen. Before the Austrians could make contact, he instructed Gardanne to withdraw by echelons, refusing his right flank so that he would come to stop with his right at Marengo, forming a line oblique to the Austrian column and taking it in the flank.[13] This meant the right-hand battalion of Gardanne's line withdrew first, then, once it had retired 100 paces, the next battalion on the right would fall back. At the same time, each battalion would have to pivot to form the new line. To execute such a manoeuvre under fire, while pressed by a superior enemy, shows the French Army of 1800 was perhaps much more tactically sophisticated than usually supposed.

We also know from Rivaud's report that Gardanne's troops executed controlled volleys when firing at the approaching Austrians. It is often said the French Army of the 1790s was incapable of anything but a *feu de billebaude* – an undisciplined voluntary fire. However, Rivaud described textbook battalion and platoon firing systems being employed at this stage of the battle. In the first, each battalion would fire a massive single volley in turn. In the second species of firing, each platoon within the battalion would fire in turn, alternating between odd numbered platoons, and then the even numbered ones. This would create a 'rolling fire' along the front of each battalion. It meant the enemy line would receive a constant rain of hits while advancing. Even if we concede that muskets were inaccurate at the best of times, and soldiers delivering the volleys would have barely had the chance to aim, Gardanne's fire must still have delivered a stinging effect.

While Gardanne executed his withdrawal, Brigadier General Olivier Rivaud prepared to defend Marengo. Victor had instructed Rivaud to place his brigade under arms with the right at Marengo, the centre opposite Spinetta and the left approaching a stream known as the Orba. On his left, Rivaud saw a regiment of dragoons, approximately 400 strong (this was the 8th Dragoons). He had no artillery, and even before the Austrians reached the Fontanone, his men were being killed by the great weight of fire coming from the approaching Austrian guns. In his own words:

'General Victor, like myself, felt the importance of the village of Marengo, which, forming a very sharp angle in the plain, afforded the enemy the advantage of uncovering our whole army without being perceived, and of directing against us a portion of his strength which he would have thought necessary to overwhelm us on a weak point.

'Scarcely had the attack commenced for half an hour, when the little division of Gardanne was already overwhelmed by numbers, and yielded step-by-step to the enemy. To maintain Marengo's important position, I placed in the front of the village the 1st Battalion of the 43rd, and I ordered the commander to defend himself with determination. Scarcely had this battalion been placed, than the troops of Gardanne, repulsed, threw themselves in disorder upon this village, and this battalion had to support the whole effort of the enemy. Melas had directed his principal forces on this village, which formed the centre of his line, and which afforded him three fine roads to debouch into the plain.'

Victor described how the earth trembled at the approach of the Austrians. The whole Austrian line, he wrote, was enveloped with 'whirlwinds of bluish smoke', out of which vomited fire and iron cannonballs.

When Gardanne's men reached the Fontanone they redeployed on the other side. A single company of grenadiers from the 101st Half-Brigade, under the command of Captain Depoge, remained on the road and is said to have protected the withdrawal of Gardanne's troops and the deployment of the reserves.[14] Once this last company was clear of his front, Rivaud's battalion in front of Marengo opened a devastating fire on the head of Hadik's troops. Gardanne's troops redeployed along the line of the Fontanone and fired into the flank of the Austrian troops. It was carnage and, as we have seen, this caused the unfortunate Hadik to break off the attack. With the first phase of the battle at an end, the advantage remained with Victor. He had taken the shock of the first attack; he had thus far only committed one battalion of Chambarlhac's division to the fray; and he had also blocked the march of FML O'Reilly's column, by placing Dampierre's detachment at Stortigliona. Better still, Lannes had begun the battle just two hours' march away at San Giuliano. His troops were already on the way to support Victor, as he had supported Lannes at Montebello. If the Austrians continued to press a frontal assault, there would be time for further reserves to come forward.

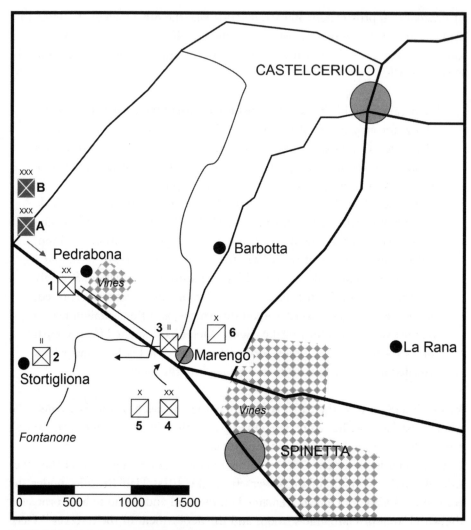

MAP 7: Tactical situation: 9.00-10.00 am

(Austrians) A – Hadik's Corps; B – Kaim's corps in second line.

(French) 1 – Gardanne's fighting withdrawal from Pederbona; 2 – Dampierre's detachment; 3 – Rivaud deploys one battalion at Marengo; 4 – Chambarlhac's division; 5 – Kellermann's brigade (and 8th Dragoons); 6 – Champeaux's cavalry brigade.

There were just two problems. Dupont points out in his memoirs that the key to the Marengo position was Castelceriolo, approximately 3km to the north-east. Like Marengo, this village offered numerous routes onto the plain, and if it fell into Austrian hands, the imperial army could fall onto the rear of the French position at Marengo. Although this threat appears to have been identified, Victor could do nothing about it. He could not weaken his position at Marengo in the face of the formidable Austrian forces before him. Reserves needed to be committed as soon as possible, and therein lay the other problem. At the time of the attack, Bonaparte's headquarters were more than 11km from Marengo. He would have heard firing at 9.00 am; he would then have received Captain Deblou's message not long after. Did the First Consul believe Victor was being attacked by Melas' entire army? It appears not.

In the aftermath of the battle, Bonaparte would have been sensitive to accusations he allowed himself to be taken by surprise by Melas. We must be mindful, therefore, of what is written on the subject, and seek only to establish the facts. Let us first retrace the First Consul's steps since the battle on the evening of 13 June. It is said that Bonaparte retired for the night believing the Austrians had retreated from Marengo beyond the bridgehead and had destroyed the bridges across the Bormida. According to Marmont, General Gardanne was the source of this intelligence, the general telling Bonaparte he had cut the bridge. His stepson, Eugène Beauharnais, also protested that Bonaparte had received false intelligence:

'The day was very stormy and we had a lot trouble passing the Scrivia, whose waters had become very strong. I was witness to the reports that several officers came to make to the First Consul at his bivouac that evening. All agreed in saying that the enemy had retired in haste and that it had broken all its bridges over the Bormida. The First Consul made them repeat this several times to be surer.'[15]

Quite who these officers were is unclear, and we know this information simply was not true. They were clearly not sent by the generals in command of the situation at Marengo. Brigadier General Rivaud at Marengo knew the Austrians 'preserved not only a bridgehead on the Bormida but maintained the outposts between the Bormida and our vanguard very close to the Bormida'. Dupont's unpublished memoir concurs with this: 'The obscurity of night had not allowed reconnoitring completely the ground and the position of the enemy, which covered Bormida.'[16]

So what was the effect of Deblou's message? Marmont had left Marengo and spent the night in a farm, continuing onto Torre Garofoli at daybreak. He was present in headquarters when Deblou arrived. He states they first heard the sound of gunfire (erroneously he says 6.00 am – it would have been 9.00 am when Hadik's artillery opened fire), then:

'Shortly afterwards an officer of General Victor arrived and reported to him a general attack of the enemy. The First Consul, astonished at this news, said that it seemed impossible to him. "General Gardanne told me," he added, "of his arrival on the Bormida, upon which he had cut the bridge." "General Gardanne," I replied, "has made a false report; I was yesterday evening closer than he to the bridgehead, and I proposed to him to attempt to seize it; but he refused it, although I had placed the cannon to support him; and the bridgehead having not been removed or blocked by our posts, the enemy might have debouched at his ease during that night, without being perceived. So you can boldly believe in the battle.'"

Despite Deblou's message and Marmont's verbal advice, the First Consul was hesitant to commit reserves. Deblou had left the field before the actual attack had begun. This attack might have been a feint – a cover under which Melas would escape Bonaparte. There was certainly no logic in Melas attacking him, having ceded the plain almost without a struggle the day before. In fact, although Bonaparte could hear the sound of battle to the west, it is unlikely he received definite news about the scale of the Austrian attack until 11.00 am at the earliest. If we suppose that Victor made a report at the end of Hadik's attack, this would have taken at least an hour to reach Torre Garofoli. Therefore, the First Consul continued making his contingencies for blocking Melas' escape. Around the time the battle commenced, Bonaparte ordered Lapoype to turn his division around and recross the Po to operate in support of Chabran. Lapoype received this message at 10.00am, and had long since departed by the time any recall was sent to him. At some point between 10.00-11.00 am, the First Consul also sent Desaix a message, instructing him to march from Rivalta in a southward direction to Pozzolo-Formigaro, where he could intercept the road from Genoa to Alessandria.

At the bridgehead, GM Nobili's cavalry brigade had come back from the battlefield and headed southwards towards Acqui. FML Ott's column was now finally able to cross over the Bormida and begin its march on Sale via Castelceriolo. Crossard was attached to this column as a staff officer, and as he crossed over he saw the seriously wounded Hadik being carried back to Alessandria. Hadik indicated to them that his men were still going forward. Ott's column took the left fork in the road and began marching to the north-east as planned. It was clear to them that the French were concentrated at Marengo, and this meant there was no one to dispute their passage. In comparison to the hell experienced by the main column, their march was fairly leisurely.

Back on the main road, FML Kaim led forward his line to repeat Hadik's attack. Kaim was not the sort of general who resorted to stratagems and ruses. The enemy was before him – he advanced. As before, the flags were unfurled and the musicians struck up their martial airs. Eager to set an example to his men, Oberst

Veimatti of IR 47 placed himself and all the staff officers of his regiment at the head of his men and advanced towards the French position. At the same time, on the left of the line, Oberst Soudain of IR 63 and Major Prince Aremberg did the same. However, the result was the same, partly because of the difficulty crossing the Fontanone, but mostly because of the intense enfilading fire from Gardanne's troops lined up along the brook, many of whom had dispersed as skirmishers, using the natural cover along the ditch – some even fighting from inside the ditch. IR 63 had almost 100 killed outright as they advanced through a hail of lead. As the regiment pushed nearer the Fontanone, the soldiers found themselves funnelled into Victor's killing ground. A huge French volley smashed into IR 63 from across the ditch, killing Oberst Soudain's horse and badly wounded him in the head and hand, while Prince Aremberg took a crippling hit in the leg. IR 47 suffered equally badly, with Oberst Veimatti and Oberst Leutenant Kovesdy included in the scores of men who fell. As Hadik had found, Kaim's men could not cross the ditch in sufficient numbers to break the French line. Captain Rauch in IR23 Toscana was also in this attack, and recalled:

'When the regiment had only advanced a little further, it was already running onto cultivated terrain – arable land, cut up by ditches, meadows and bushes; the field of view around it was limited in all directions, which gave cover to the enemy facing us and at the same time, acted as a barrier, so that our cavalry could not co-operate to support us at all. Ignoring the obstacles, we mounted a lively attack and the musketry was so ferocious, that I had never heard its like before ... I came through unwounded, but my coat and my clothes were shot through with bullet holes.'[17]

The Austrian pioneer troops were normally equipped with *Laufbrücken* (lightweight, portable bridges) which could be thrown over obstacles like the Fontanone, but for some inexplicable reason, when the *Laufbrücken* were called for, the equipment wagons were right at the tail of the army and had to wait for Ott's column to cross the Bormida before they could be brought forward.

As Kaim's men tried to bludgeon their way into Marengo, Hadik's troops reformed under the command of Bellegarde. Although quite badly mauled in the first attack, the men were still eager to resume the fight. Keeping away from Gardanne's enfilading fire, Bellegarde directed the troops to move to Kaim's left and advance up to the Fontanone opposite the farm of Barbotta. Some of the Austrian light troops managed to get across the marshy ground and onto the opposite bank. Frimont's cavalry also moved up into this sector of the battlefield. From Barbotta, a road led southward into the rear of the Marengo position. If this could be exploited, the French line could be taken in reverse.

It was now approaching 11.00 am. Just at the right moment for the French, Lannes arrived from San Giuliano. This corps had spent an ugly night at the small village, sleeping in the open. There was no shelter, no food, no wine and no brandy, and so breakfast had passed as quickly as the evening meal before.[18] Arriving in support of Victor, Lannes left the 28th and 40th Half-Brigades in reserve behind Marengo. He ordered Watrin to drive away the Austrians taking up position at Barbotta. Marching directly at the Austrians with the 6th Light, the 22nd Half-Brigade and all of Lannes' artillery, Watrin engaged the Austrians. General Champeaux led his cavalry brigade to support the attack, but fell mortally wounded at the head of the 1st Dragoons. As Bellegarde's men were pushed back across the Fontanone, the French infantry, ignorant of the depth of the muddy ditch, hesitated momentarily. Five NCOs of the 22nd threw caution to the wind and jumped in. They made the far bank with a little difficulty, although under heavy fire; inspired by that success, the rest of the line followed. Other French soldiers attacked and captured an Austrian gun, then turned it round on its former owners, serving it with skill.[19] Watrin's advance continued until a terrific barrage from the Austrian reserve batteries under the direction of Major Perczel blunted his ambitions. In this attack, General Watrin's brother, Lucien, was killed.[20]

Back in the Austrian centre, there was a discussion about getting some of the cavalry to work their way behind the French position. If they could get onto the French left flank, a brisk charge could roll up Gardanne's troops and put an end to the enfilade fire. GM Pelatti's cavalry brigade was chosen for this task and Zach was sent to give the necessary orders. According to Neipperg:

'General Zach, however, ordered the regiments of the 1st Kaiser and 4th Karaczay Light Dragoons to pass the ditch at all costs. The chiefs represented the impossibility; they had to obey; half of them remained mired, the rest could only pass one by one with infinite difficulty.'[21]

GM Pelatti was a local man, an Italian from Castellazo Bormida.[22] Approaching midday, he found a crossing point which was sheltered from view by trees and started to cross, as Neipperg describes. With the difficulties in crossing the ditch, only two squadrons of the 1st Kaiser Light Dragoons were able to assemble and form into two lines on the French flank. It was at this point that they were seen by Brigadier General Kellermann, who was located to the left of Gardanne. The French general sent an order for the 8th Dragoons to attack the Austrian horsemen. While the green-jacketed French dragoons advanced, Kellermann formed his heavy cavalry into a single line and followed a short distance behind. The art of cavalry warfare is to always have a reserve. The first clash of horses is likely to disorder both friend and foe alike, and all momentum is lost. The initiative can only be regained by the arrival of successive waves of horsemen. Kellermann knew this, and so was ready to follow. His after-action report describes the outcome:

'I ordered the 8th Dragoons to charge them; I supported them, marching in line; the 8th knocked over the enemy's cavalry; but the charge having disordered them, they were charged in turn; I ordered them to unmask me and rally behind the brigade, which advanced with *sang froid* on the enemy's line, charged it at fifty paces, routed it, and tumbled it into the ditches, even on its infantry. The enemy lost more than 100 horses in these two charges.'[23]

Neipperg agreed with the effect of light cavalry being pounced upon by heavy cavalry:

'Scarcely had this cavalry and some infantry battalions, encouraged by its example, crossed than all the enemy's cavalry threw themselves upon them, threw them into the ditch, causing them an infinite loss, and making many prisoners. The brave Lieutenant-Colonel Baron de Kees of the Kaiser Light Dragoons Regiment was caught and wounded beyond this ditch, which greatly contributed to discouraging the cavalry he commanded. These two regiments were ruined for the whole day. The enemy again occupied the ditch, and might have already enjoyed his success if he had not been stopped by the corps of grenadiers commanded by General Weidenfeld, who, at the charge, prevented the enemy from advancing further.'[24]

When Weidenfeld's grenadiers arrived, they opened fire on Kellermann's cavalry with their battalion guns. After a quarter of an hour under fire, Kellermann could see no fresh attempts to cross the ditch were going to be made, so he withdrew his brigade to its original position on Gardanne's left.

There is one last anecdote from this episode in the battle, which is drawn from the bravery citation of Grenadier Corporal Cervelle from the 101st Half-Brigade. Some of the Austrian light dragoons appear to have escaped Kellermann and fled in the direction of Gardanne's troops. Seeing the horsemen in green jackets, the French ignored them, assuming these were the same French dragoons posted on their flank. It was Cervelle who first noticed they were enemy cavalry: 'Let's charge,' he shouted. 'They are the enemy's and their horses are tired!' The officers ordered their men to open fire and within a few moments the already disordered light dragoons were being shot from their saddles.[25]

With the failure of the cavalry attack, and Lannes driving back the attempt to take the French right, Kaim also fell back from the centre to regroup. It was midday and the Austrian main column had not yet reached the start position allocated to it in Zach's plan. This force, which was supposed to deliver the hammer blow to Bonaparte's army by falling on its flank at Sale, was now a battered and bruised wreck. There is no disputing the bravery of the Austrians, particularly their officers, who led conspicuously from the front, but they had walked into something of a trap. Rather than breaking out towards Novi, O'Reilly's column had now become bogged down in a firefight with Dampierre's small force at Stortigliona. Zach stated that O'Reilly was injured by a fall from his horse in the battle, and perhaps that might explain why the French were able to hold his column up with just a few hundred men. The result of this private battle was that O'Reilly had become cut off from the main column. Much of the cavalry had been sent away at the beginning of the battle – no one thought to recall them or ask if Suchet was actually in range. The only thing which was going to plan was Ott's advance on Sale; in other words, a false march against an enemy which did not exist. However, despite this, no one on the Austrian side, with perhaps the exception of Radetzky, appears to have been thinking strategically. Zach was obsessed about enacting his plan, and Melas could not think beyond the great fatalistic 'decisive battle'. Melas was so fixated with beating his way through Marengo that he ordered his grenadiers to prepare for action. A third attempt to storm the village would be made.

So what news of the First Consul? Despite two or more hours of thundering cannonade, he was apparently still not convinced the Austrians were serious about pressing home an attack, and had remained at Torre Garofoli. Perhaps the spy Gioelli had told him the Austrians were planning to make a feint to cover their withdrawal? It is certainly possible the spy had heard this discussed. In any case, Bonaparte clearly did not want to make a false move until it was absolutely clear what Melas was intending. It appears that Berthier went to look first, and then the First Consul followed. It was not until 11.00 am that Bonaparte decided to take a look for himself.[26] We have confirmation of this from the memoirs of Horse Grenadier Joseph Petit:

'At eight o'clock in the morning, the enemy had manifested much vigour of preparation. He touched upon a few weak points, and made certain dispositions in consequence; but his intentions were not fully known at head-quarters till towards the latter part of the morning. Berthier was the first upon the field of battle. Till this time the various aides-de-camp had relieved each other in apprising the consul of the enemy's

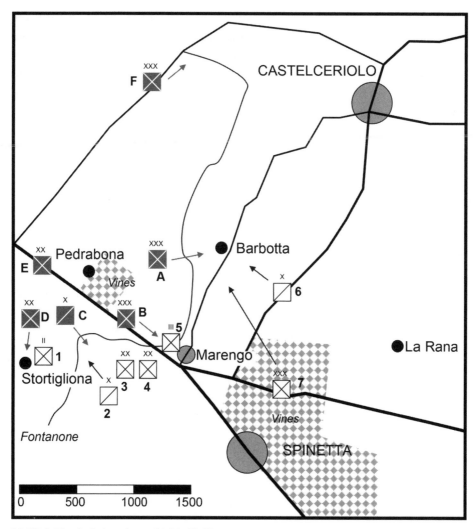

MAP 8: Tactical situation – 11.00-12.00 pm

(Austrians) A – Hadik's Corps (Bellegarde) advances on Barbotta; B – Kaim's Corps attacks Marengo; C – Pelatti's cavalry brigade attempts to cross the Fontanone; D – O'Reilly attacking Dampierre; E – division of grenadiers in reserve; Ott's column.

(French) 1 – Dampierre's detachment; 2 – Kellermann attacks Pelatti; 3 & 4 - Gardanne and Chambarlhac; 5 – Rivaud protecting Marengo; 6 – Champeaux's brigade counter-attacks; 7 Lannes' Corps drives Hadik's Corps back over the Fontanone.

steps. Numerous wounded soldiers arriving, acquainted us that the Austrians were in force. Upon these tidings, the consul mounted his favourite charger at eleven o'clock, and made great haste to the field of battle.'

The Foot Guards and Monnier's division were instructed to advance towards the battlefield at this time, and had a distance of more than 11km to march before arriving at Marengo. Moving at an ordinary rate of 4km per hour – assuming the Guard and Monnier's troops were already formed on the road, under arms and awaiting orders – the head of the column would not be due to arrive at Marengo much before 2.00 pm.

Chapter 11

The Battle for Marengo

At the time of the battle, General Soult was inside Alessandria held prisoner by the Austrians. One month before, on 14 May, he had been wounded at the Battle of Monte Creto – his right leg was shattered by a ball while leading a desperate assault against Hohenzollern's entrenchments. In driving rain and hill fog, the general could not be carried to safety. He lay on the ground protected by his two aides-de-camp (his brother, Chief of Squadron Pierre-Benoît Soult, and Lieutenant Étienne Hulot) and was taken into captivity. Soult and his ADCs were later joined by Dr Cothenet, a surgeon from the 25th Light Infantry sent by Massena to care for him, and these four were transferred to Alessandria. Soult's memoirs say he was in the Episcopal Palace at Alessandria, and on the day of battle they heard the gunfire of Hadik's first attack. Soult was bedridden, but still proves to be a valuable 'witness' of the battle:

> 'From my bed I could hear the battle very well, and from the distance and closeness of the fire I could judge which of the two parties was making progress. It was a cruel position. My brother and Lieutenant Hulot, my aides-de-camp, and Dr Cothenet, my surgeon, went alternately to watch at an observatory above the Episcopal palace, where I was staying. There, armed with a spyglass telescope, they could see the movements of the two armies well enough, and then they came to communicate their remarks to me. I was thus informed of the state of the battle, as well as possible, without taking part.'[1]

Twenty kilometres away from Soult, General Desaix also heard the opening barrage of Hadik's attack at Marengo. At 9.00 am, Desaix was still at Rivalta waiting for his command to finish crossing the Scrivia. Boudet recorded his division's actions in his journal:

> 'At the break of day, the water did not yet permit us to ford, but a boat had been secured by the help of some boatmen that a detachment had taken from Tortona during the night. The troops crossed speedily, and went to take position at Rivalta. Towards ten o'clock in the morning, the waters had fallen and the artillery was able to ford the river.

'Meanwhile, Desaix had sent to headquarters to find out what was to happen following the action of the day before. He received an order (fortunately too late) to go to Pozzolo-Formigaro, an intermediate position, from where we could move on Alessandria or to Genoa, in case the enemy tried to make its retreat that way.'[2]

As Boudet states, Desaix had informed the First Consul there were no imperial troops at Novi, but there were some at Serravalle. The bearer of this message – Desaix's ADC, Savary – had returned to Rivalta with the instruction to march on Pozzolo-Formigaro. When the sound of artillery fire was heard in the direction of Alessandria, Desaix was uneasy about it. Savary's memoirs are wildly inaccurate in their timings, but the general description of what occurred next rings true:

'We at once took up arms, and quitted Rivalta; we marched on Novi; but scarcely had day dawned, when we heard a redoubled cannonade open in the distance behind our right. The country was flat; we could only see a little smoke. General Desaix, astonished, stopped his division and ordered me to go quickly to reconnoitre Novi. I took fifty horses, which I launched at full speed on the road; I quickly reached the place where I was sent. Everything was calm and in the condition in which I had left it the day before; no one had yet appeared. I put off my detachment at a gallop, and rejoined General Desaix. I had only been two hours in my mission. It could influence the combinations of the day; I ran to announce to the first consul all was quiet at Novi, that General Desaix had suspended his movement and awaited new orders.'[3]

We know the division's artillery could not have crossed the Scrivia much before 10.00 am. Desaix would then have set off for Pozzolo-Formigaro as soon as possible, but Boudet claims the division had not got 'more than one mile beyond Rivalta' (a French 'mile' is akin to half a league; approximately 2km – or half an hour's march) when it stopped. At the earliest then, the 'redoubled cannonade' reported by Savary was either Kaim's second assault on Marengo, or more probably the point at which Lannes joined the battle. This indicates Savary set out for Novi between 10.30 and 11.00 am. He would not have returned then until 12.30 pm at the earliest. Reporting back to Desaix, Savary was then instructed to go and find the First Consul, tell him Novi was empty, that Boudet's division was halted at Rivalta and to ask for new orders. Contrary to popular legend, Desaix did not 'march to the sound of the guns'; he simply waited for confirmation before moving any further away from the main body of the army on what appeared to be a false movement.

Elsewhere on the extremities of the battlefield, Brigadier General Jean Rivaud heard the opening cannonade while at Sale with his cavalry brigade. According to the 1801 regimental history of the 21st Chasseurs, their mission was 'to contain the enemy on the right flank and become if needed the pivot of the line'.[4] At the outbreak of fighting, Rivaud sent a squadron of the 12th Hussars to scout out in the direction at the main Alessandria road. The squadron appears to have headed south in the direction of San Giuliano, then turned westwards at 10.00 am, before reaching at midday the farm of Pagella, 3km to the north-east of Castelceriolo.[5] By this time, Rivaud had begun to move the whole brigade in the direction of Castelceriolo, approaching the sound of the guns cautiously.

On the French left there were two cavalry detachments watching that wing of the army. The nearest to the battlefield was the 11th Hussars, commanded by Chief of Squadron Ismert. This force had been sent by Victor to monitor the Orba and Lemme rivers and appears to have encountered some Austrian patrols. Ismert said he executed several little charges until 11.30 am, when he was obliged to recross the Lemme. A study of a chart demonstrates Ismert had his rivers confused; he in fact would have meant the confluence of the Orba and Bormida rivers, and the Austrians he encountered were most likely scouts from Nobili's cavalry brigade which had been sent to Cantalupo. In any case, he headed in the direction of the fighting and came across Dampierre's detachment at Stortigliona. There, Ismert received an instruction from one of Victor's ADCs to remain in this position.

The last French outpost on the battlefield was Duvignau's brigade, which was positioned at Castellazo, 8km south-west of Marengo. The brigade had forded the Orba to reach this position, and on arrival the commander of the 12th Chasseurs had placed two advanced posts on the Bormida, one commanded by Lieutenant Loquette and the other by Lieutenant Besson. Chief of Squadron Müller was ordered to bivouac the regiment. He placed half the regiment in the courtyard of a 'sort of chateau', the remainder in the courtyard of a large grange.[6] The sound of the 'violent' cannonade caused the commander of the 12th Chasseurs, Chief of Brigade de France, a degree of unease, and he twice rode along his line without noticing any enemy movements. In the event of attack, a rallying point (or *place d'alarm*) was nominated a little way behind the village. Chief of Brigade de France, satisfied with his dispositions, sent a *maréchal des logis* (sergeant) with a message back to Victor detailing his actions. As it approached midday, the subaltern officers went to a lunch in the village hosted by Capuchin friars. They were blissfully unaware that two messengers sent by Victor had been intercepted and Nobili's cavalry brigade was just a few kilometres away on the other side of the Bormida at Cantalupo.

Our focus now turns to the Austrian column under the command of FML Ott. In Zach's original scheme, Ott's command was to march on Sale and distract the

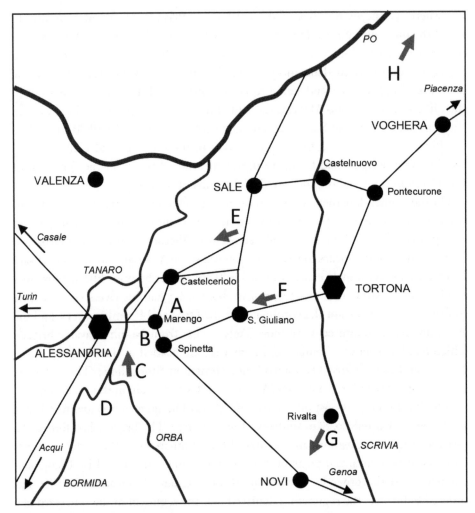

MAP 9: French positions at midday

A – Lannes and Champeaux's brigade on the right of Marengo; B – Victor and Kellermann's brigade on the left of Marengo; C – 11th Hussars moving to Stortigliona; D – Duvignau's brigade at Castellazo; E – J. Rivaud's cavalry brigade probing from Sale; F – Monnier and Consular Guard on march from Torre Garofoli; G – Desaix outside Rivalta; H – Lapoype's division marching to the Po.

French while the main Austrian column marched out of Marengo and executed a left turn at San Giuliano to fall on the flank of the French army. No one had thought to change this plan, so Ott marched away from the battle raging around Marengo and took the quiet road to Castelceriolo. Although there was a main road through the town, the surrounding area was described by Crossard as marshy and covered with vines. Stutterheim mentions there were a lot of bushes in the area, and older maps show the land to the south of Castelceriolo was cultivated with small holdings. Just outside the village was the castle, or rather a fortified manor house belonging to the Ghilini family – the lords of Castelceriolo. Before Ott's troops arrived, a small detachment of the 6th Light was sent to scout the town by Lannes. Although probably less than 100 men, it appears Ott took some time scouting the strength of the French troops before mounting an attack on the place. The French gave token resistance according to Stutterheim, and were driven off in the direction of Sale, pursued by several squadrons of the Lobkowitz Dragoons (the 6th's regimental history says the Frenchmen held out for four hours!).

When Ott's troops occupied the town and explored the land beyond it, they found two things of note. Contrary to Zach's instructions, there was no sign of the French army in the direction of Sale. Looking down towards the south, where the battle was raging, they could see an open field which extended south-eastward, behind the French position at Marengo, continuing as far as the vineyards of San Giuliano. Although it was against Zach's instructions, Ott decided he would execute a right turn and join the battle at Marengo.[7] It was not long before General Watrin saw Ott was planning to turn his flank:

'Perceiving the enemy appeared in force at Castelceriolo and seeing him deploying a strong column on my right, I made a battalion of the 22nd carry towards Castelceriolo to support the 6th Light which was going to be turned by the enemy corps which extended fully beyond our right. General Lannes seconded this movement with the 28th, which he carried at once to this point, whereas the 40th supported vigorously several cavalry charges which the enemy made at them on the main road of Marengo.'

The movement of the 28th Half-Brigade to support the right flanks is confirmed by a letter written in 1805 by the former commander of the unit, Roger-Valhubert. This key document was discovered in the papers of Dupont and is therefore not one of the documents collected by de Cugnac in the French War Archives. This letter helpfully provides a time for this phase of the battle:[8]

'At noon the 28th held the extreme right of the army, and never left it. This corps made a change of front, the left in front, which, from being parallel to the Bormida, placed it somewhat perpendicular to this river: then it faced opposite the Po and had, at around a hundred fathoms behind it, the road from Tortona to Alessandria.'

The 28th were an indomitable unit; having guarded the Alpine passes through the winter, they fought with distinction at the crossing of the Po and at Montebello. With just 998 combatants at the start of the action, the chief of brigade issued a stern instruction forbidding the carrying off of wounded men. With no formal stretcher-bearers in that era, soldiers would often excuse themselves by carrying wounded comrades to the rear – from where they did not return: such losses could not be afforded. No sooner had the unit come under fire from Ott's troops, than Roger-Valhubert was wounded by a gunshot. True to his word, he refused all treatment and grimly clung on.[9]

Watrin's report (cited above) also states the 40th Line came under cavalry attack. This unit was placed to the rear of the French position, probably level with Spinetta, directly behind Marengo. There are several indications of these attacks in the bravery citations attributed to the regiment. Grenadier François Boudier killed an Austrian horseman who was about to strike down a French officer. Fusilier Jean Pinau was notable for the way he encouraged his comrades to resist the Austrian cavalry, which charged 'seven times'. Meanwhile, Sergeant Jean-Pierre Senat led a detachment which fought off a group of horsemen trying to charge the left flank of the 40th Line's third battalion.

Melas had watched the first two attacks against Marengo fail. He now decided to commit his two grenadier brigades to breaking the French resistance at Marengo. While Melas prepared for the third attack, and Kaim's troops reformed, Victor moved some of Chambarlhac's division forward to bolster Gardanne's men. Two battalions of the 96th Half-Brigade were placed to the left of Marengo, with their right flank near the main road and the bridge; the 24th Light Infantry positioned themselves to the left of the 96th Half-Brigade. Until then, most of Chambarlhac's men had been relegated to the role of observers. Now they were up at the ditch for the first time, positioned in a wheat field which gave them a degree of shelter from view. Grenadier Coignet's account of the fighting there gives a good indication of the intensity of the battle at this stage:

> 'Suddenly the enemy's skirmishers emerged from the marshes and willows in front of us. The artillery begins to fire. A shell explodes in the first company and kills seven men. A bullet wounded the gendarme, who was a staff officer near to General Chambarlhac. The latter escaped at full speed, and we did not see him again during the day.
>
> 'A general, whose name I do not know, took his place; small, well-made, with fine blond moustaches, showing a great deal of bravery and activity … Scarcely was he at our head, when he advanced towards the first company of grenadiers to which I belonged, made us form in a single rank, and threw us into the attack. "March," he said. "Do not stop to load your weapons. When it is necessary, I will call you back with a drum roll." That said, he ran off to join his division.

'A column of Austrians, however, appeared from the groves of willows where it was hidden, deployed before us, and riddled us with its battalion volleys. Our little general responds by other battalion volleys, and here we are, between the two, sacrificed. I run behind a large willow, I lean on the trunk, and I keep shooting at the enemy column. I could not keep it up for long. The balls came in all directions. I was obliged to lie down on the ground, to protect myself from the canister bullets, which had hammered the branches and made them fall upon me. I was covered with it; I thought I was lost. Fortunately all the division advanced on my side. I got up, and found myself in one of the companies of my battalion.'

All along the banks of the Fontanone, French skirmishers found themselves in desperate battles of survival. Surrounded by enemy grenadiers, Fusilier Jean Lambert made a dash for the ditch and leapt into the water, dragging with him a grenadier whom he made prisoner. Another soldier conspicuous for his bravery was Fusilier Jacques Maitre, who stood up to his waist in water, firing on the Austrians through the thick of the action.[10] Another notable action of bravery was performed by Sergeant Louis-Jacques Châtelain of the 24th Light Infantry. The Austrians placed a gun opposite his company and began firing on the French line. Châtelain attacked the crew and chased them off. He then had the gun turned on the Austrians and opened fire himself, and remained with the gun 'until the last extremity'. A similar action was also performed by Grenadier Sergeant Pierre Monnet of the 44th Half-Brigade. Under fire from an enemy battery (probably two regimental guns), Monnet made a single-handed attack, killing or wounding the gunners and driving the rest off, even though he had been shot in the arm.[11] Along with Coignet's description of the battle, these heroic feats illustrate the intensity of the fighting over the Fontanone.

In the centre of the French position, Brigadier General Rivaud had reinforced the village with the second battalion of the 43rd Half-Brigade at midday. By 1.00 pm, these fresh troops were already running low on ammunition, and the sustained artillery bombardment had broken up their formation. Rivaud decided to throw his hand in, and advanced in person with his final reserves, the 3rd Battalion of the 43rd and the 3rd Battalion of the 96th. These were placed with their right against the village and the left extending towards the Austrians, their line occupying a space of about 200 metres. With the remainder of the 96th and the 24th Light already engaged, these two battalions were the last of Victor's fresh troops. Rivaud's account of the fighting confirms the severity of the Austrian grenadiers' assault:

'I stopped the enemy by a well-fed platoon fire, and made him fall back; he at once returned at the charge, reinforced with fresh troops; I stopped this effort, and wished to advance upon the enemy; a ravine stopped me ten paces away; then he engaged an extremely sharp fusillade at point-blank range; it lasted a quarter of an hour; the men fell like hail on both sides; at this moment I lost half my line; it was no more than a field of carnage; everyone in my brigade on horseback was killed or wounded; the chiefs of battalion and the captains were dangerously hit; my staff officers were killed; my aide-de-camp had his right thigh shot through by a bullet; I myself was wounded in the thigh by a canister bullet; the wound was horrible; but I felt if I yielded, the enemy would take possession of the village, and enter the plain with his cavalry and artillery, and take all the troops who had already taken part in the fight, and who were in disorder on the plain.'

As the grenadiers regrouped from their first attack, the two squadrons of the 1st Kaiser Dragoons launched a headlong charge at Marengo. It was desperate stuff, as described by Rivaud:

'The enemy, despairing at not being able to shake us with his infantry, formed a charge of cavalry; but this troop stopped before the fire of my battalions; not having been able to cross the ravine; they fell into disorder upon themselves, and lost about sixty men.'

Having been thwarted in three major attempts to batter their way through Marengo, over four hours into the battle, at last a breakthrough was about to occur. The Austrian pioneers had been separated from the wagons carrying their portable foot bridges as already described. Despite this, they worked their way towards the Fontanone under the cover of some trees, to the north of Marengo, and south of Barbotta, probably at a break in the line between the troops under Victor's command and those of Lannes. By now there would have been so much smoke blowing around the French position that a small group of men might well have gone unseen (there was a westerly breeze, so the smoke would have drifted towards the French). Directed by Radetzky, Major Hardegg led his pioneers up to the muddy banks of the Fontanone. The pioneer commander ordered some of his men into the water. Although almost up to their necks, the pioneers formed a single file, seventeen men deep, and, placing their hands on the shoulders of the man in front and lowering their heads, they created a human bridge. Seeing what was possible, Hardegg ordered the whole company into the ditch and by this means formed several chains over which troops from IR 63 Erzherzog Joseph got across to the far bank. These men fanned out, forming a sort of bridgehead around the human bridge. Seeing this success unfolding, General Lamarseilles drove up all the available artillery reserve to this position to support the foothold on the other side, and began battering the French at Marengo and Lannes' troops on their left. Now the pioneers' wagons arrived, and at last they were able to construct a proper footbridge at this point, despite being under fire from French troops who at last saw what was occurring.

Now came the crucial moment. Lattermann's grenadier brigade was directed across Hardegg's bridge. As they raced across, they turned southwards and charged at the farmhouse of Marengo where Rivaud was struggling to hold on.[12] Behind the grenadiers, the remainder of IR 63 also crossed, this time facing northwards, driving a wedge through the French line, which began to break and take flight. For Rivaud, the situation was now critical:

> 'I judged all was lost if we did not rally; although my wound already made me suffer greatly, I went to the centre of my two battalions, stopped the drummers who were fleeing, and put them to the front, and made them beat the charge. My troops stopped; I made them face front, and, under a very sharp enemy fire, I carried them forward; I overthrew the grenadiers, who were already passing the ravine, and I caused the enemy to retreat in his turn, as far as 300 yards from the village; then the troops of General Lannes also advanced on the front of the village, the battle was restored. It was then two o'clock in the afternoon ... Having a very swollen thigh, and unable to keep my horse, I took advantage of this fortunate situation to withdraw from the combat and go to the ambulance [field hospital] to be dressed.'

As Rivaud suggests, Lannes' troops did rally in the face of the unexpected breakthrough. The regimental history of the 6th Light records that Sergeant Gautheir, Corporals Legay and Thory and Chasseur Barillet rallied several companies which had abandoned their position for want of cartridges. Corporal Legay called out to the light infantrymen: 'Remember that Frenchmen have no need of powder. Don't you have your bayonets? Forwards, always forwards. This must be the tactic of the brave!' Watrin's light infantrymen regained their composure and charged forwards. On their right, the 22nd Half-Brigade also rallied and counter-charged, pushing back IR 63 towards the foot bridges. However, they did not press home the attack. Protected by the artillery, the Austrians retained their foothold across the Fontanone and began to regroup. However, in this push over the Fontanone, General Bellegarde suffered the fate of Hadik and fell wounded, along with General Lattermann, the grenadier brigade commander. Melas had also been injured in a fall from his horse, one of two incidents he would suffer that day, and was heavily bruised. These casualties among senior commanders would begin to tell.[13]

It appears that something of a lull descended on the battlefield; with the early afternoon sun now high above them, the hottest part of the day began. Although the immediate crisis appeared to have passed, in truth the French were in a terrible position. Rivaud's brigade could have barely formed a battalion in the defence of the village. The butchery around Marengo was extraordinary. The wounded had been piled up inside the walls of the farmhouse, but Austrian shells had landed among them. The Fontanone was choked with bodies and blood. The remainder of Victor's troops were low on ammunition and could offer not much more than a thick skirmish line in that direction. Much of the French artillery was disabled by Austrian fire. Only one half-brigade (the 40th) had yet to be fully committed into the line, and even it had faced cavalry attacks. Kellermann took this opportunity to have his men dismount to rest the horses. The period of calm was, Kellermann remarked, 'the precursor of a tempest'.[14]

The fighting around Stortigliona continued until about 1.00 pm, when, under heavy artillery fire, Dampierre's little group broke away and retreated southwards for a kilometre, rallying at Cascina Bianca. While part of O'Reilly's force pursued Dampierre, a portion of it moved into position to fire on Victor's left flank. It was the French turn to suffer from an enfilading fire.[15] As French troops turned to face this new threat, it reduced the number of muskets which could be brought to bear on the main road. By now, Gardanne's troops in particular were extremely low on ammunition, and probably formed little more than a thick skirmish line, with the battalions reduced to clumps gathered around the colours. Dupont's unpublished memoir has the following to say on the crisis concerning the lack of ammunition:

> 'Our troops were all engaged: there were no more reserves, ammunition ran out; whole regiments asked for cartridges, and General Marmont, commander of the artillery, to whom I mentioned this, denied it saying that they were almost all consumed. We realized, indeed, that the passage of the Alps had only allowed incomplete supplies.'[16]

As the above account alludes, this was the gamble the First Consul had taken. His 'thunderbolt' strategy relied on speed of movement and capturing enemy supplies. Without conventional lines of communication, there was an evident risk the troops would lack the essential equipment and munitions to succeed. All throughout the campaign, the French had relied on their enthusiasm and ingenuity to improvise solutions; but now they were in a battle of attrition, and the Austrians had the advantage in guns and powder.

Alongside Gardanne, the troops in Chambarlhac's division were equally hard-pressed. Grenadier Coignet gives a vivid description of the pressure they faced:

> 'There we were riddled with canister: everything fell on us. We held the left of the army and touched the highway of Alessandria. That was the

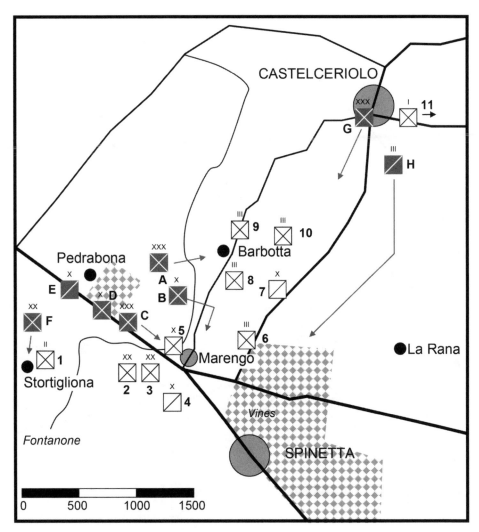

MAP 10: Tactical situation - 12.00 pm

(Austrians) A – Hadik's corps (Bellegarde) supporting crossing of Fontanone; B – Pioneers lay bridges for Lattermann's grenadier brigade to cross Fontanone; C – Kaim's infantry corps; D – Weidenfeld's grenadier brigade; E - Pilatti's cavalry brigade regrouping; F – O'Reilly; G – Ott probing south from Castelceriolo; H – Lobkowitz Dragoons probing rear of French position.

(French) 1 – Dampierre's detachment; 2 & 3 – Gardanne/Chambarlhac (part); 4 – Kellermann's brigade and 8th Dragoons; 5 – Rivaud's brigade in Marengo; 6 – 40th Half-Brigade in reserve; 7 – Champeaux's cavalry brigade; 8 – 6th Light Infantry; 9 – 22nd Half-Brigade; 10 – 28th Half-Brigade holding French right; 11 – company of 6th Light pursued from Castelceriolo.

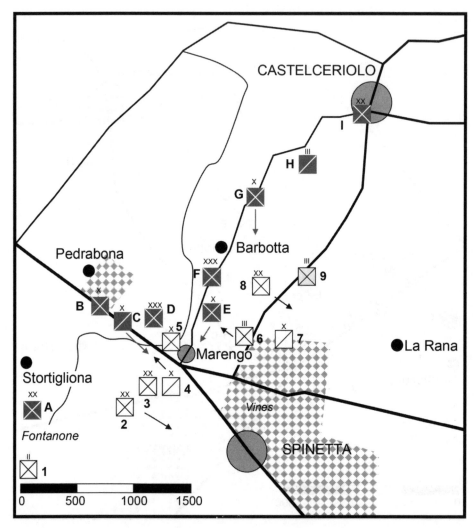

MAP 11: Tactical situation - 1.00 pm

(Austrians) A – O'Reilly clears Stortigliona; B – Weidenfeld's grenadier brigade; C – Austrian cavalry massing for attack on main road; D – Kaim's infantry corps; E – Lattermann's grenadier brigade pressing Marengo from the north; F – Hadik's corps attacking Watrin; G – Gottesheim's brigade pressing French right; H – Lobkowitz Dragoons rallying; I – Schellenberg's division.

(French) 1 – Dampierre's detachment retreating southwards; 2 & 3 – Gardanne/Chambarlhac falling back; 4 – Kellermann covering the retreat; 5 – Rivaud's brigade in Marengo; 6 – 40th Half-Brigade moving forward to support Marengo; 7 – Champeaux's cavalry brigade; 8 – Watrin (part) retreating; 9 – 28th Half-Brigade holding French right.

most difficult position. The enemy always wanted to turn us and gain the road that was so useful to them. We had to support our left to avoid being caught from behind … The smoke was so thick that you could no longer see. The shells set fire to the large cornfield which we were in the middle of. This made a revolution in the ranks. A few cartridge pouches blew up. We were forced to fall back and reform as soon as possible. This accident did us great harm, and it took all the intrepidity of our chiefs to restore us.'

Approaching 2.00 pm, General Kellermann noticed the Austrian cavalry reserve forming up.[17] The horsemen came out from the woods along the Bormida behind them and headed up the road to Marengo. This body of cavalry was preceded by a large quantity of cavalry artillery. Kellermann made a quick estimation of their strength and considered there to be 2,000–3,000 enemy horse riding confidently on, resolute in their numerical superiority. Kellermann ordered 'to horse' and took his brigade forward to meet this new threat. Straddling the road on the right of Gardanne's infantry, Kellermann placed his brigade in the same manner as he had met Pilatti's cavalry earlier. The 8th Dragoons took the first line, with the heavy cavalry in the rear supporting. Kellermann then rode over to seek General Gardanne's opinion on the situation.

With urgency in his voice, Kellermann called over to Gardanne: 'General, arrange your troops, the enemy is coming with all his forces.'

Gardanne replied grimly: 'I am without a single cartridge, without a shell.'[18]

Without ammunition, Gardanne had to get his troops onto better ground to protect them from the approaching Austrian cavalry. A little way behind Gardanne's position was a vineyard in front of Spinetta. Kellermann agreed and offered to cover this withdrawal with his brigade. Dupont noticed Gardanne's division falling back and raced towards it. 'I am going to take a better position,' Gardanne told Dupont. 'I shall hold there.'[19]

As Gardanne's skirmishers fell back, a huge shout of 'hurrah!' came up from the Austrian lines.[20] The Austrian cavalry charged up the main road, followed by a mass of infantry. The 8th Dragoons counter-charged, but were unable to stem the tide of Austrian cavalry. As the dragoons were forced to retire, Kellermann charged in and drove the lighter Austrian horse back on the infantry massing behind.[21] This charge gave long enough for Gardanne's men to reach the safety of the vines. Kellermann then broke off contact and followed the movement of retreat, protecting the main road.

It is difficult to describe the moments following Gardanne's retreat with any great clarity. As the French left fell back, the movement was followed by Lannes' troops, with the troops forming closed columns. Victor's memoir states his troops fell back for fifteen minutes only, which would have brought them into line with the village of Spinetta and the vineyards to the north of the village which extended either side of the old and new Tortona roads. In this fifteen-minute period, there was desperate fighting as the Austrians at last crossed the Fontanone at Marengo and began to deploy. Again, Coignet is extremely useful, particularly for describing the fate of Rivaud's men in Marengo:

'Opposite the centre of the division was a farm surrounded by large walls. A regiment of Austrian dragoons took advantage of it to hide and fell on a battalion of the 43rd Half-Brigade. It surrounded them, put them in disorder, and made them prisoner. This made a hole in our line, and since we had nothing behind us, we had to press on our right to fill the deficit. General Kellermann was informed of this, and hastened himself with his dragoons, charged the Austrians and stopped them for some time. Our position did not become much better. The artillery overwhelmed us. Our ranks were thinned in a glance. Only the wounded were seen, and the soldiers who carried them to the ambulance did not return again. Also, while the Austrian columns ceaselessly received further reinforcements, we weakened incessantly and no one came to support us. We could see behind us only the plain encumbered with the dying and the bearers. By dint of firing, we could no longer ram the cartridges to the bottom of our muskets. The officers, despairing, pointed out a singular remedy for this new misfortune. It consisted of pissing in the barrel and then drying it by burning loose powder. The ammunition began to fail, and we retreated, but in good order.'

A key factor in the French ability to rally at Spinetta was a rearguard action by the 40th Half-Brigade. Dupont's memoir describes how the 40th Line under Chief of Brigade Legendre 'remained in its position and this rare fearlessness still slowed down the progress of the enemy'. Accompanied by his staff, Dupont rode over to General Watrin and asked if he would attempt a charge with his troops to take back the village. Filled with 'noble ardour', Watrin replied to Dupont:

'"I don't expect anything from it," he told me with an accent deep in sorrow. "My soldiers, still brave, are overwhelmed; if you want it, we will march." His dispositions were immediately made, the charge was beaten and everything moved off. What a beautiful feat of arms had crowned the audacity of this division, if fate had been less contrary! But after so long an effort, this attempt was to be powerless.'[22]

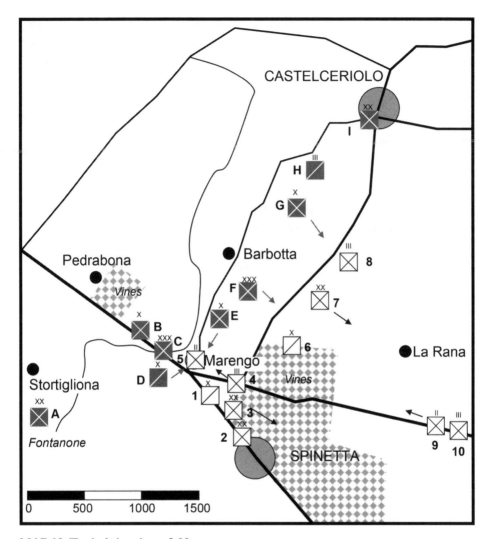

MAP 12: Tactical situation – 2.00 pm

(Austrians) A – O'Reilly in pursuit of Dampierre; B – Weidenfeld's grenadier brigade; C – Kaim's infantry corps; D – Austrian cavalry surrounds Marengo; E – Lattermann's grenadier brigade entering Marengo from the north; F – Hadik's corps advancing on Lannes; G – Gottesheim's brigade pressing French right; H – Lobkowitz Dragoons; I – Schellenberg's division.

(French) 1 – Kellermann covering the retreat; 2 & 3 – Gardanne/Chambarlhac falling back; 4 – 40th Half-Brigade attempting to attack Marengo; 5 – Battalion of 43rd cut off in Marengo; 6 – Champeaux's cavalry brigade; 7 – Watrin (part) retreating; 8 – 28th Half-Brigade holding French right; 9 – Monnier's division arriving; 10 – Foot Guard arriving.

Thus by 2.00 pm, the French were finally driven away out of Marengo. Regrouping in line with Spinetta, the lines of Lannes and Victor were reduced by as much as three-quarters their original number, with just five guns remaining in service. Against them, the Austrians deployed a line of eighty guns, with Hadik's and Kaim's troops reforming their battered corps into two lines. However, the French were about to receive a new reinforcement. The final word on this passage of the battle must go to Victor, the architect of the brilliant six-hour defence of Marengo:

'For about a quarter of an hour these brave men had retired, and with what regret! Before an enemy whom they had so often put to flight, when, suddenly, a murmur of joy and hope rose from their ranks: the man of battles and victories appeared, Bonaparte! He was preceded by Monnier's division, who was already level with our right, and was followed by the Consular Guard which advanced rapidly on [Cascina] Li Poggi.'

Chapter 12

The March of the Consular Guard

The First Consul departed Torre Garofoli at 11.00 am, instructing Monnier's division and his guard to follow him and march on Marengo. There was a distance of 11km to march to reach the French position at Marengo, as it then stood. On arrival at San Giuliano, the advancing troops encountered the army's field hospitals (*ambulances*) gathered there. From this point the column encountered wounded soldiers retreating from the field, along with a crowd of sutlers and their mules and wagons. The number of wounded made it abundantly clear a hot action was taking place. Whatever was said by later writers, the reports and oral history of the battle make it quite apparent that these reserves did not come into play until after the French evacuated Marengo, which is to say, around 2.00 pm.

Of course, Bonaparte probably rode ahead, impatient to witness the scene for himself, and we know from Horse Grenadier Petit this is the case. With so many questions unresolved about Melas' intentions, and being the experienced general he was, Bonaparte would not have ridden headlong into the fray, but would have chosen a vantage point from where he could observe the full extent of the battle, and it is likely this was on the area of high ground which later became known as 'Regione Trono', the site of the 1805 re-enactment of the battle.[1] Having quit his headquarters at 11.00 am, it is unlikely the First Consul would have arrived before noon, and we are able to confirm this because he did not arrive until after Ott's troops had taken Castelceriolo and then fallen on the flank of Lannes. We know this from the memoirs of Petit, who described the battlefield as the newcomers first witnessed it:

'The enemy's line was extended to the space of two leagues ... The enemy was particularly tenacious of its position near the bridge; but the principal point of action was at San Stefano [*sic*]. From this point the enemy could gain Voghera before we could, and thereby cut off our retreat. They, therefore, incessantly directed their attention to this weak point. By twelve o'clock we were well convinced we had the whole Austrian force against us, and that they now, in good earnest, accepted the challenge which they had declined the day before.'

If one reads Castelceriolo for 'San Stefano' (there is no record of such a place), then the description of the Austrian army extending two leagues (8km) perfectly fits the situation shortly after noon. Also, and this is crucial for understanding what he did next, Bonaparte correctly identified the critical point of the battlefield was not Marengo, where Victor and Lannes still held, but Castelceriolo, because there was nothing there to prevent the Austrians advancing eastwards and cutting off the French army's line of retreat. From his vantage point overlooking the battlefield, the First Consul would have seen the great gap in the vines running from Castelceriolo diagonally towards Cascina Grossa. This was perfect ground for the Austrian cavalry and afforded no cover for the French infantry if it was forced to retreat. The Austrians had to be driven from Castelceriolo if there was any chance to hold Marengo, or to withdraw from the battle. Petit's account reveals the First Consul's next step:

'Our general was now satisfied of the measures he had to pursue. Orders were given to the disposable troops in the rear to come forward; but the corps under the command of Desaix was still at a considerable distance.'

This statement raises an intriguing possibility. It is generally supposed that Bonaparte issued the recall to Desaix from Torre Garofoli when he left for the battlefield himself at 11.00 am. Dupont says as much in his memoirs; but Petit's statement indicates Bonaparte only issued the recall after he saw the situation for himself.

We have previously established Desaix halted half an hour's march from Rivalta in the direction of Pozzolo Formigaro. We know he could not have left Rivalta before 10.00 am because the waters of the Scrivia had not allowed the passage of artillery until then. Once the division had halted (between 10.30–11.00 am), Savary was then sent on a mission to reconnoitre Novi, which he said took him two hours to complete. This takes us until at least 12.30 pm. On his way to find Bonaparte, Savary encountered the bearer of the recall message, an ADC of the commander-in-chief, Captain Jean-Pierre Bruyère, who was travelling cross-country in the opposite direction looking for Desaix.[2] The two aides told each other where to find their respective commanders and galloped off, Savary using the rising plume of battlefield smoke 'as a compass'. As the crow flies, it is just 4km from the First Consul's headquarters to Rivalta. If the recall had been sent from Torre Garofoli, it means it took Bruyère over two hours to cover this short distance. This is surely inconceivable. Based on other movements, it would have taken a little under forty minutes to convey this message.

If we instead follow Petit's timing, this means Bruyère would have left the Spinetta area shortly after noon. If Savary left Rivalta at 12.30 pm, and both men travelled cross-country, they would have encountered one another at approximately 12.50 pm. The probable arrival time at Rivalta would have been twenty minutes later. We may conclude, therefore, that Desaix did not receive the recall before 1.00 pm. The later time of the recall also perhaps explains why Lapoype's division did not receive the same recall until 6.00 pm. By the time the messenger arrived at Lapoype's last known location, the division would have been hours on the march already.

Most commentators from the period indicate a division marching under a hot sun with artillery would have done well to maintain a pace of 4km per hour. Using the probable route later described by Pittaluga, from their position outside Rivalta to San Giuliano is approximately 10km; it was then a further 8km to Marengo. Supposing it took time for the division to turn around and reform its order of march, Desaix would not have been able to reach San Giuliano until 4.00 pm – and Boudet confirms they did not march on the battlefield until after the arrival of the ADC:

> 'My division had not got more than one mile beyond Rivalta when one of the commander-in-chief's ADCs, sent by the Premier Consul, came in haste to bring me the order to march on San Giuliano and then Marengo, where the two hostile armies had been fighting since day break.'[3]

Once his division was on the march, Boudet did allow the detachment from the 3rd Cavalry to ride off ahead, but Desaix retained the 1st Hussars to serve as an advanced-guard.[4]

On the subject of the recall, there is one last item to note, and that is the content of the message. One can take the following story as one likes; it has been dismissed and quoted in equal measure. In his memoirs, the Marquis de Faverges says he conversed with a young Hungarian who had served in the Bregenz Hussars, but was serving in the French Army as an aide in 1800. This Hungarian told Faverges he saw Bonaparte's note with his own eyes after Desaix had read it. One might argue this was not the language used by one of the greatest military commanders in history; or one might see an authentic urgency in the choice of words. In any case, the phrase has entered the mythology of the battle, so it is perhaps fitting to repeat it at this point:

> 'I thought to attack, the enemy has forestalled me; return in the name of God, if you can.'

Having recalled Desaix and Lapoype to the battlefield, Bonaparte went forward to look at the dispositions made by Victor and Lannes. As discussed above, the

First Consul was immediately concerned with the right of the French line at Castelceriolo. As for Victor and Lannes' troops, it appears Bonaparte was content with what he found (this would have been about 1.00 pm). According to Dupont: 'Arriving on the ground, the First Consul travelled the lines; he changed nothing of the dispositions already ordered and the action continued with the chances still equal.'[5]

At 2.00 pm, we reach one of the most critical parts of the battle. We have noted Victor and Lannes began their retreat around this time, and fell back for fifteen minutes, approximately 1km to a new line level with Spinetta and the vineyards extending northwards from there. Before the retreat began, Bonaparte had already decided to direct Monnier's division towards Castelceriolo and to engage the troops commanded by Ott. Monnier's after-action report states:

'The division arrived yesterday on the field of battle, at two o'clock in the afternoon. It was directed on our right, where the enemy was advancing in force. The 19th, led by General Cara-Saint-Cyr, went to the right, advanced in a close column upon the village of Castelceriolo; while the 70th, commanded by General Schilt, who followed his movements to the left, threatened to take the centre of the enemy in the rear. The columns, numerous in infantry and cavalry, could not resist our impetuous shock; they retreated in the greatest disorder in the marshes in front of the Bormida, abandoning to us two pieces of artillery and three caissons.'

Following the Ventolina and Villanova roads, there is a distance of 7km from San Giuliano to Castelceriolo, a little under two hours' march. From his position behind Torre Garofoli, Monnier's 2.00 pm timing fits. To have achieved this, Bonaparte would have made the decision to deploy Monnier on the right well before he arrived on the field, something confirmed by Victor, who spoke of Monnier already being on the right at the time of the French retreat. One thing which should be noted is that Monnier was not with the force which marched on San Giuliano; for reasons known only unto him, Monnier actually remained behind the lines at San Giuliano with two battalions of the 72nd Half-Brigade. The 3rd Battalion of this half-brigade continued on the main road to Marengo, followed by the Consular Guard.

Before describing the action in more detail, there is one other crucial point to note. We have concluded Desaix received the recall a little after 1.00 pm, and by this same conclusion, Savary would have reached the First Consul by 2.00 pm. Whatever his merits as an aide-de-camp, Savary can be extremely frustrating as a source on the battle. Having described meeting Bruyère, Desaix's ADC then spends several pages describing the battle he did not witness and blaming another

ADC (Lauriston) for providing the First Consul with false intelligence on the status of the Austrian-held bridge on the Bormida. Eventually, Savary returns to his personal account. He appears to have told Bonaparte there were no Austrians at Novi, and the First Consul made it quite clear he was no longer interested in the comings and goings of that place. Of more interest was the news Desaix had made a halt.

'At what hour did you leave him?' the First Consul asked, looking at his pocket watch.

Savary told him the time, but in his memoirs Savary does not record this time; he just wrote 'at such an hour'. He had either forgotten or, more likely, the real time was inconvenient to his general account of the battle. In any case, knowing Bruyère would have reached Desaix, and Bouder's division would now be on the march, Bonaparte gave his verdict on the news. 'Well he cannot be far off; go and tell him to form in that direction (pointing with his hand to a particular spot): let him quit the main road, and make way for all those wounded men who would only embarrass him, and perhaps draw his own soldiers after him.'[6]

By halting his march at the sound of the Austrian cannonade, Desaix had proven what an able lieutenant he was. He knew the importance that Bonaparte had placed on the arrival of Hohenzollern from Genoa, but was equally aware that facts were changing from the lack of any evidence of Hohenzollern's arrival, and the growing sound of battle to the north-west. As a result of Desaix halting his march, although the situation at Marengo was difficult for the soldiers fighting in the front line, by 2.00 pm, Bonaparte knew he had 5,000 fresh troops with artillery marching towards him. If he could stabilise the right with Monnier, and prevent Ott from breaking out beyond the new line the army was holding at Spinetta, the situation was far from desperate. He had clearly made an error of judgement in the morning, but now he was determined to regain the initiative.

Having set out the tactical situation at 2.00 pm, we should return to the thick of the fighting. While Bonaparte had been quietly touring the rear and making his plans for deploying the reserves, Coignet was fighting for his life, but was thankful for the arrival of Bonaparte and his Guardsmen. The support was as much practical as moral. Coignet wrote:

'Suddenly six hundred men of the Consular Guard arrived with cartridges in their canvas smocks and on blankets attached to their shoulders. They passed behind the ranks and made the distribution. Then the fire redoubled. At that moment we had already fallen back a lot. We were in the middle of the plain. More willows, more ravines: a bush from place to place. We saw a great part of the army, and above all we saw the Consular

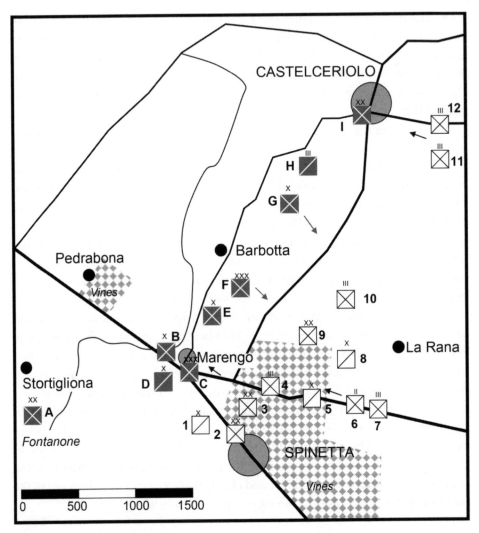

MAP 13: Tactical situation – 2.30 pm

(Austrians) A – O'Reilly; B – Weidenfeld's grenadier brigade; C – Kaim's infantry corps; D – Austrian cavalry regrouping; E – Lattermann's grenadier brigade; F – Hadik's corps; G – Gottesheim's brigade; H – Lobkowitz Dragoons; I – Schellenberg's division.

(French) 1 – Kellermann's brigade; 2 & 3 – Gardanne/Chambarlhac; 4 – 40th Half-Brigade; 5 – Bonaparte with Guard cavalry; 6 – battalion of 72nd Half-Brigade; 7 – Foot Guard arriving; 8 – Champeaux's cavalry brigade; 9 – Watrin (part); 10 – 28th Half-Brigade holding French right; 11 – 70th Line (Schilt); 12 – 19th Light (Carra-St-Cyr).

Guard. Bonaparte soon appeared. His presence was a pledge of security, a motive of confidence, an occasion of unheard-of enthusiasm.'

It was said by a later adversary that Napoleon's presence at a battle was equal to a reinforcement of 40,000 men.[7] We can easily picture the First Consul on his charger. On the day of the battle, Bonaparte was in his thirty-first year; he was still thin, not the paunchy man of later years. As befitted his rank (he was still addressed as General Bonaparte in 1800), he wore a general of division's *habit*; dark 'national blue' and double-breasted, with a red collar and beautiful gold oak leaf embroidery. This jacket was mostly covered by a simple, light grey riding coat – this neutral colour making the First Consul stand out among his suite of lavishly dressed aides and generals. Above all, what made him stand out was his black felt bicorn.[8] This was Bonaparte's trademark look – the grey coat, the bicorn – very simple clothes which associated him with the uniforms worn by ordinary soldiers.

Bonaparte and Berthier toured the lines, allowing the soldiers to see them, reassuring them that help was on its way. Despite this, the pressure on the French line was too great to prevent it from falling back towards Spinetta. As the Austrians advanced beyond Marengo, they simply deployed their artillery and pounded the retreating French formations. Many accounts mention the soldiers were alarmed at how exposed Bonaparte was to incoming enemy fire as he toured the line. There were shouts of: 'Let us save the republic! Let us save its first magistrate!'

Horse Grenadier Petit observed this first movement of retreat from near to the First Consul:

'The left wing under the command of Victor began to give way; and we perceived several corps of infantry retire in disorder, as well as platoons of cavalry pushed back. The firing drew nearer; in the centre a dreadful discharge was heard, and ceased all at once on the Bormida. I was in an inexpressible anxiety, yet still I ventured to flatter myself that our troops advanced; on the contrary, however, I saw them in a few minutes after returning but with too much haste, carrying the wounded on their shoulders. On the part of the right wing also, I saw, with concern, the enemy gained insensibly upon us.

'Bonaparte advanced in front, and exhorted to courage and firmness all the corps he met with: it was visible that his presence re-animated them. Several soldiers were observed to prefer absolute death in sustaining the retreat, to the displeasure they might give him in being a witness of their flight. From this moment his horse guards no longer continued as before, near his person; but, without being at any great distance from him, took an active part in the battle.'[9]

Another member of the Consular Guard present at the battle was Trumpet-Major Elie Krettly. Still aged 24, Krettly had joined the army as a musician in the French Guards in 1789. As a trumpeter in the cavalry, he had fought the Mamelukes at Mont Tabor in 1799, an action in which he was twice shot, and stabbed by a lance while saving an officer. Returning to France with Bonaparte, and now as a member of the horse chasseurs, he found himself part of the First Consul's escort during the battle. His memoirs talk about an action involving the de Bussy Light Horse, the imperial regiment containing French *émigrés* and part of the Austrian main column's advanced guard under Frimont. Krettly appears to be referring to the cavalry charge which cut off Marengo and caused the remainder of Rivaud's troops there to be captured:

'On this great day, I found myself on picket duty beside General Bonaparte; he sent me with one of his aides-de-camp to reconnoitre the rout caused on the left by the de Bussy Dragoons; I went forward near enough this corps; an officer presented himself to me and disputed my passage; I accepted the combat, which was not very long; within a second I had killed him and seized his horse, then I continued on my way.

'I had almost reached the 8th Dragoons, when a shell burst ten paces from us; the first consul's aide-de-camp and I were covered with a muddy earth which blinded us. After we were put back a bit by this accident, we finally reached the 8th Dragoons and we gave the commander-in-chief's orders to the colonel of this corps, and right away, the colonel put the troops into motion and stopped the rout; my mission being fortunately enough finished, I returned to the headquarters to give an account to the first consul of what had occurred.'[10]

Precious little is written on this part of the battle from the Austrian perspective. It appears the hour leading up to 3.00 pm was again something of a lull. Neipperg's account contains the most information on the fall of Marengo and the period which follows. He indicates Melas was instrumental in the final collapse of French resistance:

'As the taking of the village decided the gain of the battle, the commander-in-chief took forward two brigades of grenadiers which supported the infantry so well that by means of the artillery we succeeded in cleaning out the village, and we became masters of the outlet: we had already taken prisoner from the enemy approximately 2,000 men and ten cannons.'

French accounts of a cavalry charge capturing Rivaud's men is confirmed by the account of Dannican. He writes:

'During this time a squadron of the Kaiser Dragoons did prodigies of valour at Marengo. Captain Toussaint, who commanded it, took a whole battalion prisoner, and this action produced so great a terror to the French that a part of their centre fled to the Scrivia.'

Elsewhere, he qualifies this statement with the following:

'The French retreated methodically at first disputing the ground step by step. They stubbornly defended the village of Spinetta, which they abandoned only at the last extremity.'

With the fall of Marengo, a Piedmontese soldier, Count Vincenzo-Amedeo Ferrero-Ponziglione, decided to write to his friend in Turin, the Marquis de San Marezano. Although perhaps a little premature, he could not contain his excitement:

'Everything is turning out for the best. The centre of the enemy is in full flight. The centre and the right have also been broken. Please pass this good news to LL. EE. MM. Baron de la Tour and Chevalier de la Flechère. Tell your mother to say her prayers. Adieu. Long live our king and the emperor – Spinetta, 14 June 1800 at two thirty.'

Once resistance ceased in Marengo, it was as if Melas' army was completely exhausted. Neipperg confirmed victory at Marengo came at 2.00 pm, and he watched the French falling back on Spinetta, following the Tortona road. The French, it appeared, had little more than a line of skirmishers and some cavalry to protect the retreating columns. The retreat was, he admitted, slow, and this was because of the lack of any meaningful pursuit. The Austrian bands struck up a 'grave and pathetic' rendition of the *Grenadiermarsch* as a sign of victory. The troops began to reform their battle lines on the ground outside Marengo, which Neipperg described as a heath. It was as if all sense of urgency had been lost. The critical thing for Neipperg was the lack of a coordinated cavalry attack on the retreating French. In Napoleonic warfare, this was the moment one launched squadron after squadron of light cavalry after the retreating enemy, turning withdrawal into rout; but the cavalry had already been consumed, 'scattered, and detached on both sides, by squadrons, half squadrons, platoons, etc'. Pilatti's brigade of dragoons was 'already lost' because of the fighting over the Marengo ditch. Other than artillery fire, the only pursuit Neipperg could pinpoint was from 'a swarm of skirmishers and infantry volunteers' sent after the French rearguard. While there were specialist light troops in Austrian service, the line infantry volunteers would have been less skilled in this style of fighting. They had routinely been discouraged from skirmishing throughout the campaign, and now was perhaps a hazardous moment to adopt the tactic.

As for the arrival of Monnier's troops in Castelceriolo, Stutterheim admits they took possession of a few buildings and some of the gardens. In Captain Karl von Mras' account of Marengo, he states that Ott had troops in reserve behind the town and sent the Stuart Regiment and some artillery to clear the Frenchmen out. It is unclear exactly when this occurred (according to Soult, whose aides were watching the battle from Alessandria, the fighting at Castelceriolo did not begin until 4.00 pm). Zach was completely dismissive of the operation, telling Faverges that 'victory belonged to us; the enemy did not hold more than to Castelceriolo, and even this was by the matter of luck. A chief of battalion cut off from his regiment, forgotten, lost, defended there in desperation, and so gave those around him the time to find themselves.' The regimental history of the 70th Line states that they remained in Castelceriolo for one hour, during which time they were surrounded and escaped to the safety of a belt of vines to avoid being captured by the Austrian cavalry.[11] Later claims that the French barricaded themselves into the town and held on throughout are entirely groundless. For confirmation of this, we need only read an excerpt from a letter from Carra-Saint-Cyr to the Minister of War on 21 October 1800:

'I took the village of Ceriolo, in the face of the enemy's army, at the very moment when the army was in retreat; I operated mine, supported only by the 70th line; it has not been mentioned in the various reports, but my conduct has nevertheless been known to the whole army. On the left of Castelceriolo, General Schilt, head of the 70th, from the same Monnier division, had cleared our right by a brilliant combat, but he also had to follow the retreating movement of the whole army. The Monnier division then retired to San Giuliano, where the army rallied.'[12]

Quite what happened to these troops, where they went and where they ended up is a subject we will return to.

At Spinetta, Bonaparte would have had very little idea what was taking place at Castelceriolo. He asked Dupont to find out what was going on there, and the army chief-of-staff investigated and concluded Monnier was holding out with 'skilful vigour' at this place. From what he could see, the capture of the place had put a halt to the Austrian advance in that area and compensated somewhat for the loss of Marengo. With Victor and Lannes having restored order to their battalions and taken position level with Spinetta, there was just one real weak point in the French line. There is a distance of 3km between Castelceriolo and the main French position at Spinetta. There was a substantial gap between Lannes and the troops in Castelceriolo, and this could be exploited by the Austrians, particularly their cavalry. In order to plug this gap in his line, in terms of uncommitted infantry to hand, Bonaparte had a battalion of the 72nd Line (probably about 400 strong) and his Foot Guard, nominally 800 strong. With the time approaching 3.00 pm, and Desaix still an hour or more away, Bonaparte decided to throw his guardsmen into the hole and buy the army some more time.[13]

The march of the Guard at Marengo is one of the most iconic moments of the Napoleonic Wars – immortalized in a musical march still in the repertoire of French military bands. It is also one of the least understood and controversial actions of the battle, certainly since the Austrian claims have become wider-known among French and English-speaking audiences. To understand what happened, we should begin with a review of the Foot Guards. Under the French empire, the Imperial Guard would become an enormous force – a veritable army of praetorians. It is so much a part of the Napoleonic legend that a painting of its bearskins marching behind l'Empereur is still enough to make grown men weep in admiration. However, at the time of Marengo, this force was modest in size, not even the equivalent in size of a regular infantry battalion.

At the time of Marengo, the Foot Guard was organized into two battalions of grenadiers and a company of light infantry chasseurs ('huntsmen' – like the German jäger). It also appears to have had a number of pioneer troops, or sapeurs.[14] However, not all of the Foot Guards were sent on this campaign, and a portion of it remained in Paris carrying out guard duties. The Guard was sent from Paris in several detachments, of different sizes, and to cloud matters still further, we are told it was 800 men strong at the time of the battle, and that all its men were committed to action; but the oral histories speak only of 500 or 600 men (the original 600 reported by Coignet became 800 only when the memoirs were later 'enhanced' by a ghost writer). Unfortunately, the regimental rolls do not help us identify their strength in the battle either. Of the 1,290 men recorded in the regimental rolls in 1800, only 151 grenadiers were recorded as being present at Marengo – the records were not accurately maintained.

They were excellent soldiers. The French guardsmen were tall for the period, very lean and fierce-looking. They wore their hair powdered, unlike much of the rest of the army, and sported moustaches. The registers of the consular period Foot Guard have survived, and so it is possible to identify the type of men who formed this unit. However, the register does not appear to have been completed in terms of what happened to all the men, many of whom are simply recorded as having been struck from the registers. The average height of the grenadiers we know served at Marengo was 1.779m (5ft 10in), a good height for the period. The shortest was the 22-year-old drummer, Couboue, at 1.678m (5ft 6in), while the tallest was Grenadier Jacques Gelmont, a veritable giant for the period at 1.989m (6ft 3in). In fact, of a sample of 102 men we know fought at Marengo, forty-one of them were 'six-footers'. With their tall bearskin caps and red feather plumes, these men would have towered over the average Frenchman of the era. All were veterans, mostly from the wars of the First Coalition (1792-1797). There were also a few old soldiers in the ranks. Sergeant Pioline was born in 1749, and Jacques Géard had fought in Minorca in 1781-1782 as a soldier in the old Lyonnais Regiment. There were even some veterans from the pre-revolutionary French Guards (Gardes Françaises) at Marengo. Antoine Carrieu joined the Guards in 1783, Grenadier Vargnier in 1785 and Jean Huguin Basset in 1786. From the point of view of social history, it is remarkable that we find the same soldiers who witnessed the storming of the Bastille also present at Marengo.[15]

The chasseurs were an altogether different prospect, and our knowledge of them is more complete. These light infantrymen were formed from the 'foot guides' who had returned from Egypt with Bonaparte the previous year (in the revolutionary wars, the commanders-in-chief of each army were allowed to keep a bodyguard which were termed 'guides'). Most of them were veterans of Bonaparte's first campaign in Italy, as well as the Egyptian expedition. They had fought in the desert, beneath the walls of Acre, and protected him during revolts. They were truly battle-hardened men. Compared to the immaculate Paris guardsmen, the chasseurs must have appeared something of a *banditti* when incorporated into the Guard after *Brumaire*. According to their regimental rolls, at least 103 of the chasseurs were present at Marengo, perhaps as many as 125 (not including officers). The eldest was 37 years old and the youngest 18. Where we have data, we find ten aged 21 years or younger; nineteen of them were 30 or older; the remainder were in their twenties, the average age of a chasseur being 26. In stature, their heights ranged from 1.62m (5ft 3in) to 1.82m (5ft 11in), the average being 1.69m (5ft 6½in). Thus, we can imagine a typical chasseur at Marengo as 26 years old, standing at 1.69m.[16]

Interestingly there is no mention of chasseurs or 'foot guides' in any of the movement orders associated with the Consular Guard marching from Paris, only of grenadiers. The two units appear to be classified as the same unit. The first detachment was 300 men which set out on 11 April; a second detachment under the orders of Chief of Brigade Jean-Baptiste Bessières left Paris with 400 men on 29 April; a final detachment of 100 men set out in May. It is only on 21 May that we see references to 800 grenadiers being attached to the army. As we know, anything up to 130 of these were actually light infantry, and the figure would have included various supernumeraries, musicians and gunners. Despite later protestations the whole guard was deployed at Marengo, it is likely some of the men would have been left as sentries to guard the headquarters. We simply do not know the exact number present on the field, but we must entertain the possibility it was lower than the 800 officially reported. Nor do we know the organisation of the unit, if it formed one single battalion or two smaller ones. A case can be made for both situations. There is strong evidence that the Foot Guard actively engaged was commanded in the battle by Chief of Battalion Jérome Soulès.[17] His biography in the *Fastes de la legion d'honneur*[18] states how in his fortieth year, this veteran of the Royal Army was appointed to the Foot Grenadiers of the Guard on 3 January 1800. At Marengo, he is said to have commanded 500 grenadiers and chasseurs of the Guard, and was ordered by Bonaparte to carry them to the right of the army.

On the day of the battle, we know the Foot Guards arrived behind Victor's troops at about 2.00 pm, if not shortly before. Coignet clearly reports them handing out cartridges to the troops engaged in the morning, so this places the Guard on the main road (probably the 'old road'), level with Spinetta. Coignet then describes how the First Consul marched the Guard away:

'He placed his Guard in line at the centre of the army and made it march forward. Sometimes it formed into a square, sometimes it deployed itself in line, and immediately stopped the enemy.'

Petit also witnessed the Foot Guard being sent forward into action:

'The Foot Grenadiers of the Consular Guard now came up, in the same state they have always been beheld on the parade. They formed up in the most orderly manner, in subdivisions, and advanced against the enemy, which they met with not a hundred paces from our front. Without artillery, without cavalry, to the number of five hundred only, they had to endure the brunt of a victorious army. But, without considering the smallness of their numbers, they kept advancing, and forced everything to give way in their passage. The lofty eagle hovered everywhere around them, and threatened to tear them to pieces. The very first bullet which struck them laid three grenadiers and a quartermaster corporal (fourrier) dead on the ground, being in close order.'

One will notice that Petit called them 500 men only; however, Petit was mistaken when he said they had no artillery. It appears they had with them four small 'battalion guns'.[19]

With the Guard moving away from the centre, we must look for witnesses on the right of the French line who saw this movement. A crucial piece of evidence, not previously found in other accounts of the battle, was a letter by the commander of the 28th Line, Roger-Valhubert, written to Dupont on 23 March 1804:

'At one o'clock the 28th drew closer to the plain, but still holding the right of the army. The grenadiers of the Guard of the Consuls came to occupy it for only a moment, and having scattered a column of cavalry which very quickly came to charge them, they received the order to carry themselves to another point.'

The first sentence of this account refers to the first movements of retreat during the action to defend Marengo. Unfortunately, he does not tell us when the Guard arrived alongside his troops, but simple arithmetic places this closer to 3.00 pm (it would have taken twenty minutes to march up level with Barbotta, but first the guardsmen had to hand out cartridges, then regroup before marching off). Nor does Valhubert report seeing the Guard again, something which will become crucially important. As far as Valhubert was concerned, he remained the right flank of the army.

As Valhubert indicates, the Foot Guard's first action was against Austrian cavalry. This is a point no one contests. To understand more, we must now look to the Austrian sources, particularly Stutterheim, who was a staff officer attached to Ott's column. This first description of what occurred appears to have been almost entirely a repeat of the 1804 account given by Geppert, and therefore pre-dates Berthier's 1805 official French account of the battle:

'Shortly before this crucial moment the Guard infantry came marching on the Sale road to the centre. With these chosen men Bonaparte hoped if not to restore the battle to stop us for a while and to afford protection to his other troops that were already on the verge of flight. In a column of open sections the Guard marched across open field and had individual skirmishers accompanying their march at a distance of some 60 paces. There could not have been a more desirable sight for our cavalry. Ott, whom the Guard passed with four cannon, ordered the Lobkowitz Regiment to blow the rappel and to attack as soon as all were assembled. Only here there were circumstances – above all Colonel Fürst Taxis could not be found – as such Ott ordered Lieutenant-Colonel Graf Harrach to lead the charge against the Consular Guard; after time-consuming preparations they set off at a walk, then into trot, finally into the gallop. The Consular Guard infantry seemed to be close to disaster when at a few musket shots from its skirmishers the whole regiment turned about and ran away. Some French cavalry that had been observing this from a position behind the Guard pursued our dragoons. The situation for Ott's infantry seemed desperate as in midst of the coverless plains she had been deserted by her only cavalry.'

In Stutterheim's second account, he is more specific about the Guard's intentions. As described above, the Guard were following the route of the Sale road, which is easy to trace as it still exists today. It is the road from Spinetta which leads into the centre of Castelceriolo. His second account describes how the Foot Guard were spotted by Ott's jäger who were skirmishing against Lannes' flank. The Guard, the account states, were hidden by tall crops, but their tall red plumes gave away the location of the column. As described above, there was an element of confusion and a delay trying to form up the Lobkowitz Dragoons, but they did eventually charge. At this point, the Foot Guard's column of march was screened by the light infantry chasseurs, a standard precaution. Having spent a great deal of time in the Egyptian campaign fighting Ottoman light horse, the Lobkowitz charge does not appear to have alarmed the chasseurs. According to the Austrian accounts, they were supported by four battalion guns which the Guard had with them. This well-aimed, withering fire on the approaching horsemen broke the momentum of the charge. Meanwhile, the grenadiers, it appears, either formed square behind them, or closed up their column of march. Berthier reported this encounter in his first report (written that evening), although he incorrectly identified the regiment concerned:

'A squadron of the Latour Dragoons was entirely destroyed by the fire of the grenadiers of the Guard of the Consuls.'

There is no point of dispute on this account from either side. The cavalry which chased off the Lobkowitz Dragoons would have been Champeaux's brigade, as this was operating in the area, and had screened the advance of Monnier's men into nearby Castelceriolo. With the Lobkowitz Dragoons departed, the Guard continued its march towards Castelceriolo.

Where the accounts become confused is what happened next. The 1805 official report into the battle describes the Guard as being 'isolated at more than six hundred yards from the right of our line' and 'they appear as a block of granite in the middle of an immense plain'.[20] Petit concludes the Guard action thus:

'Charged three times by the cavalry, fusilladed by the infantry within fifty paces, they surrounded their colours, and their wounded, and, in a hollow square, exhausted all their rounds of cartridges; and then, with slow and regular steps, fell back and joined our astonished rearguard.'

Heroic stuff; the question is, which rearguard? Not the 28th Line; there is no mention in Valhubert's account of the Foot Guard coming back and rejoining him, and he continued to hold this position for the remainder of the battle quite isolated. In fact, there is scant evidence of the Foot Guard doing anything for the next three hours or so. Victor's memoir is a little fuller in what apparently occurred:

'A few hundred men, however, pretend to make an obstacle: it is the battalion of the Grenadiers of the Consular Guard, all veterans proved in a hundred battles; it is there, in open country, between Li Poggi and Villanova, formed in square, motionless. The enemy beat him at first with his volleys of cannonballs, canister and shells; it does not move. Ott throws his cavalry against him, it does not move, and this cavalry flees and disperses before his discharges and bayonets; General Gottesheim arrived with the infantry regiment of Splényi; our grenadiers are deployed on the centre and welcome these new assailants with the most murderous fire; but at this moment they are charged in the rear by the hussars of Frimont, who at last shakes them, and the enemy continues his march forward without any resistance.'[21]

Clearly we require evidence from the Austrian accounts as to what occurred. Perhaps the most partisan account is the regimental history of the Splényi Regiment. We have encountered this regiment before, driving away Gardanne's attack on the bridgehead the night before the battle. They clearly had a reputation, and despite their reduced number (probably about 650 strong after their losses on 13 June), they took on the challenge of fighting the grenadiers with a degree of relish. This excerpt from the regimental history begins after the Lobkowitz Dragoons have been driven off:

'There moves GM Gottesheim with the Splényi Regiment, in line and with music playing, under cheering hurrahs at the enemy cavalry supporting the Guard, in the middle of the plain. This falls back after the first discharge. Now the Regiment Splényi, supported by a battalion of Frölich [IR 28], turns against the "Consular Guard", which had also deployed into line, and received the attack with a lively fire. Neither side would yield, and the battle remained undecided; at this critical moment, Colonel Fronius [sic – read Frimont], with four hussar squadrons from the main column, bursts into the back of the Guard, and their fate is now sealed. A terrible massacre ensues, in which only a small part of the Guard escaped with their lives. These too are captured, the total artillery is conquered. The splendid "Consular Guard", the pride of Bonaparte, the elite troops of France were destroyed; destroyed by the feared "Legion infernale", the heroic regiment of Splényi, who were supported by a few sections of Hungarian cavalry and Bohemian infantry.'

Crossard's account of the battle concurs that the Guard, 'which Bonaparte had estimated as his most formidable reserve, had been almost fully destroyed or made prisoner'. Crossard was a staff officer attached to Ott's command, it must be remembered. Even considering the jingoistic nature of regimental histories, and the certain bias of a noble émigré, it is difficult to imagine these statements being published without there being some substance behind them.

We find the most definitive explanation of events in Stutterheim's two accounts, the first of which followed Geppert's 1804 account (to which Stutterheim probably contributed), and the second of which followed the publication of Mras' account of the battle. According to Stutterheim, when the Lobkowitz Dragoons broke, a battalion of Splényi broke from the column 'on its own impulse' and advanced on Champeaux's cavalry with bayonets lowered. This battalion fired at the French horsemen, which scattered and cleared off. GM Gottesheim was then instructed (presumably by Ott), to attack the Consular Guard with the Splényi Regiment, and a battalion of IR 28 Fröhlich. The two adversaries engaged in a fusillade with platoon-fire and volleys as if on an exercise ground. Gottesheim was wounded, but the musketry continued with no sign of either adversary backing down. Ott was unable to deploy more troops to assist, because he also had to deal with Carra-Saint-Cyr and Schilt who were bottled up in Castelceriolo. By now it was 4.00 pm. Our timekeeper in Alessandria, the wounded General Soult, stated his companions saw the action begin with the Guard (it is more likely they saw puffs of smoke at a distance of 6km rather than specific formations), followed swiftly by firing at Castelceriolo, which was the counter-attack led by Vogelsang with the Stuart Infantry Regiment.

According to Stutterheim, as Ott was engaged with Monnier's troops and the Guard, the main column was engaged in crossing the Fontanone at Marengo, and the infantry was followed by the cavalry. Among these horsemen was Frimont, the commander of the main column's advanced guard. While most of the Austrians were engaged in deploying opposite the French at Spinetta, Frimont headed northwards on exiting the village and travelled to the left (he had done the same thing earlier that morning when clearing Hadik's line deployed outside the bridgehead). With some squadrons of the Bussy Light Horse and the Nauendorf Hussars, Frimont saw the Guard deployed in line fighting against Gottesheim, and so charged into the rear. This ended the action, with the Guard's four guns being seized and, in the words of Stutterheim, 'only a very few escaped with their lives'. Stutterheim was vociferous in his defence of this account: 'The Frenchmen hid this circumstance up to now in their reports completely.' He even laid down a challenge: 'The author witnessed this whole incident and requests all who have been present with the Consular Guard at Marengo if they could dispute this account.'[22]

From the pages of history, there certainly is a challenger to this. Read Soulès' biographical account in the *fastes de la légion d'honneur*, bearing in mind he was awarded a coveted 'sabre of honour' for his conduct in the affair, and later entered the Senate and became a respected French peer:

'For five hours consecutively, he [Soulès] held this position, despite the reiterated efforts of a column of 8,000 Austrians which looked to flush them out, and he did not retire until he received a formal order from the commander-in-chief, who sent him to protect the retrograde movement of the army with around 200 men who remained with him.'[23]

We thus find ourselves at this point, like Coignet sheltering under his tree, caught between two fires. On the French side we have the Guard, immobile, like a rock of granite in the centre of the plain, albeit surrounding its colours, and making a fighting withdrawal in the direction of the French rearguard. We then have the Austrian accounts, which describe a bloody massacre. On the balance of probability, something calamitous clearly occurred. There is some evidence for all this in Petit's striking description of how the 'soldiers of the legion of Bussy had collected the caps of the grenadiers killed or wounded, and exhibited them to us, by twirling them round on their sabres'. Petit also complained about the treatment of French prisoners, how they had the earrings torn from their ears, and gave an account of the treatment one foot chasseur received:

'A chasseur on foot belonging to the Consular Guard, full of wounds, lay almost dead in the field of battle, at the moment of our retreat. Some soldiers of Bussy's legion surrounded him, and disputed among themselves for his spoils. Nothing was already disposed of but his coat, which they had already stripped him of, when an Austrian colonel by chance came up, and driving away these inhuman fellows with his cane, asked the soldier, whom he at first took for an officer, to what corps he belonged?—I belong to the Guard of the consul whom you see before you, replied the chasseur. The colonel, after paying a compliment to that body of men had his surgeon called, and the wounded prisoner was dressed in his presence, and carried to the ambulance.'

All these things indicate the Austrians gained an ascendancy in the fight and were clearly jubilant about their success. However, the French casualty returns do not support the description of butchery implied by the oral accounts. There is no surviving battlefield report from the Foot Guards. Murat adds a footnote to his report, written two days after the battle on 16 June. He admits the Foot Guard lost 121 killed or wounded. There is no report of any prisoners, which is unsurprising because Petit tells us there was a prisoner exchange that same day and all those taken by the Austrians were returned. Later in Petit's account he downplays the number of French captives and states only twenty-five guardsmen were taken captive in the battle. At the same time, he doubles the number of casualties suffered by the Foot Guard:

'The loss of the Consular Guard was considerable only in infantry. In five hundred men, there were two hundred and fifty-eight killed or put *hors de combat*.'

We also have the admission in Soulès' account that only 200 men remained when he withdrew, so what conclusions can we reach?

Stutterheim's description of a massacre appears to be based on something he was told soon after the battle by some officers of the Consular Guard he met in Milan. These told him barely 100 guardsmen had escaped being killed or captured. Stutterheim took this statement at face value; but in the way soldiers might sometimes exaggerate their successes, so too they are prone to exaggerating the dangers they faced. Had the French officers told Stutterheim the truth, or was this a flippant exaggeration?

The important fact is that after Frimont's charge, French resistance in that part of the field was broken, albeit having fulfilled its mission of preventing Ott's troops from breaking out beyond Castelceriolo and cutting of Victor and Lannes' line of retreat. Those guardsmen not tumbled over by enemy horsemen, or seized by belligerent Hungarian infantrymen, clumped around their colours and made their escape, probably numbering around 200, as Soulès' biographical entry suggests. At the same time, Monnier's troops evacuated Castelceriolo, and did so by making a break for the vines in order to protect them against enemy cavalry. Did the Consular Guard do the same? Valhubert did not see the grenadiers return in his direction, so this is perhaps the most likely conclusion.

But what of the granite redoubt in the middle of the plain, resisting everything that was thrown at it? This is so much a part of the mythology of the battle that we must explain the phenomenon. There is usually an element of truth in these accounts, so what did the Frenchmen actually see? Let us not forget Valhubert and the valiant 28th Line.[24] What happened to them after the Guard departed from their side? Valhubert tells us:

> 'After [the Guard's] departure, the 28th, being isolated, formed in battalion square, dragged some abandoned artillery, and had the fortune of resisting the cavalry charges which the enemy repeated on three of his fronts throughout the evening.'[25]

In his after-action report, Lannes singled out the 28th Line for particular praise, writing:

> 'Citizen General, the bravery of the troops at my command was so much sustained during the battle, it is impossible for me to single out any particular corps, all having fought with invincible courage. Nevertheless, I must tell you that the 28th showed the most uncommon sangfroid in all the various movements in the presence of the enemy's cavalry.'

Is this the enduring image the soldiers on the main road remembered seeing out on the far right flank – the blue-coated square, surrounding its colours, gathering in its wounded and attempting to preserve its guns from capture amid repeated cavalry charges? These men were as heroic as any on the battlefield that day, so perhaps the honour should now be fully shared.

Chapter 13

This New Thermopylae

While the action on the French right has dominated our account, we should now return to Spinetta and the struggle to hold back the Austrians in that sector. Whatever the exact circumstances of their demise, the march of the Consular Guard and the arrival of Monnier's division in Castelceriolo had served their intended purpose. As Coignet writes: 'Their efforts gave us respite for an hour.' An hour in which Desaix moved ever closer to the battlefield. It is generally supposed the French continued to retreat across the plain once they quit Marengo, all the way back to San Giuliano 7km away. This does the French a great disservice, and in fact there was much heroic fighting and desperate acts of bravery, all intended to slow the Austrian Advance. Referring to this phase of the battle, Horse Grenadier Petit called the French defence: 'this new Thermopylae'.

At the time the Guard began its march towards the right of the French line, there was a succession of uncoordinated cavalry attacks against the French. These appear to have been launched by smaller groups of cavalry and do not appear to have been massed in any way. Petit has this anecdote:

'A cloud of Austrian cavalry debouched rapidly in the plain and formed themselves before us in battle array, masking several pieces of artillery, which did not long delay playing to the destruction of our ranks. General Berthier, who, at no great distance, had his eye upon the movement of this column, was briskly charged by a part of it, and was forced to retire upon us. Murat, at the head of the dragoons, took them in flank, protected the retreat of our infantry, and preserved the right flank of Victor.'

Coignet also appears to have become involved with this action:

'The handsome grenadiers on horseback rushed at a gallop and overthrew the Austrian cavalry. But being unable to stand against the Consular Guard, the Austrian dragoons fell upon us. They broke down our first platoons and sabred us. I received a blow on the back of my head so hard that my tail was cut by half ... The blow only touched the flesh, after cutting off the coat and opening one of my epaulettes. I fell backwards in a ditch. Kellermann came running. Three times he charged at the head of his dragoons. He led them and brought them back; and all this cavalry passed over me, who was stunned in my ditch. When I recovered my senses, I got rid of my pack, my cartridge pouch and my sabre, and seized the tail of the horse of a French dragoon who was retreating. This horse carried me away. To follow him I made enormous strides, and soon I fell flat out, unable to breathe. But thank God, I was in the middle of the French lines. I easily found a gun, a pack and a cartridge pouch, the ground was covered with them; and I resumed my rank in the second company of grenadiers of my battalion.'

At the beginning of the action involving the Foot Guards, Krettly of the Guard Horse Chasseurs was in action. As part of the First Consul's escort, he watched as the Foot Guard climbed down into a ditch running along the side of the road. The Austrians saw them and fired two cannon shots in the Guard's direction. A bullet from this salvo cut Krettly's plume in half. Seeing the trumpeter unwounded, Bonaparte called out to him:

'Ah good! You have nothing?'

'Nothing, my general, but a rage in my heart and a smaller plume; but if you would allow it of me, I will take their guns.'

Bonaparte narrowed his eyebrows into a frown and stared at Krettly: 'Always the same! No, I don't want that, it is much too reckless.'

'Reckless, my general, it is, but give me only half of the picket [approximately twenty men] and the guns are ours.'

The First Consul refused him again, but Krettly pressed him. In the end, Bonaparte consented.

'Comrades,' Krettly cried, 'a little audacity! Charge in foraging order.'[1]

The score of cavalry men raced off and cut down the Austrian gunners, after which they returned to protect the First Consul. Bonaparte congratulated Krettly and put him down for an honour.

Krettly witnessed another cavalry action, this time led by Bonaparte's stepson, Eugène Beauharnais. In the same way every Austrian infantryman in a French memoir was a 'Hungarian grenadier', it appears the Bussy Light Horse accounted for every sighting of Austrian cavalry:

'I had returned to my post; Prince Eugène who commanded the horse chasseurs of the consuls, seeing come at him the corps of the Austrian de Bussy Dragoons numbering around two thousand men, commanded a charge on them; a large ditch separated us from our adversaries, we had soon crossed it and the charge was so rapid that we cut into the head of this corps in the blink of an eye; in the middle of the mêlée, the general who commanded it was removed from his horse and found himself grabbed round the neck by the brave Daumesnil, who vigorously seized him and held him so tightly that it was impossible for him to move; he conducted him in this manner to headquarters. The dragoons had made a half-turn and in the pursuit that we made of them, they received vigorous sabre cuts on their backs, which made the prisoner general addressing Prince Eugène say: "Your chasseurs have strong wrists, for my dragoons all have their backs slit open."

"General," the brave Daumesnil replied pleasantly, "it is because we took them for Paris mackerels [pimps]."[2]

More than anything else, the artillery fire was causing the French terrible problems. With every moment, the Austrians advanced more guns across the Fontanone and brought them to bear on the French. Kellermann's horsemen were suffering such terrible casualties from this artillery that he asked for volunteers to ride out and kill the gunners of the nearest pieces. Corporal Lecomte of the 8th Dragoons and six of his men rode out and charged down one of the nearest pieces, which was protected by a detachment of twenty grenadiers. Lecompte wounded the officer in charge and took him prisoner; the grenadiers were driven off and the gun taken.[3]

On the French side, artillery was very much in short supply. In the regimental history of the 1st Artillery Regiment we find two stories of heroes trying to rescue the guns during the retreat. The first was First Gunner Juillet, who attempted to fight off a group of horsemen armed only with his trail spike. He was eventually overpowered, but then escaped, joining a group of light infantry carabiniers, with whom he remained the rest of the day. Gunner Jean Renaud had already come to the attention of the First Consul on the campaign during the siege of Fort Bard, aiming a gun which had been raised up into the clock tower of the church at Bard. At Marengo, Renaud found himself manning a gun threatened by a group of Austrian horsemen. Unsupported by infantry, Renaud's colleagues ran off, but the intrepid gunner refused to quit his piece. Instead he lay on the floor close to the barrel and when the Austrian horsemen were no more than twenty paces away, he leapt up and fired a round of canister into the startled riders. The firing of the artillery piece was noticed by the First Consul, who despatched an aide to find out what had occurred. Renaud was recognized from his action at Fort Bard, so Bonaparte sent the gunner instructions to fire on a battery of guns which was firing at his guardsmen. The First Consul ensured Renaud was the first recipient of a 'grenade of honour', writing the citation in his own hand.[4]

Eventually the pressure began to tell, and the French started to retreat further eastwards, onto the higher ground behind Spinetta – the same ground Duvignau's cavalry brigade had to cut its way through the day before. Petit gives a vivid description:

'The consul who was all the while in the centre, encouraged the remains of the gallant corps which defended the road, and the defile which it crossed, shut up on the one side by a wood, and on the other by some bushy vineyards of lofty growth. The village of Marengo [*sic* – read Spinetta] flanked this cruelly memorable spot to the left. What torrents of blood were shed in that place! What numbers of brave men perished there! An invincible courage had unceasingly to struggle against numbers of the obstinate foe, perpetually increasing. Our artillery, in part dismounted or taken, had but little ammunition. Thirty pieces of cannon, actively served by the enemy, cut in two both men and trees, the branches of which, in their fall, further crushed to death those who were before wounded, and who had sought an insecure refuge under them.'

On the right, Lannes was extremely hard pressed. He later complained he was without a gun or a man on horse at the time of his retreat. In what was to become something of a long-running feud, Lannes ordered Bessières to support him with the Guard cavalry, and to mount what would have been a suicidal charge. The episode is told by Eugène Beauharnais:

'General Lannes, pressed a little briskly by the enemy, wanted to make us make a charge without success; he had in front of him, two battalions and two artillery pieces, behind which was a mass of cavalry in closed columns; his troops retired in disorder, such that, to have the time to breathe and rally them, he ordered Colonel Bessières, who commanded us, to charge on the enemy column. The terrain was not favourable, because it was necessary to traverse the vines; however we passed and arrived in musket range of these two battalions, waiting for us at support arms and in the finest bearing. Colonel Bessières, having formed us, prepared to order the charge, when he perceived that the enemy cavalry deployed itself on our left and was going to turn us. Consequently, he made a half-turn to the left, and we crossed the vines under canister fire and musketry; but, arriving on the other side, we held a good enough bearing to impose on the enemy cavalry. General Lannes was very discontented by this operation and complained bitterly. However it is probable that, if we had executed his orders, few among us would have returned.'

The horses which they reported seeing to the left were two regiments of Austrian cavalry, the 3rd Erzherzog Johann Dragoons and the 9th Lichtenstein Light Dragoons – twelve squadrons in total. The 3rd Dragoons led the way and began to head round the French left flank, to the south of Spinetta. The French position was becoming untenable. At one point Bonaparte placed himself at the head of the single battalion from the 72nd Line and ordered them to follow him forwards in a desperate last charge. They refused to obey him, exclaiming, 'We do not want the First Consul to expose himself to danger.'[5] Bullets were seen falling around him, driving up the ground between his horse's legs; Berthier was imploring him to move to safety. In the end it was Murat who rode up to the First Consul and said frankly: 'General, it is time for us to retire. There is the Austrian cavalry which will turn us.'[6]

By now it was clear the Austrians were extending on the flanks, and if the French remained in position they would be surrounded.

'I believe so,' the Bonaparte replied. 'Oh well, let us retire.'

The timing of this decision is given as 4.00 pm by Victor's ADC, Quiot. He also appears to have noticed the fighting flare up at Castelceriolo at the same time (as recorded by Soult), and confirms Monnier's men also began their withdrawal at this point. The retreating battalions formed themselves in masses, ready to form square against cavalry if necessary. The battalions retreated in a chequerboard pattern, led by those on the left of the line. The French cavalry stationed itself on the wings and prevented the Austrians from venturing too near. The line of troops soon exited the vineyards and entered a large open expanse, followed by a line of eighty Austrian guns. In this open ground, the battalion of the 72nd Line which had followed the Consular Guard to Spinetta was also engaged by cavalry. Unable to form a square in the time available, the third rank of the battalion is said to have turned round to fire on the Austrian cavalry.

One of Berthier's ADCs, Maurice Dupin, provides a vivid description of the French army at the moment of retreat:

'The right flank had been turned back by the enemy, whose artillery now formed a cross-fire with our centre. Cannonballs were raining down on all sides. At the time, the general staff was having a meeting. A cannonball passes under the belly of the horse of General Dupont's aide-de-camp. Another grazes the rump of my horse. A shell lands in our midst, explodes, and no one is hurt. They are still deliberating over what should be done. The commanding general dispatches to the left flank one of his aides-de-camp, Laborde by name, with whom I am on rather good terms. He hasn't gone a hundred paces when his mount is killed. I go [to] the left flank with the Adjutant General Stabenrath. On the way, we meet a platoon of the 1st Regiment of Dragoons. The commanding officer comes toward us sadly, shows us twelve men with him, and tells us that that is what's left of the fifty men who made up his platoon that morning. While he is talking, a cannonball passes under the nose of my mount and so stuns him that he falls over on top of me as if dead. I quickly get out from under him. I thought he was killed and was quite surprised when I saw him get up again. He wasn't hurt. I get back on, and the adjutant general and I ride off to the left flank. We find them retreating, and we do our best to rally a battalion. But hardly was that done when we see even farther off to the left a column of deserters taking to their heels. The general sends me to stop them, which is impossible. I find infantry mixed in with cavalry, baggage carts and pack horses; the wounded abandoned on the road and crushed by the caissons and the artillery. The screaming is dreadful, the dust so thick you can't see two feet in front of you. In this extreme confusion, I hurl myself out of the roadway and gallop ahead, shouting, "Halt up there, at the head of the column!" I gallop on; not one commander, not one officer. I encounter the younger Caulaincourt, wounded in the head and fleeing, carried off by his horse. Finally, I find an aide-de-camp. We set out to try and stop the disorder. We hit some with the flat of our sabres and praise some of the others, for among these poor devils there were still plenty of brave men. I dismount, I have a piece put in position, I form a platoon. I start to form a second. I had hardly begun, when the first one had already bolted. We abandon the enterprise and ride off to rejoin the commanding general. We see Bonaparte beating a retreat.'[7]

At this moment of retreat, Petit sums up the French predicament:

'In short, at four o'clock in the afternoon, I have no hesitation in saying, that in a line of five miles or more, there did not stand six thousand infantry to their colours, and only six pieces of cannon could be made any use of. Let me not be accused of exaggeration in painting this prodigious falling off: the causes of which are very easily to be made known. A third of the army was actually put *hors de combat*: the deficiency of carriages for removing the sick and wounded, occasioned the necessity for more than another third to be occupied in this painful service, not to speak of the plausible pretext this circumstance afforded to certain individuals (of which an army always contains more or less) to absent themselves at so unseasonable a conjuncture from their respective corps. Hunger, thirst and fatigue, had imperiously forced a great number of officers to withdraw also; and everyone knows what effect the absence of officers occasions. The skirmishers also had, for the most part, lost the direction of their corps: in short, what remained of the army, occupied in vigorously defending the defile already mentioned, knew nothing of what passed behind them.'

The Austrian skirmishers came forward under the protection of their artillery and began to enter the vineyards and woods. On the right, with Castelceriolo evacuated and the Guards' resistance broken, Ott resumed his march, threatening to outpace the French rearguard to the south. Despite this, Bonaparte was outwardly calm. He knew Desaix could not be far off now, and he sent the aide-de-camp Louis Lejeune off to find him, and to instruct him to hurry up. As the remains of Victor and Lannes' troops began to retreat in their little closed columns, Eugène Beauharnais and the horse chasseurs were ordered to destroy any abandoned munitions. They would wait for the Austrians to approach before setting the caissons on fire and leaping on their horses to escape.[8] Moving eastward out of the protection of the vines and into the open fields on the reverse side of the slope, the army was now entering the most dangerous phase of the battle. Everything now rested on the timely arrival of Desaix. Coignet saw the First Consul in a moment of solitary contemplation:

'Looking behind us, we saw the Consul who was seated on the bank of the ditch on the main road to Alessandria. He was alone, the bridle of his horse passed in his arm and flicked up small stones with his riding crop. He did not seem to see the balls rolling down the road. That was his habit. He never thought of his life. I only once saw him shelter from enemy fire; this was at Eylau, behind the church. When we were near him, he mounted his horse and galloped behind our ranks. "Take courage, soldiers," he cried. "The reserve is coming! Stand firm!" He went to the right of the army, and everywhere on his way the soldiers shouted: *Vive Bonaparte*!'

We have seen how the Austrians attacked the French at Spinetta with a formidable line of artillery, while calling for volunteer skirmishers from the infantry regiments. The French accounts also indicate there was a great deal of cavalry swarming around, albeit their attacks appear to have been largely uncoordinated in the Spinetta area. While these attacks were being made, the remains of the divisions of Hadik and Kaim marched out beyond Marengo and began reforming to the east of the village, in two lines, just as they had begun the battle.

This deployment appears to have been hindered by the creation of a bottleneck at the Fontanone. In addition to troops trying to march out beyond Marengo, there was a great deal of traffic heading westwards in the guise of wounded soldiers being evacuated and French prisoners being marched off towards Alessandria. One of those waiting to cross the Fontanone was Captain Rauch of IR 23 Toscana. Along with his comrades, he had seen the cavalry fall on the rear of the French inside

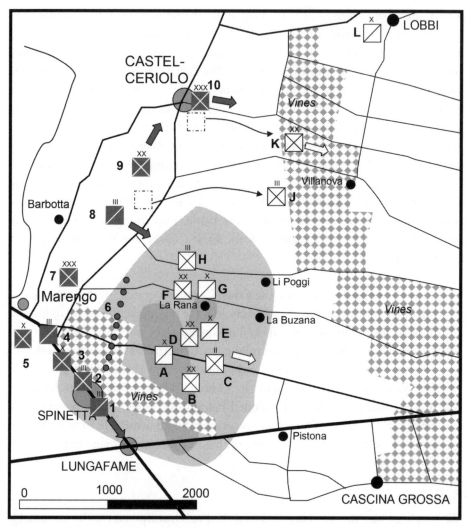

MAP 14: The French retreat, 4.00 pm

(French) A – Kellermann; B – Gardanne; C - 72nd Line; D – Chambarlhac; E – Guard cavalry;
F – Watrin; G – Champeaux; H – 28th Line; J – Foot Guard (estimated line of retreat); K – Monnier;
L – Rivaud's cavalry brigade.

(Austrians) 1 – Archduke Johann Light Dragoons; 2 – IR 11 Wallis; 3 – Lattermann's grenadiers;
4 – Lichtenstein Light Dragoons; 5 – Weidenfeld's grenadiers; 6 – Austrian skirmish and artillery line;
7 – Kaim reforming debris of main column; 8 – Frimont's light cavalry; 9 – Gottesheim; 10 – Ott's column.

Marengo and the subsequent round-up of prisoners. The great number of these prisoners, which had filed past him, filled him with joy. As they passed over the bridge and passed Marengo, Rauch could clearly see the destruction and slaughter that had taken place there.[9] The ditch was choked with bodies. The casualties of

Rivaud's brigade littered the field. There were dead and injured horses, broken artillery carriages and wagons, a scene of complete devastation. As Rauch passed Marengo, his regiment was directed to the left of the line. When they quit the Barbotta road to head eastwards, Rauch soon encountered the vines, and had to cut his way through them with his sword. Near to him, artillery pieces were dragged through the vines, which were crushed beneath the heavy wheels of the gun carriages and limbers.

In the first line, Captain Emerich Marx, commanding 2nd Battalion IR 53, found himself the senior surviving officer in his battalion, which was now at the head of a column marching towards the French. Marx's main problem was trying to coordinate a long thin column of men moving through a field of high crops and Italian-style vines totally obscuring his view. Marx was very wary he might blunder into the French without any warning, so was cautious in his advance. He soon crossed over a broad, muddy, water-filled ditch and found before him was a small rise, obscuring the enemy's position. To check this area, he sent a group of about forty men up onto the rise and ordered them to fire a few shots ahead of them into the crops. Ahead of them some republican cavalry were lying in wait, screening a body of infantry. After Marx's men fired at them, they peeled away and allowed the infantry behind to fire a massive volley at Marx's forty-man vanguard. Marx now climbed the rise himself and could saw the unmasked body of troops – probably Lannes' 40th Line. The French firing caused the Austrian column to disperse and fall back towards the second line. Unsure of the strength of the French troops before him, Marx hurried back to inform Zach that he had come under fire.

We have heard precious little of Zach since the beginning of the battle. In his account of the battle given to Faverges, the Austrian chief of staff described the losses suffered taking Marengo as 'horrifying'. Zach told Faverges:

> 'Unfortunately, our cavalry had no commanders, and we could not profit from the disordered enemy. Unfortunately also, our infantry was no less up in the air. Each regiment came and pirouetted, as the head sang to its colonel. The improvised generals who replaced their fallen colleagues, knowing nothing of our plans, answered haphazardly to the demands for direction.'

By this Zach appears to concur with Neipperg, who had earlier complained about the pursuit being held up because regimental bands were playing the *Grenadiermarsch*. The French sources also speak of the Austrians shouting their victory cry '*Vivat!*' at this time. More tellingly, it was the loss of generals and senior officers which really caused the problems. The losses were shocking. So many had been gunned down, or maimed by artillery fire. Radetzky concurred:

'The commander-in-chief had two horses wounded, the colonel-director of the artillery [Reisner] was wounded in the head. Brave Major Perczel, my worthy friend, had his thigh broken by the same bullet which assailed my horse. Captain Krapf of the engineers was killed beside the commander-in-chief, and there is not one of us who has not had some accident.'

Speaking with his comrades after the battle, Faverges wrote: 'Our regiment had lost there almost all its superior officers. The colonel had gone crazy, the Prince Arenberg had had his leg taken off.' Had the battle been so intense that it had caused a colonel to lose his mind? Apparently so; and it was the same everywhere. The Austrian officers had led from the front and had suffered heavily. This is why Captain Marx had found himself at the head of the main column, blundering into a French rearguard hidden in the crops.

The problem extended all the way to the top. As stated by Radetzky, Melas had lost two horses shot from under him, and he had fallen heavily, suffering bruises. He had been in the thick of the action and personally directed the final attack on Marengo; but now, at the moment the army desperately needed leadership to complete the victory, Melas' seventy-one years caught up with him. With the French in full retreat, Melas decided to return to Alessandria, placing command of a new advanced guard in the hands of GM Saint-Julien. According to Crossard, on leaving the field Melas told Saint-Julien:

'It is a finished affair, they retire on all points. You will not go farther than San Giuliano, where you will place the right of your infantry. You will have the enemy pursued by your cavalry and the light artillery, which will kill as many people as possible when he passes the Scrivia. As for me, I am old; I have been on horseback since midnight, so I am going to lie down.'[10]

A column was formed, at the head of which was IR 11 Wallis, followed by Lattermann's grenadier brigade. Behind the grenadiers came the 9th Liechtenstein Dragoons and three batteries of cavalry artillery, with Weidenfeld's grenadier brigade in reserve. These were directed onto the main road to follow the French withdrawal. As Melas quit the field, Zach placed himself at the head of the column on the main road with Saint Julien, as did Radetzky. If Melas had been overjoyed at the eventual success of the day's engagement, then Zach was completely ecstatic. The chief of staff believed he had both outwitted his enemies in headquarters and General Bonaparte. Ignoring the fact that the assumptions in his battle plan had been completely wrong, and the failure to adapt the plan had seen much of the army gunned down before it had even reached its start positions, Zach had never rated Bonaparte as a commander, putting his past successes down more to luck than any great judgement. He shouted out to those officers riding near him: 'Now we certainly have the great Bonaparte here, so where is this rare genius?' Zach then announced he was going to carry San Giuliano with a bayonet attack.[11]

Major Anton Volkmann was less confident.[12] This talented staff officer felt obliged to point out a few truths to his chief. Referring to Kaim's men in the centre behind them, he pointed out to Zach there was no longer a line of battle and one needed to be re-established; whole battalions were so fatigued that their commanders had allowed them to lay down and recover for a short while; the artillery had fallen behind and to carry San Giuliano it would be wise to have the guns at the front. But Zach would not listen. He said if he had listened to the advice of others like Volkmann before, he would not now be at the head of a victorious army, but running away to Milan with one eye looking over his shoulder for the pursuing French.

As for the rest of the army, the other cavalry regiment which had survived the morning battle largely intact was the 3rd Johann Dragoons. Part of this regiment was directed to the south-east, along the road to Novi to look for Desaix's column (the Austrians did not know Desaix had been delayed crossing the Scrivia and naturally assumed he had fulfilled his mission the day before). To the right of the column on the main road, IR 47 Franz Kinsky was sent towards Cascina Grossa, a hamlet 700 metres south of the main road. Out on the Austrian left, Ott began his march eastwards, taking the road from Castelceriolo towards the manor house of La Ghilina, approximately 2km north of San Giuliano. In the centre, FML Kaim took control of all the remaining infantry previously forming the main column. These troops had borne the brunt of the morning battle and many were exhausted. Whole battalions sat on the floor resting under the hot sun. Soldiers went looking for food in the houses, or for wells to refill their canteens. Others gave assistance to the wounded, or plundered the dead. Some went chasing after the herds of riderless horses now roaming the plain.[13] It clearly took some time to organize these men back into the battle lines which had begun the battle.

The wings of the army advanced first, on a front nearly 3km wide, with Ott to the north, Saint-Julien to the south on the main road and IR 47 on the extreme right. Kaim's troops advanced in the centre, lagging slightly behind the wings, probably following the line of the old road. There was also an improvised line of artillery, skirmishers and various detachments of cavalry which followed the French more closely.

Captain Rauch was with Kaim's troops and thought 'the sight of the victoriously advancing soldiers was glorious, it looked like they were engaged in drill on the parade ground'. However, he began to have concerns at the way the regiments in

Kaim's command extended themselves sideways, so rather than forming a solid, double battle line, the two lines converged to form just a single line. Rauch began to have concerns about this formation, because there was no reserve in the centre. These concerns were shared by Crossard, who was with Vogelsang and his staff. Crossard noted the detrimental effects victory was having on the troops near him. He felt that the ranks were disordered, many men having quit them to pillage the dead. Those remaining in the ranks were marching without a care in the world, with less discipline than if walking down a road in peacetime. The officers were slapping one another on the backs, giving and receiving congratulations, totally unconcerned about the French. It seemed as though the army had had a great weight lifted off it since breaking out across the Fontanone, that they were all just grateful to have survived.

In his order before the battle, Radetzky had warned the army not to become complacent, even if the French appeared to be retreating. They would have done well to heed this advice. Crossard kept muttering to himself: 'What disorder! Why do we not we reform the army?' He was surprised when FML Vogelsang, normally a man full of gentle kindness, turned around and said in an aggressive tone, 'What is the meaning of this screeching? Do you not see that there are two regiments there in total?', pointing to troops to the south of them. This tirade from one whom Crossard considered to be one of the best generals in the army left him in despair.[14]

At this point it is necessary to survey the actions on the wings of the battle in order to gain a complete picture of the French predicament. First we must check on the progress of the Austrians sent to Cantalupo, then on the cavalry brigades of Duvignau and Rivaud, and Dampierre at Cascina Bianca - not to mention the Austrian garrison of Tortona, which also played a part in the day.

To recall, Nimpsche had been sent south from Alessandria to Cantalupo to guard against the approach of Suchet from Acqui. This redeployment across the Bormida had caused a lengthy delay in Ott's march to Castelceriolo, and one wonders the outcome had the brigade instead been directed to seize that place, and what would have been the impact of Ott perhaps arriving there at 11.00 am, not at noon. This is to speculate. Arriving at Cantalupo, Nimpsche ordered Major Fulda to ride to Acqui with an advanced guard formed of two squadrons of hussars. They entered Acqui and chased away the French dragoons: many of the French were on exhausted horses and were thus made prisoner. From interrogating them, Fulda learned that Suchet was still too far away to have an impact on the battle. Fulda sent his findings back to Nimpsche who, without orders to do anything but monitor Suchet, now felt more confident to intervene in the battle raging away to the north-east.

He began to send his troopers towards a ford on the Bormida near to the town of Castellazo. This was the place Duvignau's brigade had taken up position at earlier in the morning. When we last checked on their progress, the officers of the 12th Chasseurs were going to lunch courtesy of some Capuchin friars. Blissfully unaware of the presence of a large Austrian brigade at Cantalupo less than 3km away, and seemingly ambivalent about the battle raging to the north, the officers sat down to dine. This was about the same time that Rivaud was marching his last reserve into Marengo for the desperate firefight with Lattermann's grenadiers.

Halfway through their meal though, there was an alert and everyone hurried back to rejoin the regiment. Perhaps made anxious by the heavy gunfire to the north, the French pickets had become jumpy. They thought they had seen enemy skirmishers coming through the fields, but these were reported to be peasants going about their daily business. Everyone breathed a sigh of relief. The main force retreated back to the village, the officers disgruntled at having had their lunch disturbed. Instead of returning to their meal, they decided to go and take a nap to catch up on their lack of sleep the night before.

Lieutenant Besson was in charge of the post overlooking the Bormida. He watched the build-up of Nimpsche's cavalry across the river, but they did not appear to be interested in him. However, after a long period of inactivity, 200 Austrian troopers began crossing the river by a ford and headed straight for Castellazo. While transfixed by the approach of this column, Besson was unaware that he was being stalked by another set of Austrian troopers who had already infiltrated the area. Before he knew it, Besson and his picket found themselves surrounded and taken prisoner by Nimpsche's hussars. Behind Besson, Lieutenant Loquette saw what was happening and rushed off to raise the alarm in the village. Captain Estienne was sent with reinforcements to support Loquette, and Chief of Squadron Muller went to examine the situation himself, riding behind the detachment just sent. Pistol shots rang out nearby. Muller paused and saw six enemy hussars just ahead of him. He galloped back to the village and noticed for the first time that the whole area was swarming with Austrians.

The officers were just dozing off when the trumpeters blared 'to horse'. The slumbering officers raced to get on to their horses and reach the rally point outside the village. A column of Austrian hussars rode into the village behind them. At the same time, the column that Besson had watched fording the Bormida came round trying to cut them off. Led by Lieutenant Démont, the chasseurs made two small charges and opened a pathway back towards the Orba and the presumed safety of the French army at Marengo. They galloped for their lives.

The 12th Chasseurs had decided to make a stand once they had crossed the Orba. They found a position from where their flanks were protected by hedges and ditches, hoping the Austrians would not be able to make their numerical superiority count. Across the Orba, Nimpsche's various detachments began to regroup and form up into a column, the size of which would overwhelm the 12th Chasseurs, who had already lost half their number killed or captured. As this column formed, a corporal from the 8th Dragoons arrived. He had been sent by Victor once the retreat from Marengo had begun. At outset of his journey, he had been given an escort of four dragoons, all of whom had been taken prisoner or killed on the way. As a footnote to the corporal's message, he told de France that the army had been utterly destroyed. It was grim news indeed. Chief of Brigade de France watched as Nimpsche took up his place at the head of the column ready for the charge. Realizing resistance there was futile, he ordered his remaining 100 or so chasseurs to head eastwards at the gallop.[15]

To the north of Cantalupo, we now rejoin Dampierre's little detachment, which by 2.00 pm was taking refuge in Cascina Bianca, pursued by O'Reilly's troopers. With Dampierre was Chief of Squadron Pierre Ismert of the 11th Hussars. His after-action report gives a clear description of his activities, and how he took an opportunity to escape O'Reilly's clutches:

'About two o'clock the enemy forced us, by his superiority, to retire. His artillery and infantry made great ravages. We were without guns and ammunition. So we retreated 400 fathoms. The enemy assailed us on all sides without engaging us. Their cavalry, who had cut off the retreat, executed a charge upon us. The obstacles which it had to traverse brought a little disorder into its ranks. I took advantage of it, and executed a vigorous charge; I succeeded in piercing their line, and I rallied my troop four or five hundred fathoms from this last action.

'While the enemy was occupied with our infantry, which I could no longer assist, I gave orders to have all the fugitives picked up. This search procured for me some fifty infantrymen, a captain of the 2nd Cavalry, and twelve men who had been sent out for supplies, which served me very usefully. I divided my hussars into three parts: the right commanded by Captain Sainte-Marie, the left by Captain Briche and the centre, where I had placed the cavalry of the 2nd and the infantry under my direction.

'The enemy cavalry, who had become more audacious by the little capture it had just made, came to charge me. My infantry ambushed them and fired a discharge, and on my side I made a light charge and withdrew my infantry. The enemy, who had become more circumspect, followed me, but without fury.

'The brave Captain Briche recognized a column of cavalry which came out on my left, coming from San Carlo. This intelligent officer immediately pulled away from me, in order to attract the enemy towards the Lemme, so as not to allow him time to know where I was. This little manoeuvre was perfectly successful. For my part, I took advantage of all the advantages of these positions, and retired to San Giuliano.'

The location 'San Carlo' does not now appear in maps, but finding the patrol from the 2nd Cavalry indicates Ismert had headed southwards from Cascina Bianca, in the direction of Frugarolo. The Austrian cavalry reported by Ismert was most likely the detachment of the 3rd Johann Dragoons which had been despatched south-eastwards looking for Desaix's approach from Novi. What is most interesting about Ismert's account is the small remark that the 2nd Cavalry had been sent out to procure supplies. This detail was quite probably the same one sent out by General Kellermann before the action to procure supplies from the convent of the Holy Cross and All Saints at Bosco Marengo. Bourrienne tells the story of how convents were always well supplied, and so always sought out by French soldiers. Bonaparte's secretary states that Kellermann's men procured an abundant quantity of supplies and wine from this convent, in return for a guard to 'protect' them from pillage. These supplies instead ended up in headquarters and formed the ingredients of the meal given to the First Consul and his ravenous staff after the battle. This meal became known to history as Chicken Marengo (*Poulet Marengo*).

To the north of the battlefield, we last encountered Jean Rivaud's cavalry brigade in the vicinity of Sale, probing in the direction of Castelceriolo, albeit via a circuitous route across the plain. At 3.00 pm, Rivaud's advanced guard (a squadron of the 12th Hussars) encountered Ott's cavalry scouts beyond the village of Lobbi. The rival horsemen fired on each other from a distance with their carbines, then the French withdrew, believing the Austrians were in large numbers. In fact, Ott's cavalry was about to head off to engage the Consular Guard, so the French were not rigorously pursued. Two kilometres away, the advanced guard rejoined Rivaud, who was now on the main road at Pagella. Surprised the pursuit did not materialize, Rivaud formed his brigade into a column of platoons (i.e. quarter-squadrons), 12th Hussars at the head, followed by the 21st Chasseurs. He then began to advance cautiously towards Castelceriolo.[16]

Far behind the French lines, there was further trouble. The Austrian garrison in Fort San Victor at Tortona was commanded by Generalmajor Wenzel Karl Brigado. As the sounds of battle had raged to the west, Brigado ordered an attack to be made out of Fort San Victor in the direction of Rivalta. Oberleutnant Wratzfeld led a detachment of the 3rd Battalion IR 24 out towards the town. Corporals Georg Rase and Heinrich Müller captured ninety-one prisoners and a large quantity of stores, including a French pay chest. The two corporals found themselves having to defend the chest from their own men, who naturally wanted to plunder it. Calm was restored by the arrival of Oberleutnant Wratzfeld. While this anecdote serves as something of an historical footnote (both corporals were awarded the gold bravery medal), if the French did find themselves pushed back over the Scrivia, the loss of Tortona would likely prove a formidable obstacle to a retreating army.[17]

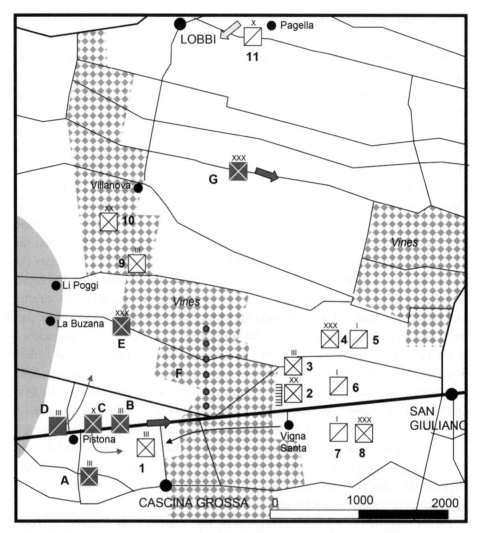

MAP 15: French positions – Approx. 5.00 pm

A – IR 23 Franz Kinsky heading to Cascina Grossa; B – IR 11 Wallis (St-Julien); C – Lattermann's Grenadiers; D – 9th Lichtenstein Dragoons; E – Kaim's Corps; F – line of skirmishers and artillery following French; G – Ott's corps.

1 – Boudet with 9th Light Infantry; 2 – Guénand's brigade with Marmont's battery; 3 – 72nd Line (Monnier); 4 – Lannes' corps; 5 – Champeaux's dragoons; 6 – Horse Guard; 7 – Kellermann's brigade; 8 – Victor's corps; ; 9 – Foot Guard (approx); 10 – Monnier's division sheltering in vines (approx); 11 – Rivaud's cavalry brigade.

Chapter 14

Vengeance!

Aide-de-camp of the commander-in-chief, Louis Lejeune, had been sent by Bonaparte to hurry the arrival of Desaix. The ADC encountered Boudet's division half a league (2km) from the battlefield. Watching the approaching column of infantry, Lejeune remarked that Desaix's troops 'were marching as gaily as if they were bound for a ball'.[1] Having rested the whole morning waiting for the Scrivia to subside, and then for fresh orders to arrive from headquarters, the division was as fresh as could be that hot afternoon. It had at least 4,500 men present, and eight guns, including two 12-pdrs, four 8-pdrs and two 6in howitzers.[2] The division was preceded by a strong squadron of the 1st Hussars. Boudet's journal records his first impressions arriving at San Giuliano, which had become the rallying point for the army's wounded:

'My division, accelerating its march, was soon arrived at San Giuliano. It witnessed there the disorder that was starting to reign within the army; the disorder was caused, in part by the movement of a great number of wounded and their comrades who assisted them, blocking the road and, on the other, the encumbrance of wagons and a crowd of domestics, sutlers, and of bad soldiers who had joined in with them.'

Commanding Boudet's second brigade was 44-year-old Louis Charles Guénand, a professional career officer and graduate of the Paris École Militaire. In 1793, he had been denounced as a nobleman and suspended for the remainder of the wars of the French Revolution. This did little for his promotional prospects.[3] Command of this brigade was his first employment since suspension, and it appears he was anxious to make an impression. Somewhat unfortunately, his report and several letters he penned describing the battle have never been used in the accounts of the battle. This has been a terrible omission, as his brigade was to play a pivotal part in the battle:

'The advanced-guard and corps of the line were all in such a rout it was impossible for General Guénand to enter by the road that went to San Giuliano which found itself so encumbered by the fugitives he had to abandon it to go forwards rapidly, crossing through the fields at this point.'

Guénand was clearly unimpressed by the debris of the army he encountered, which in contrast to his well-ordered brigade was clearly something of a mob. In a letter to the First Consul dated 25 June 1800, Guénand indicates that Bonaparte was present to witness the arrival of Boudet's division:

> 'I am writing this to see if you recall what might be my name, my face and above all my bearing at the moment when I arrived on the field passing through our fugitives to offer you my brigade in the fine order in which you saw it arrive.'

Bonaparte's presence at the arrival of the division is confirmed in his own memoirs, writing about the confidence the arrival of Boudet's troops inspired. Speaking of Boudet's first brigade, the 9th Light, he wrote:

> 'I truly never had with me better troops than the 9th Legion [*sic*] ... One saw them pass, with their determined air; the calm of brave men, their resolution. I judged they looked certain of victory and presumed the enemy would be stopped and thrown back.'[4]

Dupont concurred with the high state of morale among Desaix's troops. He wrote of the division in his memoir:

> 'It formed its ranks in front of the First Consul; he showed himself with a serene front, and we heard the soldiers say in seeing him: "It's not going too badly; he laughs, the little Corporal." This omen was precious in such a moment, and it is a noble testimony of the French character. Nothing is indeed more remarkable than the fine countenance of that division in the middle of the movement of retreat which took place, and we cannot too much praise the enthusiasm with which these three half-brigades, the only hope of success, went forward under the command of Desaix.'

Once the division was past San Giuliano, there was a break in the vineyards, and the ground formed something of an open plain. Here Boudet deployed his division:

> 'On the left of the main road, I placed my first brigade, a portion of which was deployed, the other in closed column. I also ordered my second brigade to assume the same dispositions on the right of the road.'

The sight of Boudet's division was an enormous boost to the morale of French troops retreating towards San Giuliano. Coignet was part of the French rearguard.

Coignet's captain gave him a swig of rum and congratulated him on surviving, but they were hard-pressed keeping the Austrians at bay, periodically firing volleys in the direction of their assailants. The guns fouled and the Frenchmen were again required to urinate into the musket barrels to unclog them. Then this most welcome of news arrived:

> 'The battle was lost, when an aide-de-camp came rushing past, asking where the consul was, and announcing the reserve. The consul himself passed a little later, crying out to us that we should be supported. Our poor little platoons, harassed with fatigue, were revived at these words. Each one turned his eyes towards Montebello, towards the place where our saviours were to appear. At last cries resound everywhere: "Here they are!" "Here they are!"
>
> 'General Desaix's division advanced at *l'arme au bras* [support arms]. The artillery was placed in the intervals between the half-brigades, and a regiment of heavy cavalry closed the march. They arrived on the same road to Alessandria on which we had been fighting since the morning. We saw it perfectly, because we were then at the extremity of the plateau of Marengo, at the place where the ground is inclined and descended. We saw Desaix's division below us. It was like a forest of bayonets. As for the Austrians, less advanced than our platoons, they were deceived by the folds of the ground, and did not suspect the arrival of our reinforcement. For the sake of happiness, Desaix, on approaching us, found a position, in order to put himself in line, which seemed to have been chosen beforehand. To his left was a gigantic hedge, perpendicular to the main road, protected by a kind of slope, and behind which all the troops were hidden. We did not even see the cavalry.'

This account is very useful because it helps us understand where Coignet was at the time the reserve arrived. Pittaluga's plan of the battlefield (dated 31 December 1896) shows the extent of the higher ground which Coignet describes as the 'plateau'. The ground has changed considerably in our own time, and is today occupied by an industrial estate. The reverse incline of this plateau extends between the farmhouses of Li Poggi and Pistona. The giant hedge which Coignet reports appears to be a tree-lined road approximately 1km to the east of Pistona. This tree-lined road runs perpendicular from the main road, southwards to Cascina Grossa. It is shown in Lejeune's painting of the Battle of Marengo, and survives to this day as the Via della Libertá (Liberty Way). Like many roads in the area, it is embanked to guard against flooding. Just behind this road is the point where the old and new Alessandria–Tortona roads converge before continuing to San Giuliano; if the position had been picked in advance as Coignet suggests, it was a perfect one.

Although Boudet deployed his division outside San Giuliano as previously described, it did not all remain there. While the army was retreating and Guénand's division was deploying (it would have taken at least half an hour for the tail of the division to reach the point of deployment), Desaix and Boudet went ahead and came up with something of a plan. Boudet writes:

> 'Lieutenant General Desaix and I, considering the position of the army, decided to send forward my first brigade, composed of the 9th Light. The order was thus given for this movement, the execution of which would at least remind the retreating troops of their courage, and by result, make them return.'

This would take the half-brigade far in advance of Guénand's brigade, beyond the vine belt in front of them, out beyond the French rearguard. The mission was equally clear – to buy time for Guénand to deploy, and to perform a feat of arms which would inspire the army and restore to the ranks all the soldiers around San Giuliano who had quit on the pretext of assisting the wounded, or through lack of ammunition. Before the Ninth advanced, there was a small action which is never mentioned. With Boudet's division were 100 or so troopers from 1st Hussars. The regiment's colourful regimental history records how the hussars (formerly known as the Berchény Hussars) swept the area clear of the Austrian skirmishers which had been following the French rearguard:

> 'It was therefore Captain de Juniac with the blue dolmans of Berchény, preceding Desaix's corps, which arrived first before the cannons of Marengo to save the day. It executed the boldest charges, killed twenty-six Austrians and made a number prisoner. This squadron obtained considerable success; its intrepidity was of great help on all the points where it found itself. It put a number of the enemy out of action. Desaix, admiring its valour, testified his satisfaction and took the name of Captain de Juniac who was in command to give to the first consul. He had successively removed seventeen Austrian posts; Hussar Bricogne-Visconti and Hussar Michel in removing one took the commanding officer prisoner.'[5]

The only other mention of such an action is found in Kellermann's *Truth on the battle of Marengo* pamphlet, in which he writes: 'The enemy skirmishers were repulsed until the village of Cascina Grossa.' It is unclear if these skirmishers were found on the main road and were preceding Saint-Julien's infantry, or if they were the same Austrian volunteers who had followed the centre. The result of the action was that the Austrians were unaware of the advancing French half-brigade.

The 9th Light Infantry was 2,000 men strong in three battalions. The first and second battalions formed line, with the third battalion remaining in column 200 paces to the rear.[6] The three elite carabinier companies were formed as a single unit, placed towards the right of the first battalion. Coignet describes how the advancing Austrians were walking in a leisurely fashion, muskets at the shoulder as if going home. Coignet passed the 9th Light by about 300 paces when it was launched forward, leaping through the tall hedge 'like rabbits' and propelling itself to within musket range of Saint-Julian's column. The original version of Coignet describes hearing the command: 'Battalion fire – oblique to the right!' This indicates the Ninth greeted the Austrians with a volley, the soldiers in the ranks aiming their muskets to the right at the road. Boudet does not mention this, only that he halted within musket range and threw out skirmishers to attack the Austrians.[7] These were not inexperienced volunteers like the Austrians were employing in their skirmish line, but trained light infantrymen. Racing out of their ranks, they swarmed towards the head of the Austrian regiment in column on the road, making a rapid, well-aimed fire.

The sudden arrival of the 9th Light came as a complete surprise to IR 11 Wallis – a blue wall several hundred metres long appearing as if from nowhere, racing towards them. Zach tried to get the regiment to deploy, but, as they did so, they simply provided a larger target for the skirmishers. Some French guns on the main road began firing. The balls crashed into IR 11 Wallis, which was becoming completely disordered. Finally, the Austrians broke off and ran for the safety of Lattermann's grenadier brigade behind.[8]

While Boudet led the 9th Light forward to attack the Austrian column, Desaix joined the First Consul and held a council of war. This appears to have been held behind Guénand's brigade, to the north of the main road. Having observed the deployment of Boudet's division, Bonaparte was surrounded by his senior generals and the staff. He climbed down from his horse and looked towards a figure approaching on horseback. He raised his riding crop over his brow to shield his eyes from the bright sun; he recognised Desaix, who, as was his habit, was dressed in civilian clothes with no badges or marks of distinction:

'Well-well, General Desaix, quite a skirmish!'

'Well, General,' replied Desaix as he dismounted. 'I have arrived; we are all fresh, and if we must, we will go and get killed.'[8]

Much has been written about this meeting under artillery fire, and matters have been clouded by subsequent writings which describe a pre-ordained change of frontage in the French army, often described as the Castelceriolo pivot. All serious commentaries of the battle dismiss this as a post-battle attempt to rationalize the French tactics, or in the words of Zach: 'It was long after the deed that one invented the famous line of Castelceriolo, Villanova and San Giuliano. The truth is that the French held on nowhere and went away in disarray towards the Po.'[9] That said, we know the First Consul had been aware of Desaix's location and probable time of arrival since 2.00 pm. When he consented to withdraw from Spinetta at 4.00 pm to avoid being outflanked, he must have known Desaix could not have been far from San Giuliano. Although his army was in retreat, his situation was far from desperate, and there were opportunities to be exploited. Of all the accounts, the one which best summarizes the tactical situation as it stood at 4.30 pm is again found in Petit:

'General Melas, then finding too many obstacles in the centre, thought that, by extending his wings, he might surround us, and thereby entirely cut us off. He therefore directed [the] great part of his force to these points, imagining he had sufficiently concealed his movements, and that he should be quite able to check us by his artillery. Thus, not being able to discover what passed with us, and ignorant of these reinforcements which had just arrived, he laid the foundation of his own disaster. In fact, Bonaparte, always placed in the post of honour, and to whose perspicacious eye nothing escaped, seized this favourable opportunity: his orders flew everywhere in a moment.'

It appears that some French generals saw the arrival of Desaix as an opportunity to protect the withdrawal of the army across the Scrivia. There were merits in this, because it would draw the French closer to Lapoype, and they could also summon assistance from Duhesme. However, with so many wounded at San Giuliano, and with Austrians in Tortona behind them, a retreat could be perilous – which is to say nothing of the impact a retreat would have on Bonaparte's reputation. Having said he would make good the calamities of 1799, Bonaparte could not afford the loss of a major battle in Italy. Some, including his ADC Rapp, have said Desaix was in favour of a retreat; others, like Bourrienne, have Desaix pulling out his pocket watch and declaring there was still time enough to win another battle. Of all the descriptions of the council of war where these matters were debated, perhaps the most interesting is found in the unpublished memoirs of Dupont. Witness his observation of the dynamic between Bonaparte and Desaix:

'[Bonaparte] consulted Desaix on the new dispositions. We saw he attached a great price to the opinion of this general who answered him with a noble

frankness, such as the gravity of the circumstances required of him …
This sort of council of war was very remarkable for me. I saw for the first
time Bonaparte on a battlefield. Clothed in power and surrounded with
a long prestige of glory, he grappled at the moment with fortune and all
the luck seemed against him. No emotion however showed itself in him.
He struck the sand with his riding crop, as if playing, a distraction which
was familiar to him, and he calmly addressed his questions to Desaix.
General Desaix was also for me a new and precious object to observe.
One of the lieutenants of Moreau in the army of the Rhine, he had left
this great banner of the Germanic glory for that of Bonaparte, the fame
of which had entrained him. He arrived from Egypt a few days before,
and I knew him only of this moment. I appreciated with a deep interest
all I saw in him; his words and his bearing, in that sudden crisis, deserved
his reputation. Never has so prompt a concert preceded such a fortunate
change in the fate of the fighting.'

The account continues, and it appears Desaix advised against some of the First
Consul's suggestions. More than anything, it indicates the two men were happy to
talk as equals in military matters, perhaps in a way the likes of Murat, Lannes and
Victor would not have done. Dupont continues:

'Several plans of operation were successively designed by Bonaparte, but
to these diverse plans his severe council always opposed this reflection
that we had no artillery, the ammunition was spent: "Let us do like at
Tagliamento", added the First Consul finally, and he asked for his horse.'

This statement is intriguing. At the Battle of Valvasone (16 March 1797), the French
were attempting to cross the Tagliamento River. After feigning an attack, the French
performed something of a ruse on the Austrians, pretending to withdraw and to
begin forming a camp. Assuming the French were bedding down for the night,
the Austrians did the same. Once the Austrians were thus occupied, the French
launched a sudden and decisive attack. We can deduce from this that Bonaparte
and Desaix's plan was to recall Boudet's first brigade, and trick the Austrians into
thinking the French were continuing their retreat, drawing the Austrians onto
Guénand's infantry brigade, which would launch a decisive counter-attack.

The actions of Guénand's brigade have been overlooked too long. While the
council was taking place, Guénand's brigade was deploying north of the road.
This brigade is traditionally depicted as forming in a 'mixed order' of columns
and lines. Guénand described it as having formed in 'columns by echelons,
mixed with some deployed battalions'. It is possible, therefore, that the brigade

formed something of a diagonal line, the right-hand battalion foremost and the left rearmost. In terms of the division's strength, there is something which has been previously overlooked. The 30th Line was formed only of two battalions (the third was with the Army of Italy), although it is possible Guénand brigaded his five grenadier companies to form a sixth battalion – something which was quite common in the wars of the revolution. What has not been previously noted is that upon arrival at San Giuliano, Desaix's troops encountered the two battalions of the 72nd Line which Monnier had left in reserve, probably 800 men strong. These joined Boudet's division, as confirmed by Guénand, who wrote: 'It is to be noted that two battalions of the 72nd, which were detached from the division of General Monnier, perfectly assisted the right wing of the division Boudet.' This brigade was therefore somewhere in the region of 3,500-4,000 men strong at 5.00 pm. This brigade was further strengthened by having all the remaining French artillery placed in front of it. It was therefore at least as strong, if not bigger than, either the divisions of Gardanne or Monnier were at the outset of the battle.

The concentration of the artillery into a single large battery was to prove an important factor. The commander of the artillery, General Marmont, was present at the council of war, and had a discussion with Desaix about how best to use it:

'It was about five o'clock, and the division Boudet, on which rested our safety and our hopes, had not arrived. Finally, shortly after, it joined us. General Desaix preceded it by some moments, and came to join the First Consul. He found the affair in this annoying state, [and] he had bad opinion of it. We held on horseback a sort of council which I attended; he told the first consul: "There must be a lively artillery fire imposed on the enemy, before attempting a new charge; otherwise it will not succeed: it is thus, general, that one loses battles. We absolutely need a good cannonade." I told him I was going to establish a battery with the pieces still intact and to the number of five; by joining five pieces left on Scrivia, and newly arrived, and, furthermore, eight pieces of his division, I had a battery of eighteen pieces. "That's good," Desaix told me; "see, my dear Marmont, some cannons, some cannons, and make the best possible use of them." Eighteen pieces were soon put in battery. They occupied the right half of the front of the army, so much was this front reduced. The pieces on the left were to the right of the road to San Giuliano.'[10]

While the council had been deliberating, the Austrians had not remained inactive. In front of Guénand's brigade was a belt of vines in which the Austrian artillery line had taken position. His report describes the Austrians in front of him:

'On the right of the road, a formidable artillery, some infantry in the vines, supported by cavalry. The enemy artillery, perfectly served and that we estimated as fifty guns, continued its devastation on all the line.'

Guénand's account of the battle states his men were appealing to him for the order to attack so they could close on the enemy from which they were taking fire, with no reply.[11] Boudet reported: 'Every instant saw files of our troops cut down, which increased the impatience to get to close quarters.' Guénand in turn petitioned Desaix, who was at that moment still with Bonaparte. The First Consul told Guénand: 'Order the attack', and Desaix rode off to rejoin Boudet and to order him to bring his troops into line.

As Desaix had urged, Guénand's attack was preceded by an artillery bombardment. This lasted for twenty minutes, according to Marmont. Although a formidable escalation in the battle, the sheer number of guns on the Austrian side meant the contest was unequal.[12] When Guénand began his advance towards the vines, forming his battalions into a line of closed columns, Marmont ordered his gunners to cease fire, and to turn their pieces round so they could march forward with the advancing columns. The gunners ignored him and continued to fire through the intervals in the French battalions. For Guénand's soldiers, many of whom were conscripts seeing a large-scale action for the first time, having balls coming at them from in front and behind must have been terrifying, but they did not waiver. Marmont had to ride down the line of the battery and, piece by piece, order the gunners to follow their instructions. Even then, the ones near the main road continued to fire.

On entering the vines, Guénand's brigade found itself engaged in a short but violent combat. He described the Austrian infantry there as being 'entrenched to the teeth' in the vines. There was nothing for it but a bayonet charge to clear them out. However, just 100 paces into the vines, Guénand was struck in the right groin. Wincing in pain, he was amazed to discover the enemy ball had struck his pocket and had flattened and bent the coins it contained. Although heavily bruised from the strike, he was able to continue, albeit extremely lucky to have survived. As he recovered from the shock, Boudet arrived with new orders from Desaix. Boudet put himself at the head of the 59th Line and spurred on the brigade.

The bravery citations of the men in Guénand's brigade bear witness to the intensity of the fighting. On the right, the Austrians managed to get themselves and a few guns inside some of the farm buildings there. One group of Austrians actually made a dash at the 59th Line's flag; Sergeant-Major Aiginy only managed to save it at the price of a nasty sabre cut. Chief of Battalion Pastre of the 59th Half-Brigade led his men into the fray. He was on the left of Guénand's line and encountered some fierce resistance. In quick succession, three balls hit him as he exhorted his men to charge. The Austrians lost two more flags to this brigade. Sergeant-Major Blien of the 30th led a charge on one, accompanied by two sergeants, Corporal Promel and a few of the men. In the scramble that followed, it was a conscript named Georges Amptil who seized the trophy and got it into the clear. Captain Jolle of the 59th led the way and fought his way to another standard, seconded by Lieutenant Robin. As Jolle grabbed the pole, a larger than usual Austrian tried to prevent him; in spectacular fashion, Robin threw himself at this man, knocking him to the floor, where he was obliged to surrender.

Opposed to this advance was Captain Rauch. His account describes the terrible momentum of Guénand's attack columns:

'Kaim came riding up to IR23 Toscana and shouted, "Men! Up to now, we have attacked; make yourselves ready to be attacked in response." With these words, he rode off and everyone prepared themselves for an attack. Immediately after that, the French smashed into us with a terrible shout. In these moments, which were otherwise only filled with the shock and dreadful scenes of killing, I felt the purest joy, which could only come over me as a soldier in this situation; for as the enemy attack happened, which overthrew our entire deployed line as far as my eye could see and forced everyone to turn back, my company stood its ground isolated there for a few minutes, against the whole mass of French, who stormed in on us, and I and my Oberleutnant [Vuchetich] directed half-company volleys at them several times, then I set off on the retreat with my men in close order, ignoring the superior enemy numbers, as though I was manoeuvring on the drill square. This fact is evidenced and is no boast. The steadiness of isolated small groups of troops and their confidence in their officers has certainly only rarely been displayed as it was here … Their brave resistance against the above-mentioned attack by enemy lasted, as stated, only a few minutes, also as long as was humanly possible, they then closed up on the other companies of the regiment, which were engaged in establishing a new position to the rear.'[13]

Once Marmont's battery had opened fire and Guénand's brigade began preparing for the attack, attempts were made to rally the remainder of the army which had fought in the morning. The fields around San Giuliano were awash with soldiers who had lost their corps for one reason or another. According to Petit:

'The consul, the commander-in-chief [Berthier], the generals, the officers of the staff, ran through the ranks, and everywhere inspired that confidence which precedes and creates great successes. This work took up an hour, which was a terrible one to pass; for the Austrian artillery was bearing cruelly upon us. Every discharge mowed down whole ranks. Their ricochet bullets carried away with them, both men and horses. They received death amidst them in this manner, without moving a step, except to close their ranks over the dead bodies of their comrades. This thundering artillery reached even the cavalry who rallied in the rear of us, as well as a great number of foot-soldiers of different corps, who, encouraged by Desaix's division, which they had seen pass, ran anew to the field of honour.'

True enough, the generals were everywhere, recalling the men to their ranks. There was a great unity of purpose, and despite their fatigues and wants, the French soldiers showed remarkable resilience in gathering themselves back into ranks to support Desaix. Dupont had already considered the need to rally these men. He had ordered Chief of Brigade Rigaud, the commander of the headquarters, to gather all the troops he could and to lead them in support of Boudet's division. When Berthier instructed Dupont to form a reserve, he was able to announce the command had already been executed. Bonaparte then began touring the lines, haranguing the troops as he went: 'We have gone back far enough today. You know that my custom is always to sleep on the battlefield.' Another account has the First Consul turning to his soldiers while pointing at the Austrians: 'My friends! There is peace, go and fetch it!'[14]

We must now retrace our steps and rejoin the 9th Light Infantry. After the retreat of IR 11 Wallis, Lattermann's grenadier brigade had deployed and set its sights on fighting the newly arrived French infantry. The memoirs of Faverges state:

'Zach stayed to direct the charge of the grenadiers but now, whereas these moved forward in fine order, a terrible musketry came from the nearby vines taking them suddenly in the flank. The grenadiers forgot San Giuliano and threw themselves on their aggressors.'

At this critical moment, Boudet now received the order to pull back into line with Guénand:

'I was far more advanced than the rest of my line with my first brigade, and I would not have been delayed long before the 9th Light became engaged along its entire front, when General Desaix sent me the order to retire my troops by echelons. This manoeuvre would have become, in truth, essential, if the general attack was delayed; but it also compromised the skirmishers I had out in front. I ordered the movement however, executing it at a very slow pace, and I went very quickly to Lieutenant General Desaix to present my observations to him.'

Boudet reached Desaix and told him what was taking place in front, and that his skirmishers were heavily engaged. He would lose as many men retreating as he would advancing because of Austrian fire. Boudet insisted the order to attack had to be given then, before it was too late. Desaix agreed. He told Boudet to halt the 9th Light at once. Satisfied, Boudet swung his horse about and galloped back to them.[15]

Desaix, meanwhile, turned to his aide de camp, Savary, and told him:

'You see how matters stand. I can no longer put off the attack without danger of being myself attacked under disadvantageous circumstances: if I delay I shall be beaten and I have no relish for that. Go then in all haste and apprise the First Consul of the embarrassment I experience; tell him that I cannot wait any longer; that I am without cavalry and that he must direct a bold charge on the flank of that column whilst I charge it in front.'

Savary went off to find the First Consul. In so doing he passed a wounded artillery lieutenant named Conrad, who had been struck in the leg by an Austrian cannonball. Refusing to be taken to the rear, Conrad had crawled forward to observe the effect of his battery's fire. Savary saw the poor man was calling out to him. Thinking he was asking for assistance to the rear, Savary replied: 'Have patience, we will come back for you later.'

'It's not that,' replied Conrad. 'Please do me the pleasure of telling my gunners to aim a little lower!'

Savary continued his mission and found Bonaparte, passing on Desaix's request for cavalry support. After reflecting for a moment, the First Consul replied: 'Have you well examined the column?'

'Yes General.'

'Is it very numerous?'

'Extremely so, General.'

'Is Desaix uneasy about it?'

'He appeared uneasy as to the consequences that might result from hesitation. I must add his having particularly desired I should tell you that it was useless to send any other orders than that he should attack or retreat – one or the other; and that the latter movement would be at least as hazardous as the first.'

'If this be the case, let him attack: I shall go in person to give him the order. You will repair yonder [pointing to a black spot in the plain] and there find General

Kellermann, who is in command of that cavalry you now see; tell him what you have just communicated to me and desire him to charge the enemy without hesitation as soon as Desaix shall commence his attack.'

When Boudet reached the Ninth it had retired, according to Boudet, no more than 200 paces. Seeing the French pull back, the grenadiers had indeed become over-confident and were pressing forward. Desaix then arrived with the 9th Light and ordered Boudet to go to his second brigade. He was given specific instructions to pierce the enemy line and 'to drive it in with enough rapidity to separate it entirely and to thereby disrupt their plan of operations'. By this Desaix wanted Boudet to aim at the Austrian centre, driving through it and ensuring the columns on the wings were unable to link up. Boudet arrived at Guénand's brigade shortly after the latter was struck in the groin. He directed the brigade through the vines and out beyond to the other side. In his letter of 25 June 1800, Guénand writes:

'At the exit of the vines the terrain offered nothing but an open plain. On our flanks there were some houses where the enemy was taking action with a perfectly served artillery and infantry well under cover. Opposite was a numerous cavalry in the finest order of battle. On debouching, we had gone at least a mile beyond the rest of the line. It was a feat of strength to rally my troops, I succeeded there beyond my hopes and in an instant they were re-established in their original order, in column by echelons mixed with a few battalions deployed.'

The cavalry Guénand could see before him was the 9th Liechtenstein Dragoons, which had deployed north of the road, having followed Lattermann's grenadier brigade from Spinetta. His main concern was on his left flank, where the 9th Light and Lattermann's grenadiers were coming to blows. He described the situation as 'up in the air', and admits hesitating 'for a few seconds' before Boudet authorized him to resume the advance.

Shortly before Guénand broke out into the plain, Savary arrived at Kellermann's brigade and conveyed Desaix's instructions to launch a cavalry attack on the flank of the Austrian column. The various charges in the morning and the artillery fire during the retreat had severely reduced Kellermann's brigade. At 5.00 pm, there were just 150 men left on horseback, and of the twenty-eight officers only eight were still in the saddle.[16] In his 1828 account, Kellermann said he had 300 cavalry, indicating he may have been joined by the 3rd Cavalry, which had ridden ahead of Desaix. Their regimental history is silent on the matter, except for pointing out that the unit did suffer casualties, and therefore must have been engaged at some point.

Savary relayed the instructions of Desaix and the First Consul, which were (according to Kellermann): 'To march level with the corps of General Desaix and support him in the new battle that was about to be engaged.'

'I have been fighting since six in the morning,' replied Kellermann. 'I have made six charges, I have lost half my men, my troop is exhausted, replace us with some others.'

'There is only you,' Savary replied. 'All have disappeared or are too far away; you must go.'

The ADC then pointed at the remains of Champeaux's brigade: 'There is the debris of two regiments of dragoons, rally them to your column.'[17]

These dragoons (they came from half a squadron of the 1st Dragoons, two squadrons of the 8th Dragoons and the remainder from the 6th Dragoons) increased Kellermann's strength by another 150-200 sabres. In total, then, there were 400-500 men.

As the two men spoke, they heard the din of musketry open up on the left of the French line. Kellermann set his brigade in motion. His after-action report says he followed Desaix's division in a single line, 200 fathoms (approximately 400 metres) to the right of the main road – in other words he was behind Guénand. In later accounts, Kellermann changes this, saying he was level with the infantry – but in fact this would have made him nearer 800 metres from the road. In other accounts, he says he was in a column because he had to pass through vines. Importantly, he also says his forward movement was masked by the vines, which were suspended from mulberry trees.

Given his distance from the road, and from comments Kellermann later made to Guénand (saying his attack was facilitated by Guénand's advance), it appears Kellermann was in fact following the infantry brigade, and probably in column to better move through the broken ground. He would have then exited the vines and entered the open plain. Kellermann would have seen what was occurring on the left as he drew level with the troops commanded by Desaix. His battlefield account records what he saw and did:

'I perceived that the infantry which marched on the left of the road to Marengo, level with Cascina Grossa, began to give way, and that the enemy grenadiers charged it at the run. I thought there was not a moment to lose, and that a speedy movement could bring the victory back to our standards. I stopped the line, and commanded: "Platoons to the left and forwards!"'[18]

Kellermann's brigade turned to the left and formed a narrow-fronted column.[19] Kellermann looked at the unprotected flank of Lattermann's grenadiers and the re-formed IR 11 Wallis. There was a loud discharge as the grenadiers fired at Desaix's troops, seconds after which Kellermann gave the order to charge. At this same moment, on the main road, General Marmont was having something of a disagreement with the gunners of the Consular Guard. With some difficulty, he had the rest of his battery cease fire and follow Guénand's brigade forward. The gunners of the Guard had continued firing. His account tells the following:

> 'I had arrived at the left near the road where were three guns, two 8-pounders, and a howitzer served by the gunners of the Guard of the Consuls; by means of threats, I put them to movement, and the horses were harnessed to the pieces, to the gun carriages, to make the about-turn, when suddenly I saw in front of me and to the left the Thirtieth Half-Brigade in disorder and in flight. I promptly [had] the three guns put back into battery and loaded with canister; but I waited to open fire. I perceived at fifty paces from the Thirtieth, in the middle of the thick smoke and dust, a mass in good order; at first I believed it French, soon I recognized that it was the head of a big column of Austrian grenadiers. We had time to fire on them four shots of canister with our three guns, and, right after that, Kellermann, with four hundred horses, the rest of his brigade, passed in front of my pieces, and made a strong charge on the left flank of the enemy column, which laid down its arms. If the charge had been made three minutes later, our pieces would have been taken or withdrawn; and maybe that, not being any more under the influence of the surprise caused by the rounds of canister, the enemy column would have better received the cavalry. It would maybe have been the same if the charge had preceded the salvo; thus it was needed this precise combination to assure a success so complete, and, it is necessary to say it, unhoped-for. Never had fortune intervened in a more decisive way; never had a general showed more *coup d'œil*, more vigour and presence of mind than Kellermann in this circumstance.'[20]

We must suspend time at this moment and analyze Marmont's account. There is no other reference to the 30th Line fleeing in disorder. At this moment, the 30th Line would have been to the right of Guénand's brigade, nearly half a kilometre from the road. Nor does Boudet or Guénand have anything but praise for this half-brigade. If anyone was running in disorder, the soldiers had to have come from the 9th Light Infantry. Kellermann has indicated this half-brigade was retreating and was apparently hard-pressed. In fact, nothing could be further from the truth.

There is one last element to describe before the sabres of Kellermann's cavalry brigade begin hacking down on the Austrian infantry. When Boudet left the 9th Light, it had begun a movement of withdrawal. Boudet states they had fallen back only 200 paces, but having earlier claimed the Ninth were far in advance of the rest of the line, one imagines they had indeed retreated further. The Austrians saw them falling back and became encouraged. Desaix arrived and decided to lead the charge himself, sending Boudet with instructions for Guénand's brigade. Having prepared the action with an artillery bombardment, and requested a cavalry charge against the Austrian flank, Desaix had set in motion one of the greatest combined arms attacks of the Napoleonic Wars. Alas, he did not survive long enough to witness the effect of it.

We might imagine Desaix, near the road, at the head of the carabiniers of the 9th Light. Lejeune has painted this scene for us. We see the carabiniers in their shakos with tumbling red horsehair plumes; their light cavalry-style trousers, with a red stripe down the outer leg, tucked into short gaiters. We see a shell explode, having just killed six men on the right of the line. We see the young drummer boys standing next to their captain, no more than 14 years old – children of the corps, beating the charge. We see the light infantrymen stamping down the poles of the recently planted vines. Behind them we see the tree-lined road to Cascina Grossa. Bayonets are lowered. The officers are pointing forwards; and, illuminated by the flash of musketry, we see the figure of Desaix in a general's uniform, falling mortally wounded from his rearing horse, with an ADC behind, arms outstretched to catch him. The reality was somewhat different.

Perhaps the most authentic account of Desaix's final moments is found in an unsigned letter dated Milan, 19 June 1800. The letter has been attributed by de Cugnac to 32-year-old Chief of Brigade Jacques Jean Alexandre Bernard Law de Lauriston. Serving as an ADC to the First Consul, Lauriston was present at the fatal moment:

> 'The enemy, animated by its success, drove at us sharply. All the generals were behind the line to make it advance. Our fire was very murderous and forced it to stop. General Desaix had gone to his column and had put himself at the head of the 9th. General Bonaparte had ordered me to accompany him. General Boudet and Dalton made our left [*sic*] with two half-brigades. I preceded General Desaix. We marched with the 9th. A regiment placed in some vines, was at no more than ten paces, and received us with a very lively musket fire; behind these was the enemy army's chief of staff. It was then, and on beginning the charge, that General Desaix was struck by a ball that was coming obliquely. It hit him above the heart and exited though the right shoulder; if it had come directly, it is I that would

have received it, for I was in front of him, on horseback. I turned round and I saw him fall. I approached; he was dead. He only had time to say to Lefèbvre [Desnouettes], who was near to him: "Dead!" As he had no uniform, the soldiers did not notice. Lefèbvre had him carried away, and I continued to advance with the 9th. At that moment General Kellermann made, from the left, a cavalry charge on the troops we were opposed to.'

Several remarks can be made on this episode. In the 1830s, a Captain Dubois compiled all the surviving correspondence in the French war archives relating to the 9th Light Infantry during the Revolution and First Empire. Dubois then went on to write a manuscript history of the regiment, in which he was a serving officer. As part of his research, Dubois interviewed a number of survivors from the regiment, including the former Sergeant Major Nicolas Fouquet, who took the regiment's eagle from Napoleon's hands in 1804, and became guardian of a flag awarded to the 9th Light in reward for its bravery at Marengo. We do not have Dubois' original correspondence, but we can treat his account of the battle as part of the oral history of the regiment.[21] Taken from the words of veterans of the battle, the following account is a very convincing one:

'The fusillade was engaged in the vineyards by the skirmishers. General Desaix having approached them to reconnoitre the enemy, was shot in the chest, and fell among the skirmishers of the half-brigade. This loss only served to excite the ardour of the officers and soldiers who rushed furiously upon the Austrian grenadiers.'

Desaix was a brave general and carried the scars of many engagements; however, he was a famously calm general. Although he perhaps had a presentiment of death before the battle, it does not make any sense for him to have ridden at the head of an infantry charge like some medieval paladin, sacrificing himself to enemy fire for no useful gain. The Dubois account at last gives context to his actions. Arriving at the 9th Light, the view in front of him would have been obscured by gunpowder smoke. Unlike Boudet, he had not seen the Austrian forces himself. So, while the main line of the 9th Light advanced, it appears he rode ahead to get up among the skirmishers and look out beyond them. Alas the smoke was so thick he perhaps did not realise the grenadiers were so close. He was struck and killed, suffering the fate of General Joubert at Novi the year before – shot through the heart in the skirmish line.[22]

After Desaix fell, the Ninth continued to advance and, after exchanging a point-blank volley with the grenadiers, launched a furious bayonet charge. Victor's memoir fast-forwards the action:

'The 9th Light shouted "vengeance!" and rushed with rage upon the grenadiers of Lattermann. The shock is terrible! Kellermann sees it, and he feels that the decisive moment has come. He set off at a grand trot with his line of cavalry, and when he drew level with the enemy: "Halt" he commands; then, immediately afterwards: "Platoons to the left and to the front!" The movement is executed, and our platoons of cavalry fall, one after the other, like a thunderbolt, on the flank of the Austrian battalions, which, attacked in front and with fury by the 9th Light, [was] stunned, terrified, losing all energy, and engaged almost without resistance to the bayonets and sabres of our soldiers.'

Indeed, when Kellermann's heavy cavalry struck, the grenadiers' muskets would have been unloaded. The French horsemen would have sped through the intervals between the companies, slashing and stabbing as they went. Men would have been knocked to the ground by the horses. Already shaken from its first encounter with the 9th Light, the Wallis Regiment probably took the brunt of the cavalry charge (it suffered a 70 per cent casualty/prisoner rate). In the chaos, Zach was captured by Cavalier Le Riche of the 2nd Cavalry, who unceremoniously grabbed him and called on him to surrender while pressing the point of his sword into his back. The 2nd Cavalry's 1801 history, signed by Chief of Brigade Yvendorff, has the following to say on the affair:

'The enemy infantry lost its artillery in an instant, General Kellermann perceived this, he ordered the 2nd and 20th cavalry to charge the flank of a corps of grenadiers: Quicker than lightning, four hundred cavalrymen made six battalions captive. The first flag was taken by Chief of Squadron Alix, the second by Citizen Cavalier Beouf. Cavalier Le Riche made a prisoner of General Zach, chief of the enemy army's general staff, and Cavalier Pasteur seized two cannons.'[23]

The 20th Cavalry's version of events is similar:

'The enemy was stopped by some pieces of light artillery and by Desaix's division which had already set off. Having the head of the column, the regiment charged in concert with the 2nd Cavalry level with Cascina Grossa, amid a hail of balls and canister, [and] the Hungarian grenadiers lowered their arms to the number of six thousand. For its account, the regiment took six hundred prisoners, four cannons, a caisson and a flag.'[24]

These two unpublished documents are interesting because they clearly indicate where the charge took place ('level with Cascina Grossa') and that it was *after*

Desaix's troops had stopped the Austrians.[25] Given Guénand and Kellermann's description of having passed through vines and opened into a plain, we can see this cavalry charge was executed in the location shown in Lejeune's famous painting of the battle, to the west of the tree-lined road.

Having completed the charge against the Austrian infantry, Kellermann rallied 200 horsemen and launched a charge at the Liechtenstein Dragoons, who had deployed into line and were now facing Guénand's advancing brigade. Kellermann does not say he crossed swords with the enemy horse, only 'it was restrained; it even began to withdraw'. A footnote perhaps, but Berthier's 1805 history indicates Kellermann held half of his brigade back from the charge 'to block the corps of enemy cavalry opposite him and to mask the brave blow which he was going to make'. All of this happened so quickly that it is unsurprising to find so many contradictory accounts.

For further clarity, we should now consult the Austrian accounts to discover their opinion of the disaster which bore down upon them. Melas' report of the battle described a 'violent and accelerated fire' which dismantled their artillery and caused the troops to hesitate. The report describes how General Zach advanced 'the three battalions of the Wallis Regiment, with the hope of being able, by this means, to re-establish order; but this regiment itself yielded'. The grenadiers then advanced 'with the greatest enthusiasm and courage through the broken lines of the Wallis regiment and renewed the attack'. However, at the moment the grenadiers' fire was at its most intense, the 'French cavalry appeared'.

Neipperg's description of the attack indicates the Austrians believed Desaix was nothing more than a rearguard come to protect the withdrawal of the French army. However, when faced with the attack, Neipperg said the Austrians were gripped by 'indecision, a stupefaction, I may even say a general panic'. He described Kellermann's charge as 'more imprudent than bold', but agreed this threw the infantry into disorder and caused the cavalry to flee at full gallop. Indeed, if the appearance of the Ninth had caused hesitation, the arrival of Guénand's formidable brigade in the centre must have startled the Austrians. When Kellermann's heavies fell upon the Austrians, it was the last of a series of consecutive blows.

As previously stated, at the point that Boudet's division unmasked itself, the 9th Liechtenstein Dragoon Regiment (approximately 1,000 sabres strong) deployed from the main road onto the fields to the left of Saint-Julien and Lattermann. Almost every Austrian account blames this cavalry for failing in the face of the French counter-attack. Radetzky wrote of his frustration that the Austrian cavalry had remained motionless during the preliminary fighting and Marmont's bombardment:

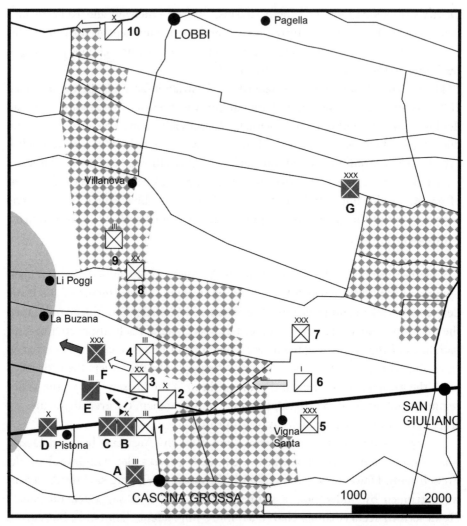

MAP 16: Kellermann's charge – Approx. 5.30 pm

(French) 1 – Desaix with 9th Light Infantry; 2 – Kellermann's brigade (with Champeaux's dragoons); 3 – Guénand's brigade; 4 – 72nd Line (Monnier); 5 – Victor's corps (rallying); 6 – Horse Guard; 7 – Lannes' Corps; 8 – Monnier's division; 9 – Foot Guard; 10 – Rivaud.

(Austrians) A – IR 47 Franz Kinsky; B – Lattermann's grenadiers; C – IR 11 Wallis (St-Julien); D – Weidenfeld's grenadiers; E – 9th Liechtenstein Dragoons; F – Kaim (retreating); G – Ott's corps.

'None of the cavalry generals had the audacity to turn and to take this battery. During this stagnation the enemy made a cavalry charge on ours and, will you believe it? This renowned cavalry, the mainstay of the monarchy, shamefully fled and carried along our brave infantry while throwing disorder and terror everywhere. Several infantry generals offered to put themselves at the head of the cavalry, but everything was in vain; this misfortune caused us the absolute loss of the battle.'

Zach's account, as relayed by Faverges, also expresses frustration at the lack of support from the cavalry. Typically for Zach, his rather academic analysis identifies a systemic failing in the training of Austrian cavalry, blaming the timidity of the horses rather than any tactical faults. Faverges writes:

'Zach ran up to the head of the Liechtenstein Dragoons; the dragoons turned their bridles. Zach led them back once, twice; he wanted to be killed. "We had," he told me, still under the impression of this terrible moment, "we had on the battlefield the result of the instruction which we give to the men and to the horses in peacetime. All the bravery of the riders will frankly not make the horses approach in war an infantry which they have been trained to be afraid of and to avoid in the training camps. The battle of Marengo was lost because we had taught too much contradance to the horses." That is what Zach told me.'

Stutterheim's account also follows a similar narrative:

'The commanders of each dragoon regiment were unable to deploy their troops and come to the aid of the infantry in distress. Still in the process of deploying, they were overturned by Kellermann's far weaker force and put to flight. General Zach is sure that as soon as they saw the French cavalry, which moreover initially stopped short and certainly did not appear to want to attack ours, who were superior to them, the 9th Liechtenstein Light Dragoons immediately turned about and carried away the other regiment with them. It was later disbanded.'

Certainly we see the 9th Liechtenstein Dragoons singled out for particular criticism. What does not quite add up is the number of accounts of Austrian cavalry attacks on Boudet's troops, in particular the 9th Light. Boudet's account has the following to say about the Austrian cavalry:

'This corps of grenadiers was supported by a very strong cavalry which extended beyond the wings of my first brigade; their resistance was very stubborn; but the valour of the 9th Light rendered it null, and a fortunate charge by our cavalry crowned this attack … On several occasions, the enemy cavalry attempted to turn and to surround the 9th Light; but it was received so as to be discouraged.'

Dubois' 1839 history of the 9th Light states the third battalion of this half-brigade was forced to form square at one point. We also find among this unit's bravery citations a number of situations where the light infantrymen fought against cavalry. For example:

'JACQUES, sergeant. Being at the head of the skirmishers, and having been charged by the enemy's cavalry, whose object was to fall upon the battalion, he dismounted several cavaliers, and contained the rest.

'MACQUART, sergeant. At the head of a picket of six men, he showed great firmness, resisting successfully a charge of twelve enemy cavalry.

'BENOIST, sergeant. Detached as a skirmisher, and charged by two Austrian cavaliers, he dismounted one, and made the other prisoner.

'MAHUT, corporal of grenadiers. Seeing an officer of dragoons on the point of falling into enemy hands, he killed one of the Austrians, put the others to flight, and received a gunshot when he seized the horse of the cavalier whom he had killed.

'CAMUS, carabinier. Dismounted two horsemen whom he took prisoners.

'SALLIOR, carabinier. Detached as a skirmisher and charged by two Austrian cavalrymen, he killed one and dismounted the other.

'VINOT, chasseur. He detached as a skirmisher, and, assailed by two Austrian cavaliers and a Hungarian grenadier, dismounted one of the cavaliers, forced the other to retire, and with a bayonet thrust put the grenadier out of action.

'LAMBERT, chasseur. Detached as a skirmisher, and charged by two Austrian cavalrymen, he killed one and dismounted the other.

'PIESSEVAUX, chasseur. Detached as a skirmisher, and attacked by two Hungarian horsemen, he put one out of action, and forced the other to retire. Charged almost at the same moment by six Austrian cavalrymen, who gave him several sabre cuts and left him for dead, he arose, as soon as they had abandoned him, ran to the grenadier whom he had put to flight, struck him, and brought him back as a prisoner.'

These citations for 'muskets of honour' indicate Austrian cavalry was active quite early in the attack, while the Ninth had its skirmishers deployed to slow the advance of the Austrian column. It is unlikely these troopers belonged to the

9th Liechtenstein Dragoons, but from other units which had followed the main column on the road, for example those of Pelatti's brigade.

In the wake of Kellermann's charge, Zach and Saint-Julien were both captured. In the latter case, Saint-Julien was lucky. In the confused aftermath of the charge, he was rescued by 22–year-old Corporal Atmann of the 4th Karacsay Dragoons, who rode among the crowd of French infantry and scooped him up to take him back to safety, for which he was later rewarded with the Gold Bravery medal. Zach was not so lucky. Radetzky elaborates on the circumstances of the chief of staff's capture:

> [A]bout 3-400 horse chasseurs [*sic*] jumped out from their rearguard, which had just arrived and the grenadiers, previously positioned in the middle, but now marching at the front in four battalions, fell into such a panic at the sight of them, that they threw away their guns and fled in disorder. The two light dragoon regiments [9th Liechtenstein and 3rd Erzherzog Johann Light Dragoons], seized by the same panic, likewise fled and so the panic spread, until everyone was running. Zach, I and some staff officers were located in front of a ditch filled with water to the side the road. Zach remained frozen to the spot, but I and the officers jumped over the ditch, followed by some shots from the pursuing horse chasseurs, but Zach was captured.'[26]

Having so loudly boasted about his success, Zach ultimately failed in both his predictions; namely to carry San Giuliano with a bayonet charge or to be killed in the battle in the event of a defeat. With his capture, Zach must have had a terrible feeling that his enemies in headquarters would now blame him for the catastrophe unfolding around him. In fact some would even claim he deliberately allowed himself to be captured. Led away towards Torre Garofoli, there was nothing more he could do.

One question about Desaix's counter-attack remains. Kellermann expressly said the 9th Light were in retreat when he charged; Marmont also says he saw men to the left of the road running before the grenadiers. What did they see? The logical answer is quite simple. Ahead of the 9th Light were several hundred of its skirmishers. Seeing themselves about to be overtaken by the grenadiers on one side, and their comrades on the other, the skirmishers must have run to clear the front of the unit. Some would have run through the intervals of the battalions, but some must have run near the road in the direction of the guns of the Consular Guard. Were these the disordered men Marmont saw?

In 1828, Kellermann claimed the 9th Light Infantry was unable to withstand the shock of the grenadiers. He wrote of the half-brigade: 'It stops, staggers, retires hastily, and draws the line with it.' This accusation met from an angry response by Savary:

> 'Took to flight! This is the first time I read such an assertion. Undoubtedly I have no right to give it a positive denial, since it is vouched by General Kellermann, and I was engaged in conveying to him the First Consul's orders at the moment when the flight is alleged to have occurred. But from the point where he was stationed with his troop, neither of us could discover Desaix's division. He therefore makes so grave an assertion upon nothing more than hearsay. I may then be allowed to doubt its accuracy.
>
> 'The first line of General Desaix consisted of the 9th Light Regiment, one of the most formidable in the army, which was commanded by Colonel La Bassée, who is still alive. This regiment, and its chief, were wont to affix their names to every field of battle upon which they had to contend. They were never known to hesitate at the sight of danger; and I can attest that, as I was proceeding after Kellermann's charge, to overtake the division which was debouching, upon the left of San Giuliano, I beheld at the head of the column the 9th Light Regiment, which certainly bore no resemblance to a regiment just broken in.
>
> 'This accusation is rendered still more improbable by another circumstance. The First Consul was fully aware of all the occurrences of the day. The reports could not have left him in ignorance of those acts of weakness or of courage which had marked the vicissitudes of the battle. Nevertheless, he congratulated the 9th Light Regiment upon its conduct, and assigned to it the title of the incomparable regiment. Now, it is a fact of general notoriety that, however well disposed to distribute praises, he was never lavish of them.'[27]

As will be seen, at the end of the battle, Berthier declared the performance of the Ninth to be 'incomparable'. Boudet was equally full of praise, saying:

> 'It is absolutely to the bearing and to acts of valour of this corps that such marked advantages were achieved on the left and above all the capture of the artillery and prisoners. The cavalry has equally contributed with much timeliness and courage.'

The cost of this success was extremely high. Accurate casualty returns for the French are notoriously difficult to find, but the 1839 history of the Ninth records one-third of its number were killed or wounded in the fighting – between 600-700 men. This is comparable with half-brigades which had been engaged since the morning.

A final word here on Desaix, whose body now lay among the dead light infantrymen. Having relayed Desaix's request to Kellermann, Savary returned to the Ninth. When he arrived, the Ninth's commander, Chief of Brigade Mathieu Labassée, told him Desaix was dead. Savary was distraught and went looking for the body of his mentor so it would not be condemned to an unmarked mass grave. The ground was littered with the dead, and, as was the custom at the time, the dead were immediately stripped. Immediately after being killed, a sergeant of the Ninth took Desaix's coat. He first asked Adjutant-Major Pierre Barrois if he could keep it; after all, he said, Desaix had no further use for the garment.[28] The body was then stripped, except for the shirt, which was bloodstained and fouled by gore. Savary eventually found Desaix's body 'not two hundred yards' from where he had last spoken with him.[29] He recognized Desaix's corpse because of his long, loosely tied hair and the battle scars on his tanned face. He tried to mop up the blood with his handkerchief, but there was too much. Savary then thought to remove Desaix's heart so it might be embalmed and returned to his family, but the organ had been destroyed by the fateful ball, which had exited through his right shoulder blade. Savary instead attempted to cut a lock of the general's hair, but this became soiled by the blood on Savary's handkerchief. The body was wrapped in a horse blanket and led away to the rear by a young hussar. News of Desaix's death soon reached the ears of the First Consul. He was left numb by the shock. With the battle still raging, and victory by no means certain, Bonaparte did not have time to mourn. He simply said: 'Why am I not allowed to weep?'

Chapter 15

Victory

Melas had taken his time to leave the battlefield, speaking to wounded men who had been collected around Marengo to have their wounds dressed before being evacuated by cart to Alessandria. Eventually the commander-in-chief rode off to his quarters and a well-earned rest. Cavour, a curious Piedmontese observer of the battle, was near to him at the time and noticed the early evening sky began clouding over, making it seem prematurely dark. He was surprised when they saw several carts full of French prisoners rather than Austrian wounded. Exhausted, they had pleaded to be transported and the drivers had consented. One never can tell how much truth there is in these things, but Petit claimed the church bells of Alessandria were rung in celebration of the Austrian victory and that the priests of that city 'manifested a baseness and cruelty' to the French prisoners, and even 'exhibited poniards' to threaten them.

Around this time, Adjutant-General Dampierre was finally captured at Cascina Bianca. Two-thirds of his men were casualties and they were out of ammunition. When they had stopped firing, a prince serving in the Nauendorf Hussars rode up to the Frenchmen and invited them to surrender, promising the officers they could keep their swords. Dampierre consented, but had no sooner done so than a mob of hussars descended on him, took his sabre and pulled off an epaulette 'like thieves'. The Austrian officer hit his men with the flat of his sword and drove them off, but the articles were not recovered. Dampierre and his men were marched off towards Alessandria. In his absence, French troops would later pillage his baggage.

Meanwhile, the wounded General Soult had been lying in his bed quite cheerfully, hoping victory would go to his compatriots. An old Austrian surgeon-major walked into his room to check on him.

'Well doctor, how is the affair going?' inquired Soult.

'Ah general, what a battle! We do not know where to put our wounded; we have more than 5,000 up until now and, although the battle has finished, at this moment they are still arriving by hundreds. Our brave General Hadik is in that number, several other generals and a quantity of officers. Your loss is also very considerable.'

'But to which side goes the victory?'

'To ours, General, and that is the only consolation for the price it has cost us.'

Soult was unconvinced: 'Are you sure, Doctor?'

'Without a doubt, General Melas is coming back and did you hear his staff just pass by in the street?'

Soult realized he had just heard the sound of horses going by, so perhaps the doctor was telling the truth. All the time, though, he could hear a number of guns in the distance. The doctor had claimed that the battle was over, so Soult quizzed him on this.

'It can only be the French rearguard that General Zach is pursuing.'

Soult listened again; the sound seemed to be coming closer:

'If there is a rearguard engaged, it would seem to be yours?'

This time the doctor listened more carefully. It was true; the guns were coming nearer. A look of concern came over the doctor's face; he left the room hurriedly.

In the wake of Desaix's attack, prisoners were rounded up and led to the rear by the cavalry. Soldiers laid claim to the guns they had seized in the hope of reward. Ranks were redressed and the French began the pursuit of the fleeing Austrians. Rallying behind Desaix's troops were the soldiers of Victor and Lannes. Suddenly aware of the reversal of fortune in the battle, there appears to have been a sense of eagerness to regain the initiative. Anyone who witnessed the French army at 4.00 pm would have scarcely believed this was the same body of men two hours later. Petit describes the moment the order for a general advance was given:

> 'What was now to happen had been foreseen – was calculated upon; the battalions burnt with impatience; the drummer's eye fixed upon the drum-major's cane, waits for the signal; the trumpeter, with his arm raised up prepared his breath. The signal is given: the terrible *pas de charge* is heard. All the corps are put in motion at once; the mettlesome fire of the French, like a torrent, carries everything away with it that opposes its passage.'

Coignet summed the moment up nicely in his usual colourful manner: 'The charge rang out everywhere. Each of us turned round and ran forward. We did not shout any more, we roared!'

The aide de camp Lejeune had returned to Berthier's side after delivering his message to Desaix. With the Austrians in full flight, he witnessed many harrowing scenes about him. Amid all the horror, his attention was drawn to one particularly poor wretch of an Austrian officer who was writhing in agony on the floor. Lejeune went over to this man and dismounted, looking to see if he could offer any assistance. The Austrian officer had been shot through the lower torso by a cannonball, but had not been killed outright. The officer begged Lejeune to kill him and finish the job. Lejeune could not bring himself to do this in cold blood.

He did, however, offer the man his pistol to perform the terrible deed. The man sat forwards and put the pistol in his mouth. Lejeune turned his head and shielded his face with his hand as the Austrian pulled the trigger and blew his brains out. Happier moments were to come though. Young Georges Amptil, a conscript from the 30th Line, came running towards the commanding general's entourage. He was holding aloft the flag that he had captured and wanted to present it to Berthier. Lejeune led the conscript forwards and introduced him to Berthier. It was a symbol of the triumphs being made all over the field by Republican troops.[1] Up until this point, Bonaparte had viewed the proceedings with great anxiety. However, as the advance began the nearby band of the 6th Light Infantry struck up an impromptu performance which the band master aptly named 'An Air to Victory'.[2]

Boudet led his division in the direction of Marengo, heading diagonally across the open plain, following the line of the old road, with the divisions of Watrin and Chambarlhac to their rear and right. They drove back Kaim's troops ahead of them. Captain Rauch was witness to the flight of the Austrian army in the centre:

> 'Our cannon were withdrawn and the artillery falling back at the gallop immediately gave the signal for a general flight. Only he who was an eyewitness to the panicked shock at this hour of the engagement can have any idea of the terrible confusion, which resulted from the disordered retreat. The officer put his life and honour at risk, but he was no longer heard; his orders were no longer followed; he shouted hoarsely: "Halt, halt", but in vain. Everyone shouted "Halt" after him and fled. Some threw their guns away and ran where they could, others fired their muskets randomly into the air, or not infrequently, at their brave comrades, who were still faced forward and better behaviour could no longer be expected from the men, who were seized with panic, from the moment it set in. At such a moment, the enemy musketry often doubled its murderous effect; most of the prisoners taken and the guns lost were at that stage.'[3]

During this pursuit of the Austrian centre, Valhubert states that the 28th Line maintained its square and supported the right of Boudet's division. The 40th Line were also reported to be in this area, as were the 24th Light Infantry, who followed directly behind Monnier's men. This report of Monnier perhaps also clears up the mystery of the whereabouts of the French Foot Guards. Speaking of the troops who had fought at Castelceriolo earlier, Monnier writes: 'The attack having recommenced, they attacked, assembled with the Guard of the Consuls, led by Adjutant-General Léopold Stabenrath.'

Léopold Stabenrath was an officer on Berthier's staff. We encountered him briefly before, with Maurice Dupin at the time of the French retreat. What was this staff officer doing at the head of the Consular Guard? In 1803, the Count de Castres attempted to prepare an account of the battle. He interviewed officers from Carra-Saint-Cyr's brigade as part of this work and (according to de Cugnac, *Campagne de l'Armée de Réserve en 1800*, Vol. 2, p.458) they claimed the following:

> 'They said they had executed this [retreat] through vineyards, which had protected them against the Austrian cavalry; that it was five-quarters of an hour, or an hour and a half, after they had left the village, and that they were marching in isolation and without any knowledge of the rest of the French army, when an aide-de-camp met them and told them that they should carry themselves forward, and that he had been sent to give orders to all the troops he would meet to resume the offensive.'

It appears likely that Stabenrath was the ADC identified by Carra-Saint-Cyr; in which case, if Monnier's troops were found in the vines, it is entirely plausible Stabenrath first found the Foot Guard in the same area.[4]

Having retreated from Castelceriolo, Carra-Saint-Cyr headed straight back to the place when told to advance. It appears the Foot Guards went with him. At the same time, Rivaud's light cavalry brigade at last decided to advance boldly onto the battlefield, coming down from the Sale road also heading for Castelceriolo. Admittedly uncoordinated, these two pincers moving towards Castelceriolo overtook Ott's column, which had continued its march eastwards and was not far off being level with San Giuliano. Ott's column, not yet seriously engaged, was now in danger of being cut off.

When the firing had begun at San Giuliano, Ott ordered his troops to halt while the new situation was assessed. FML Vogelsang was in favour of falling on the French right flank, just as they had done at noon when the French held Marengo. They were still strong, and Vogelsang was all the more emboldened because he had collected various detachments of cavalry during the advance. This time Ott was more hesitant. He looked instead for advice from his principal staff officer, Colonel de Best.

Crossard saw de Best and Stutterheim together. His account describes the conversation he had with de Best.

'Colonel, the enemy has arrived in the centre.'

'I know.'

'Should we not, with the greater part of our left, fall on their flank?'

'But do you know what has happened on the right?'

'No.'

'Well, we must retire.'

Stutterheim gives a different rendition of what occurred, albeit the result was the same. He states de Best rode towards the San Giuliano road to observe what was taking place there. This must have taken some time. On his return he urged caution, telling Ott the coming darkness would not allow them to see the enemy's strength. Stutterheim then states that 'a voice' rang out and assured Ott his men 'would certainly not make any difference alone, that moreover everything was lost, so it would be best, if we gave up waging war and that those who were responsible for all our misfortunes should be hung'.[5] Ott ordered a retreat back to Castelceriolo.

Stutterheim does not identify the man behind the voice, but it was almost certainly de Best. Here we reach the climax in the conflict between Zach and his deputy, and indeed, the operational leadership of the imperial army in Italy. It is uncertain if Ott's intervention in the battle would have changed the results, but we see in this conversation the principal cause of the Austrian defeat. The French army was fully united behind Bonaparte. Witness the way the French rallied to support Desaix's attack. Now witness the advice given to Ott by the deputy chief of staff. Zach and his sponsor, Thugut, were the architects of this disaster and upon them would fall the blame. These were the men de Best thought should be hanged.

Unfortunately for Ott, he did not enjoy an easy journey back to Alessandria. Lannes advanced against Ott's column, supported by Chambarlhac's division and, it appears, the surviving Foot Guards. Schellenberg's infantry did not wait idly for this attack, but launched one of their own against the oncoming French. As two sets of bayonets stabbed and parried, the outcome of the affair was by no means guaranteed to favour the French. The 96th Line in particular came under heavy attack and became entangled in a fierce mêlée. Quartermaster-Corporal Leroy was carrying the battalion flag, when he found himself surrounded by Austrians eager to dispossess him of this prize. It was only after the intervention of a handful of Leroy's comrades that the battalion's honour was saved, although only after Leroy had been savagely wounded. In another incident, Grenadier Bisson watched as his captain was dragged away captive. He threw off his haversack so as not to be encumbered and called for two of his comrades to help him rescue the officer. The three men flew after the Austrians and succeeded in releasing the grateful captain again. Coignet was also in the thick of it. A Hungarian infantryman had thrust at him with his bayonet, and although Coignet parried it, the bayonet still nicked him on the eyelid. Blood poured into Coignet's eye, half-blinding him, but still he managed to make a thrust of his own, killing his assailant. All around individual fights began to go the way of the French, and the Austrians, disordered by their charge, began to fall back. Corporal Daumas of the 6th Light walked boldly to within four paces of one group of Austrians, and calmly shot their senior officer dead. Rather than exact their revenge, the Austrians ran away in disorder, unsure what to do in the chaos.

As Rivaud approached Castelceriolo, he encountered the debris of Pilatti's cavalry brigade and the Lobkowitz Dragoons. This force of cavalry was attempting to maintain Ott's line of retreat, because by now it was clear the French counter-attack had driven in the Austrian centre and appeared headed for Marengo. Rivaud formed his brigade into a column of platoons, 12th Hussars at the front, 21st Chasseurs in the rear, and pursued the Austrian cavalry. Unfortunately for the latter, when they arrived at Castelceriolo, they found Carra-Saint-Cyr had reoccupied the place at 8.00 pm. Some Austrian infantry formed square to protect themselves from Rivaud's troopers, but Corporal Coliboeuf shot an officer with a pistol as he rode by.[6]

Finding Castelceriolo blockaded, Vogelsang led his troops to attack. Within a moment, the general was wounded and had to be carried off to safety – another Austrian general fallen victim to the battle. Ott's troops had to bludgeon their way through the village, being fired on by French troops all the way. Crossard took over a company of the Bach Light Infantry in the vineyards outside the village. For a moment he was able to direct fire into the French right flank and halt their advance, but he was unsupported. The other Austrian troops simply used this moment to make good their escape. Crossard says it was as if the army was gripped 'by enchantment'. He saw the cavalry escaping, and among them Prince Max de Latour Taxis, the commander of the Lobkowitz Dragoons. Crossard looked imploringly at the prince, but admitted he did not have sufficient rank to order him to stand and fight, and his own horse was by now extremely fatigued. With Melas absent, Zach captured and so many generals wounded, the Austrian army was leaderless at the moment it needed leadership the most. Worse still, the headlong flight had to pass over the Fontanone ditch at Marengo, and then cross the Bormida in order to reach safety. 'What finer ground could offer itself to the victor to complete the defeat,' Crossard wrote. 'Where could the ruin of this army be better consumed than in the passage of a river?'[7]

The final act of the battle has a certain savage, poetic justice to it. Throughout the campaign, Zach's plan had been to lure the Army of the Reserve out onto the open plain, where he could destroy it with superior forces of artillery and cavalry. The Austrian artillery had played its part in the battle, and the fields were littered with dead and maimed Frenchmen as a testament to its skilful employment. However, when the French retreated, the Austrian cavalry did not have its great moment. We have seen the reasons for this as the battle unfolded. So it is with some sense of irony that it was left to the numerically weaker French cavalry to deliver the knockout blow. While Kellermann's charge was a severe blow to the Austrians, helping turn the tide of the battle, it was a French cavalry charge which ended the battle and administered to the Austrians the terminal *coup de grâce*.

Before describing this charge, we must return to the main road and review events since the capture of Zach. From studying casualty returns, it appears the Paar battalion of Lattermann's brigade was able to disengage from Desaix's attack, and make off in the direction of Spinetta in reasonably good order. This battalion of grenadiers perhaps acted as a rallying point for the Austrian fugitives escaping Desaix's attack. On the right, IR 47 had reached Cascina Grossa, but had then fallen back when the results of the French counter-attack became clear.[8] This regiment headed towards Spinetta, where Weidenfeld's grenadier brigade had taken up position, deployed across the road. On the opposing side, it took some time for the 9th Light Infantry to regroup after securing prisoners and passing these to the cavalry to escort to the rear. The half-brigade advanced along the main road, supported by an assortment of troops from Victor's command, who had rallied at San Giuliano. These advanced westwards and encountered Weidenfeld in the vineyards behind Spinetta and on the high ground.

Captain von Ostoich was the interim commander of the right-hand grenadier battalion. When he saw the French advancing towards him, he seized the battalion flag and advanced with it towards the enemy. Grenadier Heinrich Eichelmann ran over to Ostoich and offered to take his place, promising not to abandon the standard and to advance as far forward as ordered. To loud cheers, Eichelmann began advancing towards Victor's soldiers; Ostoich ordered the battalion to advance in support. It was a brave but foolhardy gesture. The French directed their fire on Eichelmann, who fell wounded, with eight shots also hitting the flag. Another soldier, Franz Graf, ran out of the line and recovered the flag before the French could reach it, and Eichelmann was rescued.[9] The fighting now became more intense as Weidenfeld's whole brigade opened up with volleys of musketry. However, without orders, Weidenfeld began to fall back in the direction of Marengo lest he be cut off from his own line of retreat. Behind Weidenfeld, a body of Austrian cavalry began to form. This included the detachment of the Archduke Johann's Light Dragoons, who had been sent to scout the Novi road, and also some of O'Reilly's troopers. This force of horsemen rode round Weidenfeld's left flank into the centre opposite Marengo.

While Victor was engaged with Weidenfeld, Murat advanced with the cavalry of the Consular Guard. Kellermann rode up to support Murat with his heavies and the remains of Champeaux's dragoons. As they advanced across the plain, Kellermann ordered the 8th Dragoons to send some men forward to act as mounted skirmishers and screen their advance. Night was beginning to draw in. At Marengo there was terrible confusion as the debris of the Austrian centre attempted to negotiate the bottleneck of the bridge over the Fontanone. Infantrymen were mixed pell-mell with the artillery and cavalry. Murat saw this and realized now was the moment for the French cavalry to turn retreat into utter rout. Petit describes the scene:

'Night was coming on; the troops of the enemy in disorder: cavalry, infantry, artillery, were heaped one upon another towards the centre; in the throng, many of their own men were thrown off the bridge into the river. The artillery which they had drawn back at the commencement of our good fortune, for fear that by its being taken it might be turned against themselves, was, in the present circumstance of more injury than use to them, as it intercepted their passage. Murat, seeing the importance of precipitating their retreat, and increasing their confusion, made us advance on a full trot, when we, in a short time, got before a part of their infantry, which had no resource but to be made prisoners, or to be cut to pieces. The Horse Grenadiers, and the Chasseurs of the Guard, kept the right of the road, to the number of 200, four or five hundred men of the 1st, 6th, 8th dragoons, and 20th cavalry, occupied the left: Murat flew from one side to the other. The decisive moment was come: Chief of Brigade Bessières, filled with the same ardour which inspired us all, and, exciting a desire in each corps to distinguish itself, gave orders for the trumpet to sound a charge, that we might fall upon the enemy's infantry, already out of breath.'

As these 600 horsemen advanced, Bessières perceived an Austrian cavalryman thrown on the floor, holding out his hands, pleading for the French horsemen not to crush him. In a moment of humanity, Bessières called out: 'My friends, open your ranks; let us spare this unfortunate man.'

Just before the French cavalry charged, they saw the arrival of the Austrian cavalry coming out from behind Weidenfeld's brigade. Petit continues the account:

'The Austrian cavalry, resolving to save the infantry, came up to us in column, and their rapid pace obliged us to give loose to the reins. We inclined to the left, by obliquing on them. At the distance of about thirty paces, was a ditch, which again separated us. The crossing it, taking sword in hand, surrounding the two first platoons, all was but a work of five minutes. Stunned by this proceeding, and probably intimidated by the height of the men, whose hairy caps seemed to add to their natural stature, they but ill defended themselves and were therefore cut down or thrown into disorder. We made no prisoners, nor did we take any horses. While all this was doing the dragoons took the same column in the flank, and added to the general carnage.'

According to Eugène Beauharnais, the melee lasted no more than ten minutes.[10] Having crossed two ditches, the French cavalry crashed into the Austrians at the moment they were deploying. In the melee, Trumpeter Faniel of the 8th Dragoons was particularly noticeable; in his left hand were his reins and trumpet, on which he sounded the charge relentlessly, while in his right hand was his sword, with which he battled at the same time. He saw his chief of squadron fall from his horse wounded and rode over to protect him, escorting him to the rear. Once the commander was safe, Faniel, sounding his continual charge once more, rode back into the fray, killing two, dismounting another and capturing a new horse.

The Horse Grenadiers and Kellermann's heavies were among the biggest men in the army, and were mounted on the largest horses. They pushed the lightly mounted Austrian cavalry towards Marengo. Gripped with terror, the Austrian horsemen rode into the throng of fugitives around Marengo and stampeded across them. Men were crushed and drowned in the ditch, which was already choked with bodies. Those who made their way across it fled towards the Bormida. There the crush began again as men rushed to pass through the bridgehead. By now Melas had been told of the disaster. He returned to the battlefield, but it was too late for him to do anything but issue instructions for men to reform where they had camped the night before. He posted a battalion from the city garrison to help restore order, and directed an officer in the bridgehead to shout down the assembly orders to the retreating men.[11] As the queue at the bridgehead built up, some attempted to swim the Bormida, but were swept away in the current. One artillery driver chanced his luck by taking his team through the water, gun still in tow. Improbably, he was successful, and seeing this others followed. The wheels of the wagons and limbers churned the bed of the river into a complete morass, and these hopefuls now found themselves stuck. Twenty guns were lost this way.

While all this took place, Murat had recalled his cavalrymen and formed a line in front of Marengo. Boudet's division also formed a line overlooking the village, and together they watched the last of Weidenfeld's grenadiers fall back across the ditch. O'Reilly had also returned, his light troops forming a defensive rearguard. At around 9.00 pm, Boudet's troops assaulted Marengo and reoccupied the place. Within an hour, Gardanne was back at Pedrabona. Dupont had thought it a wise precaution to place troops near the Austrian bridgehead to await the dawn. At 10.00 pm, the battle concluded. It had been a remarkable day. Fourteen hours before, the Austrians had crossed over the bridgehead and the two sides had fought one of the most intense battles ever known. Yet there they were, back where it had all begun: Gardanne watching the bridgehead, wondering what the Austrians would do next?

The account of Count Cavour has some interesting remarks on the latter part of the battle. He said night began to fall at 7.30 pm, and it was only at this time that

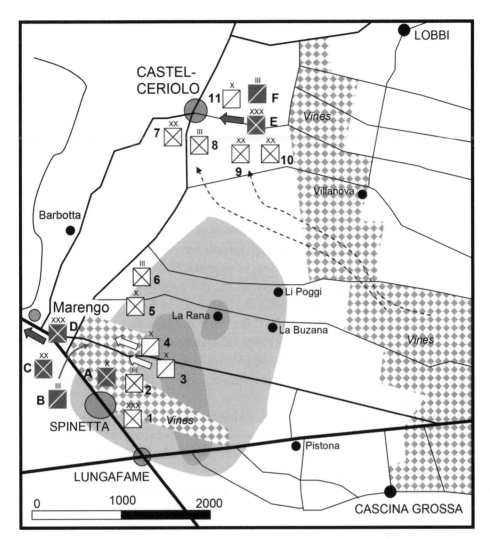

MAP 17: The Austrian retreat – Approximately 8.00 pm

(French) 1 – Gardanne; 2 – 9th Light Infantry; 3 – Kellermann's brigade (with Champeaux's dragoons); 4 – Guard cavalry; 5 – Guénand's brigade; 6 – 72nd Line (Monnier); 7 – Monnier; 8 – Foot Guard; 9 – Chambarlhac; 10 – Watrin; 11 – Rivaud's cavalry.

(Austrians) A – Weidenfeld's grenadiers and remains of Lattermann; B – Archduke Johann's Light Dragoons; C – O'Reilly; D – Kaim (retreating); E – Ott's corps; F – various Austrian cavalry units.

Melas arrived in Alessandria. He was with Melas at this point, near the drawbridge into the city, and they heard the sound of gunfire off to the east while watching the arrival of wagons loaded with wounded. They dismissed the gunfire as belonging to some lost French patrols making a desperate last stand. As it began to darken, the sky became stormy, but everyone was happy, believing victory had been gained. At 8.00 pm, Cavour saw General Lamarseille and paid him his compliments. The Austrian general replied: 'Looks like I caught it in the arm.'

Cavour saw the Austrian had been bruised by a gunshot, and asked: 'But finally the battle is won?'

'Yes, but the resumption has been a little strong and it is there that I caught this shot.' Wondering what exactly Lamarseille had meant by the resumption, Cavour went up to the bastions around the city to try to see what was going on, but found it too dark to see anything. He instead went to the bridgehead at the Bormida to see what he could learn. When the bells sounded 9.00 pm, he was in a house. There he learned of the arrival of Count Poncillon, a Piedmontese gentleman in Austrian service. Poncillon had commanded a squadron of the Bussy Light Horse during the battle, and had been heavily engaged. Cavour was surprised by his appearance. The scabbard of his sabre was missing, as were the tassels from his sash, a piece of his jacket and a part of his horse's cover. He had been brushed by a cannonball which had carried the missing articles away, leaving the lucky man with nothing but a slight bruise. Cavour asked him if the battle had been won, and was told: 'It had been until around seven o'clock, then the troops were assailed on all sides. The French have retaken their first position with the exception of the village of Marengo which is still occupied by two squadrons of my regiment. General Zach has been made a prisoner, I do not know how.'

Cavour continued to quiz Poncillon, asking him what he thought would happen next. 'As far as I have been told, tomorrow we attack again; if meanwhile tonight we don't make a shameful capitulation; but I am going to hang around headquarters and I will tell you if there is anything more.'[12]

Another anxious spectator was General Soult, in his bed in Alessandria. At about 11.00 pm, the old doctor came back to Soult's room. He spoke of his disappointment:

> 'We are lost, our troops are recrossing the bridge at this moment! One had thought the battle won, and, like I told you, General Melas came back to Alessandria, when it was announced to him that your army had made a new attack. He returned with all haste, but he was not in time. Everything had changed, General Zach had been taken and we had been broken. There was nothing more left than for General Melas to cover the retreat. I do not know what General Melas will do to get us out of this situation.'

It became Soult's turn to console the doctor, who left shortly afterwards. That night Soult could barely contain his joy.

With the veil of night drawn over them, the living sat down among the dead and wounded, friend mixed with foe, fearful of the night. By all accounts it was a clear night – the evening clouds had passed overhead. Everyone would have been deafened by gunfire, with ears ringing, tormented with thirst, starving hungry now the adrenaline of battle began to subside. Coignet describes the moment:

> The whole army, with the exception of Desaix's division, was in a state of unbelievable weariness. Most of the soldiers had not eaten since the day before. We spent the day biting our cartridges. It was our only food. We were black with powder. Our legs were so stiff, that after a moment's rest we could not get up again. About ten o'clock my captain Merle sent for me by his domestic to take supper with him. There, my wounds were dressed, my hair restored, my powers revived; I had more happiness than my poor companions.'

On the Austrian side, Wenzel Rauch had safely crossed the Bormida with a group of about sixty or so men he had collected on his way. He was relieved to see the cavalry was held back from crossing until the infantry had all got across – he believed the bridge would collapse from the weight if they too tried to pass. Once across, he could not pass through all the fugitives to the camp of the night before, so he sat down where he could and allowed his sensations to overwhelm him. Hunger and a terrible thirst tortured him. He replayed moments of the battle in his head, in particular one when the colonel had prevented him from resisting the French attack. The thirst was so bad that he would gladly have paid a gold sovereign to quell it, even for just a drop of water; but there was none. He then began to feel cold, so much so he that could not even close his eyes, let alone sleep. Instead, he gazed up at the stars.

Across the scenes of devastated crops and smashed bodies, another man looked up at the stars: it was General Guénand. The French army was bivouacked in line behind Marengo, and most of the younger generals had returned to headquarters to lay claim to their successes. Guénand did not follow, and it is likely this is why his role in the battle has been ever since overlooked. Guénand was instead content to sit among his men and let his emotions subside. He considered the day's events and the conduct of the soldiers, who seemed so young to him; they had made him proud. If he was remembered in history for anything, he thought to himself, it was that he had commanded these brave boys at the Battle of Marengo.

When victory was concluded, the First Consul returned to his headquarters at Torre Garofoli. He was followed by the Horse Guard. Joseph Petit said they were all exhausted and in danger of dozing off in the saddle had it not been for the shouts of the wounded on the road side. The battlefield presented a terrible sight, even at night. Burning buildings illuminated harrowing scenes as the wounded were evacuated by their weary comrades. Wounded horses limped about on three legs, neighing in distress and unsettling Petit's horse. Caissons and guns had been tipped off the road into the ditches, completing the scene of destruction. The darkness added to the feeling of dread. Here and there were small groups of Austrian soldiers who had escaped their captors, but were then turned back to resume their captivity. Eventually the Horse Grenadiers reached Torre Garofoli and fell off their saddles to sleep among the heaps of dead and the dying, still holding their horses' bridles in their hands. The screams of the unfortunates around them were not enough to prevent Petit and his comrades from falling into a heavy, deep sleep.

Earlier that evening, the 12th Chasseurs had arrived at headquarters. De France looked for someone to report to, and finding no one but the First Consul, he made his report to him. Bonaparte requested that de France remain at headquarters until further notice, in case his men were needed for headquarters duties.[13] Ismert of the 11th Hussars had also arrived back in headquarters. With him was the small detachment that had been sent out to find food for Kellermann's dinner. Bonaparte's staff saw these provisions and lightened the load of the cavalrymen in order to prepare the First Consul's dinner. His chef, Dunan, prepared a meal of chicken cooked in wine. This relatively simple dish has now passed into culinary history as *Poulet Marengo* (Chicken Marengo).

Bonaparte expressed his sadness to Bourrienne over Desaix's death. He also said: 'Little Kellermann made a fine charge – he did it just at the right time – we owe him much; see what trifles decide these affairs.'[14] Bourrienne was still shocked that they had won the battle. Bourrienne had remained with Bonaparte's other private staff at San Giuliano the whole time Bonaparte was absent from them. One minute someone would come by and announce victory, then defeat and then victory once more. He and the valet, Constant, had both been worried by the approach of the Austrian guns and had noticed the stream of wounded pass by with increasing regularity; but sure enough the day had been won.

As the night went on, more and more reports of the scale of the victory came pouring in. Melas had been well beaten, but French losses had also been heavy. The first formal report of the battle was written by Berthier, dated 'on the battlefield of Saint-Juliano, 25 Prairial Year 8 [14 June 1800], at nine o'clock in the evening'. This report must have been dictated while the Austrians were still fleeing back to the bridgehead, and before Gardanne reached Pederbona. Of all the French reports which followed, it is perhaps the most accurate battle account in terms of identifying the key phases, and suffers very little from any self-promotion. It described how the French army had advanced after the the Battle of Montebello and 'repelled the enemy' up to Marengo. It described the attack on the evening of

13 June and then Melas' attack the following morning. It described the Austrians working their way onto the wings of the French army, of 100 guns pounding the French line. It described the collapse of the French left, and the support rendered by the cavalry, describing how Lannes in the centre had been forced to retreat in line with Victor, and how the right, supported by the grenadiers of the Guard of the Consuls, maintained its position 'until the moment of the arrival of the division Boudet, under the orders of General Desaix' (by which we can infer the right retreated at 4.00 pm, when Desaix began to arrive at San Giuliano). The account continues to describe the evening battle – how Desaix's troops attacked the enemy centre at the charge. Then to quote part of the report in full:

'The 9th Light Half-Brigade, incomparable by its bravery, was in the front line; General Desaix marched at its head. Your presence gave the army this impetus which decided, so many times, the victory. The charge was beaten; all the new line moved off, followed by the divisions which had fought since morning. General Kellermann, who had supported the movement of retreat of our left, seized the moment when the enemy infantry, having been shaken, tried to attack again. He charged impetuously, made more than 6,000 prisoners, took ten cannon and General Zach, chief of staff of the army.'[15]

The report now focused on the fighting against Ott. It described Watrin's division being 'supported by some Foot Grenadiers of the Consuls, who distinguished themselves during all the battle' (note the description of *some* Foot Grenadiers). It described Bessières at the head of the Horse Guards, and Monnier attacking Castelceriolo. Losing the correct chronology once, finally it described how a 'squadron of the Latour [*sic* – read Lobkowitz] Dragoons was entirely destroyed by the fire of the grenadiers of the Guard of the Consuls'. The French had taken 7,000 or 8,000 prisoners, many cannon and at least twelve flags. The Austrians had suffered 6,000 killed and wounded.

Berthier sent this report to headquarters, and told Kellermann the First Consul would probably want to congratulate him on his impressive achievements. Kellermann entered Bonaparte's headquarters believing he was about to be promoted to full general of division, but it was not to be. 'You made a pretty good charge,' Bonaparte told him coldly. Then turning to Bessières, he said with deliberate volume: 'Bessières, the Guard has covered itself in glory.' Kellermann was disgusted. He stalked moodily around headquarters, telling anyone who would listen that he had replied to Bonaparte: 'My *pretty good charge* has placed the crown on your head.'[16] Bourrienne believed Kellermann had not said these words to the First Consul directly, but they became so well known that Bonaparte soon learned of them and therefore did not give Kellermann the promotion he probably deserved. This slight was to fuel a sense of injustice in Kellermann until his death in 1835.

On retiring to his private chamber, Bonaparte considered the loss of Desaix. While valets Constant and Hambard busied themselves around him, Bonaparte talked about how he had lost his best friend: 'No one knew how much goodness nor how much genius was in his head. My dear Desaix always wanted to die like that. But need death have been so prompt in granting his wish?'[17]

Furnished with Berthier's report, Bonaparte looked to write his own account of the battle. He was a brilliant writer, able to embue his bulletins with a sense of drama and glory.

Bourrienne writes:

'After supper was over the First Consul dictated to me the bulletin of the battle. When we were alone I said to him, "General, here is a fine victory! You recollect what you said the other day about the pleasure with which you would return to France after striking a grand blow in Italy; surely you must be satisfied now?" – "Yes, Bourrienne, I am satisfied. But Desaix! Ah, what a triumph would this have been if I could have embraced him tonight on the field of battle!" As he uttered these words I saw that Bonaparte was on the point of shedding tears, so sincere and profound was his grief for the death of Desaix. He certainly never loved, esteemed, or regretted any man so much.'[18]

By now the clock had passed midnight. The bulletin embellished Berthier's account, following the main themes, but adding a greater sense of drama. The bulletin speaks of the uncertainty before the battle. 'The enemy seemed to have no plans and was very uncertain of its movements,' he wrote. The battle ebbed and flowed until 3.00 pm, when '10,000 cavalrymen [sic] overtook our right in the superb plain of San Giuliano. They were supported by a line of cavalry and much artillery' (clearly he was describing the emergence of Ott's Corps). Then there is one of the most iconic sentences in Napoleonic history:

'The grenadiers of the Guard were placed like a granite redoubt in the midst of this immense plain. Nothing could hurt them. Cavalry, infantry, artillery, all were directed against this battalion; but in vain; it was then one really saw what a handful of brave men can do.'

Monnier's division then arrived at Castelceriolo and seized the village at bayonet point; but now Austrian cavalry arrived on the French left and this movement precipitated a retreat. The enemy advanced with 100 guns firing canister:

'The roads were covered with fugitives, wounded, and debris. The battle seemed lost. The enemy was allowed to advance as far as a gun-shot from the village of San Giuliano, where the division of Desaix was in line, with eight pieces of light artillery in front, and two battalions *en potence* on the wings. All the fugitives rallied behind. Already the enemy made mistakes which foreshadowed his catastrophe. He stretched his wings too far. The presence of the First Consul rekindled the morale of the troops. "Children," said he, "remember that my habit is to sleep on the field of battle." To the cries of "Long live the Republic! Long live the First Consul!" Desaix approached at the charge and by the centre. In a moment the enemy is overthrown. General Kellermann, who, with his brigade of heavy cavalry, had protected the retreat of our left all day, executed a charge with such vigour and timing, that 6,000 grenadiers, and General Zach, chief of the staff, were captured, and several enemy generals killed.'

Seizing on Berthier's description of the half-brigade, the bulletin announced the 9th Light had 'merited the title of Incomparable'. He would later award the unit with special flags emblazoned with this device. Bonaparte then came to the death of Desaix:

'But a sharp loss felt by the army, which will be felt by the whole Republic, closes our hearts to joy. Desaix was struck with a bullet at the beginning of the charge of his division. He died instantly. He had only time to tell young Lebrun, who was with him: "Go and tell the First Consul that I die with regret that I have not done enough to live in posterity."'

Again, Desaix's final words are such an iconic part of the myth of the battle (along with the fallacy he spontaneously marched to the sound of guns) that they merit a few words of analysis. The statement above was a pure piece of political theatre. 'Young Lebrun' was the son of the Third Consul, Charles-François Lebrun, and serving with the army as an aide-de-camp to Desaix. As Bourrienne states in this memoirs, these last words, as dictated to him by the First Consul, 'were imaginary'. The doctors who later embalmed Desaix's body concluded the wound was so substantial that the man would have said nothing. It will be remembered that Lauriston wrote Desaix barely had the chance to say 'Dead!' when struck. After the battle, Lefèvre-Desnouettes assured everyone that Desaix fell 'without proffering a word'.[19]

Interestingly, Boudet also indicates Desaix said something: 'Death came to carry this great captain from his brothers in arms. He recommended, with his last words, concealing his fate, in the fear that this news would produce some alarm and be harmful to the victory.' Adjutant-General Dalton also wrote about last words in his after-action report: 'He fell in the first ranks of our soldiers, where he was always found; he lived a few minutes and recommended not to speak to the troops of his wound, in the fear that it might slow their enthusiasm. He was hardly able to say that his wound was mortal.'[20] Boudet and Dalton's accounts of the campaign are among the most credible documents which exist, but they were not present at the time of Desaix's death. The only way we might find some truth in these statements is if Desaix said something before he rode forward to the Ninth's skirmish line.

So the bulletin was written, and with that it appears fatigue finally overcame the First Consul. At 2.00 am, General Dupont entered his quarters to give Bonaparte an account of the positions taken up by the army that night. Here is how he found the man who had just enjoyed the greatest victory of the age:

'He slumbered in an old leather armchair. The fragments of the most modest of meals was placed next to him, on an unrefined table, and it is in this poor cubbyhole that he enjoyed the charms of the most important, most surprising, most compete victory by its results, and which, in the morning of the same day, he would have found hard to believe.'[21]

Chapter 16

The Convention of Alessandria

hat must Melas have felt watching the debris of his army fleeing back across the Bormida? What must he have felt when told of Zach's capture? Surprise? Anger? A sense of relief? Whatever rest Melas managed to snatch that night could not have been much comfort to the man, already badly bruised by the falls from his horse in the battle. His army was in a state of chaos and somehow, inexplicably, they had thrown away one of the greatest victories ever won by a Habsburg army. He was furious at Zach in particular.[1] The chief of staff was cursed and referred to in 'words of abuse'. Several senior officers, Radetzky prime among them, went so far as to accuse Zach of deliberately allowing himself to be captured when things turned in favour of the French.[2] Neipperg dismissed this, concluding Zach had been captured because he was poorly mounted on a bad horse.[3]

Regardless of this, everyone agreed Zach was liable for the defeat and for not properly communicating his plans to his subordinates on the general staff, in particular his deputy, de Best. Radetzky severely reproached Zach's handling of the campaign, blaming the politician 'Thugut and his cherished Zach' for the disaster.[4] Rather than wasting time in Turin, Radetzky complained, Zach should have attacked the French before they broke out from the Alps. Ott could have advanced up from Genoa via Casale and joined forces, and Bonaparte's army would have been blockaded in the mountains unable to gain provisions. This strategic failure was the result, he believed, of a 'brave and respectable army' being placed in the hands of a man whose only talents were a 'profound scholastic erudition and a ridiculous pedantry'; one who was, moreover, 'scheming, mean, rampant and who has no other resources in himself at the most critical moment other than the blackest and the most hideous deceit'.

Most agreed they should never have attempted to fight the battle at all. The senior officers had wanted to cross the Po at Casale, but had been overruled on Zach's advice. This had been a critical mistake. Even if they had driven Bonaparte beyond the Scrivia the night before, they would still have to fight the French in the defiles of Casteggio and Stradella. If they managed this, they would have to fight their way across the Po at Piacenza. All the while, the French would be falling back on their line of march, picking up reinforcements along the way.

Having determined to give battle, why had Zach squandered so many troops on 'false marches'? Not privy to Zach's labyrinthine deception strategy, his subordinates queried, if the object was to gain the Scrivia, why had Ott been directed to march on Sale? Why had O'Reilly been detached to the south-east? Why were battalions detached to Casale? Why hadn't the army been concentrated? Why had Hohenzollern been left at Genoa? Why hadn't the garrisons of the smaller fortresses been summoned? In total, 25,000 men had sat idle on their hands while the fate of the war was played out. Imagine the result if Hohenzollern had arrived late in the day, not Desaix.

As for the battle itself, they could not believe Zach did not know about the difficult ground in front of Marengo and the Fontanone ditch. Neipperg complained that plans of the countryside had been drawn up and that the army had manoeuvred over this ground almost continually for a year. It was 'impossible' for Zach not to realize that bridging equipment would be required to cross the Fonantone, but this same equipment was stuck with the army's baggage in the rear. The delay in bringing this equipment forward had been fatal.

The decision to 'sacrifice' the Kaiser and Karaczay dragoons in the Fontanone early on in the battle was also criticized. Neipperg believed the cavalry never recovered from being attacked by Kellermann as it attempted to reform on the other side of the ditch. If the cavalry had been kept fresh until the army advanced onto the plain, perhaps things would have been different? The decision to detach Nimptsch with fourteen squadrons to Cantalupo on the Acqui-Alessandria road to observe Suchet and Massena was also criticized. This elite cavalry was in very good condition. Its appearance on the field in the afternoon could have been decisive. Other than Zach, most blame was laid at the door of the cavalry. Firstly, Radetzky wondered, why hadn't the cavalry simply charged Marmont's battery from the flank? Why had these same troopers then turned and fled the field, causing panic everywhere their mad stampede took them?

As the casualty reports came in, everyone began to realize the scale of the defeat the day before. As Radetzky put it: 'After two campaigns of fatigue, pain, and suffering; having sacrificed brave men, we found ourselves almost without the means to defend our Hereditary Lands.' The casualty returns were frightful by any measure of the imagination. Hadik was dying. Lattermann, Vogelsang, Bellegarde, de Brie, Lamarseille and Gottesheim had been wounded and were in no state to serve. Zach was in enemy hands. In addition, twenty-six senior and 300 subaltern officers had been killed, wounded or captured. The army had lost 9,069 men and 1,493 horses:[5]

	Generals	Officers	Men	Total	horses
Dead	0	14	949	963	479
Wounded	7	238	5,274	5,519	683
Captured	1	74	2,846	2,921	331
Total	8	326	9,069	9,403	1,493

In terms of materiel, they had left a dozen cannon on the battlefield and one howitzer. More were in the Bormida, stuck in the mud. In the camping area in front of the bridgehead, the army was in a state of 'indescribable confusion'. Stutterheim compared the army to a 'Tartar' camp, with thousands of men flung out on the ground where they fell; and he complained about the panic caused by false alarms from random musket shots and shouts through the night.

At first light on Sunday 15 June, Melas held a council of war with Field Marshal Lieutenants Kaim, Ott and Schellenberg. As the senior staff officer, de Best stood in for Zach. Radetzky was also present, along with the other senior aides. As usual Melas said very little, but left the talking to Radetzky and de Best. In their discussions, four realistic options emerged. The first was to make a second attack on Bonaparte. However, with losses of over 9,000 men and so many battalions without officers, with the French again in possession of the 'Marengo ditch' and the route to Mantua barred by French troops at Piacenza, this option was quickly discounted. The next option was the escape route via Valenza or Casale, over the Po and beyond Milan; or thirdly, they could make a run for Genoa. The fourth option was different altogether. The three options thus far discussed all raised the risk of the army being totally destroyed. Despite the mauling it had suffered on 14 June, it was still a considerable army. Would it not be better to negotiate with Bonaparte and to return this army and its equipment and baggage to the Hereditary Lands?

The last three options were hotly debated. The option of crossing the Po at Casale or Valenza had been the preferred course of many to fighting the battle. However, it is believed the odds of them reaching safety with their artillery and baggage intact were now as low as 10:1. Marching on Genoa had been suggested by Major Nugent, and the scheme certainly had its merits. Melas would reunite with Hohenzollern troops and be able to receive supplies and reinforcements from Lord Keith's ships. However, to keep ahead of the French, it would mean abandoning the baggage and artillery. Deliberating on this, FML Ott said: 'As for the baggage, I do not care much about it. I will gladly sacrifice what I have to the good of the state.'

Kaim responded with an angry outburst which silenced Ott: 'Yes, and what do you have with you? A little victuals wagon with a pair of old nags? If I had nothing else with me, the French could take everything at the manger; but I've got my whole fortune with me, and that's not so easily shaken out of the sleeve.'[6]

At one point de Best raised a completely different idea, as suggested to him by Neipperg: an invasion of France through the Mont Cenis Pass. By Neipperg's own admission, this was an imprudent idea and Neipperg later confessed that 'through a combination of circumstances' he had 'lost his head' at this moment. However:

> 'Absurd as my reasoning was, I believed that if we should absolutely
> pass through a dishonourable capitulation, it would certainly have been

more honourable to conclude it at the gates of Lyons than at Alessandria. Perhaps our rapid movements towards the frontiers of France would have given a completely different turn to our affairs.'[7]

Melas listened to de Best and then jumped out of his chair with uncharacteristic energy, asking why he had not put such a madman under arrest?[8]

Of all the options available, a negotiated settlement appeared the most prudent. If the army was destroyed in a new attack, it would leave Austria exposed. No troops could be spared from the German front, so Vienna would be open to a French advance through Italy, as had occurred in 1797. The greatest responsibility was to protect the Hereditary Lands, and the safest means of returning the army intact was through negotiation. Melas had done the honourable thing in fighting on 14 June, but now the situation called for a different approach. However, at first no one really wanted to admit this, and so the council reached an impasse. A compromise was required, and this came in the suggestion that 'time gained was everything gained'. It was agreed they would ask Bonaparte for a forty-eight-hour ceasefire in which to bury the dead. During the ceasefire, Melas could consider his options more deeply and see what events arose. Neipperg spoke excellent French, so was sent to parley with French forward posts and to arrange for emissaries to be sent to the First Consul. Meanwhile, the commander of the citadel of Alessandria, General Major Skal, was chosen as the negotiator, accompanied by Major Torres. The pair were jokingly referred to as 'Thugut's Benjamins' by de Best – the name Benjamin meaning 'right-hand son' in Hebrew.

On the way to the bridgehead, this group passed the French émigré Crossard. Having spent the night in a house caring for the wounded Vogelsang, Crossard had gone outside to observe a spate of firing between the rival forward posts. Seeing Torres, Crossard asked if there was any news. 'Leave me,' Torres replied impatiently. 'The commander-in-chief has sent me to Bonaparte's headquarters to make some proposals.' Crossard ran back inside the house to tell Vogelsang that Melas was attempting to negotiate with the French.

A short while later, the Austrian party came in view of the French pickets. There was some firing, but Neipperg ordered the Austrian outposts to cease fire and rode forward under a flag of truce. General Gardanne was summoned, and Neipperg explained how Melas wished to send two officers to recommend a forty-eight-hour armistice. Gardanne was initially sceptical, but Neipperg said his opinion changed when he saw the look of resignation on the faces of Skal and Torres. Gardanne foresaw the Austrians had come not to dictate terms, 'but to receive them'. He consented and had the emissaries escorted to Bonaparte's headquarters, in the meantime agreeing a ceasefire would remain in place until the emissaries returned.

As the two Austrians rode towards Torre Garofoli, the French army was reforming and preparing for further fighting. Boudet had the 30th Line take a position on the reverse of the Fontanone to enfilade the main road. More troops were sent up towards Castelceriolo, where part of Ott's column was still roaming around. The sight of Austrian officers coming to negotiate raised everyone's morale because it indicated there would be an end to the fighting. In Boudet's division, the soldiers made use of the temporary truce to replenish their ammunition from discarded Austrian cartridge pouches. New flints were found and handed round. Meat and bread were also distributed so the men could make soup, and a ration of brandy was issued as well. There was a major problem with regard to the hundreds of corpses, as Adjutant-General Dalton records:

'The division finds itself camped on the battlefield, and among the dead: it has neither pickaxes nor shovels to be able to bury them. Soon the place will no longer be bearable. The air already smells of mephitis.'

Horse Grenadier Petit woke up to an empty stomach. He led his horse to the great farm complex at Torre Garofoli to see if anyone there had anything to eat. As he entered into the courtyard he was met with a terrible sight: thousands upon thousands of men were packed into every space available while they waited to go under the surgeon's knives and saws. Austrian and French soldiers lay compacted together, uttering a near constant moan; those undergoing the butchery that passed for surgery cursed their tormentors with every oath imaginable. Petit began to recognize the faces of some of his comrades among those imploring him for food and water. He soon forgot his own wants and spent the next few hours fulfilling the role of medical orderly. All the time more and more wounded were brought in, along with prisoners that had been taken in the night. A major battle like Marengo was far beyond the resources of the medical services of the era.

Coignet also visited Torre Garrofoli. Before joining the army he had sold horses to the Guard, and he wanted to visit them. His reflections echo those of Petit:

'Passing through the courtyard, a heart-rending spectacle was offered to us. The wounded of the Guard were there stretched out on the straw, and amputations were made. Everywhere shouts! I left with a sorry heart. In the plain, it was still worse. We saw the battlefield covered with soldiers, Austrians and French, who picked up the dead, dragged them along with the straps of their muskets and piled them. Soldiers and horses were all put together in the same heap, and burned to protect us from the plague. ·As for the corpses too far from the others, we contented ourselves with throwing a little earth on them.'

Many of the generals began writing their battle reports that morning. Rivaud's brigade had suffered enormous losses defending Marengo in the morning battle:

> 'The battalions of the 43rd and the 3rd [Battalion] of the 96th, which have acted before my eyes, have conducted themselves very well in this affair. The four battalion commanders were wounded, 45 other officers and 700 non-commissioned officers and soldiers were killed or injured. When I have received the details of what has happened during the rest of the day, I will give a more detailed report, in which I shall make known the names of the braves who have particularly distinguished themselves and who deserve promotion.'[9]

He later added a postscript to this report which confirmed the six battalions of his brigade had lost eighty-two officers killed or wounded and 1,900 non-commissioned officers and soldiers – a casualty rate of over 50 per cent. Watrin also counted his losses:

> 'The division, according to the reports of the commanding officers, had 13 officers killed, 83 wounded and nearly 2,000 men killed, wounded or taken. It suffered a lot from enemy fire.'

Watrin's thoughts were clouded while writing this report, because he had learned his brother, Lucien, had been killed in the battle while charging at the head of the 22nd Line.

Victor put his total losses at 'more than 3,000'. Among these were around sixty officers, many of whom had been killed. Lannes put his total losses at 'around 1,800 men wounded or taken by the enemy; but the number of prisoners is very small. 14 officers were killed and 83 wounded; around 300 non-commissioned officers and soldiers were killed.' Among the senior officers wounded can be found generals Malher, Mainoni and Citizen Valhubert, chief of brigade of the 28th. Monnier reported up to 800 men missing at roll call, although more were still coming back in from the battlefield all the time. Boudet was silent on his losses; but they were significant. Lauriston estimated the losses at 600–700 killed, 2,000 wounded and 1,500 prisoners (Berthier's 1805 account later admitted 1,100 killed, 3,600 wounded and 900 prisoners).

As the cost of battle was counted, some were concerned that their conduct would be called into question. Brigadier General Duvignau would be castigated by Murat for missing the battle 'under the pretext of illness'. Chief of Brigade de France of the 12th Chasseurs was concerned he too would come under scrutiny – after all, his regiment had been surprised by Austrian horsemen while the officers were taking a nap after lunch. Called to report to the First Consul, he was naturally concerned, as described in the memoirs of Aubry:

'Our regiment had suffered greatly at Marengo; it had been detached on the left wing, and had to deal with a numerous cavalry. Therefore, in spite of its good countenance, it had lost many prisoners. Our colonel, obliged the next day to appear before the First Consul, thought he was done for, and feared a severe remonstrance. What was his surprise when Bonaparte, on the contrary, gave him a magnificent reception, complimented him, congratulated him on the services rendered by his regiment, bravely heading against superior forces, and maintaining by his fine conduct a cavalry which could have changed the luck of the battle!'[10]

Clearly Bonaparte was in a generous mood, but as ever there was some truth in the praise. Duvignau's brigade had unwittingly tied up a massive force of Austrian cavalry and kept them busy enough not to take part in the battle. Bonaparte also met with Zach at Torre Garofoli and had a long interview. Zach was well treated, but was held in a room and prevented from looking out of the window by a guard. Stutterheim claimed the French had in fact spent the night preparing to retreat beyond the Scrivia, and this is what Zach was prevented from seeing, but this seems unlikely. If anything, the carts seen heading eastwards by the Tortona garrison were carrying French wounded. Speaking of being attacked, Bonaparte allegedly told Zach: 'I did not expect this. In truth it was amazing, especially after losing Marengo the day before.'[11] This remark at least must have assured Zach he had not been openly betrayed by the spy, Gioelli.

It appears a rider had gone ahead to alert the First Consul about the arrival of the Austrian emissaries. The musicians of the Consular Guard were assembled and the Guard drawn up in parade. At first Bonaparte appeared very eager to hear what General Skal had to say, but when he realized the Austrians had not come to capitulate, only to request a forty-eight-hour truce, his mood changed. Adopting a dictatorial air, he stated he would not enter into any armistice unless it did not lead to full negotiations on the fate of Italy. The French army was preparing to attack, he said, and he would not allow pointless negotiations to delay this attack. Bonaparte went to one side and in his own hand wrote out the main points of a convention, which he handed over to Berthier, quietly instructing him to go to Alessandria and talk to Melas directly. Having received Bonaparte's outline proposal, Berthier assembled a large group of generals and aides, then rode up to the Austrian forward posts and announced Melas wanted to see him. Having seen Skal riding out in the other direction earlier in the day, the outpost commander assumed the invitation was genuine and waved the Frenchmen through.

Melas, meanwhile, remained in his quarters. In the afternoon there was a great commotion outside, with the sound of many horses entering through the building's gateway. Radetzky looked out of the window to investigate the cause of the disturbance and was stunned to see a large party of French horsemen. He raced off to Melas' room and was just informing him there were French cavalry at the gates, when the door to the room burst open and in walked, without any ceremony, the French commander-in-chief and his party. To poor Melas it was like he had fallen into some sort of dream, a fantasy. How had the commander of the French army passed through his forward posts and simply opened the door to his quarters without his knowledge? As Melas sat dumbstruck, the French generals noisily praised him; he, the brave Austrian who in his wisdom had performed heroically and had through no fault of his own ended up in so sad a predicament. They told him he was assured a place in history, alongside Bonaparte; two men who brought the war to an end. Melas the hero! Melas the peacemaker!

Neipperg was livid at the sight of the officers accompanying Berthier and the other generals:

'A swarm of French adjutant-generals and aides-de-camp, all covered with gold and silver, with the imprint of French arrogance on the physiognomy which never detracts from success. This gilded scum filled all the apartments in the town house where our commander-in-chief lived, and seemed already to dictate the law before the treaty had even concluded.'[12]

Stutterheim listened to the exuberant French officers boasting of their successes. Stutterheim realized nothing more could be expected of old Melas now, although he did think it might be beneficial if somebody brought up a company of infantry to arrest these unexpected guests. Radetzky alone appeared to restore some kind of order to the situation. He walked into the room and drew Melas to one side as if receiving an order from him. After a few moments he turned and declared to the assembled officers that His Excellency, General Melas, wished to speak alone to the commander of the French army, therefore would everybody else please go to the room next-door where refreshments would be provided?

Outside the building there was a growing interest in the arrival of the French entourage. In front of the guardhouse in the main square of the city quite a crowd of officers and even a few generals could be seen demanding the arrest of the Frenchmen. The word 'treason' was spoken, for no one knew what was being negotiated in the room between the two army commanders. Only with difficulty was a bloodbath in the city prevented and tempers calmed by a degree. As for the negotiations, there was only going to be one outcome. When Radetzky had cleared the room so Melas and Berthier could talk alone, Kaim had whispered to Neipperg in German: 'I'll pack up my baggage to send it to the Minico.'

Neipperg was furious that Melas had been left alone with Berthier:

> 'This is the instant when the excess of my patriotism, my enthusiastic love for the army in which I have the honour to serve, does not allow me to pass over in silence the indefinable conduct of Count D.B. [de Best], then quartermaster general; of Colonel Count R. [Radetzky], adjutant-general, and generally of all the officers composing the suite of the commander-in-chief, Baron Melas. These gentlemen retired to the different apartments, leaving this respectable old man, *with his morale as trembling as his physique*, prey to the astuteness and arrogance of the French negotiator. In such a decisive moment, when everybody should have sacrificed themselves for the good of the state and the army, everyone went his own way, and asserted the egotistical and noble principle *of not interfering in anything, not having to answer for anything*, having always the charming proverb in the mouth: *I wash my hands.*'[13]

While Berthier had been travelling to Alesssandria, Bonaparte had continued his interview with Skal. The First Consul told Skal he wanted Genoa and Savona handed over to him, and for the Austrians to evacuate all of Piedmont and its fortresses. He concluded his position with the words:

> 'Sir, bear my final determination to your general, and return quickly: it is irrevocable. Know, that I am as well acquainted with your position as you are yourselves, I did not begin to make war yesterday. You are shut up in Alessandria; you are encumbered with sick and wounded; you want provisions and medicines. I occupy the country in your rear. You have lost in killed and wounded the flower of your army. I might insist upon more, and my position authorizes it; but I moderate my demands through respect for the grey hairs of your general, whom I esteem.'

Skal received his intense monologue with a growing sense of resignation. Bonaparte's terms were written down and handed over to him. As he was conducted out of the room, Skal turned to Bourrienne and said: 'These terms are very severe, particularly the giving up Genoa, which surrendered to us only a fortnight ago, after so long a siege.'[14]

After this interview was concluded, Skal and Torres returned to Alessandria with Dupont, the French chief of staff. Crossard had noticed the party of Frenchmen riding by. Crossard had long been curious about the identity of the French chief of staff, having studied at the old college of Laval-Magnac with a young man with a similar name. Now having seen the man in question up close, he realized Dupont was his onetime classmate. Crossard followed Dupont to Melas' apartments and followed them in. After Radetzky had called everyone into the other room for refreshment, Crossard made a happy reunion with his old friend.

'I knew from MacDonald that you were here,' Dupont said.

'Where were you yesterday?'

'To our left.'

'And I myself was to our right.'

'So we could have killed one another?'

'What rank do you have?'

'I am a lieutenant.'

'What? Are you not sorry for such a slender existence? What fortune you would have made among us! Come, come back. The first consul endeavours to get rid of everything the revolution has created. MacDonald and I will take care of your progress.'[15]

Crossard remained silent on the offer – probably a genuine one – being uneasy about a return to the country that had been so unstable and violent. He had once pledged his service to a king and he would continue to support the Allies of that same ill-fortuned family. Noting Crossard's silence, Dupont changed the subject and introduced General Boudet to him.

'Do you remember our old comrade Boudet?' Crossard looked at him but he had aged much since they had last met. 'It was he that gave you the final blow,' Dupont continued.

'Yes,' Boudet replied with a modest pride. 'It was my division that finished the affair.'

Elsewhere that day, Rauch had found his way back to camp and emersed himself in water to quench his thirst before taking a little food. Before he could even think about resting, his battalion was ordered to Riverone, four hours' march away, to watch the road from Sale; he gathered up the remains of his company and broke camp. When he at last arrived at the place, Rauch walked into the nearest manor house, found himself a bed and collapsed fully clothed. In the evening, Rauch was woken and informed that his hosts had prepared a dinner. Still half asleep, Rauch was led out into the peaceful garden, where he found a table set for four beneath a pergola. Without even knowing the name of his generous hosts, Rauch ate and made small talk in the shade of the canopy of plants and flowers around him. It all seemed so strange, so unreal; Rauch believed himself to be in an enchanted place. Apart from the sound of softly spoken voices, there was an empty quality about the place. Where were the bugles, the drums, the shouts and gunfire? Where was all the slaughter he had witnessed just a matter of hours ago? The poor captain simply could not understand it all; but he ate, drank and smiled politely all the same.

Inside Alessandria, General Soult remained in his sick bed, having spent a satisfied night contemplating the reversal of fortunes he had followed the previous day. As confirmation of the seriousness of the Austrian defeat, an officer came into his quarters and informed him that he was to be transported over the Tanaro River into the citadel to the west of the city. Soult was naturally concerned about being moved. His wound had been serious, and had been 'menaced' by gangrene at one point. He feared his wound might be aggravated by any attempt to move him. The Austrian replied that he could only remain in his quarters if Soult gave his parole. This would mean Soult would be unable to serve against the Austrians for the remainder of the war if he was released. It was a weighty decision, so Soult conferred with his physician. Dr Cothernet advised him to give his parole rather than risk further injury.[16] With hindsight, he should have tried to stall his captors a few hours, as hostilities were drawn to a close.

While Melas and Berthier negotiated, de Best called a meeting of the staff officers to discuss what they should do if the negotiations failed. Stutterheim recommended they attack the French a second time. They still had 5,000 cavalry and a large amount of artillery and ammunition. The infantry should assault the French at Marengo, supported by the fire of 100 cannons, while the cavalry crossed the Bormida half an hour upstream. It should then fall, via Spinetta, on to the rear and flank of the French army. In case of a reverse, the infantry would fight its way down to Genoa while the cavalry made a dash for Mantua via Parma. Volkmann reiterated his earlier idea of escaping northwards over the Po, which had been endorsed by Hadik, but Zach had rejected before the battle. This time de Best and Biking supported him, and a plan was drawn up in accordance. While the army crossed the Po at Casale, Oberst Frimont would lead a cavalry force 1,500 strong to Valenza. He would cross the Po and cover the army's right flank as it headed for Milan.

Meanwhile, the negotiations went into the night. At the conclusion there was a dinner for the thirty French officers, with Melas and Neipperg alone representing the imperial army. Neipperg complained how the French each boasted about their part in the battle, and he was forced to maintain his composure while inside his blood was boiling. One of these beribboned, boastful young men was Maurice Dupin, who later wrote to his mother about the evening, writing, somewhat disrespectfully, they had gone to dinner with 'Papa Melas' and dictated peace terms to him. One can see why Neipperg was so angry. When the supper was concluded, Berthier was impatient to return to Torre Garofoli and present Bonaparte with the treaty. It was favourable to the French, but at the same time it also achieved Melas's objective of escaping the net which the First Consul had thrown around the imperial army. The truth is, the moment the Army of the Reserve was allowed to break out of the mountains and commence its march on Milan, the imperial army was done for. Holding the army at Turin and waiting for the French to arrive was a grave strategic error on the part of Zach. However, at least Melas would be able to lead a substantial army with its guns and baggage back to protect the Austrian frontier. It was the best that could be hoped for in the circumstances.

Neipperg was given the dubious honour of escorting Berthier back to Torre Garofoli to have the document presented to Bonaparte for political confirmation. The one-eyed veteran had been educated in France, was well spoken in that language, firm and confident. His scars attested to his bravery in action, something they hoped would impress Bonaparte. Neipperg was instructed to bring the completed treaty back for Melas to sign, and Stutterheim instructed him to seek clarification on the line of demarcation of the Po near Ferrara. He was also given a secret instruction not to show himself under any pretext to General Zach, in case he should meet him at the French headquarters.

Neipperg says it was 1.00 am when they departed Alessandria. Their pathway across the battlefield was illuminated by dragoons carrying torches. Riding alone with the French commander-in-chief, Neipperg struck up a conversation with him, asking him about various events. His record of this conversation is an interesting one. At a strategic level, Berthier claimed their objective was the relief of Genoa, and Bonaparte had been taken by surprise when it capitulated. Conversely, Berthier expressed surprise that the Austrians had tried to invade the Riviera, as they must have known about the Reserve Army at Dijon. The subsequent crossing of the Alps was, Berthier 'modestly' claimed, a feat which had exceeded Hannibal. Berthier was also surprised that the Austrians attacked on 14 June. He referenced the 'ruined and dilapidated' state of Elsnitz's corps as a factor in not expecting battle. He also admitted the French had been beaten, and he never expected such a 'rapid success' in the evening battle, attributing this to Bonaparte's 'lucky star'. On Melas and Zach, Berthier told him:

'He would never have believed Melas was so old, that the preceding campaign did him infinite honour, but that he believed that at his age, in spite of all his talents, his activity and even his passion for glory must have infinitely lost its energy. He also told me about General Zach, believing him to be very learned and capable of very profound military calculations, but he seemed to doubt his talents for execution and believed he had little knowledge in handling soldiers and the art of serving the troops.'

At daybreak they arrived at Torre Garofoli. Bonaparte's suite was on foot; the Consular Guard bivouacked in front of the farmhouse, while the courtyard was full of cavalry and staff officers sitting around fires. To continue Neipperg's narrative:

> 'As one can imagine, we were expected like the Messiah. The triumphant air, which radiated on the face of General Berthier, when he got out of the carriage, gave sufficient information to all those around us that the mission was fulfilled beyond all expectation. He went immediately to the First Consul's apartment, and I was conducted to General Murat, who received me very affably. After a few moments the First Consul summoned me, and told me a thousand flattering things about the brilliant manner in which we had fought on the 14th, and declared that he owed all his success to the superiority and bravery of his cavalry.'[17]

Without wasting time on pleasantries, Neipperg went onto specifics, raising the issue of Ferrare. Although Neipperg does not include this in his memoirs, Crossard reports the one-eyed officer as saying the following to Bonaparte: 'Do not think that you have annihilated us; you will see us, if you like, reappearing perhaps stronger than when we began the battle. We have lead, powder, bayonets and cannon; break everything off; attack us and you will do us a service.'[18]

According to Neipperg, Bonaparte seemed disinterested in a triviality like Ferrare, and just asked if Melas would confirm what his intentions were and he would acquiesce. The reason for this is that the terms of the agreement were so generous to the French, there was little point quibbling on them. Genoa would be handed over to the French, along with all the fortresses in Piedmont. The imperial army would evacuate the country and retreat westwards behind the Minico. This would undo most of the major Austrian gains of the preceding year.

While a breakfast was prepared, Neipperg went out for a moment onto a balcony overlooking the courtyard. There he saw Zach, and despite his instructions not to approach him, he called out to him in German, telling him why he was there in headquarters. A French officer then intervened and forbade Neipperg from discussing the matter further. For all of his faults, Zach was part of Thugut's pro-war party, and it is clear Neipperg found the whole idea of an armistice and treaty completely dishonourable. It was as if Neipperg wanted Zach to intervene somehow and prevent the army from being dishonoured.

After eating his meal, Neipperg was presented to the First Consul again, and given two originals of the treaty for Melas to sign. Bonaparte said to him: 'You will hand them over to Baron Melas, assuring him of my esteem, desiring nothing more ardently than to find an opportunity of being able to prove it to him.'

Neipperg took the documents and then asked if they would allow Zach to return to headquarters, on his word of honour, to settle his private affairs. Bonaparte agreed, saying Zach must catch up with him in Milan, his next destination. Zach was released and followed Neipperg back across the battlefield to Alessandria. Neipperg did not admit his hand in Zach's temporary release, but he felt it might help put the army in a better state of affairs if he was present.

One can imagine the reaction in Melas' headquarters when Zach walked into the room behind Neipperg. They were astounded. It was as if a ghost had appeared. Feeling totally humiliated, Zach returned to the room where he kept his papers. He took a chair, sat at the table and began to work. Being Zach's replacement, de Best also went to the room; but rather than confer with Zach, he placed another table on the far side of the room, took up a book and began to read. Crossard then entered the room and approached Zach, wanting to tell him there was still some spirit in the army, and many were angry at the decision not to fight on. 'My friend,' Zach replied, 'I cannot listen to anything; I am a prisoner.' Crossard looked at de Best and when he received no response, quit to escape the awful atmosphere of the room. This poison between Zach and the other senior officers had proved utterly fatal to the Austrian cause.

As Zach and de Best endured one another's company, Neipperg presented the convention to Melas for signature. The terms were harsh in terms of territory and fortresses lost, but at the same time they guaranteed the Austrians could maintain their arms and baggage. While the convention was sent to Austria for final ratification, hostilities would cease, and the imperial army would evacuate Piedmont and Liguria. The exact terms were as follows:

Convention between the commanders-in-chief of the French and Imperial armies in Italy

ART. 1. There will be an armistice and suspension of hostilities between the army of His Imperial Majesty and that of the French Republic in Italy until the reply from Vienna.

ART. 2. His Imperial Majesty's army shall occupy all the lands between the Mincio, the Fossa-Maestra, and the Po, that is to say, Peschiera, Mantua, Borgo-Forte, and from there the left bank of the Po and on the right bank, the city and the citadel of Ferrara.

ART. 3. His Imperial Majesty's army will also occupy Tuscany and Ancona.

ART. 4. The French army will occupy the lands between Chiese, Oglio and the Po.

ART. 5. The land between the Chiese and the Mincio shall not be occupied by either of the two armies. The army of His Imperial Majesty will be able to draw provisions from the parts of this country which were part of the Duchy of Mantua. The French army will draw food from the countries which were part of the province of Brescia.

ART. 6. The castles of Tortona, Alessandria, Milan, Turin, Pizzighettone, Arona, and Piacenza, will be handed over to the French army, from 16 to 20 June.

ART. 7. The fortress of Coni, the castles of Ceva, Savona, the city of Genoa, will be handed over to the French army from 16 to 24 June.

ART. 8. Fort Urbain will be handed over on 26 June.

ART. 9. The fortress artillery will be classified as follows:

1. All the artillery of the Austrian foundries and calibres shall belong to the Austrian army.

2. Those of the Italian and Piedmontese and French foundries and calibres shall be handed over to the French army.

3. The supplies of food will be divided: half will be at the disposal of the commissariat officer of the Austrian army, half that of the disbursing officer of the French army.

ART. 10. The garrisons will leave with military honours, and will proceed with arms and baggage to Mantua by the shortest route.

ART. 11. The Austrian army shall proceed to Mantua by Piacenza in three columns: the first, from 16 to 20 June; the second, from 20 to 24 June; the third, from 24 to 26 June.

ART. 12. Messrs. General Saint-Julien; de Swrtnick of the artillery; du Brons of the engineers; Felsegi, commissioner of food; the citizens: General Dejean, Inspector Daru, Adjutant General Léopold Stabenrath;

the chief of brigade of the artillery Mossel, are appointed commissioners for the purpose of filling in the details of the execution of the present convention either for the formation of inventories, or for the provision of subsistence and transport, or for any other purpose.

ART. 13. No person shall be ill-treated on account of services rendered to the Austrian army or political opinion. The general-in-chief of the Austrian army will release those who have been arrested in the Cisalpine Republic for political opinions, and who are still in the fortresses under his command.

ART. 14. Whatever may be the reply of the court of Vienna, neither of the two armies can attack the other except by warning them ten days in advance.

ART. 15. During the suspension of arms, no army shall send detachments to Germany.

Made at Alessandria, on 15 June 1800.

Alex. Berthier. 　　　　　　　　Melas, General of the Cavalry.

With the ink barely dry on the convention document, the First Consul returned to Milan to announce his victory. Marengo did not bring an end to the war or the much-coveted peace, but the gain of so many fortresses and the removal of Melas' army from the frontiers of France was a significant victory – one worthy of laudation. It would take Moreau's victory at Hohenlinden (3 December) before Austria signed the Treaty of Lunéville on 9 February 1801. The war with England would continue for another year after that.

Berthier initially remained with his army and sent copies of the treaty to Suchet, who was now at Acqui, and to Massena, who was still at Finale. One of Suchet's men reported that he heard the battle from the village of Rocchetta, about 25km west of Marengo. At the time they were not sure if the rolling artillery fire was from the plain of Alessandria or from a naval engagement at sea.[19] Once the outcome of the battle was confirmed, the Army of Italy moved forward to reoccupy the places previously lost to the Austrians. Berthier also moved his headquarters to Tortona because of the 'infection' caused by all the bodies on the battlefield. Torre Garofoli was no place for the fit and healthy. Most of the campaign had been fought in overcast and wet weather, but now the sun broiled the men in the bivouacs and field hospitals around the place. There was hardly any food to be had, and there was only one well for 1,400 men at Garofoli, Maurice Dupin complained.

The clean-up after the battle was a grim task that no one really wanted. The dead were scattered far and wide, and not all were recovered in the immediate aftermath of the battle. For weeks after the battle, as the civilians returned to their properties, more corpses were discovered all the time. Lists survive showing the Marchese of Cassine found forty bodies on her land. Citizeness Fontanile of Spinetta had three in her property. The fathers of San Marco found two bodies, and so it went on. Then there were those wounded who died in the hospitals of Alessandria. Everywhere were bodies. As late as 1846, bones were still being ploughed up by farmers, so much so that the chemist Antonio Delavo built an ossuary at Marengo to collect the human remains.[20]

While awaiting further instructions, many took the opportunity to write home. Some of the letters were fairly simple in nature. Simon-Joseph Lepersonne was a 22-year-old soldier who reported to his mother on the cost of victory. His letter must have been fairly typical:

'I cannot tell you how many men were lost on both sides. Some say at least twenty thousand men were out of action, either killed or wounded. My dear mother, you cannot believe how much we suffered but I thank God for preserving my life and sparing me from being wounded. Of my detachment, the son of Franquinais of Doneux was killed as well as the son of Inglaibert of Justanville. All the others are well. Lebout and Janson and Collettre Pouhaut and the son of Chavois send their regards to their parents. We all hope to come back with the triumphant laurels of victory. My dear mother, this is all I can tell you now.'[21]

Perhaps the most accurate description of the experience of battle was penned by Berthier's ADC, Dupin, writing to his uncle:

'Piff, paff, pouf, pow! Forwards! Sound the charge! Retreat! Into battery! We're lost! Victory! Every man for himself! To the right, to the left, to the middle! Come back, stay, leave, hurry up! Station the howitzer! At the gallop! Heads down, here comes a ricochet ball … The dead, the wounded, legless, arms taken off, prisoners, baggage, horses, mules, cries of rage, shouts of victory, cries of pain, a devilish dust, hot as hell, effing and blinding, shit, a clatter, a confusion, a magnificent brawl: and there you have, my dear, kind uncle, in a few words, a clear and concise view of the battle of Marengo, from which your nephew has returned safe and sound after having been bowled over, together with his mount, by a passing cannonball, and after having been treated by the Austrians, for fifteen hours, to the fire of thirty pieces of artillery, twenty howitzers, and thirty thousand muskets.'[22]

Adopting a more formal tone, the Norweigan officer on Marmont's staff, Lieutenant Rustad, wrote to Crown Prince Fredrik from Tortona on 18 June:

'Gracious Lord!

'The first act of the solemn play "The conquest of peace" is happily ended. Perhaps it will only consist of one act; perhaps a definite peace will be its result. The better for the world, for suffering mankind. Your Royal Highness will already be informed about the battle of Marengo (at [the] banks of the Bormida, opposite Alessandria) on the 13th and 14th this month and its important results, that must be the wonder of the world. I could not aspire to compete with the rumour and to praise this news.'[23]

His letter went on to describe the fighting on 13 June, of bodies being dragged through the mud by the artillery; of the French infantry covered in dirt from the poor roads, and of the battle itself, the ferocious French bayonet charge in the evening, and the casualties inflicted by the Horse Guards thundering into the retreating Austrian army.

The French prisoners in Alessandria were released on 16 June. Coignet said there were about 1,200, and there was something of a fete on their return. Not all were welcomed with open arms. The officer who surrendered in Marengo with 500 of Rivaud's men was sentenced to a court martial. It was said he could have held on longer, an order of the day declared, but this seems harsh considering the intensity of the fighting. In another move, General Duvignau was dismissed from the army for missing the battle. He protested about being injured the night before, but was ordered back to Paris to receive instructions from the Minister of War.

As the Austrians prepared to evacuate Alessandria, Berthier announced a series of inspections for 19 June. He instructed the troops to wear 'greenery' in their hats as a sign of victory – aping the tradition of victors wearing oakleaf garlands. The two armies then set off marching for the line of the Minico. Again, Coignet was a witness. He said they were stupefied at the masses of infantry, cavalry and artillery which marched out of Alessandria. He was glad an armistice had been signed. The two adversaries marched along the same roads together; the officers sharing tables in the cafés along the route. It was during this time that Stutterheim spoke with the officers of the Consular Guard. Had one of them taken a little too much wine? How surreal it must have been; quarrels must have broken out. Galy-Montaglas had his money stolen by a group of chasseurs from the 'incomparable' 9th Light Infantry – plundered by one's own side! A manor house was looted on the way. A sutleress was found with her apron filled with stolen goods. She had her head shaved and was paraded naked on the back of a donkey for everyone to see. Reaching Cremona, Coignet boiled his clothes to kill the lice he was infested with. The clothes disintegrated in the boiling water and he was left naked, forced to write to his family, begging them to send money. Even Eugène Beauharnais spoke of the marked contrast between the troops of the Consular Guard, 'thin, exhausted and covered in dust', compared to their comrades back at the depot.[24]

As for the First Consul, he remained in Milan while the conditions of the convention were enacted. When he first arrived in the Lombard capital on 2 June, there was an element of warmth in the way he was greeted, but people were so surprised by the French army's appearance (and wary the Austrians might come back) that there was a certain reserve. This time round, the reception was much stronger. On his visit to Milan before the Battle of Marengo, Bonaparte requested an audience with the famous castrato singer Luigi Marchesi. The *artiste* had to be begged to grant Bonaparte an audience. Unusually star-struck, Bonaparte politely asked Marchesi if he would do him the honour of singing him an air. Marchesi replied in the most impertinent manner possible: 'Signor General, if it is a good air which you desire, you will find an excellent one in making a little tour of the garden!'[25]

The singer was quickly bundled out of Bonaparte's presence, but an angry First Consul had him imprisoned. After Marengo, the singer was given a second chance. This time he was much more polite. A concert was held. One of the other performers was Giuseppina Grassini. Berthier arrived to meet Bonpare the morning after the concert, and found Grassini at breakfast with Bonaparte having spent the night with him. In the words of Bonaparte's valet, she had become 'another conquest' of the great general. On top of his official duties, Berthier was instructed to deliver Grassini to Paris (she would one day become mistress to Wellington).

The First Consul was also generous to Melas. Before leaving Milan, he sent the Austrian commander-in-chief a Mameluke sword with the following note:

> 'I am sorry that circumstances did not allow me to make your acquaintance. I beg you, General, to permit me to offer you a sabre which I conquered from the barbarians in Egypt, and to receive it as a proof of the special consideration which the courage of your army inspired in me on the fields of Marengo.'[26]

Melas was flattered. He said he would go to Paris to visit Bonaparte, or perhaps even Egypt. In fact, Melas returned to Bohemia after being replaced as commander of the army by Heinrich von Bellegarde, brother of the general wounded in the battle. Given his advanced years and the onset of illness remarked on by several observers, Bellegarde's arrival must have come as a great relief. After all, command of the army in Italy was not an appointment he craved. Radetzky was sent to join the army in Germany. Somewhat ironically, he would go on to command an army in Italy while in his eighties during the First Italian War of Independence (1848-1849).

Zach was required to arrive in Milan on 19 June before 5.00 pm. He was thenceforth sent to Paris, where he remained a short time. If hostilities were to recommence, Bonaparte wanted the Austrian chief of staff as far away from Italy as possible. During his capture, he was in contact with the unfortunate Foissac-Latour and confirmed he had read his mail during the siege of Mantua. He also visited the armament works at Versailles and was impressed. Bonaparte made a gift to him of a fine pair of pistols, and then pointed out the difference in his treatment compared to the way the British had treated Desaix. Despite Radetzky's anger at Zach, his career continued, and he found himself reprising his role of chief of staff in Italy in 1805.

There was also the matter of payment for the spy from Alba, Carlo Gioelli. After the battle, he went to see Bonaparte, as is recounted by Bourrienne:

'The information given by this man proved so accurate and useful that on his return from Marengo Bonaparte ordered me to pay him the 1,000 Louis. The spy afterwards informed him Melas was delighted with the way in which he had served him in this affair, and had rewarded him handsomely. He assured us that he had bidden farewell to his odious profession. The First Consul regarded this little event as one of the favours of fortune.'[27]

What are we to make of the spy? From the Austrian point of view, he was clearly of critical importance, as much for delivering the deception before Marengo, as his earlier work at Mantua and Cuneo in particular. Desaix was diverted away from the battlefield on 13 June with a very strong division, the reappearance of which was to prove decisive to the eventual French victory. What if Desaix had crossed the Scrivia on 13 June, and had marched further than Rivalta? What if he had been two hours further from the field? Fortune perhaps smiled on Bonaparte with this intervention of nature in the guise of heavy rainfall. The surprise expressed by Bonaparte to Zach perhaps also indicated that Gioelli had not betrayed the Austrians. So what benefits came Bonaparte's way with the spy, and why was he paid so handsomely? Firstly, the spy had been able to describe Melas' concentration at Alessandria. When negotiating with Skal after the battle, Bonaparte was able to tell the Austrian he knew the real condition of the Austrian army in the city, with its sick, and the baggage train. More than anything, Gioelli had been a channel through which Bonaparte could communicate false intelligence to the Austrians; magnifying his strength, playing to the Austrian fears of being surrounded and outnumbered. So what became of Gioelli? With Zach now in French hands, it appears Gioelli did make good his intention to retire – at least for the short term anyway. There is much to learn about this spy, who must become a rival to the double agent of 1805, Charles Schulmeister. The hunt goes on for the mysterious *l'art d'espionnage* pamphlet reported by Gachot. We know Gioelli lived beyond the campaign and there are tantalising clues that he played his duplicitous game once again.

Command of the army was given to Massena, who joined Bonaparte in Milan and was praised for his heroic defence of Genoa. The First Consul then quit Milan on 24 June and travelled to Paris via Mont Cenis, passing through Lyon, arriving in the capital on 2 July at night. One can imagine the scenes of celebration the following day. He had been absent from the capital for just eight weeks, in which time his armies had traversed the Alps, conquered Italy, restored honour to the army and confirmed himself as the greatest soldier of the age. The war was far from ended, but the primary objective had been achieved: France united behind the leadership of Napoleon Bonaparte. Kellermann was right: Marengo did place the crown of France upon Napoleon's head; and despite the great victories to come, Marengo always remained the cornerstone of his legitimacy. Marengo was the battle which ended the French Revolution and gave birth to the Napoleonic era.

Endnotes

Prologue: On the battlefield of Marengo

1. Napoléon I, *Mémoires de Napoléon Bonaparte*, p.36.
2. Plon, *Correspondance de Napoléon Ier*, Vol.10, p.266.
3. Plon, *Correspondance*, Vol.10, p.332.

Chapter 1: 1799: A Secret History

1. Feldzeugmeister (ordnance-master) was a senior general of the artillery branch of an army, with the French equivalent of lieutenant-general.
2. MacDonald, *Souvenirs*, Vol.1, p.269.
3. MacDonald, *Souvenirs*, Vol.1, p.277.
4. Radetzky, *Erinnerungen*, Vol.1, p.47.
5. Melas to Tige, letter of 7 December 1799, Hüffer, Vol.1, p.510. See Vaccarino, *Giacobini Piemontesi*, p.917. The name Gioelli is pronounced in English something like Joy-elly.
6. Foissac-Latour, *précis*, p.475.
7. Foissac-Latour, *précis*, p.471.
8. The spy's late arrival is also mentioned in Maubert's *Relation du blocus et du siége de Mantoue, et exposé des causes qui ont contribué a sa reddition* (Paris: 1800), p.15.
9. Foissac-Latour, *précis*, p.221.
10. Melas, Hüffer, Vol.1, pp.510–14.
11. The note has survived in the Austrian Kriegsarchiv attached to Melas' report under HKR 1799 Italien XI 19d. Suchet had evidently signed the paper in advance. The other documents carried by Gioelli have also been preserved.
12. Crossard, *Mémoires*, Vol.2, p.206. The sum of money was generous, but not huge. A ducat was worth 9 shillings, 4 pence in 1799; thus 1,000 ducats was the equivalent of £460 Sterling. This was perhaps in the region of £47,000 in 2017 prices.
13. Crossard, *Mémoires*, Vol.2, p.207.
14. The story of Cuneo is related in Melas' report of 7 December 1799 to Tige (Hüffer: vol.1, p.331). and Crossard, *Mémoires militaires*, Vol.2, pp.205–07.
15. Vaccarino, *Giacobini Piemontesi*, p.917.
16. Radetzky, *Erinnerungen*, Vol.1, p.48.

Chapter 2: *Brumaire*

1. See Sparrow, *Secret Service*. This book offers the tantalising possibility that the British deliberately allowed Bonaparte to leave Egypt in return for him supporting a Bourbon restoration.
2. Gohier's memoirs can be found in *Mémoires de Contemporains, pour server a l'histoire de France, et principalement a celle de la république et de l'empire* (Paris: Bossange Frères, 1824), pp.199-202.
3. Bouvier, *Historique du 96e régiment*, p.41.
4. Cugnac, de, *Campagne de l'Armée de Réserve en 1800*, Vol.1, p.4.

Chapter 3: The Savona plot

1. Much of the following account is taken from the memoirs of Henri de Faverges. The original manuscript remains unpublished in full, but extracts were published by Faverges' great-nephew, the author and historian Costa de Beauregard, in the French periodical 'La Revue Hebdomadaire', Vol.9, September 1908. The article is titled *Mon Oncle le general – Douze ans d'émigration en Autriche*. It is highly recommended.
2. Hüffer, *Quellen zur Geschichte*, Vol.2, pp.506-07.
3. Criste, Oskar, *Erzherzog Carl von Österreich: Ein Lebensbild*, Vol.2 (Vienna: Braumüller, Wilhelm, 1912), p.39.
4. Stutterheim's account, Hüffer, Vol.2, pp.41-42.
5. Crossard, *Mémoires militaires*, Vol.2, p.47.
6. See *Eine Denkschrift Zach's aus dem Jahre 1798* in *Mittheilungen des k.u.k. Kriegs-Archivs: Dritte Folge, II Band* (Wien: L.W. Seidel & Sohn, 1903).
7. Crossard, *Mémoires militaires*, Vol.2, p.325.
8. Hüffer, *Quellen zur Geschichte*, Vol.2, p.229.
9. Hüffer, *Quellen zur Geschichte*, Vol.2, p.200.

Chapter 4: French Preparations

1. Cugnac, de., *Campagne de l'Armée de Réserve en 1800*, Vol.1, p.61.
2. Bourrienne, *Mémoires*, Vol.4, p.85.

Chapter 5: Melas attacks

1. OMZ: 1811-13, Vol.2.
2. Hüffer, *Quellen zur Geschichte*, Vol.2, p.207.
3. Hüffer, *Quellen zur Geschichte*, Vol.2, p.199.
4. Hüffer, *Quellen zur Geschichte*, Vol.2, pp.45-46.
5. Hüffer, *Quellen zur Geschichte*, Vol.2, p.222.
6. Bancalari, *Beiträge zur Geschichte des österreichischen Heerwesens*, pp.142-44.
7. Hüffer, *Quellen zur Geschichte*, Vol.2, pp.225-26.
8. Hüffer, *Quellen zur Geschichte*, Vol.2, p.246.
9. Cavour, in Bouvier, *Une relation inédite de la bataille de marengo*, p.55.

Chapter 6: Over the Alps

1. Cugnac, de, *Campagne de l'Armée de Réserve en 1800*, Vol.1, p.178.
2. Cugnac, de, *Campagne de l'Armée de Réserve en 1800*, Vol.1, p.194.
3. Cugnac, de, *Campagne de l'Armée de Réserve en 1800*, Vol.1, p.190.
4. Cugnac, de, *Campagne de l'Armée de Réserve en 1800*, Vol.1, p.282.
5. Cugnac, de, *Campagne de l'Armée de Réserve en 1800*, Vol.1, p.352.
6. Cugnac, de, *Campagne de l'Armée de Réserve en 1800*, Vol.1, pp.353-54.
7. The failure to pay the villagers of Bourg-Saint-Pierre became the subject of a long-running complaint. In 1984, President Mitterand symbolically honoured the debt with the gift of a bronze medallion depicting Bonaparte crossing the Alps.
8. Cugnac, de, *Campagne de l'Armée de Réserve en 1800*, Vol.1 p.422-23.
9. Marmont, *Mémoires*, Vol.2, p.118.
10. Cugnac, de, *Campagne de l'Armée de Réserve en 1800*, Vol.1, p.520.
11. Stutterheim's account, Hüffer, Vol.2, p.71. The link between the spy recruited at Mantua and used at Cuneo, and in the Marengo campaign, is confirmed by Radetzky, *Erinnerungen*, p.48.
12. Bourrienne, *Mémoires*, Vol.4, pp.105-07.
13. See Landrieux's memoirs for details on this bureau's activities.
14. Gachot, *Deuxième Campagne d'Italie*, p.247.
15. Gachot, *Deuxième Campagne d'Italie*, pp.153-55.
16. Since first learning of *l'art d'espionnage* in 1998, all attempts to trace it have failed. Gachot said the Milan libraries did not hold the document, which he found inserted into another document belonging to a collector in Aosta. The archives at Aosta apparently suffered a major fire since Gachot's time. In 2017, I visited the monastery on the Great St Bernard looking for the note of Luder confirming the arrival of 'Toli'. I did not find this note in the surviving papers. Nor did I find the *relation de Luder*, which Gachot cites in his book. The account by an anonymous monk which survives today is written by a different hand to that of Luder. Perhaps more tellingly, a 1999 local history account by Léonard Closuit called *Passage de Bonaparte au Grand-Saint-Bernard en mai 1800*, fails to mention the spy. Closuit was evidently aware of Gachot's account, as it is cited in his bibliography. Perhaps the most concerning element of Gachot's account is that it fails to link the 'Milan' spy with later events at Marengo.
17. Duhesme, *Essai historique sur l'infanterie légère*, pp.167-68.

Chapter 7: The Fall of Genoa

1. Hüffer, *Quellen zur Geschichte*, Vol.2 p.256.
2. Hüffer, *Quellen zur Geschichte*, Vol.2, p.257.
3. Hüffer, *Quellen zur Geschichte*, Vol.2, p.257.
4. Hüffer, *Quellen zur Geschichte*, Vol.2, p.264.
5. Hüffer, *Quellen zur Geschichte*, Vol.2, p.266.

6. Hüffer, *Quellen zur Geschichte*, Vol.2, p.265.

7. Hüffer, *Quellen zur Geschichte*, Vol.2, p.566.

8. Stutterheim's account, Hüffer, Vol.2, p.63.

9. Stutterheim's account, Hüffer, Vol.2, p.66.

10. Cugnac, de, *Campagne de l'Armée de Réserve en 1800*, Vol.2, pp.228-31.

11. Montaglas, *Historique du 12e chasseurs*, p.76.

12. Montaglas, *Historique du 12e chasseurs*, pp.76-78.

13. The Austrian casualties were: 659 dead including six officiers; 1,445 wounded including fifty-three officiers; 2,171 prisoners including forty-five officiers. From Mras, cited in de Cugnac, *Campagne de l'Armée de Réserve en 1800*, Vol.2, p.269.

14. Bourrienne, *Mémoires*, Vol.4, p.112.

15. SHD GR1 M857. *Historiques des corps de troupe.* 21st Chasseurs.

Chapter 8: The Armies Concentrate

1. 1 Louis = 1 GBP = £105 in 2017 – i.e. 1,000 Louis is over £100k.

2. Brinner, *Geschichte des K. K. Pionier-Regiments*, p.579.

3. Archivio di Stato di Alessandria, Mappa dei tenimenti di Spinetta Marengo e del cantone Marengo, 1762.

4. Brinner, *Geschichte des K. K. Pionier-Regiments*, p.582.

5. Weissenbacher, *Geschichte des k.u.k. Infanterie-Regimentes Nr.19*, p.315.

6. Hüffer, *Quellen zur Geschichte*, Vol.2, p.303.

Chapter 9: 'This time we have this Bonaparte'

1. Hüffer, *Quellen zur Geschichte*, Vol.2, pp.305-06.

2. Hüffer, *Quellen zur Geschichte*, Vol.2, p.306.

3. Stutterheim's account, Hüffer, Vol.2, p.73.

4. By divisions it means quarter companies or squadrons.

5. Rauch, *Erinnerungen*, p.370.

6. Hüffer, *Quellen zur Geschichte*, Vol.2, pp.313-14.

7. The depth was reported by the Norwegian officer attached to the French artillery staff, Lieutenant Rustad. See: Skarstein, Karl Jakob, *Under fremmede flagg: nordmenn i utenlandsk krigstjeneste 1800-1900* (Oslo: Forsvarsmuseet, 2002).

8. Cugnac, de, *Campagne de l'Armée de Réserve en 1800*, Vol.2, p.364.

9. See Duvignau's report in de Cugnac, Vol.2, pp.341-42.

10. Cugnac, de, *Campagne de l'Armée de Réserve en 1800*, Vol.2, p.339.

11. Cugnac, de, *Campagne de l'Armée de Réserve en 1800*, Vol.2, p.339, quoting the 1803 relation of the battle.

12. Cugnac, de, *Campagne de l'Armée de Réserve en 1800*, Vol.2, p.319.

13. Cugnac, de, *Campagne de l'Armée de Réserve en 1800*, Vol.2, p.342.

14. Cugnac, de, *Campagne de l'Armée de Réserve en 1800*, Vol.2, p.343.

15. i.) Radetzky, *Erinnerungen*, Vol.1, p.54); ii.) Stutterheim's account, Hüffer, Vol.2, p.75.

16. Maendl, Maximilian, *Geschichte des K. und K. Infanterie-Regiments Nr. 51*, Vol.1, p.560.
17. This account was told to Musset by the marquess after the Battle of Marengo. See: Musset, *Voyage en Suisse et en Italie, fait avec l'armée de réserve*, pp.171-72.
18. Dalton's report indicates there was one 12-pdr only, but after the battle he says there were two. Most sources agree Boudet had eight guns.
19. Pittaluga, *La battaglia di Marengo*, p.58.
20. Oliva, *Marengo Antico e Marengo Moderno*, p.265.
21. The detachment of the 3rd Cavalry is confirmed in the regiment's own 1801 history of the Revolutionary Wars: (SHD/GR1 M856). This document states that most of the unit spent the night with the carabiniers of the 9th Light, having swum the Scrivia.

Chapter 10: That Miserable Ditch

1. Radetzky's account of 29 June 1800 in Hüffer, Vol.2, p.354.
2. Dannican in Bouvier, *Une relation inédite de la bataille de marengo*, p.49.
3. Hüffer cites a biography of Radetzky (Biographischen Skizze) which says Zach had gone to bed exhausted. Given the descriptions of him in Stutterheim, this is entirely plausible. According to this account, Radetzky wanted to turn the French right. Hüffer, Vol.2, p.76.
4. One could render oneself insane attempting to rationalize all the different times provided by the witnesses of this battle. All one can reasonably hope to do is establish the correct sequence of events and then establish times based on typical marching rates and by comparing evidence. Clocks would have been set according to the ringing of church bells, and these would have been set to local solar time by a sun dial. Standard times did not arrive until after the railways. On 14 June, solar time at Alessandria is as follows: twilight begins at 2.25 am; sunrise at 4.39 am; the solar noon is at 12.27 pm; sunset at 8.14 pm; and twilight ends at 10.46 pm.
5. Cavour in Bouvier, *Une relation inédite de la bataille de marengo*, p.61.
6. Crossard, *Mémoires militaires*, Vol.2, p.291.
7. Neipperg's account, Hüffer, Vol.2, p.118.
8. Neipperg's account, Hüffer, Vol.2, p.108.
9. Marx, *Geschichte des 53ten ungarischen Linien-Infanterie-Regiments*, p.151.
10. Amon von Treuenfest, *Geschichte des K. K. Infanterie-regimentes NR. 47*, p.417.
11. Titeux, *Le Général Dupont*, Vol.1. p.98.
12. Cugnac, de, *Campagne de l'Armée de Réserve en 1800*, Vol.2, pp.375-76.
13. Perrin, *Extraits des memoires inédits de feu*, pp.168-69.
14. Rouby, *Historique du 101e régiment d'infanterie*, p.58.
15. Beauharnais, *Mémoires*, pp.81-82.
16. Titeux, *Le Général Dupont*, Vol.1, p.98.
17. Rauch, *Erinneningen*, p.372.

18. 356 AP 1. *Souvenirs de Jean Chenevier, officier au 22e régiment de ligne sous la Révolution et l'Empire*, p.215. (Archives privées du Centre historique des Archives nationales.)
19. Both incidents are found in *Résumé Historique du 22e régiment d'infanterie*. It is worth noting that some accounts state Lannes pushed the Austrians all the way back to the Bormida. This does not appear accurate. Where the Fontanone was quite wide at this part of the field, perhaps they were confused?
20. The death of Watrin's brother is noted in Jean Chenevier's memoirs.
21. Neipperg's account, Hüffer, Vol.2, p.109
22. GM Giovanni Francesco Conte Pelatti della Torre di Mombisaggio was born at Castellazo Bormida on 3 October 1749.
23. Kellermann's report of 15 June 1800; de Cugnac, *Campagne de l'Armée de Réserve en 1800*, Vol.2, p.404.
24. Neipperg's account, Hüffer, Vol.2, p.109.
25. Perrin, *Extraits des memoires inédits de feu*, p.505.
26. The account attributed by de Cugnac to the ADC, Lauriston, states Bonaparte went to the battlefield at 9.00 am. De Cugnac throws doubt on this claim, pointing out the battle did not commence until nine, and so the First Consul would not have arrived on the battlefield before 10.00 am. From reading the many accounts, Bonaparte does not appear to have arrived until noon at the very earliest, which indicates an 11.00 am notification.

Chapter 11: The Battle for Marengo

1. Soult, *Mémoires du maréchal-général Soult*, Vol.3, p.275.
2. SHD/GR1 M466, *Boudet's journal*.
3. Savary, *Memoirs*, Vol.1, p.174.
4. SHD/GR1 M857, *21e Chasseurs à Cheval*.
5. Bourqueney, *Historique du 12e régiment de hussards*, p.61.
6. Montaglas, *Historique du 12e chasseurs*, p.80.
7. Stutterheim's account, Hüffer, Vol.2, p.78.
8. Letter from General of Brigade Roger-Valhubert to General Dupont, 2 Germinal Year XII. Cited in Titeux, *Le Général Dupont*, Vol.1, p.101.
9. Simond, *Le 28e de ligne*, p.81.
10. Rouby, *Historique du 101e régiment d'infanterie*, p.59
11. Lievyns etc, *Fastes de la Légion-d'Honneur. Biographie de tous les décorés, accompagnée de l'histoire législative et réglementaire de l'ordre* (Paris: Bureau de l'administration, 1844), Vol.2, p.97.
12. Brinner, *Geschichte des K. K. Pionier-Regiments*, pp.582-83.
13. Stutterheim's account, Hüffer, Vol.2, p.81.
14. Kellermann, *Napoléon: journal anecdotique ...*, Vol.1, p.520.
15. Perrin, *Extraits des memoires inédits de feu*, p.173.

16. Titeux, *Le Général Dupont*, Vol.1, pp.98–99.

17. Cugnac, de, *Campagne de l'Armée de Réserve en 1800*, Vol.2, pp.403–08.

18. Kellermann, *Deuxième et dernière réplique*, p.4.

19. Titeux, *Le Général Dupont*, Vol.1, p.99.

20. Perrin, Claude-Victor, duc de Bellune, *Extraits des memoires inédits de feu*, p.174.

21. Kellermann. See his letter entitled 'Bataille de Marengo' in the 1834 periodical *Napoléon. Journal Anecdotique et Biographique de l'Empire et de la Grande Armée*, p.521.

22. Titeux, *Le Général Dupont*, Vol.1, p.99.

Chapter 12: The March of the Consular Guard

1. A further clue to this is found in de Cugnac (Vol.2, p.411), who cites a quote in the *Mémoires de Napoléon*, '*Le Premier Consul arriva sur le champ de bataille à 10 heures du matin, entre San-Giuliano et Marengo.*' While one would dispute the timing, the location is interesting. This area between San-Giuliano and Marengo is where the high ground is located.

2. Jean Pierre Joseph Bruguière (1772-1813) went by the name 'Bruyère'. He was promoted to chief of squadron after Marengo and married Berthier's niece. He had both legs taken off by a cannonball at the Battle of Reichenbach (22 May 1813) and died on 5 June that year.

3. SHD/GR1 M466, *Boudet's journal*.

4. SHD/GR1 M857, *3e Cavalerie*.

5. Titeux, *Le Général Dupont*, Vol.1, p.98.

6. Savary, *Memoirs*, Vol.1, p.177.

7. This quote is attributed to the Duke of Wellington.

8. In 2014, the hat allegedly worn at Marengo was sold at auction for €1.9 million. From the tailoring of the coat he wore at Marengo, it is estimated that Bonaparte stood 1.68m tall (5ft 6in), slightly above the average conscript's height of 1.66m – by no means as short as portrayed in contemporary British cartoons, which lampooned him as a bloodthirsty midget.

9. Petit, *Marengo*, p.24.

10. Grandin, *Souvenirs historiques du capitaine Krettly*, pp.150–51.

11. *Historique du 70e régiment d'infanterie de ligne*, p.31.

12. Titeux, *Le Général Dupont*, Vol.1, p.90.

13. The 3.00 pm timing is supported by Foudras' *Bonaparte en Italie, en l'an VIII de la République*, p.72.

14. When the unit passed over the Great St Bernard, the monks recorded grenadiers à pied and sapeurs as a single entity.

15. SHD/GR20 YC5, *1er régiment de grenadiers à pied*.

16. SHD/20 YC37, *Registre Matricule Chasseurs de la Garde Consulaire*.

17. Brossier's account of the battle (see de Cugnac) identifies the chief of battalion leading the Guard as Goulez. This appears to be a phonetic misinterpretation of

the name Soulès. A Chef de brigade, Louis Fuzy, was also present at the battle, but his biographical entry in *Fastes de la Légion-d'Honneur* does not associate him with this action.

18. Lievyns etc, *Fastes de la Légion-d'Honneur*, Vol.2, pp.172-73.

19. The flamboyant history of the Imperial Guard, *Anatomy of Glory*, by Henri Lachoque at first says the guard had no artillery, but then within the same paragraph tells the story of Grenadier Brabant, 'a grenadier of uncommon strength' working a 4-pdr gun alone for half an hour! See p.17 of the Anne S.K. Brown translation.

20. If one places the 28th Line level with the Barbotta farm, and projects 600 metres beyond this on the Sale road, one can now use photographic mapping software to measure the distance to this place from the gatehouse of Torre Garofoli, via the old Tortona Road, via Spinetta. It is 12km – or 12.8km if one follows the 'new' road. A French military pace is 0.65metres; in other words, the guard marched at least 18,461 steps. At the route pace (ninety steps per minute), this would have taken three hours and twenty-five minutes, not allowing for disruption encountering the wounded at San Giuliano or the break to pass cartridges to Victor's troops at Spinetta. It is more likely the guard remained on the better new road, and so this would have taken almost exactly four hours. Any account which puts the guard action before 3.00 pm must be viewed with caution.

21. Victor places this action in the 'open ground' between Villanova and Li Poggi. The ground directly between these two places was mostly covered by vineyards in 1800. The actual location is about 2km west of this position, towards the 'Sale road' (now the Str. Cascinagrossa), a short distance to the north of the Cascina Gilendu farm. It is said the firefight with Gottesheim took place across the Cavo Fontanone stream.

22. Stuttheim account, Hüffer, pp.82-83.

23. Cugnac, de, *Campagne de l'Armée de Réserve en 1800*, Vol.2, p.173.

24. Valhubert was overlooked in the distribution of arms of honour after the battle. The officers of the 28th Line petitioned the First Consul, and this resulted in the award of a sword of honour. He was made a general of brigade on 11 December 1803, and admitted into the Legion of Honour the following year. He was stuck by a shell fragment at Austerlitz in 1805 and died five days later.

25. Titeux, *Le Général Dupont*, Vol.1, p.102.

Chapter 13: This New Thermopylae

1. Grandin, *Souvenirs historiques du capitaine Krettly*, pp.151-53

2. Grandin, *Souvenirs historiques du capitaine Krettly*, pp.154-55. Daumesnil had a certain way with words. Rising to the rank of brigadier general, he lost a leg at Wagram in 1809. In 1814, he was the governor of the Chateau de Vincennes. When called upon to surrender, he said: 'I shall surrender Vincennes when I get my leg back.'

3. Lemaréchal, *Historique du 8e dragons*, p.185.

4. Corda, *Le Régiment de la Fère et le 1er Régiment d'Artillerie*, pp.152-53. Renaud was a brave man, but his luck ran out in 1805 when he was killed trying to rescue a comrade from a burning house.

5. Cugnac, de, *Campagne de l'Armée de Réserve en 1800*, Vol.2, p.427 (Berthier's second report).

6. This conversation was overheard by Dupont's ADC, Léopold. Crossard, *Mémoires militaires*, Vol.2, p.313.

7. Letter dated Torre di Garofolo, 16 June 1800. Albert Le Roy's *Georges Sand et ses amis*, p.7.

8. Beauharnais, *Mémoires*, p.84.

9. Rauch, *Erinneningen*, p.372.

10. Crossard, *Mémoires militaires*, Vol.2, p.298.

11. Stutterheim's account, Hüffer, Vol.2, p.83.

12. Cavour incorrectly rendered Volkmann as Icklmann in his notes. Cavour in Bouvier, *Une relation inédite de la bataille de marengo*, p.61.

13. Stutterheim's account, Hüffer, Vol.2, p.86; Neipperg's account, Hüffer, Vol.2, pp.109-11.

14. Crossard, *Mémoires militaires*, Vol.2, pp.296-97.

15. The events told here have been reconstructed from the 1801 manuscript history of the 12th Chasseurs (SHD/GR1 M856); the regimental history of the 12th Chasseurs (Signorel, J., *Historique*, 1792-1801); and the memoirs of Galy Montaglas, p.79.

16. Bourqueney, *Historique du 12e régiment de hussards*, p.61.

17. Procházka, *Geschichte des k. k. Infanterie-Regimentes Nr. 24*, p.336.

Chapter 14: Vengeance!

1. Bell, *Memoirs of Baron Lejeune*, Vol.1, p.21.

2. In this report, Dalton says he had one 12-pdr; in his post-battle report, he says they have two 12-pdrs. Most sources indicate Boudet had eight guns in total.

3. Guénand described the revolutionary zealots as 'horrible cannibals'.

4. Fleuriot de Langle, *Général Bertrand, Cahiers de Sainte-Hélène*, p.436.

5. *Historique du 1er régiment de hussards*, p.113.

6. See Quiot, in Perrin's *Extraits des memoires inédits de feu*, pp.426-27.

7. This figure comes from a remark made by Bonaparte that Desaix was later at the head of 200 'scouts' from the 9th Light. See Gourgaud, *Mémoires pour servir à l'histoire de France sous Napoléon*, Vol.1, p.292.

8. Letter attributed to Lauriston by de Cugnac, *Campagne de l'Armée de Réserve en 1800*, Vol.2, pp.412-14.

9. Costa de Beauregard, *Mon Oncle le general*.

10. Marmont, *Mémoires*, Vol.2, p.132.

11. Titeux, *Le Général Dupont*, Vol.1, p.103.

12. SHD/GR1 M466, *Boudet's journal.*
13. Rauch, *Erinneningen*, pp.374-75.
14. Montaglas, *Historique du 12e chasseurs*, p.84.
15. SHD/GR1 M466, *Boudet's journal.*
16. SHD/GR1 M857, *Historique du 2e cavalerie.*
17. Kellermann, *Réfutation de M. le duc de Rovigo,* pp.10-11.
18. Cugnac, de, *Campagne de l'Armée de Réserve en 1800,* Vol.2, pp.404-07.
19. A platoon was a tactical subdivision of a company, or half squadron. As the force was an amalgamation of so many regiments, it is unclear how they organized themselves.
20. Marmont, *Mémoires,* Vol.2, pp.133-34.
21. SHD/GR1 M842, Dubois, Captain L., *Historique du 9e Régiment d'infanterie légère de 1788 à 1839* (La Rochelle: 20 September 1839).
22. It was a day for coincidences. At the same time Desaix fell at Marengo, General Kléber was assassinated in Cairo by a knife-wielding fanatic.
23. SHD/GR1 M857, *Historique du 2e cavalerie.*
24. SHD/GR1 M857, *Historique du 20e cavalerie.*
25. Guénand and Kellermann later discussed the battle in Milan. Guénand writes the latter agreed that 'without the impetuosity and success of my attack he could never have made the cavalry charge'. SHD/GR1 M610: *Note to General Dumas,* 21 November 1801.
26. Radetzky, *Erinnerungen,* Vol.1, pp.55-56.
27. Savary, *Memoirs,* Vol.4, p.237.
28. Bourrienne, *Mémoires,* Vol.4, p.128. Barrois went on to become colonel of the 96th Line, then a noted general in the First Empire, and lived until 1860.
29. Local tradition places the spot Desaix fell in the grounds of the Vigna Santa farm by a small tree. A memorial was placed there in 2002 by Alessandria-based re-enactors. This is several hundred metres east of where the 9th Light probably fought. Interestingly, the Duchess of Abrantes visited the battlefield in 1818 and was shown the tree where Desaix's body was taken. Perhaps this is after all the spot where Savary found him? (Abrantes, *Mémoires,* Vol.3, p.51.)

Chapter 15: Victory

1. These scenes are portrayed in Lejeune's 1801 *La bataille de Marengo.* As a serving officer and participant in the battle, viewing the painting is very much like watching a piece of newsreel rather than a single moment of the battle. For artistic reasons, Lejeune painted Kellermann's charge hitting the right flank of the grenadiers.
2. Gremillet, *Historique du 81e de ligne.* A fragment of this composition has survived and is recorded in that work.
3. Rauch, *Erinneningen,* pp.375-76:
4. Local tradition has it a great number of French troops sheltered in the farmhouse of Villanova during the battle, and many wounded men were left there. There is

no way of verifying if these troops were Monnier's men or guardsmen, but it is an intriguing possibility.

5. Stutterheim's account, Hüffer, Vol.2, p.89.

6. Brémond d'Ars, *Historique du 21è chasseurs à cheval*, p.8.

7. Crossard, *Mémoires militaires*, Vol.2, p.301.

8. Two cannonballs were lodged in the front facade of the church at Cascina Grossa. This indicates some fighting took place there.

9. Baich von Lovinac, *Geschichte des KK inf. Reg 23*, Vol.1. Both Graf and Eichelmann were awarded the silver bravery medal.

10. Beauharnais, *Mémoires*, p.84.

11. Neipperg, *Aperçu militaire*, p.15.

12. This conversation is related by Cavour in Bouvier, *Une relation inédite de la bataille de marengo*, p.60.

13. Carnet de la Sabretache, *Le Colonel de France et le 12e régiment de chasseurs*, p.334.

14. Bourrienne, *Mémoires*, Vol.4, p.124.

15. Cugnac, de, Vol.2, p.415.

16. Bonaparte later learned what had been said when he saw the contents of a letter Kellermann wrote to his friend Lasalle. The letter had been opened by censors. Bourrienne, *Mémoires*, Vol.4, p.126.

17. Constant, *Mémoires de Constant*, Vol.1, p.62.

18. Bourrienne, *Mémoires*, Vol.4, p.127.

19. Kellermann, *Réfutation* …, p.15.

20. Titeux, *Le Général Dupont*, Vol.1, p.97.

21. Titeux, *Le Général Dupont*, Vol.1, p.95.

Chapter 16: The Convention of Alessandria

1. Stutterheim's account, Hüffer, Vol.2, p.89.

2. Stutterheim's account, Hüffer, Vol.2, p.89.

3. Neipperg, *Aperçu militaire*, p.23.

4. Radetzky's letter of 29 June, Hüffer, Vol.2, p.357.

5. Stutterheim, Hüffer, Vol.2, p.89.

6. Stutterheim's account, Hüffer, Vol.2, p.92.

7. Neipperg, *Aperçu militaire*, pp.25-26.

8. Stutterheim's account, Hüffer, Vol.2, p.92.

9. Cugnac, de, Vol.2, p.382.

10. Aubry, *Souvenirs*, p.211.

11. Stutterheim's account, Hüffer, Vol.2, p.90.

12. Neipperg, *Aperçu militaire*, p.27.

13. Neipperg, *Aperçu militaire*, p.27.

14. Bourrienne, *Mémoires*, Vol.4, p.130.

15. Crossard, *Mémoires militaires*, Vol.2, p.307.

16. Soult, *Mémoires*, Part 1, Vol.3, pp.276-77.

17. Neipperg, *Aperçu militaire*, pp.30-31.

18. Crossard, *Mémoires militaires*, Vol.2, p.311.

19. Guillaume, E., Maison, G., and Moerman, Y., *Les trente batailles du sergent Denis Moreau, journal de campagne, 1794-1809* (Bruxelles: Memogrames éditions, 2011), p.179.

20. An analysis of these remains showed, unsurprisingly, that the bones were of men between 20 and 35 years, with heights ranging from 1.63-1.75 metres. See Gino Fornaciari's *Bone lesions from the Napoleonic Battle of Marengo, Italy, 14 June 1800* (paleopatogia.it).

21. Wilkin, *Fighting for Napoleon*, pp.51-52.

22. Le Roy, Albert, *Georges Sand*, p.7.

23. Skarstein, Karl Jakob, *Under fremmede flagg: nordmenn i utenlandsk krigstjeneste 1800-1900* (Oslo: Forsvarsmuseet, 2002), trans. Karl Jakob Skarstein.

24. Beauharnais, *Mémoires*, p.86.

25. Constant, *Mémoires de Constant*, Vol.1, pp.73-74.

26. Hüffer, *Quellen zur Geschichte*, Vol.2, p.320.

27. Bourrienne, *Mémoires*, Vol.4, p.107.

Orders of Battle

Army of the Reserve at Marengo, 14 June 1800
Commander-In-Chief, Alex. Berthier
Chief of Staff, General of Division Dupont

Lieutenant-General	Division	*Brigade*	Unit	Strength
Victor	Gardanne	*Dumoulin*	44th Line	1,748
			101st Line	1,890
	Chambarlhac	*Herbin*	24th Light	1,801
		Rivaud	43rd Line	1,901
			96th Line	1,586
Lannes		*Mainoni*	28th Line	998
	Watrin	*Gency*	6th Light	1,114
		Mahler	22nd Line	1,255
			40th Line	1,716
Desaix	Monnier	*Schilt*	19th Light	914
		Cara-St-Cyr	70th Line	1,460
			72nd Line	1,240
	Boudet	*Musnier*	9th Light	2,014
			1st Hussars	120
			3rd Cavalry	120
		Guénand	30th Line	1,430
			59th Line	1,872
Murat		*Kellermann*	2nd Cavalry	300
			20th Cavalry	100
		Champeaux	1st Dragoons	450
			8th Dragoons	328
		Rivaud	12th Hussars	300

Lieutenant-General	Division	*Brigade*	Unit	Strength
			21st Chasseurs	359
			11th Hussars	200
		Duvignau	6th Dragoons	345
			12th Chasseurs	340
		Marmont	Artillery and train	618
		Bessières	Foot Grenadiers	800
			Horse Grenadiers & Chasseurs	360
			Light Artillery	72

Summary

Infantry	23,739
Cavalry	3,322
Artillery	690
Total	**27,751 men**

Order of Battle, Austrian Forces
(The following OB is taken from Geppert's 1804 study)

Commander:	Gdk Melas
General Adjutant:	Oberst Graf Radetzky
Chief Of Staff:	GM Zach
Director of Artillery:	Oberst Reisner, Oberst-Lt Perzel
Commander Pioneer Battalion:	Major Graf Hardegg
Commander of Engineers:	Major Vincenz Krapf

Advanced Guard:

	Mariassy Jäger*	4 companies	164
	3rd Bach Light Battalion	1 battalion	277
	4th Am Ende Light Battalion	1 battalion	291
Oberst Frimont	1st Kaiser-Dragoons	2 squadrons	272
	Bussy-Jäger zu Pferde	2 squadrons	186
	Pioneers	1 company	100
	Cavalry artillery	1 battery	

Main column:

FML Hadik	GM Pilatti	1st Kaiser-Dragoons	3 squadrons	309
		4th Karaczay Dragoons	6 squadrons	1,053
	GM Bellegarde	IR 53 Jellacic	2 battalions	613
		IR 52 Erzherzog Anton	2 battalions	855
	GM Saint Julien	IR 11 Michel Wallis	3 battalions	2,209
	GM de Briey	IR 47 Franz Kinsky	2⅓ battalions	1,640
FML Kaim	GM Knesevich	IR 23 Grossherzog von Toscana	3 battalions	2,188
	GM Lamarseille	IR 63 Erzherzog Joseph	3 battalions	1,111
FML Morzin	GM Lattermann:	Paar Battalion		357
		St. Julien Battalion		580
		Schiaffinati Battalion		408
		Kleinmayer Battalion		378
		Weber Battalion		393
	GM Weidenfeld	Khevenhuller Battalion		384
		Pieret Battalion		226
		Pertusi Battalion		555
		Perss Battalion		293
		Gorschen Battalion		291
		Weissenwolf Battalion		491
		Pioneers	4 companies	400
FML Elsnitz	GM Nobili	3rd Erzherzog Johann Dragoons	6 squadrons	859
		9th Lichtenstein Dragoons	6 squadrons	1,014
	GM Nimbsch	7th Hussars	8 squadrons	1,353
		9th Erdödy Hussars	6 squadrons	988
		The Artillery Reserve		
		Summary (with advanced guard)		**20,238**

The second, or left column FML Ott

Advanced-Guard:	GM Gottesheim	Mariassy Jäger*	1 company	40
		10th Lobkowitz-Dragoon	2 squadrons	248
		IR 28 Fröhlich	1 battalion	523
		Cavalry artillery	1 battery	
The Column:				
FML Schellenberg		Pioneers	1 company	100
	GM Retz	IR 28 Fröhlich	2 battalions	1,046
		IR 40 Mittrowsky	3 battalions	853
	GM Sticker	10th Lobkowitz-Dragoons	4 squadrons	492
		IR 51 Spleny	2 battalions	737
		IR 57 J. Colloredo	3 battalions	1,369
		Artillery		
FML Vogelsang	GM Ulm	IR 18 Stuart	3 battalions	1,282
		IR 17 Hohenlohe	2 battalions	912
			Summary	**7,602**

Right Column

FML O'Reilly	GM Rousseau	Mariassy Jäger*	1 company	40
		8th Nauendorf-Hussars	3½ sqdns	426
		5th Hussars	2 squadrons	230
		4th Banater Grenzer	1 battalion	533
		1st Warasdin-Kreuz Grenzer	1 battalion	755
		3rd Ogiliner Grenz Regiment	1 battalion	602
		3rd Ottocac Grenz Regiment	1 battalion	298
		8th Würtemberg Dragoons	1 squadron	113
		Cavalry artillery	1 battery	
			Summary	**2,997**

* *Note*: the Mariassy Jäger do not appear in Zach's Order of Battle.

Author's note on the sources

The history of Marengo is an interesting tale in itself. In the memoirs of Madame Junot (later the Duchess of Abrantes), we find the heroes of Marengo telling the story of the battle at the dinner table. One can imagine the exaggerations which flourished over goblets of wine and which later found their way into memoirs and accounts:

> 'Frequently, during this same year of the battle of Marengo, which was also that of my marriage, have I been party to a dinner prolonged till nine o'clock, because Bessières, Lannes, Eugène, Duroc, or Berthier, or some others of his companions in arms, or altogether, explained to Junot, who was greedy of the most trifling details, all those of this memorable affair. The table then became the plain of Marengo; a group of decanters at the head stood for the village, the candelabras at the bottom figured as the towns of Tortona and Alessandria, and the pears, the filberts, and bunches of grapes represented, as well as they might, the Austrian and Hungarian regiments, and our brave French troops.'

On the French side, the official report of the battle was written by the commander-in-chief of the Army of the Reserve, General Berthier, and published in 1805. While this account has its merits, it famously fell victim to what one might politely call an over-rationalization of the battle on the part of Napoleon. As this account states, the First Consul was far from expecting a battle, and even when it was fully engaged, he took much convincing of the fact, not leaving his headquarters until 11.00 am. Until the arrival of Boudet's division at 5.00 pm, the First Consul could do very little but play for time and react to the Austrian attack. Only after 5.00 pm could he fully seize the initiative. The authorized account reduced some of the urgency of the situation, and described how Bonaparte set up and controlled the evening battle. In this account, Monnier's division held Castelceriolo and the French army redeployed to form an oblique line across the plain to San Giuliano, where Boudet arrived. The 1805 account must therefore be seen in the context of Bonaparte's coronation and elevation to emperor. It is much the same as viewing David's painting of Bonaparte dramatically crossing the Great St Bernard mounted upon Alexander's horse, Bucephalus, when in reality he made the final ascent on a donkey. History and art were an important part of state propaganda. We should not be ignorant or squeamish of this fact.

In the late 1990s, I began researching the Battle of Marengo with a view to writing a regimental history of the French 9th Light Infantry. This regiment played a celebrated role in the battle and was awarded the title 'Incomparable' for its heroic actions. My research led to several collaborations, and these resulted in two publications marking the bicentennial of Marengo in 2000. The first book was an Italian work by Marco Gioannini and Giulio Massobrio called *Marengo: La battaglia che creò il mito di Napoleone*. The second was Osprey Publishing's 'Campaign Series' book by David Hollins, *Marengo: Napoleon's Day of Fate*. The collaboration leading up to these publications (Hollins concentrating on the Austrian archive sources, myself on the French, and Gioannini and Massobrio on the local Italian perspective) uncovered a wealth of material which had not appeared in previous accounts of the battle. With hindsight, it might have been better to have awaited publication of a full English-language work first because the 'Campaign Series' format did not permit extensive footnotes or space to elaborate on the claims made by Austrian participants. With Hollins, I had prepared a first draft of a much larger work entitled *Marengo: Napoleon, Melas and the Spy*. However, it was impossible to deliver this project in time for the bicentennial, although it was equally impossible to ignore the new material uncovered in our research for it. When, in 2000, Hollins' *Marengo* arrived in the English-speaking market, like Napoleon's army appearing over the Alps, it came as something of a thunderbolt. Without the full account and the footnotes to support it, the Austrian version of the action involving the French Foot Guards was interpreted as deliberately provocative in some quarters. A lively debate was waged on-line about the merits of this work, with partisans on both sides of the debate quoting accounts with little understanding of the full context of the new research. Since these works were published, I have concentrated on other projects and have played something of a waiting game on Marengo to see what new significant material might come to light over the bicentennial celebrations of the Napoleonic Wars. The pause has been worth it, with more sources coming to light, and the availability of digital collections aiding research in a way no generation has previously enjoyed. Given full access to the fruits of Hollins' Vienna research, in 2015 I returned to 'Marengo' and began preparing this account.

Authors should declare any bias. Before I am labelled as a Habsburg partisan, or a perfidious Albionite, for the record I have dedicated a large part of my adult life to the serious study of the French Army of the Napoleonic Wars. I consider myself a Francophile, as much as an Englishman can be. Bonaparte, in my opinion, was a genius; his capacity for intellectual exercise was vast; whether planning military campaigns or in his civil and legal capacities. Between 1800 and 1805, he was at the height of his powers and energy. That said, he was capable of tyranny and was unmatched in the art of self-propaganda. One of the most intriguing parts of this research project has been getting to know the personalities in the Austrian camp. One of my objectives has been to properly introduce readers to the likes of Melas, Zach and Radetzky.

In terms of the sources now available, there are two key authors to introduce. On the French side we have Captain Gaspar Jean Marie René de Cugnac, who in 1900 published a two-volume compilation of primary source material found in the French *Archives de la guerre*. The following year, a two-volume compilation of Austrian documents was produced by the German historian Herman Hüffer. Combined, these four volumes form the backbone of any study into the subject.

Between myself and Hollins, we collected a great many of the official histories of regiments which fought in the battle. The majority of these date from the second half of the nineteenth century. In many cases they are simple rehashes of standard accounts, but in some cases the authors have done an excellent job of searching through the regimental archives to find specific details of the regiment's feats of arms. These are invaluable as sources. One discovery of particular importance was a set of French regimental histories which were compiled by the serving officers of infantry and cavalry in 1801 following an order by the Minister of War. These histories provide significant details, particular in relation to Kellermann's famous cavalry charge in the battle.

For the best part of 200 years, the main Austrian source on the battle was the 1822 account by Captain Karl von Mras, published in the Austrian military journal '*Österreichische Militärische Zeitschrift*' (OMZ), a publication for Austrian officers to study past campaigns and other military subjects. Written two decades on from the event by an author who did not witness the affair, the Mras account clearly must have limitations. However, as a staff history written for fellow officers (not a self-aggrandizing memoir), the account clearly has merit. It has more merit still when one sees the provenance of it; that it was based on several earlier staff reports written by men who were veterans of the 1800 campaign.

In the course of research made for this book, we have found an unpublished staff report which appears to have been a key source for Mras. The document was discovered in the Vienna War Archive by David Hollins in 2015, and was subsequently photographed by our colleague, Michael Wenzel. Entitled *Geschichte des Feldzugs in Italien im Jahre 1800 bis 1801*, the manuscript is written in the old German *Kurrent* script and dates from 1804. The author was Major Menrard von Geppert, who, while not actually present at Marengo, was a staff captain attached to the corps of FML Hohenzollern at Genoa on the day of battle. Serving on the staff of the imperial army, Geppert was well-acquainted with the key participants of the battle, and would have had access to them very soon after the event. He is likely to have had access to the reports and notes of his fellow staff officers which have not survived. Geppert therefore provides the earliest written Austrian account of the action involving the French Foot Guards, which concludes fatefully: '*und nur wenige entkommen ließ*' ('and only allowed a few to escape'). Interestingly this account pre-dates by a year the official publication of French Minister of War General Alexandre Berthier's 1805 *Relation de la bataille de Marengo*; but by this time the description of the Consular Guard being a rock of granite in the plain was a well-established part of the mythology of the battle.

From Geppert, we move to the subsequent report of Joseph von Stutterheim. Like Geppert, Stutterheim was a staff officer attached to the general-quartermaster staff of Melas' army. Unlike Geppert, he was actually present at the battle, and witnessed some of the key events (including the Guard action) and the armistice negotiations which followed. Following the creation of the OMZ in 1808, Stutterheim was charged with writing a history of the 1799 campaign, which was published in 1811/1812. Stutterheim then wrote a report on the 1800 campaign in Italy, which was an expansion on Geppert's work and in places is a direct copy of it. Stutterheim's report was described by Hüffer as 'fresh' and possessing a 'convincing descriptiveness', which is difficult to discount. This is something of an understatement – Stutterheim's report was frank in the extreme. He called into question not just the actions, but the personalities and health of the most senior commanders; including men who were alive when he wrote it. Although drafts were no doubt circulated, the account was not published in the OMZ. Before there was any time to review the account, in 1812 Stutterheim became adjutant to Field Marshal Lieutenant Schwartzenberg, who commanded the Austrian contingent in Napoleon's invasion of Russia. After this, Stutterheim was busily engaged in the final campaigns of the Napoleonic era, and his time for writing would have been somewhat diminished. After the wars, Stutterheim returned to his draft and made a new start. The best indications are that his second draft was prepared in 1822 – around the time Mras' account appeared in the OMZ. One imagines he was advised, or felt inclined, to tone down the original account, not because anyone questioned its veracity, but to formalize it and make it read more like a professional staff history. This document remained unpublished, and we see later additions made to the document – there is a note added remarking on Bourrienne's 1829 memoirs. It is important to state that the two Stutterheim accounts (Hüffer labels them as A and B) vary little in content. When Hüffer came to publish his collection of documents, he published the B account in full, but provided excerpts from the A account where he felt the two accounts were different. In terms of their veracity, Stutterheim appears a very credible source, and his personal observations are indispensable to understanding the Marengo campaign and battle. A staff officer in 1800, Stutterheim rose to the rank of field marshal lieutenant (FML) by the end of the Napoleonic Wars and had a distinguished service, being made a baron in 1819. In 1824, he became part of the Hofkriegsrat (High Military Council), the body responsible for advising the Habsburg emperor on military policy. Two years later, we find the composer Ludwig van Beethoven dedicating his String Quartet No.14 to Stutterheim; it is said in gratitude for taking his nephew Karl into the army after a failed suicide attempt. The reason for stating the above is to show Stutterheim was a man of some talent, very much part of the Austrian military establishment, not a scurrilous sensationalist writing an account on the wings.

Of the remaining Austrian accounts, perhaps the most important is the autobiography of Count Radetzky, the Austrian general adjutant in 1800. These memoirs unlock the story of the Piedmontese spy and are verified by contemporary reports in Hüffer. Crucially, it establishes that the Marengo spy who delivered Zach's deception at Marengo, was the same found at Mantua and Cuneo in 1799. Published in 1887 as *Erinnerungen aus dem Leben des Feldmarschall Grafen Radetzky*, this memoir emphasizes the author's dislike of Zach, the army chief of staff. The others are better known because they have appeared in French. Two are by Stutterheim's fellow staff officers. The first account is from Count Adam Neipperg, published in French in 1906 (a German version is published in Hüffer's second volume). The other is by French émigré Baron de Crossard. His six-volume account forms an interesting and useful record of the Napoleonic era. He repeats Stutterheim's claim about the Foot Guards being 'almost entirely destroyed or taken prisoner' in the action; but is equally critical of the performance of the Austrian leadership at the critical moment – the crisis of the battle. One can dismiss his claims as the work of an anti-Bonapartist, but actually his verdict on the Guard is delivered matter-of-factly, as if it were already an accepted fact. He also dedicates several paragraphs to the Piedmontese spy who forms a central part of this new account.

Also on the Austrian side, we find the memoirs of the French émigré August Danican and the Piedmontese Franchino di Cavour published by Félix Bouvier in 1900 in the Italian *Centenario della Battaglia di Marengo*. One work which remains unpublished in its entirety is the memoirs of Henri de Faverges. A relatively recent find on my part, I was alerted to Faverges' highly readable account by a footnote in Kellermann's son's history of the campaign (published 1854). Excerpts from Faverges' memoirs were published in the 1908 *La Revue Hebdomadaire* by his nephew, the author and historian Charles Costa de Beauregard. Technically an émigré, Faverges was from Savoy, part of the Kingdom of Sardinia annexed by France. Faverges served the imperial army after the fall of the House of Savoy in 1798. Although wounded prior to the commencement of the campaign, Faverges is an extremely important source. After Marengo, his brother married the daughter of the Austrian chief of staff, Generalmajor Anton Zach – a pivotal figure in this account. Although Zach did not leave a memoir, he did speak about the battle with Faverges, and the latter recorded their conversation. Although an anecdotal source, when combined with criticisms made by Crossard about Zach's capabilities as staff officer, it reveals key mistakes on the part of the Austrian chief of staff which are critical for understanding the campaign and battle.

Another unpublished memoir on the Napoleonic Wars is that of the French chief of staff at Marengo, General Etienne Dupont. One of the most brilliant generals of the French army, Dupont fell from favour in 1808 after surrendering an army at Bailen in Spain. In 1903, Eugène Titeux published an epic, three-volume biography called *Le general Dupont: une erreur historique*. The first volume of this series contains excerpts from Dupont's memoirs and numerous other documents, including the report of General of Brigade Guénand. I had previously found some unpublished letters written by Guénand at Vincennes, and these were complimented by the information I discovered in Titeux's work. Guénand's brigade was effectively airbrushed from the official history – not through any fault of the general, but, I believe, simply because the story of his brigade's advance across the battlefield did not fit the narrative begun by the First Consul's bulletin, subsequently enshrined in Berthier's history. Guénand pushes the action away from San Guiliano, westwards towards Cascina Grossa. It also provides some interesting clues about how Kellermann's charge was so effective. Also of great interest in Titeux's work were letters by Valhubert (colonel of the 28th Line) and Dalton, a staff officer in Boudet's division. With colleagues, I have made an attempt to track down the original of Dupont's manuscript, because it is worthy of publication in itself; but at the time of writing, this has drawn a blank.

Other than the documents compiled by de Cugnac, the main French memoirs are by Savary, Marmont, Kellermann, Lejeune, Krettly, Marbot, Coignet, Petit, Prince Eugène, Victor and Soult. These are all well-known to English-speaking readers and need little introduction. One should point out the argument between Savary and Kellermann in the late 1820s, with the latter effectively claiming he was responsible for the victory, not Desaix. The argument was bitter and one feels there was personal animosity between the two parties. Of course Kellermann gave the order to charge and was responsible for judging the exact timing of it; but Desaix had requested the charge to be made.

The memoirs of Horse Grenadier Joseph Petit have proven particularly valuable. At first I was suspicious of the account, published so soon after the battle; but I found Petit described phases of the battle which went unmentioned except in the Austrian sources. I have taken a liberty with the ever-popular memoirs of Jean-Roch Coignet. His notebooks would one day form one of the best-known memoirs of the Napoleonic Wars. Living until 1865 and the ripe old age of 89 years, Coignet survived long enough to be photographed, so we can look upon the actual living face of a veteran of Marengo. Even in old age, he has broad shoulders and a large jaw. His memoirs were first published under the title *Vingt ans de gloire avec l'empereur* in 1851 in Auxerre with a limited print run of 500; they were then republished in 1883 by the author Lorédan Larchey. Around 2000, I was provided with a French transcription of Coignet's original text. When compared to the 1883 version, we can see where Larchey has polished the original prose. In some areas, small technical details are changed, and these are very important – for example, he increases the strength of the Foot Guard from 600 to 800 men. Some of the technical language has also changed. The excerpts from Coignet given in this book are my translations of the original version.

The letters of Maurice Dupin appeared from an unexpected source. This staff officer wrote a series of amusing letters about the campaign, which later appeared in a biography of his daughter – the author George Sand. In the course of this work, I was contacted by Karl Jakob Skarstein, who provided me with the letters of Lieutenant Rustad, a Norweigan officer attached to the French artillery staff. Almost on my deadline, Skarstein contacted me again, this time with the unpublished *Souvenirs de Jean Chenevier*, an officer in the 22nd Half-Brigade.

No doubt more memoirs, letters and accounts will materialize in the future, and our understanding of the battle will evolve yet further. At the bicentennial commemorations at Marengo in 2000, I met the late Dr David Chandler, author of the seminal *The Campaigns of Napoleon*. When David Hollins and I described some of the new sources coming to light, Chandler encouraged us, stating *The Campaigns of Napoleon* was just a starting point and further work was needed to uncover the detail. With that endorsement ever in mind, one hopes this work will act as a spur for further research over the present century. If nothing else, our collective efforts hopefully demonstrate that the serious study of military history cannot be a one-sided narrative written by the victors alone. All voices must be heard if we are to understand and learn from conflicts old and new.

Acknowledgements

This has been a project of twenty years. In that time many people have furnished information or given practical, sometimes unwitting, advice, guidance or inspiration. I have limited the following list to those who provided me with material assistance with this project, and I of course take responsibility for all the views expressed, as they are entirely my own. Without the assistance of David Hollins, my research would have been entirely one-sided. For twenty years he has generously and patiently shared his research and ideas on the Habsburg forces. Our collaboration will continue beyond this project, seeking out the spy, and taking a broader look at the role of secret intelligence in Napoleon's Italian campaigns – it is a fascinating and worthwhile subject for further research. The majority of German translation in this book was carried out by David Hollins, although I must also acknowledge Michael Wenzel for some help in this matter, and also for answering the many queries I have sent his way over recent years. My thanks go also to Pierre-Yves Chauvin, who arranged our visit to the archives of the monastery on the Great St Bernard in 2017; also for photographing Guénand's papers at Vincennes and helping with the transcription. I must thank Ian Edwards, who copied many of the French regimental histories at Vincennes in the days before eBooks, and introduced me to Dave Hollins twenty years ago. I also received support from Pierre Liernaux at the Musée Royal de l'Armée et d'Histoire Militaire in Brussels, who copied a number of works for me. I would like to thank Martin Lancaster for his continued encouragement and interest over the years, particularly for sponsoring my first visit to the battlefield in 1999. Martin also introduced me to Andrea Puleo, who arranged my last visit to Marengo in 2017 and in turn introduced me to Gian Lorenzo Bernini, who conducted us passionately and expertly to various locations, including Vigna Santa, where a memorial to Desaix now stands. I must acknowledge and thank the staff of the British Museum, the Vienna Kriegsarchiv, the Service Historique de la Défense (Vincennes), the French Bibliotheque Nationale and its fabulous 'Gallica' service. I must thank Peter Harrington, Curator at the Anne S.K. Brown Military Collection. I would also like to thank the Congrégation des Chanoines du Grand-Saint-Bernard for their hospitality and advice. As ever, I must thank my editor at Pen and Sword, Philip Sidnell, and last but never least my wife Sarah, who supported me with endless patience and encouragement as this long project drew to an end.

Bibliography

1. Regimental Histories

Note: Many of the regiments which fought at Marengo were subsequently retitled, renumbered, disbanded or reformed. It is therefore sometimes difficult to trace the ancestry of a regiment. The following list will help readers locate the correct regiments.

A. Austrian Empire

I. Cavalry regiments

1st Kaiser Dragoons:
- Pizzighelli, Cajetan, *Geschichte des k. u. k. Ulanen-Regimentes Kaiser Joseph II. No. 6* (Wien: 1908).

4th Karaczay Dragoons:
- Theimer, Alexander, *Geschichte des k. k. 7. Uhlanen-Regimentes Erzherzog Karl Ludwig von seiner Errichtung 1758 bis Ende 1868* (Wien: 1869).

8th Würtemberg Dragoons:
- Dedekind, Franz, *Geschichte des k. k. Kaiser Franz Joseph I dragoner-regimentes Nr.11* (Wien, 1879).

9th Lichtenstein Dragoons:
- Amon von Treuenfest, Gustav Ritter von, *Geschichte des k. u. k. Bukowina'schen Dragoner-Regimentes General d. Cavallerie Freiherr Piret de Bihain Nr. 9 von seiner Errichtung 1682-1892* (Wien: 1892).

10th Lobkowitz Dragoons:
- Grosser, *Beitrag zur Regiments Geschichte des 3ten Chevauleger-Regiments* (1805).
- Thürheim, Andreas Graf, *Geschichte des k. k. 8. Uhlanen-Regimentes Erzherzog Ferdinand Maximilian* (Wien: 1860).

5th Hussars:
- Amon von Treuenfest, Gustav Ritter von, *Geschichte des k. k. Feldmarschall Graf Radetzky Husaren-Regimentes Nr. 5 (1798-1884)* (Wien: 1885).

7th Hussars:
- Anon., *Geschichte des k. k. Husaren-Regimentes Nr. 7 von dessen Errichtung im Jahre 1798 bis 1855* (Wien: 1856).

8th Nauendorf Hussars:
- Amon von Treuenfest, Gustav Ritter von, *Geschichte des k. k. Husaren-Regimentes Alexander Freiherr von Koller Nr. 8 (1696-1880)* (Wien: 1880).

9th Erdödy Hussars:
- Korda, Ignác *Geschichte des k. u. k. Husaren-Regimentes Graf Nádasdy Nr. 9 (1688-1903)* (Sopron: 1903).

II. Infantry regiments

IR 11 Michael Wallis:
- Jäger, Franz, Masak, Stefan, and Novak, Wenzel, *Schicksale und Thaten des K. u. K. Infanterie-Regiments Georg Prinz von Sachsen Nr. 11* (Wien: 1901).

IR 23 Grossherzog Toscana:
- Babich von Lorinach, A, *Geschichte des K. K. Infanterie Regiments 23* (1911).

IR 17 Hohenlohe:
- Steiner, D. Franz, *Geschichte des K. K. Prinz Hohenlohe-Langenburg Infanterie-Regiments Nr. 17 seit dessen Errichtung 1632 bis 1851* (Leykam: 1858).
- Strobl von Ravelsberg, F., *Geschichte des K. u. K. Infanterie-Regiments Ritter von Milde Nr. 17. 1674-1910* (Laibach: 1911).

IR 18 Stuart:
- Amon von Treuenfest, Gustav Ritter, *Geschichte des K. K. Infanterie-Regimentes Nr. 18, Constantin Grossfürst von Rußland, von 1682 bis 1882* (Wien: 1882).
- Novak, Friedrich: *Achtzehner 'immer vorwärts!': Kriegsgeschichten vom K. und K. Infanterie-Regimente Erzeherzog Leopold Salvator Nr. 18* (Theresienstadt: 1896).
- Padewieth, Mansuet von, *Geschichte des kaiserl. Königl. 18. Linien-Infanterie-Regiments Grossfürst Constantin von Russland* (Wien: 1859).
- IR 28 Fröhlich:
- Schmedis, Emil, *Geschichte des K. K. 28. Infanterie-Regiments FZM. Ludwig Ritter von Benedek* (Wien: 1878).

IR 40 Mittrowsky:
- Posselt, Oskar, *Geschichte des k. und k. Infanterie-Regiments Ritter v. Pino Nr. 40* (Rzeszow: 1913).

IR 47 Franz Kinsky:
- Amon von Treuenfest, Gustav Ritter: *Geschichte des k. u. k. Infanterie-Regimentes Nr. 47* (Wien: 1890).
- Vogelsang, Ludwig Freiherr von, *Das Steierische Infanterie-Regiment Graz Nr. 47 im Weltkrieg* (Graz: 1932).

IR 51 Splényi:
- Maendl, Maximilian, *Geschichte des K. und K. Infanterie-Regiments Nr. 51* (Klausenburg: 1897-1899).

IR 52 Erzherzog Anton:

- Ascher, Adolph: *Geschichte des k. u. k. Infanterieregiments FZM Erzherzog Friedrich Nr. 52* (Wien: 1905).
- Herzmann, Franz: *Geschichte des k. und k. 52. Linien-Infanterie-Regiments Erzherzog Franz Carl* (Wien: 1871).

IR 53 Jellacic:

- Hostinek, Oberst: *Geschichte des k. k. 53. Infanterie-regimentes erzherzog Leopold Ludwig; verfasst im auftrage des regiments-commandos* (Tulln: 1881).
- Marx, Anton, *Geschichte des 53ten Ungarischen Linien-Infanterie-Regiments* (Wien: 1838).

IR 57 Joseph Colloredo:

- Maciaga, Joseph: *Geschichte des k. u. k. galizischen Infanterie-Regimentes Feldmarschall Friedrich Josias Prinz zu Sachsen-Coburg-Saalfeld Nr. 57* (Wien: 1898).
- Pillersdorff, Albert Freiherrn, *Das 57. Infanterie-Regiment Fürst Jablonowski und die Kriege seiner Zeit* (Wien: 1857).

IR 63 Erzherzog Joseph:

- Schneider, Michael, *Geschichte des K. u. K. Infanterie Regiments Nr. 63*, (Bistritz: 1906).

III. Grenzer regiments

Ogiliner Grenzer:

- Kussan P., *Kurzgefasste Geschichte des Oguliner dritten National-Grenz-Infanterie-Regiments* (Wien: 1852).

3rd Ottochaner Grenzer:

- Bach, Fr., *Otocaner Regiments-Geschichte* (Karlstadt: 1851-1852).

IV. Unattached grenadier brigade companies

(IR 4) - Amon von Treuenfest, Gustav Ritter, *Geschichte des K. K. Infanterie-Regimentes Hoch- und Deutschmeister Nr. 4* (Wien: 1879).

(IR 10) – Anon., *Geschichte des K. u. K. Infanterie-Regimentes Oskar II. Friedrich, König von Schweden und Norwegen, Nr. 10* (Wien: 1888).

(IR 13) - Mandel, Fryderyk, *Geschichte des K. u. K. Infanterie-Regiments Guidobald Graf von Starhemberg Nr. 13* (Krakau: 1893).

(IR 24) - Prochazka, Wilhelm, *Geschichte des K. K. Infanterie-Regimentes FML Hreiherr v. Rheinänder Nr. 24* (Wien: 1886).

(IR 26) - Wrede, Alphons, *Geschichte des K. u. K. Infanterieregimentes Michael Groszfürst von Ruszland Nr. 26 vpm seiner Errichtung bis zur Gegenwart 1717-1909* (Györ: 1909).

(IR 27) – Anon., *Geschichte des K. u. K. Infanterie-Regimentes Leopold II. König der Belgier Nr. 27* (Wien: 1881).

(IR 36) – Paiir, Franz, *Geschichte des K. K. 36. Linien-Infanterie-Regiments* (Prag: 1875).

(IR 40) – Posselt, Oskar, *Geschichte des K. und K. Infanterie-Regiments Ritter v. Pino Nr. 40* (Rzeszow: 1913).

(IR 44) – Branko, Franz von, *Geschichte des k. k. Infanterie-Regimentes Nr. 44 Feldmarschall Erzherzog Albrecht, von seiner Errichtung 1744 bis 1875* (Wien: 1875).

(IR 45) – Dragoni Edler von Rabenhorst, Alfons, *Geschichte des K. u. K. Infanterie-Regimentes Prinz Friedrich August, Herzog von Sachsen, Nr. 45. Von der Errichtung bis zur Gegenwart* (Brünn: 1897).

(IR 55) – Nahlik, Johann Edler von, *Geschichte des kais. kön. 55. Linien-Infanterie-Regimentes Baron Bianchi* (Brünn: 1863).

(IR 59) – Leiler, A., *Geschichte des K. K. Infanterieregimentes No. 59 seit seiner Errichtung 1682 bis zum Schlusse des Jahres 1855* (Salzburg: 1864); Wück, Alois, and Knorz, Justus, *Geschichte des k. k. Infanterie-Regiments Erzherzog Rainer Nr. 59 von seiner Errichtung 1682 bis 3. Juni 1882* (Salzburg: 1882-1901).

V. Pioneers

Brinner, Wilhelm, *Geschichte des K. K. Pionier-Regiments in Verbindung mit einer Geschichte des Brückenwesens in Österreich* (Wien: 1878-1881).

B. French Republic

I. Cavalry regiments

2nd Cavalry:
– Rothwiller, Antoine Ernest, *Histoire du deuxième régiment de cuirassiers, ancien Royal de Cavalerie, 1635-1876* (Paris: E. Plon & Cie, 1877).
3rd Cavalry:
– Maumené, Charles, *Historique du 3è Regiment des Cuirassiers: ci-devant du commissaire général, 1645-1892* (Paris: Boussod, Valadon & Cie, 1893).
20th Cavalry:
– Ruff (Chief of Brigade), *Historique du régiment rédigé en l'an 9* (SHD/MS 1856, 1801).
1st Dragoons:
– Sisson (Sub-Lieutenant), Serve (Commander), *Historique du 1er régiment de dragons, 1656-1890*, (Manuscrit des Archives Historiques de la Guerre, 1894).

6th Dragoons:
- Anon., *Historique du 6e régiment de dragons* (Paris: Delagrave, 1898).

8th Dragoons:
- Lemaréchal (Lieutenant), *Historique du 8e dragons* (Manuscrit des Archives Historiques de la Guerre, 1894).

12th Chasseurs:
- Anon., *12e chasseurs à cheval* (SHD/MS 1856, 1801).
- Anon., *Carnet de la Sabretache No. 10, Le Colonel de France et le 12e Régiment de Chasseurs, 1800 à 1805* (Paris: Berger-Levrault & Cie., October 1893).
- Aubry, Thomas Joseph, *Souvenirs du 12e Chasseurs 1799-1815* (Paris: Maison Quantine, 1889).
- Dupuy, *Historique du 12e chasseurs de 1788 à 1891* (Paris: Person, 1891).
- Montaglas, Galy, *Historique du 12e chasseurs à cheval depuis le 29 avril 1792 jusqu'au traité de Lunéville, 9 février 1801* (Paris: Chapelot, 1908).

21st Chasseurs:
- Anon., *21e chasseurs à cheval* (SHD/MS 1856, 1801).
- Brémond d'Ars, Théophile Charles, Comte de, *Historique du 21e chasseurs à cheval, 1792-1814* (Paris: H. Champion, 1903).

1st Hussars:
- Anon., *Historique du 1er régiment de hussards, d'après le manuscrit du commandant Ogier d'Ivry* (Valence: Imprimerie Jules Céas, 1901).

11th Hussars:
- Lassus (Lieutenant) de, *Historique du 11e régiment de hussards* (Valence, Imprimerie Jules Céas, 1890).

12th Hussars:
- Bourqueney (Lieutenant) de, *Historique du 12e régiment de hussards* (Paris: Charles-Lavauzelle, 1902).

II. Infantry half-brigades

6th Light:
- Gremillet, Paul, *Un régiment pendant deux siècles, 1684-1899. Historique du 81e de ligne, ancien 6e léger «l'Intrépide» ... etc.* (Paris: Chapelot, 1899).

9th Light:
- Crowdy, T.E., *Incomparable: Napoleon's 9th Light Infantry Regiment* (Oxford: Osprey Publishing, 2011).
- Labassée, M., *Notice sur les Batailles, Combats, Actions, Sièges et expéditions ou ces différents corps se sont trouvée depuis le mois de Septembre 1792 jusqu'è ce jour. 2 Messidor An IX* (SHD MR1856).

– Loÿ, L., *Historiques du 84e régiment d'infanterie de ligne 'Un Contre Dix'; du 9e régiment d'infanterie légère 'l'Incomparable'; et du 4e régiment de voltigeurs de la Garde 1684–1904* (Lille: L. Danel, 1905).

22nd Line:

– Anon, *Résumé Historique du 22e régiment d'infanterie* (Montélimar: Astier & Niel, 1895).

24th Light:

– Anon., *Historique du 99e régiment d'infanterie* (Manuscrit des Archives Historiques de la Guerre, 1889).

28th Line:

– Simond, Émile, *Le 28e de ligne. Historique du régiment d'après les documents du ministère de la guerre* (Rouen: Mégard et O., 1889).

30th Line:

– Taboureau (Captain), *Petite bibliotheque de l'armée francaise. Historique abrégé du 30e régiment d'infanterie* (Paris: Charles-Lavauzelle, 1887).

– Yvert, Louis, *Historique du 30e régiment d'infanterie, 1667-1896* (Annecy: Hérisson et Cie, 1896).

40th Line:

– Coste, Emile, *Historique du 40e régiment d'infanterie de ligne* (Paris: Chamerot, 1887).

43rd Line:

– Anon., *Historique abrégé du 43e régiment d'infanterie* (Lille: Imprimerie du 43ᵉ régiment, 1893).

44th Line:

– Casanova, Mathias, *Historique du 44e régiment d'infanterie* (Lons-le-Saulnier: Declume, 1892).

59th Line:

– Barthas (Lieutenant), *Petite bibliotheque de l'armée francaise: Petit historique du 59e régiment rédigé sous la direction du colonel Durupt* (Paris: Charles-Lavauzelle, 1903).

– Maury (Lieutenant), *Aux Soldats. Histoire d'un régiment* (Foix: Gadrat, 1899).

70th Line:

– Anon., (publication de la réunion des officiers), *Historique du 70e régiment d'infanterie de ligne* (Paris: Imprimerie Dutemple, 1875).

– Godbert (Captain), *Historique du 70e régiment d'infanterie de ligne, 1674-1889* (Vitré: E. Lécuyer, 1890).

96th Line:

– Bouvier, J.B. (Captain), *Historique du 96e Regiment D'Infanterie* (Lyon: A. Storck, 1892).

101st Line:
- Anon., *Historique du 101e régiment d'Infanterie* (Laval: Moreau, 1892).
- Rouby, Lieutenant G., *Historique du 101e régiment d'infanterie* (Manuscript, Archives Historiques de la Guerre, 1890).

III. Artillery regiments

1st Artillery Regiment:
- Corda, Henri, *Le Régiment de la Fère et le 1er Régiment d'Artillerie, 1670-1900* (Paris: Berger-Levrault, 1906).
2nd Artillery Regiment:
- Anon., *Historique du 2ème régiment d'artillerie, 1720-1898* (Grenoble: Falque et Perrin, 1899).
5th Artillery Regiment:
- Anon., *Historique sommaire du 5e régiment d'artillerie à partir l'année 1720,* (Beasnçon: Dodivers & Cie, 1883).
6th Artillery Regiment:
- Anon., *6e régiment d'artillerie. Résumé historique, 1756-1903* (Valence: J. Céas et fils, 1903).

IV. Consular Guard

Lachouque, Henri, and Brown, A.S.K., *The Anatomy of Glory: Napoleon and his Guard - A Study in Leadership* (Providence: Brown University Press, 1961).
Saint-Hilaire, Émile Marco de, *Histoire anecdotique, politique et militaire de la Garde Imperiale* (Paris: Eugène Penaud & Cie, 1847).

2. Archive sources consulted

A. Service Historique de la Défense (Château de Vincennes)

- B3 236. Armée de Réserve. *Correspondance et ordres du général en chef Berthier, du 29 germinal au 1er messidor an VIII (19 avril-20 juin 1800).*
- GR1 M462. 1. *Relation des mouvements et des combats des différents corps de l'armée de réserve, depuis le 23 floréal jusqu'au 24 prairial an VIII,* par le chef de bataillon Blein. 2. *Lettre du chef de bataillon Chabrier au général Sanson, directeur du dépôt de la guerre, 16 fructidor an X, Renseignements statistiques sur le champ de bataille de Marengo.* 3. *Renseignements demandés en l'an XIII (1805) sur la bataille de Marengo par le général Sanson, et notes diverses.*
- GR1 M463. *Relation de la bataille de Marengo, par le lieutenant-général Quiot, alors aide-de-camp du général Victor.* Rédigée en 1845.

- GR1 M465. *Lettre du lieutenant-colonel de Castres, en date de Lille, le 23 octobre 1819, relative à la même bataille.*
- GR1 M466. *Rapport des marches et opérations de la division Boudet, à compter de son départ d'Aoste jusqu'à la capitulation de l'armée ennemie* (1800), par le général Boudet.
- GR1 M467. *Notes sur la campagne de l'an VIII et la bataille de Marengo*, par le général Pelet.
- GR1 M468. *Journal de la campagne de l'armée de Réserve*, par l'adjudant commandant Brossier.
- GR1 M610. Notes rectificatives employées par le général Mathieu Dumas pour le 2e volume de son *Précis des événements militaires sur les campagnes de 1799 et 1800 en Helvétie et en Italie*, savoir: 8. *Notes du général de brigade Guenand au général Mathieu Dumas sur la bataille de Marengo. 8 bis. Dix lettres particulières de l'adjudant général Dampierre au général M. Dumas sur les événements qui précédèrent et suivirent la bataille de Marengo. 9. Notes pour servir au précis historique des premières marches de l'armée de Réserve, devenue Armée des Grisons.*
- GR1 M842. Notes Brahaut, etc. *Historique du 9e régiment d'infanterie légère, de 1788 à 1839*, par le capitaine L. Dubois, La Rochelle, 20 septembre 1839.
- GR1 M856 *Historiques des corps de troupe, établis en l'an IX par les soins des chefs de corps et des conseils d'administration, sur l'ordre du ministre de la guerre (infanterie).*
- GR1 M857. *Historiques des corps de troupe ... (cavalerie).*
- GR20 YC5 *1er régiment de grenadiers à pied, 1799-1814. Nivôse an VIII-16 ventôse an X.*
- GR20 YC37 *Registre Matricule Chasseurs de la Garde Consulaire 13 nivose an VIII – 9 décembre 1807*

B. Kriegsarchiv des Österreichischen Staatsarchivs

- KA MS Manuskripte zur Kriegsgeschichte 152. *Geschichte des Feldzugs in Italien in Jahre 1800 bis 1801 der K. K. Armee bearbeitet vom damaligen HR Major Br Menrad von Geppert.*
- KA MS Manuskripte zur Kriegsgeschichte 154. *Belchreibung der Schlacht von Marengo den vierzehn Juny 1800 verfafst Carl v: Mras.*
- KA MS Manuskripte zur Kriegsgeschichte 155/7. *Feldzug in Italien. 1800. II Hauptstück. I. Abschnitt von Hauptman von Mras.*
- KA MS Manuskripte zur Kriegsgeschichte 155/8. *Feldzug in Italien. 1800. II Hauptstück. II. Abschnitt von Hauptman von Mras.*
- KA MS Manuskripte zur Kriegsgeschichte 155/9. *Feldzug in Italien. 1800. II Hauptstück. III. Abschnitt von Hauptman von Mras.*

- KA MS Manuskripte zur Kriegsgeschichte 155/10. *Feldzug in Italien. 1800. II Hauptstück. IV. Abschnitt von Hauptman von Mras.*
- KA MS Manuskripte zur Kriegsgeschichte 155/11. *Feldzug in Italien. 1800. II Hauptstück. V. Abschnitt von Hauptman von Mras.*
- KA MS Manuskripte zur Kriegsgeschichte 155/12. *Feldzug in Italien. 1800. II Hauptstück. VI. Abschnitt von Hauptman von Mras.*
- KA MS Manuskripte zur Kriegsgeschichte 155/13. *Beilagen zur Geschichte des Feldzugs 1800. Von Hauptman von Mras.*

Note: Most of the original documents (including those cited by Hüffer) can be found in the series Alte Feldakten (AFA). They are listed as KA AFA 1800 Italien. Of particular interest are the detailed casualty reports: KA AFA 1800 Italien VI 328.

C. Archives du Grand Saint Bernard

- AGSB 2742 (*1798, 2 avril - 1800, 23 novembre*). *Passages de troupes françaises avant celui de mai 1800. Documents relatifs au passage et aux fournitures faites; mémoires et correspondance.*
- AGSB 2746 (*1800, 13 avril et 13 mai*). *Adieux des officiers français aux religieux du St-Bernard. Poésie écrite par Vivenot, chef de bataillon. Extrait d'une chronique sur le passage de Napoléon à Martigny, écrite par un prêtre du Valais; 1800, 13 mai.*
- AGSB 2748 (*1800, février - 20 juillet*). *Bordereaux des fournitures de l'hospice aux armées qui se rendent en Italie, l'armée du Rhin, l'armée de Réserve, du 3 mai au 9 juillet et l'armée d'Italie.Lettre de Dalbon, commissaire des guerres au prieur du St-Bernard pour lui dire qu'il passera à l'hospice le 9 juillet.*
- AGSB 2749 (*1800, 31 mai - 16 décembre, Valais et Genève*). *Documents relatifs aux sorts de la voiture de Napoléon laissée à Martigny.*
- AGSB 2752 (*vers 1800 - continué jusqu'en 1809*). *Copie d'une petite chronique du passage de Napoléon I et des faits antérieurs et postérieurs, de 1719 à 1809. Extrait du journal d'un paysan de Bourg-St-Pierre, écrit en partie à l'époque du passage et en partie en 1808 et 1809. Ce journal se trouvait chez Adolphe Genoud, président de Bourg-St-Pierre. Anonyme.*
- AGSB 2757 (*1792, septembre - 1815, 22 juin*). *Chronique de ce qui se passe au Gd-St-Bernard, de 1792 à 1815, des émigrés français et surtout des mouvements de troupes avec nombre de détails sur le passage de Napoléon. Anonyme mais d'un témoin oculaire, un chanoine probablement.*
- AGSB 0917/11 (*1776–1801*). *Lettres et épistolier du prévôt Luder de 1776 à 1801.*
- AGSB 0917/17 (*1806, 11 septembre*). '*Vie du très illustre et révérendissime Louis-Antoine Luder, prévôt crossé et mitré du monastère hôpital du Grand Saint-Bernard'. Ecrit par Jean-Joseph Ballet, curé de Sembrancher.*

3. Memoirs & Primary Source Collections

- Abrantès, Laure Junot (duchesse d'), *Memoires de Madame la Duchesse D'Abrantes*, Vol.3, (Paris: Chez Ladvocat, 1831).
- Anon., *Centenario della Battaglia di Marengo Memorie storiche del periodo Napoleonico pubblicate a spese del Municipio di Alessandria per cura della Società di storia della Provincia* (Alessandria: G. Chiari, 1900-1901).
- Anon., *The Campaign of the Reserve Army in 1800 according to documents collected by Captain de Cugnac* (Fort Leavenworth: United States Army Command and General Staff School Library, 1922).
- Anon., *Campagne des Français en Italie en 1800 par W ... officier attaché à l'état-major.* (Leipsic: Reinicke et Hinrichs, 1801).
- Beauharnais, Eugène, *Mémoires et correspondance politique et militaire du prince Eugène*, Vol.1 (Paris: M. Lévy frères, 1858).
- Bell, (Mrs) Arthur, *Memoirs of Baron Lejeune aide-de-camp to Marshals Berthier, Davout and Oudinot,* translated and edited from the original French by Mrs Arthur Bell with an introduction by Major-General Maurice, C.B., Vol.1 (London: Longmans, Green, and Co., 1897).
- Berthier, Alexandre, *Relation de la bataille de Marengo, gagnée le 25 prairial an VIII par Napoléon Bonaparte sur les Autrichiens aux ordres du lieutenant-général Mélas* (Paris: Imprimerie impériale, 1805).
- Bourrienne, *Mémoires de M. de Bourrienne, ministre d'état sur Napoléon, le directoire, le consulate, l'empire et la restauration,* Vol.4 (Paris: Chez Ladvocat, 1829).
- Coignet, Jean-Roch, *Trente ans de gloire avec l'empereur: Mémoires du capitaine Jean-Roch Coignet, Chevalier de la Légion d'Honneur* (Auxerre: 1850).
- Constant, Wairy, *Mémoires de Constant, premier valet de chambre de l'empereur, sur la vie privée de Napoléon, sa famille et sa cour,* Vol.1, (Paris: Maison Ladvocat, 1830).
- Costa de Beauregard, Charles, *Mon Oncle le general – Douze ans d'émigration en Autriche, La Revue Hebdomadaire,* Vol.9 (Paris: Librarie Plon, 5 September 1908).
- Crossard, Jean Baptiste Louis, baron de, *Mémoires militaires et historiques pour servir à l'histoire de la guerre depuis 1792 jusqu'en 1815,* Vol.2 (Paris: Migneret, 1829).
- Cugnac, Gaspar Jean Marie René, comte de, *Campagne de l'armée de Réserve en 1800,* 2 Vols (Paris: R. Chapelot, 1900-1901).
- Fleuriot de Langle, Paul (ed.), *Général Bertrand, Cahiers de Sainte-Hélène* (Paris: Albin Michel, 1959).
- Foissac-Latour, François Philippe de, *Précis ou journal historique et raisonné des opérations militaires et administratives qui ont eu lieu dans la place de Mantoue* (Paris: Magimel, 1800).

- Foudras, Alexandre, *Campagne de Bonaparte en Italie, en l'An VIII de la République, rédigée sur les mémoirs d'un officier de l'état-major de l'armée de réserve* (Paris: Instructions Décadaires, 1801).
- Foudras, *Marengo or the Campaign of Italy by the Army of Reserve*, translated from the French of Joseph Petit, Horse-Grenadier in the Consular Guard (London: J.S. Jordan, 1801).
- Gohier, Louis Jerome, *Mémoires de Contemporains, pour server a l'histoire de France, et principalement a celle de la république et de l'empire* (Paris: Bossange Frères, 1824).
- Gourgaud, Général, *Mémoires pour servir à l'histoire de France sous Napoléon, écrits à sainte-helene, sous la dictée de l'empereur, par les généraux qui ont partage sa captivité et publiés sur les manuscrits entièrement corrigés de sa main*, Vol.1 (Paris: Bossange Père, 1830).
- Grandin, F., *Souvenirs historiques du Capitaine Krettly: ancien tromette-major*, Vol.1 (Paris: Berlandier, 1839).
- Hüffer, Hermann, *Quellen zur Geschichte des Zeitalters der Französischen Revolution. Erster Teil. Quellen zur Geschichte der Kriege von 1799 und 1800. Aus den sammlungen des K. und K. Kriegsarchivs, des haus-, hof-, und Staatsarchivs und des Archivs des Erzherzogs Albrecht in Wien. Erste Band. Quellen zur Geschichte des Krieges von 1799* (Leipzig: B.G. Teubner, 1900).
- Hüffer, Hermann, *Quellen zur Geschichte des Zeitalters der Französischen Revolution. Erster Teil. Quellen zur Geschichte der Kriege von 1799 und 1800. Aus den sammlungen des K. und K. Kriegsarchivs, des haus-, hof-, und Staatsarchivs und des Archivs des Erzherzogs Albrecht in Wien. Zweiter Band. Quellen zur Geschichte des Krieges von 1800* (Leipzig: B.G. Teubner, 1901).
- Kellermann, François Étienne de, *Bataille de Marengo, Napoléon. Journal Anecdotique et Biographique de l'empire et de la Grande Armée* (Paris: Bureau du Journal, 1834).
- Kellermann, François Étienne de, *Deuxième et dernière réplique d'un Ami de la Vérité a M. Le Duc De Rovigo* (Paris: Rosier, 1828).
- Kellermann, François Étienne de, *Réfutation de M. le duc de Rovigo, ou La vérité sur la bataille de Marengo* (Paris: Rosier, 1828)
- Landrieux, Jean, *Mémoires de l'adjudant-général Jean Landrieux, 1795-1797* (Paris: A. Savine, 1893).
- Larchey, Lorédan, *Cahiers du capitaine Coignet* (Paris: Hachette & Cie, 1883).
- MacDonald, Etienne-Jacques-Joseph-Alexandre, duc de, *Souvenirs du Maréchal MacDonald, duc de Tarente*, Vol.1 (Paris: E. Plon, Nourrit, 1892).
- Marmont, *Mémoires du maréchal duc de Raguse de 1792 à 1832*, Vol.2 (Paris: Rotin, 1857).
- Maubert, (Chief of Brigade), *Relation du blocus et du siége de Mantoue, et exposé des causes qui ont contribué a sa reddition* (Paris: Magimel, 1800).

- Musset, Victor Donatien de, *Voyage en Suisse et en Italie, fait avec l'armée de réserve. Par V. D. M ...* (Paris: Moutadier, 1800).
- Napoléon I, *Mémoires de Napoléon Bonaparte: manuscrit venu de Sainte-Hélène* (Paris: Baudouin Frères, 1821).
- Neipperg, Comte de, *Aperçu militaire de la Bataille de Marengo* (Saint-Amand: Imprimerie Scientifque et Littéraire Bussière, 1906).
- Perrin, Claude-Victor, duc de Bellune, *Extraits des memoires inédits de feu* (Paris: J. Dumaine, 1846).
- Petit, Joseph, *Maringo, ou Campagne d'Italie, par l'armée de réserve, écrite par Joseph Petit, ... Seconde édition, revue et augmentée par l'auteur* (Paris: Favre, 1800).
- Plon, Henri (editor), *Correspondance de Napoléon Ier: publiée par ordre de l'empereur Napoléon III,* Vol.10 (Paris: J. Dumaine, 1862).
- Radetzky, *Erinnerungen aus dem Leben des Feldmarschall Grafen Radetzky. Eine Selbstbiographie. Mitteilungen des K. und K. Kriegsarchivs, Neue Folge,* Vol.1 (Wien: L.W. Seidel & Sohn, 1887).
- Rapp, Jean, *Memoirs of General Count Rapp, Aide-de-Camp to Napoleon, Written by himself, and published by his family* (London: Henry Colburn & Co., 1823).
- Rauch, Josef, *Erinnerungen eines Offiziers aus Altösterreich* (München: Georg Müller, 1918).
- Sand, George, *Histoire de ma vie,* Vol.2 (Paris: Michel Lévy Frères, 1856).
- Savary, Anne-Jean-Marie-René, duc de Rovigo, *Mémoires du duc de Rovigo,* Vols1 & 4 (Paris: Bossange, 1828).
- Savary, Anne-Jean-Marie-René, duc de Rovigo, *Memoirs of the Duke of Rovigo,* Vols1 & 4 (London: Henry Colburn, 1828).
- Skarstein, Karl Jakob, *Under fremmede flagg: nordmenn i utenlandsk krigstjeneste 1800-1900* (Oslo: Forsvarsmuseet, 2002).
- Soult, Napoléon Hector, *Mémoires du maréchal-général Soult duc de Dalmatie,* Part 1, Vol.3 (Paris: Librairie d'Amyot, 1854).
- Thiébault, Paul Charles François Adrien Henri Dieudonné, *Journal des Opérations Militaires du Siége et du Blocus de Gênes* (Paris: Magimel, 1801).
- Titeux, Eugène, *Le Général Dupont, une erreur historique,* Vol.1 (Puteaux-sur-Seine: Prieur et Dubois et Cie, 1903).

4. Select Bibliography

- Anon., *Eine Denkschrift Zach's aus dem Jahre 1798* in *Mittheilungen des k.u.k. Kriegs-Archivs: Dritte Folge, II Band* (Wien: L.W. Seidel & Sohn, 1903).
- Anon., *Mitteilungen des K. und K. Kriegsarchivs, Dritte Folge,* Vol.6 (Wien: Seidel & Sohn, 1909).

- Bancalari, Gustav, *Beiträge zur Geschichte des österreichischen Heerwesens*, Band 1 (Vienna: L.W. Seidel & Sohn, 1872).
- Bonnal, E., *Histoire de Desaix: armées du Rhin, expédition d'Orient, Marengo, d'après les archivs du dépot de la guerre* (Paris: Dumaine, 1881).
- Bülow, Dietrich Heinrich (trans., Sévelinges, Charles Louis de), *Histoire de la campagne de 1800, en Allemagne et en Italie* (Paris: Magimel, 1804).
- Chandler, David G., *The Campaigns of Napoleon* (London: Macmillan, 1966).
- Charles (Archduke of Austria), *Oestreichische militärische zeitschrift, 1811-13*, Vol.2 (Wien: A. Strauss, 1835).
- Closuit, Léonard-P., *Passage de Bonaparte au Grand-Saint-Bernard en mai 1800* (Martigny: Association Saint-Maurice d'études militaires, 1999).
- Colin, J., *La Tactique et la Discipline dans les Armées de la Révolution. Correspondance du Général Schauenbourg du 4 avril au 2 août 1793* (Paris: CHAPELOT & Cie., 1902).
- Corréard, F., *Desaix* (Paris: Hachette, 1882).
- Costa de Beauregard, Charles, *Mon Oncle le general – Douze ans d'émigration en Autriche, La Revue Hebdomadaire*, Vol.9 (Paris: Librarie Plon, 5 September 1908).
- Criste, Oskar, *Erzherzog Carl von Österreich: Ein Lebensbild*, Vol.2 (Vienna: Braumüller, Wilhelm, 1912).
- Crowdy, T.E., *Napoleon's Infantry Handbook* (Barnsley: Pen & Sword Military, 2015).
- Crowdy, Terry, *The Enemy Within: A History of Espionage* (Oxford: Osprey Publishing, 2006).
- Cugnac, Gaspar Jean Marie René, comte de, *La campagne de Marengo* (Paris: R. Chapelot, 1904).
- Daunou, Pierre-Claude-François, *Rapport fait par Daunou sur un message des consuls relatif à la victoire remportée par l'armée de la République à Maringo. Séance du 3 messidor an VIII*, (Paris: Impr. nationale, 1800).
- De Castres, (General), *Rapprochement entre diverses relations de la bataille de Marengo, Journal des Sciences Militaires des armées de terre et de mer*, Vol.12 (Paris: M.J. Corréard, 1826).
- Dumas, Mathieu comte, *Précis des Evénements Militaires ou Essais Historiques sur les Campaignes de 1799 à 1814, Campagne de 1800* (Paris: Treuttel & Wurtz, 1816).
- Esposito, Vincent J., and Elting, John R., *Military History and Atlas of the Napoleonic Wars* (London: Faber and Faber Limited, 1964).
- Furse, George Armand, *Marengo and Hohenlinden*, 2 Vols (London: Clowes, 1903).

- Gachot, Edouard, *Histoire militaire de Massena: le siége de Gênes, 1800* (Paris: Plon-Nourrit, 1908).
- Gachot, Edouard, *La Deuxiéme Campagne d'Italie, 1800* (Paris: Perrin & Cie, 1899).
- Heller von Hellwald, Friedrich, *Der k.k. österreichische Feldmarschall Graf Radetzky: Eine biographische Skizze nach den eigenen Dictaten und der Correspondenz des Feldmarschalls* (Stuttgart: J.B. Cotta, 1858).
- Herrmann, Alfred Julius Moritz, *Marengo* (Münster: Aschendorff, 1903).
- Hollins, David, (illustrated by Hook, Christa), *Marengo 1800: Napoleon's day of fate* (Oxford: Osprey Military, 2000).
- Kellermann, François-Christophe-Édouard de, *Campagne de 1800* (Paris: J. Dumaine, 1854).
- Le Roy, Albert, *Georges Sand et son amis* (Paris: P. Ollendorff, 1903).
- Mras, Karl, *Geschichte des Feldzuges 1800 in Italien* (Wien: Oesterreichische Militarische Zeitschrift, 1822-1823).
- Oliva, Pietro, *Marengo Antico e Marengo Moderno* (Alessandria: Giacinto Moretti, 1842).
- Pittaluga, Vittorio Emanuele, *La battaglia di Marengo, 14 giugno 1800* (Alessandria: G. Chiari, 1900).
- Rothenberg, Gunther E., Napoleon's Great Adversaries: Archduke Charles and the Austrian Army 1792–1814 (London: B.T. Batsford Ltd, 1982).
- Sargent, Herbert Howland, *The campaign of Marengo, with comments* (Chicago: McClurg & Co, 1897).
- Six, Georges, *Dictionnaire biographique des généraux et amiraux français de la Révolution et de l'Empire, 1792-1814*, (Paris: Librarie Historique & Nobiliaire, 1934).
- Sparrow, Elizabeth, *Secret Service: British Agents in France, 1792-1815* (Woodbridge: Boydell Press, 1999).
- Vaccarino, Giorgio, *I Giacobini Piemontesi, 1794-1814*, Vol.2 (Rome: Ministero Per I Beni Culturali E Ambientali, 1989).
- Wilkin, Bernard, and Wilkin, René, *Fighting for Napoleon: French soldiers' letters 1799–1815* (Barnsley: Pen and Sword Military, 2015).

Index